Praise for
America: The Farewell Tour

"The most engaging parts of the book are the searing portraits [Hedges] presents of individuals victimized in six arenas that he explores in detail: drug addiction, pornography, gambling, the criminal justice system, extremist groups and the search for meaningful, well-paid work. He takes the reader inside these issues in ways that are often telling and memorable."

—Thomas Carothers, *The Washington Post*

"Chris Hedges wants us to face realities. Our society is unraveling, institutionally and structurally, and is being replaced by the corporate state of merging big business and government. Commercialism overwhelms civic values, impoverishes its subjects, and reaches into childhoods bypassing parental authority. Poverty, addiction, gambling, and hopelessness spread like epidemics. Only we the people can reverse the disintegration of democracy by plutocracy. In *America: The Farewell Tour,* Hedges depicts the horrifying truths on the ground from which resistance rises to jolt us into an active, realizable culture of reconstruction."

—Ralph Nader

"Passionate, and provocative . . . certain to arouse controversy but offering a point of view that needs to be heard."

—*Booklist*

"Hedges writes a requiem for the American dream. . . . [A] fiery sermon that weighs the nation and finds it wanting."

—*Kirkus Reviews*

"Hedges's latest critique of late-stage capitalist America is forceful and direct."

—*Publishers Weekly*

"Chris Hedges is perhaps today's most important public intellectual, and *America: the Farewell Tour* is perhaps his most important book. If we as a society are able to move past our current 'sickness unto death,' as Kierkegaard put it, it will be in great measure thanks to books like this one."

—Derrick Jensen, author of *A Language Older Than Words* and *The Culture of Make Believe*

ALSO BY CHRIS HEDGES

Unspeakable
(with David Talbot)

Wages of Rebellion:
The Moral Imperative of Revolt

War Is a Force That Gives Us Meaning

Days of Destruction, Days of Revolt
(with Joe Sacco)

The World as It Is:
Dispatches on the Myth of Human Progress

Death of the Liberal Class

Empire of Illusion:
The End of Literacy and the Triumph of Spectacle

When Atheism Becomes Religion:
America's New Fundamentalists

Collateral Damage:
America's War Against Iraqi Civilians
(with Laila Al-Arian)

American Fascists:
The Christian Right and the War on America

Losing Moses on the Freeway:
The 10 Commandments in America

What Every Person Should Know About War

AMERICA

The Farewell Tour

CHRIS HEDGES

SIMON & SCHUSTER PAPERBACKS
New York   London   Toronto   Sydney   New Delhi

Simon & Schuster Paperbacks
An Imprint of Simon & Schuster, Inc.
1230 Avenue of the Americas
New York, NY 10020

Copyright © 2018 by Summit Study, Inc.

All rights reserved, including the right to reproduce this book
or portions thereof in any form whatsoever. For information,
address Simon & Schuster Paperbacks Subsidiary Rights Department,
1230 Avenue of the Americas, New York, NY 10020.

First Simon & Schuster trade paperback edition August 2019

SIMON & SCHUSTER PAPERBACKS and colophon are registered
trademarks of Simon & Schuster, Inc.

For information about special discounts for bulk purchases,
please contact Simon & Schuster Special Sales at 1-866-506-1949
or business@simonandschuster.com.

The Simon & Schuster Speakers Bureau can bring authors to your
live event. For more information or to book an event, contact the
Simon & Schuster Speakers Bureau at 1-866-248-3049
or visit our website at www.simonspeakers.com.

Interior design by Lewelin Polanco

Manufactured in the United States of America

5 7 9 10 8 6

The Library of Congress has cataloged the hardcover edition as follows:

Names: Hedges, Chris, author.
Title: America : the farewell tour / Chris Hedges.
Description: First Simon & Schuster hardcover edition. |
New York : Simon & Schuster, 2018. | Includes bibliographical references and index.
Identifiers: LCCN 2017058039| ISBN 9781501152672 (hardback) |
ISBN 150115267X (hardback)
Subjects: LCSH: Working class—United States. | Unemployment—United States.
| Drug abuse—United States. | BISAC: HISTORY / United States / 21st Century.
| POLITICAL SCIENCE / Government / General. | POLITICAL SCIENCE
/ Public Policy / Environmental Policy.
Classification: LCC HD8072.5 .H43 2018 | DDC 305.5/620973—dc23
LC record available at https://lccn.loc.gov/2017058039

ISBN 978-1-5011-5267-2
ISBN 978-1-5011-5268-9 (pbk)
ISBN 978-1-5011-5269-6 (ebook)

For Eunice,

She's all states, and all princes, I,
Nothing else is.
Princes do but play us; compared to this,
All honor's mimic, all wealth alchemy.

Actually, I hardly feel constrained to try to make head or tail of this condition of the world. On this planet a great number of civilizations have perished in blood and thunder. Naturally, one must wish for the planet that one day it will experience a civilization that has abandoned blood and horror, in fact, I am . . . inclined to assume that our planet is waiting for this. But it is terribly doubtful whether we can bring such a present to its hundred—or four-hundred-millionth birthday party. And if we don't, the planet will finally punish us, its unthoughtful well-wishers, by presenting us with the Last Judgment.

WALTER BENJAMIN, *letter from Paris, 1935*[1]

This nothingness into which the West is sliding is not the natural end, the dying, the sinking of a flourishing community of peoples. Instead, it is again a specifically Western nothingness: a nothingness that is rebellious, violent, anti-God, and antihuman. Breaking away from all that is established, it is the utmost manifestation of all the forces opposed to God. It is nothingness as God; no one knows its goal or its measure. Its rule is absolute. It is a creative nothingness that blows its anti-God breath into all that exists, creates the illusion of waking it to new life, and at the same time sucks out its true essence until it soon disintegrates into an empty husk and is discarded. Life, history, family, people, language, faith—the list could go on forever because nothingness spares nothing—all fall victim to nothingness.

DIETRICH BONHOEFFER, *Ethics*[2]

CONTENTS

1

DECAY

Hard as it may be for a state so framed to be shaken, yet, since all that comes into being must decay, even a fabric like this will not endure forever, but will suffer dissolution.

PLATO, *The Republic*[1]

I walked down a long service road into the remains of an abandoned lace factory. The road was pocked with holes filled with fetid water. There were saplings and weeds poking up from the cracks in the asphalt. Wooden crates, rusty machinery, broken glass, hulks of old filing cabinets, and trash covered the grounds. The derelict complex, 288,000 square feet, consisted of two huge brick buildings connected by overhead, enclosed walkways. The towering walls of the two buildings, with the service road running between them, were covered with ivy. The windowpanes were empty or had frames jagged with shards of glass. The thick wooden doors to the old loading docks stood agape. I entered the crumbling complex through a set of double wooden doors into a cavernous hall. The wreckage of industrial America lay before me, home to flocks of pigeons that, startled by my footsteps over the pieces of glass and rotting floorboards, swiftly left their perches in the rafters and air ducts high above my head. They swooped, bleating and clucking, over the abandoned looms.

The Scranton Lace Company was America. It employed more than 1,200 workers on its imported looms, some of the largest ever built.[2] I stood in front of one. The looms, weighing nearly twenty metric tons and manufactured in Nottingham, England, were twenty feet tall. They stretched across the expanse of the old factory floor. The word "Nottingham" was embossed on the black arms of the machines. Another age. Another time. Another country.

The factory, started in 1891, was once among the biggest producers of Nottingham lace in the world.[3] When it closed in 2002—the company's vice president appeared at mid-shift and announced that it was shutting down immediately—it had become a ghost ship with fewer than fifty workers.[4] On the loom before me, the white lace roll sat unfinished. Punch cards, with meticulous, tiny holes for the needles to pass through, lay scattered on the floor. The loom was stopped in the middle of production, arrested in time, an artifact of a deindustrialized America.

For more than a century, the factory stood as a world unto itself. I wandered through the remains. The old bowling alley, the deserted cafeteria with its rows of heavy cast iron stoves, the company barbershop, a cluttered and dusty gymnasium, the auditorium with a stage, the infirmary, and outside, the elegant clock tower with the cast iron bell and large whistle that once signaled shift changes.

The company had its own coal mines and cotton fields. It made products that the workers, including Hillary Clinton's father and grandfather, viewed with pride.[5] They could hold them in their hands. Curtains. Napkins. Tablecloths. Valances. Shower curtains. Textile laminates for umbrellas. During World War II, the facility manufactured bomb parachutes and mosquito and camouflage netting. The employees had unions. The unions ensured that workers were paid overtime and had medical care, pensions, and safe working conditions. But the company gave more than a wage to the thousands of men and women who worked here. It gave them dignity, purpose, pride, a sense of place, hope, and self-esteem. All of that was gone. It had been replaced in Scranton and across America by desperation, poverty, drift, a loss of identity, and a deep and crippling despair.

Scranton mayor Christopher Doherty, when I interviewed him, was fifty-four, trim, articulate, and the father of six children. He had been mayor for eleven years. He did not seek reelection in 2014 and was replaced by another Democrat who accelerated the selling off of city assets.

Doherty spoke to me in his shirtsleeves. The room was stuffy in the summer heat. The air-conditioning was turned off to reduce electric bills. The mayor had just negotiated a deal with his antagonistic five-member City Council to pull Scranton back from bankruptcy. By the summer of 2012, banks would no longer lend the city money.[6] With only $5,000 left in its bank account and facing a $1 million payroll in July, Scranton was forced to reduce every city employee's income, including the mayor's, to the minimum wage: $7.25 an hour.[7] His deal to save the city from default included a 29 percent increase in real estate taxes over the next three years, less than half of the 78 percent he proposed,[8] along with a new commuter tax, a sales tax, an amusement tax, and higher real estate transfer fees, license and permit fees, and business and mercantile taxes.

The plan came with requisite austerity measures. City departments saw their budgets cut by $1.6 million, which meant further job losses.[9] Doherty had already reduced the city employment rolls from five hundred to four hundred.[10] Scranton's universities, including the University of Scranton and the Commonwealth Medical College, were asked to contribute $2.4 million—instead of the current $300,000—to the city's $70 million operating costs.[11] The University of Scranton complied with the city's request.[12] Borrowing and refinancing raised nearly $17 million[13] to bridge the budget gap, but unless the city created reliable new revenue streams, disaster was, Doherty admitted, merely postponed. The Scranton school district has an annual deficit of more than $20 million.[14] Seventy percent of the residents pay less than $500 a year in property taxes.[15] The average per capita annual income is about $20,000 and less than $38,000 for a family.[16]

"We are government, education, and medicine," Doherty said of the city's principal institutions, "and if you look at all cities, that is what they are. There is really no manufacturing anywhere."

This is not quite true. Scranton makes munitions. Weapons are one of the last products still produced in America. The Scranton Army Ammunition Plant (SCAAP), surrounded by high fencing with coils of razor wire, makes a series of projectiles, including 105-millimeter and 155-millimeter shells. It is housed in a brick complex that once repaired locomotive steam engines. Most of the shells end up as useless shards of metal in Iraq or Afghanistan. SCAAP is part of America's militarized capitalism, which plows vast sums into a permanent war economy. Upward of half of all federal dollars are spent on the war industry. The Pentagon consumes nearly $600 billion[17] a year. Our real expenditure on the military, when military items tucked away in other budgets are counted, is over $1 trillion a year.[18]

The heaviest strain on the budget, the mayor said, are municipal employees' pensions and health care costs. The 2008 economic crisis wiped out as much as 40 percent of the city's investments.[19] Scranton, like many cities and institutions, invested in Wall Street financial cons such as collateralized debt obligations (CDOS)—pooled assets such as subprime mortgages, bonds, loans, and credit card debt that the banks often knew were toxic. This high-risk investment was certified by ratings agencies such as Standard & Poor's as AAA—meaning the investment had "an exceptional degree of creditworthiness." When the financial bubble burst, financial firms saw their assets plummet. American International Group (AIG) posted a quarterly loss of $61.7 billion[20] and turned, like most of the big banks, to the U.S. Treasury to bail them out. But no one bailed out the victims.

I asked Doherty what worried him most about the city's future.

"The ability to generate revenues so cities can make their payments," he answered immediately. "If they can't, you will see a breakdown of the city. You will see it in education. You will see it in crime. What happens is a domino effect, as you have in Baltimore, where even though you have these great educational institutions, the city still has a problem with crime."

The current mayor of Scranton, Bill Courtright, sold the city sewer authority to Pennsylvania American Water, a subsidiary of American Water Works Company Inc., for $195 million.[21] Pennsylvania American Water already owns Scranton's drinking water system.[22] The city's sewer system authority is shared with the town of Dunmore.

The money from the sale was used to pay off the $70 million sewer authority debt.[23] After 20 percent of the money was given to Dunmore, the city was left with $70 million.[24] This money will repair infrastructure, such as roads, and pay shortfalls in the pension funds for city employees. The city was able to pay $29.3 million in back pay to police and firefighters, including retirees.[25] It put $1.59 million into the city's public pension funds.[26]

Mayor Courtright, who declined to grant me an interview, also sold the city's parking authority to National Development Council for $32 million.[27] It costs 25 cents more an hour under the for-profit parking authority to park at a meter in the city and 50 cents more to park in one of the city's parking garages.[28]

But after the last city assets are sold, what is next? No one has an answer.

Karl Marx knew the peculiar dynamics of capitalism, or what he called "the bourgeois mode of production."[29] He knew that reigning ideologies—think corporate capitalism with its belief in deindustrialization, deregulation, privatization of public assets, austerity, slashing of social service programs, and huge reductions in government spending—were created to serve the interests of the economic elites, since "the class which has the means of material production at its disposal, has control at the same time over the means of mental production"[30] and "the ruling ideas are nothing more than the ideal expression of the dominant material relationships . . . . the relationships which make one class the ruling one."[31]

The acceleration of deindustrialization by the 1970s created a crisis that forced the ruling elites to devise a new political paradigm, as Stuart Hall (with cowriters) explains in *Policing the Crisis*.[32] This paradigm, trumpeted by a compliant media, shifted its focus from the common good to race, crime, and law and order. It told those undergoing profound economic and political change that their suffering stemmed not from corporate greed, but from a threat to national integrity. The old consensus that buttressed the programs of the New Deal and the welfare state was attacked as enabling criminal black youth, welfare queens, and social parasites. The parasites were to blame. This opened the door to an authoritarian populism, begun by Ronald Reagan and Margaret Thatcher, which supposedly championed family values, traditional morality, individual autonomy, law and order, the Christian faith, and the return to a mythical past, at least for white Americans. Donald Trump capitalized on this perceived threat to national integrity and authoritarian populism to take power.

Marx warned that capitalism had built within it the seeds of its own destruction. There would come a day when capitalism would exhaust its potential and collapse. He did not know when that day would come. Marx, as Meghnad Desai, the economist and Labour politician in the United Kingdom, wrote, was "an astronomer of history, not an astrologer."[33] Marx was keenly aware of capitalism's ability to innovate and adapt. But he also knew that capitalist expansion was not eternally sustainable. And as we witness the denouement of capitalism, Karl Marx is vindicated as the system's most prescient and important critic.

In the preface to *A Contribution to the Critique of Political Economy*, Marx wrote:

> No social order ever disappears before all the productive forces for which there is room in it have been developed; and new higher relations of production never appear before the material conditions of their existence have matured in the womb of the old society itself. Therefore, mankind always sets itself only such tasks as it can solve; since looking at the matter more closely, we always find that the task itself arises only when the material conditions necessary for its solution already exist, or are at least in the process of formation.[34]

Socialism, in other words, would not be possible until capitalism had exhausted its ability to expand and increase profits. That the end is coming is hard now to dispute, although one would be foolish to predict when. Global capitalism, in its final iteration, may replicate China's totalitarian capitalism, a brutal system sustained by severe repression where workers are modern-day serfs.

The end stages of capitalism, Marx wrote, would be marked by developments that are intimately familiar to Scranton. Unable to expand and generate profits at past levels, the capitalist system would begin to consume the structures that sustained it. It would prey upon, in the name of austerity, the working class and the poor, driving them ever deeper into debt and poverty and diminishing the capacity of the state to serve the basic needs of ordinary citizens. It would, as it has, increasingly automate or relocate jobs, including both manufacturing and professional positions, to countries with cheap pools of laborers. This would trigger an economic assault on not only the working class but the middle class—the bulwark of a capitalist democracy—that would be disguised by massive personal debt as incomes declined or remained stagnant and borrowing soared. Politics would, in the late stages of capitalism, become subordinate to economics, leading to political parties hollowed out of any real political content and abjectly subservient to the dictates of corporations.

But as Marx warned, there is a limit to an economy built on austerity and the scaffolding of debt expansion. There comes a moment, Marx knew, when there would be no new markets available and no new pools of people who could take on more debt. This is what happened with the subprime mortgage crisis. Once the banks could not conjure up new subprime borrowers, the scheme fell apart and the system crashed.

Capitalist oligarchs, meanwhile, hoard huge sums of wealth—$7.6 trillion stashed in overseas tax havens—exacted as tribute from those they dominate, indebt, and impoverish.[35] Capitalism would, in the end, Marx said, turn on the so-called free market, along with the values and traditions it claims to defend. It would in its final stages pillage the systems and structures that made capitalism possible. It would resort, as it causes widespread suffering, to harsher forms of repression to maintain social control. It would attempt, in a frantic last stand, to extract profit by looting and pillaging state institutions, contradicting its stated nature.

Marx and Friedrich Engels foresaw that in the later stages of capitalism global corporations would exercise a monopoly on the world's markets. "The need of a constantly expanding market for its products chases the bourgeoisie over the entire surface of the globe," they wrote. "It must nestle everywhere, settle everywhere, establish connections everywhere."[36] These corporations, whether in the banking sector, the fossil fuel industry, agricultural and food industries, the arms industries, or the communications industries, would use their power, usually by seizing the mechanisms of the state, to prevent anyone from challenging their global monopolies. They would fix prices to maximize profit. They would, as they have been doing, push through trade deals to further weaken the nation-state's ability to impede exploitation by imposing environmental regulations or monitoring working conditions. In the end these corporate monopolies would obliterate free market competition.

A May 22, 2015, editorial in *The New York Times* headlined "Banks as Felons, or Criminality Lite," gives us a window into what Marx said would characterize the late stages of capitalism:

> As of this week, Citicorp, JPMorgan Chase, Barclays and Royal Bank of Scotland are felons, having pleaded guilty on Wednesday to criminal charges of conspiring to rig the value of the world's currencies. According to the Justice Department, the lengthy and lucrative conspiracy enabled the banks to pad their profits without regard to fairness, the law or the public good.[37]

THE *TIMES* WENT ON:

> The banks will pay fines totaling about $9 billion, assessed by the Justice Department as well as state, federal and foreign regulators. That seems like a sweet deal for a scam that lasted for at least five years, from the end of 2007 to the beginning of 2013, during which the banks' revenue from foreign exchange was some $85 billion.

The terminal stages of what we call capitalism, as Marx grasped, is not capitalism at all. Corporations feast on taxpayer money. The government is committed to spending $348 billion[38] over the next decade to modernize our nuclear weapons and build twelve new *Ohio*-class nuclear submarines, estimated at $8 billion each.[39] Whether we need these submarines is irrelevant. No Democrat or Republican dares challenge the expenditures by the Pentagon, whose budget has never been audited, despite legal requirements to do so since 1996. That totals $10 trillion in taxpayer dollars that is unaccountable.[40] But to challenge the war industry and the empire, as even Bernie Sanders knows, is political suicide. We spend some $100 billion a year on intelligence—read surveillance—and 70 percent[41] of that money goes to private contractors such as Booz Allen

Hamilton, which gets 99 percent of its revenues from the U.S. government.[42] The Department of Education spends $68 billion a year. Wall Street and hedge funds, which are behind the charter school industry, view public education as one more source of revenue.

The fossil fuel industry swallows up $5.3 trillion a year worldwide in hidden costs to keep burning fossil fuels, according to the International Monetary Fund.[43] This money, the IMF notes, is in addition to the $492 billion in direct subsidies offered by governments around the world through write-offs and write-downs and land-use loopholes.[44] In a rational world, these subsidies would be invested to free us from the deadly effects of carbon emissions caused by fossil fuels and rebuild the nation's decaying infrastructure, but we do not live in a rational world.

Bloomberg News reported in a 2013 editorial, "Why Should Taxpayers Give Big Banks $83 Billion a Year?," that economists had determined that government subsidies lower the big banks' borrowing costs by about 0.8 percent.[45]

"Multiplied by the total liabilities of the 10 largest U.S. banks by assets," the editorial said, "it amounts to a taxpayer subsidy of $83 billion a year."

"The top five banks—JPMorgan, Bank of America Corp., Citigroup Inc., Wells Fargo & Co. and Goldman Sachs Group Inc.—account," the editorial went on, "for $64 billion of the total subsidy, an amount roughly equal to their typical annual profits. In other words, the banks occupying the commanding heights of the U.S. financial industry—with almost $9 trillion in assets, more than half the size of the U.S. economy—would just about break even in the absence of corporate welfare. In large part, the profits they report are essentially transfers from taxpayers to their shareholders."

Government expenditure accounts for 41 percent of GDP.[46] Public lands, prisons, schools, water and power utilities, parking authorities, sewer systems, garbage collection, and health services are being sold off or privatized by desperate towns, cities, and states. None of these seizures of basic services by for-profit corporations makes them more efficient or reduces costs. That is not the point. It is about extracting money from the carcass of the state. This process ensures the disintegration of the structures that sustain capitalism itself. All this Marx got.

Marx illuminated these contradictions within capitalism. He understood that the idea of capitalism—free trade, free markets, individualism, innovation, self-development—works only in the utopian mind of a true believer such as Alan Greenspan, never in reality. The hoarding of wealth by a tiny capitalist elite, Marx foresaw, along with the driving down of wages of workers, leaves populations unable to buy the products capitalism produces.

The assault on the working class has been happening for several decades. Salaries have remained stagnant or declined since the 1970s.[47] Manufacturing has been shipped overseas, where workers in countries such as China earn a dollar an hour,[48] or Bangladesh, where they earn 32 cents an hour.[49] The working class is forced to compete against labor pools of modern-day serfs. Industries such as construction, which once provided well-paying unionized jobs, are the domain of underpaid, nonunionized, often undocumented workers. Corporations import foreign engineers and software specialists who do professional work at one third of the normal salary on H-1B, L-1, and other work visas. All these workers are bereft of the rights of citizens.

The capitalists respond to the collapse of their domestic economies, which they engineered, by becoming global loan sharks and speculators. They lend money at exorbitant interest rates to the working class and the poor, even if they know the money can never be repaid, and then sell these bundled debts, including credit default swaps, bonds, and stocks to pension funds, cities, investment firms, and institutions. This late form of capitalism is built on what Marx called "fictitious capital."[50] And it leads, as Marx knew, to the vaporization of money.

Once subprime mortgage borrowers began to default, as the big banks and investment firms knew was inevitable, the government bailed out the banks and imposed austerity to pay for the bailouts. What saved us from a full-blown depression was, in a tactic Marx would have found ironic, massive state intervention in the economy, including the nationalization of huge corporations such as AIG and General Motors.

What we saw in 2008 was an example of our welfare state for the rich, a kind of state socialism for the financial elites that Marx predicted. But with this comes an increased and volatile cycle of boom and bust, bringing the system closer to disintegration and collapse. We have undergone two major stock market crashes and the implosion of real estate prices in just the first decade of the twenty-first century.

The half dozen corporations that own most of the media have worked overtime to sell to a bewildered public the fiction that we are enjoying a recovery. Employment figures, through a variety of gimmicks, including erasing those who are unemployed for over a year from unemployment rolls, are a lie, as is nearly every other financial indicator pumped out for public consumption. Marx knew that once the market mechanism became the sole determining factor for the fate of the nation-state, as well as the natural world, both would be demolished.

As deteriorating infrastructure and ongoing layoffs continue to beset the nation's cities, more dramatic signs of neglect will appear. Garbage will pile up uncollected on curbsides. Power grids will blink on and off. There will not be enough police, firefighters, or teachers. Pensions will be slashed or paid sporadically. Decent medical care will be reserved for the rich. Those who die because they cannot afford health care—now 45,000 uninsured people a year[51]—will perish in greater numbers. Fuel and food prices will climb. Processed food laden with preservatives, sugar, and fat will become the staple diet. At least a quarter of the population will lack adequate employment. Law and order will break down. Crime will become endemic, and in a nation where nearly anyone can get a gun, death rates from violence will rise. Riots, if the unraveling is not halted, will erupt across the country like wildfires. Random and mass shootings will grow more common. Hate groups will proliferate like lice. And widespread disgust with the political elites, as well as the uncertainty and chaos, will make some kind of militarized solution increasingly attractive to embittered, demoralized Americans.

The ruling corporate kleptocrats are political arsonists. They are carting cans of gasoline into government agencies, the courts, the White House, and Congress to burn down any structure or program that promotes the common good. Steve Bannon correctly named this assault as the "deconstruction of the administrative state."[52] Trump's appointees are diminishing or dismantling the agencies they were named to lead and the programs they are supposed to administer. That is why they were selected.

Rex Tillerson at the State Department, Steven Mnuchin at the Treasury Department, Scott Pruitt at the Environmental Protection Agency, Rick Perry at the Department of Energy, Ben Carson at the Department of Housing and Urban Development, and Betsy DeVos at the Department of Education are dynamiting the foundations of democratic institutions.

William S. Burroughs in his novel *Naked Lunch* created predatory creatures he called "Mugwumps." "Mugwumps," he wrote, "have no liver and nourish themselves exclusively on sweets. Thin, purple-blue lips cover a razor-sharp beak of black bone with which they frequently tear each other to shreds in fights over clients. These creatures secrete an addictive fluid through their erect penises which prolongs life by slowing metabolism."[53] Those addicted to this fluid are called "Reptiles."[54]

The addiction to the grotesque, to our own version of Mugwumps, has become our national pathology. We are entranced, even as the secretion of Trump's Mugwump fluid repulses us. He brings us down to his level. We are glued to cable news, which usually sees a decrease in viewership after a presidential election. Ratings for the Trump-as-president reality show, however, are up 50 percent.[55] CNN had its most profitable year ever in 2016. It projected increasing this in 2017 to a billion dollars in profit.[56] *The New York Times* added some 500,000 net subscribers over a period of six months.[57] *The Washington Post* saw a 75 percent increase in new subscribers in a year.[58] Subscriptions to magazines like *The New Yorker*[59] and *The Atlantic*[60] have also grown.

This growth is provoked not by a sudden desire to be informed, but by Americans' wanting to be continually updated on the political soap opera that epitomizes politics. Which country will the president insult today? Mexico? Australia? Sweden? Germany? Which celebrity or politician will he belittle? "Liddle Bob Corker"? "Lyin' Ted"? "Crooked Hillary"? What idiocy will come out of his mouth or from his appointees? Can Kellyanne Conway, who pitched Ivanka Trump's product line on cable television, top her claim that microwave ovens were turned into cameras to spy on Donald Trump?[61] Will DeVos say something as stupid as her assertion that guns are needed in schools to protect children from grizzly bears?[62] Will Trump again mangle historical fact, insisting that President Andrew Jackson, who died in 1845, opposed the Civil War, which began in 1861? Can he top his apparent belief that Frederick Douglass is among the living? Tune in.

"Trump found the flaw in the American Death Star," Matt Taibbi writes. "It doesn't know how to turn the cameras off, even when it's filming its own demise."[63]

It is entertainment all the time. The media long ago gave up journalism to keep us amused. Trump was its creation. And now we get a daily "Gong Show" out of the White House.[64] It is good for Trump. It is good for cable news networks' profits. But it is bad for us. It keeps us distracted as the kleptocrats transform the country into a banana republic. The Trump presidency is lifted from the pages of Gabriel García Márquez's novel *The Autumn of the Patriarch*, in which the "eternal"[65] dictator was feared and mocked in equal measure.

The most ominous danger we face does not come from the eradication of free speech through the obliteration of net neutrality or through Google algorithms that steer people away from dissident, left-wing, progressive, or antiwar sites. It does not come from the 2017 tax bill that abandons all pretense of fiscal responsibility to enrich corporations and oligarchs and prepares the way to dismantle programs such as Social Security. It does not come from the opening of public land to the mining and fossil fuel industry, the acceleration of ecocide by demolishing environmental regulations, or the destruction of public education. It does not come from the squandering of federal dollars on a bloated military as the country collapses or the use of the systems of domestic security to criminalize dissent. The most ominous danger we face comes from the marginalization and destruction of institutions, including the courts, academia, legislative bodies, cultural organizations, and the press, that once ensured that civil discourse was rooted in reality and fact, helping us distinguish lies from truth, and facilitate justice.

Trump and today's Republican Party represent the last stage in the emergence of corporate totalitarianism. Pillage and oppression are justified by the permanent lie. The permanent lie is different from the falsehoods and half-truths uttered by politicians such as Bill Clinton, George W. Bush, and Barack Obama. The common political lie these politicians employed was not designed to cancel out reality. It was a form of manipulation.

Clinton, when he signed into law the North American Free Trade Agreement, promised "NAFTA means jobs, American jobs and good-paying American jobs."[66] George W. Bush justified the invasion of Iraq because Saddam Hussein supposedly possessed weapons of mass destruction. But Clinton did not continue to pretend that NAFTA was beneficial to the working class when reality proved otherwise. Bush did not pretend that Iraq had weapons of mass destruction once none were found.

The permanent lie is not circumscribed by reality. It is perpetuated even in the face of overwhelming evidence that discredits it. It is irrational. Those who speak in the language of truth and fact are attacked as liars, traitors and purveyors of "fake news." They are banished from the public sphere once totalitarian elites accrue sufficient power, a power now granted to them with the revoking of net neutrality. The iron refusal by those who engage in the permanent lie to acknowledge reality, no matter how transparent reality becomes, creates a collective psychosis.

"The result of a consistent and total substitution of lies for factual truth is not that the lie will now be accepted as truth and truth be defamed as a lie, but that the sense by which we take our bearings in the real world—and the category of truth versus falsehood is among the mental means to this end—is being destroyed," Hannah Arendt wrote in *The Origins of Totalitarianism.*[67]

The permanent lie turns political discourse into absurdist theater. Trump, who lies about the size of his inauguration crowd despite photographic evidence, insists that in regard to his personal finances he is "going to get killed" by a tax bill that actually will save him and his heirs more than $1 billion.[68] Treasury secretary Steven Mnuchin claims he has a report that proves that the tax cuts will pay for themselves and will not increase the deficit—only there never was a report. Senator John Cornyn assures us, countering all factual evidence, that "this is not a bill that is designed primarily to benefit the wealthy and the large businesses."[69]

Two million acres of public land, meanwhile, are handed over to the mining and fossil fuel industry as Trump insists the transfer means that "public lands will once again be for public use."[70] When environmentalists denounce the transfer as a theft, Representative Rob Bishop calls their criticism "a false narrative."[71]

FCC chairman Ajit Pai, after ending net neutrality, effectively killing free speech on the internet, says, "[T]hose who've said the internet as we know it is about to end have been proven wrong. . . . We have a free internet going forward."[72] And at the Centers for Disease Control and Prevention, phrases such as "evidence-based" and "science-based" are banned.[73] ←— WTF

The permanent lie is the apotheosis of totalitarianism. It no longer matters what is true. It matters only what is "correct." Federal courts are being stacked with imbecilic and incompetent judges who serve the "correct" ideology of corporatism and the rigid social mores of the Christian right. They hold reality, including science and the rule of law, in contempt. They seek to banish those who live in a reality-based world defined by intellectual and moral autonomy. Totalitarian rule always elevates the brutal and the stupid. These reigning idiots have no genuine political philosophy or goals. They use clichés and slogans, most of which are absurd and contradictory, to justify their greed and lust for power. This is as true for the Christian right as it is for the corporatists that preach the free market and globalization. The merger of the corporatists with the Christian right is the marrying of Godzilla to Frankenstein.

"The venal political figures need not even comprehend the social and political consequences of their behavior," psychiatrist Joost A. M. Meerloo wrote in *The Rape of the Mind: The Psychology of Thought Control, Menticide, and Brainwashing*. "They are compelled not by ideological belief, no matter how much they may rationalize to convince themselves they are, but by the distortions of their own personalities. They are not motivated by their advertised urge to serve their country or mankind, but rather by an overwhelming need and compulsion to satisfy the cravings of their own pathological character structures. The ideologies they spout are not real goals; they are the cynical devices by which these sick men hope to achieve some personal sense of worth and power. Subtle inner lies seduce them into going from bad to worse. Defensive self-deception, arrested insight, evasion of emotional identification with others, degradation of empathy—the mind has many defense mechanisms with which to blind the conscience."[74]

When reality is replaced by the whims of opinion and expediency, what is true one day often becomes false the next. Consistency is discarded. Complexity, nuance, depth, and profundity are replaced with the simpleton's belief in threats and force. This is why the Trump administration disdains diplomacy and is dynamiting the State Department. Totalitarianism, wrote novelist and social critic Thomas Mann, is at its core the desire for a simple folktale. Once this folktale replaces reality, morality and ethics are abolished.

"Those who can make you believe absurdities can make you commit atrocities," Voltaire warned.[75]

Mass culture in the hands of corporate power is a potent and dangerous force. It creates a herd mentality. It banishes independent and autonomous thought. It destroys our self-confidence. It marginalizes and discredits dissidents and nonconformists. It depoliticizes the citizenry. It instills a sense of collective futility and impotence by presenting the ruling ideology as a revealed, unassailable truth, an inevitable and inexorable force that alone makes human progress possible. It uses the cant of nationalism and patriotic symbols to mount a continuous celebration of American power and virtues. It disconnects the working class in one country from another—one of the primary objectives of the capitalist class.

Nationalism, the revolutionary theorist Rosa Luxemburg warned, is always a tool used to betray the working class. It is, she wrote, "an instrument of counterrevolutionary class policy."[76] It unleashes powerful forms of indoctrination.

As the contagion of nationalism erupted at the outbreak of the First World War, liberal European parties, including the German Social Democrats, swiftly surrendered to right-wing nationalists in the name of the fatherland despite many years of antiwar rhetoric. Luxemburg saw this betrayal as evidence of the fundamental moral and political bankruptcy of the liberal establishment in a capitalist society. By the time the war was over, eleven million soldiers on all sides, most of them working-class men, were dead. Capitalists, who had grown rich from the slaughter, had nothing to fear now from the working class. They had fed them to the mouths of machine guns.

Mass culture is an assault that, as the Italian Marxist philosopher

Antonio Gramsci wrote, results in a "confused and fragmentary"[77] consciousness, or what Marx called "false consciousness." It is designed to impart the belief to the proletariat that its "true" interests are aligned with those of the ruling class. It transforms legitimate economic and social grievances into psychological and emotional problems. It uses nationalism to discredit class interests.

We are not a product of nature, Gramsci understood, but of our history and our culture. If we do not know our history and our culture, if we accept the history and culture manufactured for us by the elites, we will never free ourselves from the forces of oppression. The recovery of memory and culture in the 1960s by radical movements terrified the elites. It gave people an understanding of their own power and agency. It articulated and celebrated the struggles of working men and women and the oppressed rather than the mythical beneficence of the powerful. It exposed the exploitation and mendacity of the ruling class. And that is why corporatists spent billions to crush and marginalize these movements and their histories in schools, culture, the press, and in our systems of entertainment.

"Not only does the people have no precise consciousness of its own historical identity," Gramsci lamented under fascism, "it is not even conscious of the historical identity or the exact limits of its adversary."[78]

If we do not know our history we have no point of comparison. We cannot name the forces that control us or see the long continuity of capitalist oppression and resistance. A failed democracy, Plato warned, creates the conditions for tyranny based on popular support. This is what happened in fascist Germany and Italy. It is what happened with the election of Trump. When a right-wing populism or fascism takes power our goal is not, as Gramsci said, to rouse "the civic consciousness of the nation,"[79] but to nurture and recreate a civic consciousness that has been lost. This is where we are historically.

Democracy throughout most of the history of the West was an anomaly. After the suppression of Athenian democracy in 322 BC by the Macedonians—and this democracy was only for men and excluded slaves—it was two thousand years before another democratic government came into existence. It has only been in the latter part of the twentieth century that democratic governments were able to flourish, however imperfectly. Our own system of government, if one takes into consideration the exclusion of African Americans, Native Americans, men without property, and women, could not be defined as a full democracy until the middle of the last century. And we are now rolling back toward a more familiar despotism.

Gramsci edited the paper in Turin, *Ordine Nuovo* or "The New Order," during the labor uprisings in 1919 that saw workers take over factory floors and form workers' councils. He and the other writers on the paper—who inexplicably ceased publication at the height of the unrest to devote themselves to organizing—did not advocate positions until they had canvassed and spoken at length to the workers' councils. These councils, Gramsci wrote, not only gave workers power over their work lives but broke down the wall barricading the private citizen from participation in political life.

Capitalist states seek to keep workers unconscious, Gramsci wrote, because no worker under a capitalist system will ever receive the full amount for his or her labor. This would destroy capitalism. Any worker who truly understood his or her interests would be dedicated to the overthrow of capitalism.

Revolution for Gramsci did not come from above but from below. It was organic. And the failure, in his eyes, of revolutionary elites is that they were often as dictatorial and disconnected from workers as capitalist elites. The masses had to be integrated into the structures of power to create a new form of mass politics—hence his insistence that all people are intellectuals capable of autonomous and independent thought. A democracy is possible only when *all* of its citizens understand the machinery of power and have a role in the exercising of power.

Gramsci would have despaired of the divide in the United States between our anemic left and the working class. The ridiculing of Trump supporters, the failure to listen to and heed the legitimate suffering of the working poor, including the white working poor, ensures that any revolt will be stillborn. Those of us who seek to overthrow the corporate state will have to begin locally. This means advocating issues such as raising the minimum wage, fighting for clean water, universal health care, and good public education, including free university education, that speak directly to the improvement of the lives of the working class. It does not mean lecturing the working class, and especially the white working class, about multiculturalism and identity politics. We cannot battle racism, bigotry, and hate crimes, often stoked by the ruling elites, without first battling for economic justice. When we speak in the language of justice first, and the language of inclusiveness second, we will begin to blunt the proto-fascism embraced by many Trump supporters.

Revolt without an alternative political vision, Gramsci knew, was doomed. Workers are as easily mobilized around antidemocratic ideologies such as hyper-nationalism, fascism, and racism. If they lack consciousness, they can become a dark force in the body politic, as history has shown and as we see at Trump rallies and with the proliferation of hate crimes.

"But is it enough that a revolution be carried out by proletarians for it to be a proletarian revolution?" he asked. "War too is made by proletarians, but it is not, for this reason alone, a proletarian event. For it to be so, other, spiritual factors must be present. There must be more to the revolution than the question of power: there must be the question of morality, of a way of life." [80]

The ruling elites, terrified by the mobilization of the left in the 1960s, or by what the Harvard political scientist Samuel P. Huntington called America's "excess of democracy," [81] built counter-institutions to delegitimize and marginalize critics of corporate capitalism and imperialism. They bought the allegiances of the two main political parties by purging from its ranks New Deal Democrats and corporate and imperial critics. They imposed obedience to corporate capitalism and globalization within academia and the press. This campaign, laid out by Lewis Powell in his 1971 memorandum titled "Attack on American Free Enterprise System," was the blueprint for the creeping corporate coup d'état that today is complete. [82]

The destruction of democratic institutions, places where the citizen has agency and a voice, is far graver than the ascendancy to the White House of the demagogue Trump. The coup destroyed our two-party system. It destroyed labor unions. It destroyed public education. It destroyed the judiciary. It destroyed the press. It destroyed academia.

It destroyed consumer and environmental protection. It destroyed our industrial base. It destroyed communities and cities. And it destroyed the lives of tens of millions of Americans no longer able to find work that provides a living wage, cursed to live in chronic poverty or locked in cages in our monstrous system of mass incarceration.

This coup also destroyed the credibility of liberal democracy. Self-identified liberals such as Bill and Hillary Clinton and Barack Obama mouthed the words of liberal democratic values while making war on these values in the service of corporate power. The revolt we see rippling across the country is a revolt not only against a corporate system that has betrayed workers, but also, for many, liberal democracy itself. This is very dangerous. It will allow the radical right to cement into place an Americanized fascism.

It turns out that those who truly hate us for our freedoms are not the array of dehumanized enemies cooked up by the war machine—the Vietnamese, Cambodians, Afghans, Iraqis, Iranians, or even the Taliban, al Qaeda, and ISIS. They are the financiers, bankers, politicians, public intellectuals and pundits, lawyers, journalists, and businesspeople cultivated in the elite universities and business schools who sold us the utopian dream of corporate capitalism and globalization.

Wealth is no longer created by producing or manufacturing products. It is created by manipulating the prices of currencies, stocks, and commodities and imposing a crippling debt peonage on the public. Our casino capitalism has merged with the gambling industry. The entire system is parasitic. It is designed to prey on the desperate—young men and women burdened by student loans, underpaid workers burdened by credit card debt and mortgages, towns and cities forced to borrow to maintain municipal services.

Casino magnates such as Sheldon Adelson and hedge fund managers such as Robert Mercer add nothing of value to society. They do not generate money. They redistribute it upward to the one percent. They use lobbyists and campaign contributions to build monopolies—this is how the drug company Mylan raised the price of the EpiPen, used to treat allergy reactions, from $57 in 2007 to about $500—and to rewrite laws and regulations.[83] They have given themselves the legal power to carry out a de facto tax boycott, loot the U.S. Treasury, close factories, send jobs overseas, and gut social service programs. They have, at the same time, militarized our police, built the most sophisticated security and surveillance apparatus in human history, and used judicial fiat to strip us of our civil liberties. They are ready should we rise up in defiance.

These mandarins are, if we speak in the language of God and country, traitors. Financial speculation in seventeenth-century England was a crime. Speculators were hanged. The heads of most of today's banks and hedge funds and the executives of large corporations, such as Walmart and Gap, that run sweatshop death traps for impoverished workers overseas deserve prison far more than most of the poor students of color I teach within the prison system, people who never had a fair trial or a chance in life.

When a tiny cabal seizes power—monarchist, communist, fascist, or corporate—it creates a mafia economy and a mafia state. Trump is not an anomaly. He is the grotesque visage of a collapsed democracy. Trump and his coterie of billionaires, generals, half-wits, Christian fascists, criminals, racists, and moral deviants play the role of the Snopes clan in some of William Faulkner's novels. The Snopeses filled the power vacuum of the decayed South and ruthlessly seized control from the degenerated, former slaveholding aristocratic elites. Flem Snopes and his extended family—which includes a killer, a pedophile, a bigamist, an arsonist, a mentally disabled man who copulates with a cow, and a relative who sells tickets to witness the bestiality—are fictional representations of the scum now elevated to the highest level of the federal government. They embody the moral rot unleashed by unfettered capitalism.

"The usual reference to 'amorality,' while accurate, is not sufficiently distinctive and by itself does not allow us to place them, as they should be placed, in a historical moment," the critic Irving Howe wrote of the Snopeses. "Perhaps the most important thing to be said is that they are what comes afterwards: the creatures that emerge from the devastation, with the slime still upon their lips. . . .

Let a world collapse, in the South or Russia, and there appear figures of coarse ambition driving their way up from beneath the social bottom, men to whom moral claims are not so much absurd as incomprehensible, sons of bushwhackers or muzhiks drifting in from nowhere and taking over through the sheer outrageousness of their monolithic force. They become presidents of local banks and chairmen of party regional committees, and later, a trifle slicked up, they muscle their way into Congress or the Politburo. Scavengers without inhibition, they need not believe in the crumbling official code of their society; they need only learn to mimic its sounds." [84]

The kleptocrats—and, now, those they con—have no interest in the flowery words of inclusivity, multiculturalism, and democracy that a bankrupt liberal class used with great effectiveness for three decades to swindle the public on behalf of corporations. That rhetoric is a spent force. Barack Obama tried it when he criss-crossed the country during the 2016 presidential campaign telling a betrayed public that Hillary Clinton would finish the job started by his administration.

Political rhetoric has been replaced by the crude obscenities of reality television, the deformed and stunted communication on Twitter, professional wrestling, and the daytime shows in which couples discover if their husband or wife is having an affair. This is the language of Trump, who views the world through the degraded lens of television and the sickness of celebrity culture. This is why he is so effective as a politician. He may be a crass New York billionaire, but he, like much of the public, is also entranced and almost exclusively informed by whatever he sees or hears on television. These electronic hallucinations for him, and many Americans, have replaced reality.

When a society laments the past and dreads the future, when it senses the looming presence of death, it falls down the rabbit hole. And as in the case of Alice in *Alice in Wonderland*, who "went on saying to herself, in a dreamy sort of way, 'Do cats eat bats? Do cats eat bats?' and sometimes, 'Do bats eat cats?' for, you see, as she couldn't answer either question, it didn't much matter which way she put it," [85] language becomes unmoored from reality. Public discourse is reduced to childish gibberish.

CIVILIZATIONS OVER THE PAST SIX thousand years have the habit of eventually squandering their futures through acts of colossal stupidity and hubris. We are not an exception. The physical ruins of these empires, including the Mesopotamian, Egyptian, Greek, Roman, Ottoman, Mayan, and Indus, litter the earth. They elevated, during acute distress, inept and corrupt leaders who channeled anger, fear, and dwindling resources into self-defeating wars and vast building projects. These ruling elites, consumed by greed and hedonism, retreated into privileged compounds—the Forbidden City, Versailles. They hoarded wealth as their populations endured mounting misery, hunger, and poverty. The worse it got, the more the people lied to themselves and the more they wanted to be lied to. Reality was too painful to confront.

Societies in acute distress often form what anthropologists call "crisis cults," which promise recovered grandeur and empowerment during times of collapse, anxiety, and disempowerment. A mythologized past will magically return. America will be great again. The old social hierarchies, opportunities, and rules will be resurrected. Prescribed rituals and behaviors, including acts of violence to cleanse the society of evil, will vanquish the malevolent forces that are blamed for the crisis. These crisis cults—they have arisen in most societies that faced destruction, from Easter Island to Native Americans at the time of the 1890 Ghost Dance—create hermetically sealed tribes informed by magical thinking. We are already far down this road. Our ruling elites are little more than Ice Age hunters in Brooks Brothers suits, as the anthropologist Ronald Wright told me, driving herds of woolly mammoths over cliffs to keep the party going without asking what will happen when the food source suddenly goes extinct.

"The core of the belief in progress is that human values and goals converge in parallel with our increasing knowledge," the philosopher John Gray wrote. "The twentieth century shows the contrary. Human beings use the power of scientific knowledge to assert and defend the values and goals they already have. New technologies can be used to alleviate suffering and enhance freedom. They can, and will, also be used to wage war and strengthen tyranny. Science made possible the technologies that powered the industrial revolution. In the twentieth century, these technologies were used to implement state terror and genocide on an unprecedented scale. Ethics and politics do not advance in line with the growth of knowledge—not even in the long run."[86]

We are entering this final phase of civilization, one in which we are slashing the budgets of the very agencies that are vital to prepare for the devastation ahead—the National Oceanic and Atmospheric Administration, the Federal Emergency Management Agency, and the Environmental Protection Agency, along with programs at the National Aeronautics and Space Administration dealing with climate change. Hurricane after hurricane, monster storm after monster storm, flood after flood, wildfire after wildfire, drought after drought will gradually cripple the empire, draining its wealth and resources and creating swaths of territory defined by lawlessness and squalor.

These dead zones will obliterate not only commercial and residential life but also military assets. As Jeff Goodell points out in *The Water Will Come: Rising Seas, Sinking Cities and the Remaking of the Civilized World*, "The Pentagon manages a global real estate portfolio that includes over 555,000 facilities and 28 million acres of land—virtually all of it will be impacted by climate change in some way."[87]

Three key military facilities in Florida were evacuated in September 2017 because of Hurricane Irma—the Miami-area headquarters of the U.S. Southern Command, which oversees military operations in the Caribbean and Latin America; the U.S. Central Command in Tampa, in charge of overseas operations in the Middle East and Southwest Asia; and the Naval Air Station in Key West. There will soon come a day when obliteration of infrastructure will prohibit military operations from returning. Add to the list of endangered military installations Eglin Air Force Base in the Florida Panhandle, the U.S. missile base in the Marshall Islands, the U.S. naval base on Diego Garcia, and numerous other military sites in coastal areas and it becomes painfully clear that the existential peril facing the empire is not in the Middle East but in the seas and skies. There are 128 U.S. military installations at risk from rising sea levels, including Navy, Air Force, Marine, and Army facilities in Virginia.[88] Giant vertical rulers dot the highway outside the Norfolk naval base to allow motorists to determine if the water is too deep to drive through. In two decades, maybe less, the main road to the base will be impassable at high tide.

Cities across the globe, including London, Shanghai, Rio de Janeiro, Mumbai, Lagos, Copenhagen, Vancouver, New Orleans, Miami, San

Francisco, Savannah, and New York, will become modern-day versions of Atlantis, along with countries such as Bangladesh, the Marshall Islands, and large parts of New Zealand and Australia. There are ninety coastal cities in the U.S. that endure chronic flooding, a number that is expected to double in the next two decades. National economies and internal cohesion will disintegrate as central authority and basic services disappear. Hundreds of millions of people, desperate for food, water, and security, will become climate refugees. Nuclear power plants, including Turkey Point, which is on the edge of Biscayne Bay south of Miami, will face meltdowns, like the Fukushima nuclear plant in Japan after it was destroyed by an earthquake and tsunami. These plants will spew radioactive waste into the sea and air. Exacerbated by disintegration of the polar ice caps, the disasters will be too overwhelming to manage. We will enter what author and social critic James Howard Kunstler calls "the long emergency."[89] When that happens, our experiment in civilization will terminate.

"The amount of real estate at risk in New York is mind-boggling: 72,000 buildings worth over $129 billion stand in flood zones today, with thousands more buildings at risk with each foot of sea-level rise," writes Jeff Goodell. "In addition, New York has a lot of industrial waterfront, where toxic materials and poor communities live in close proximity, as well as a huge amount of underground infrastructure—subways, tunnels, electrical systems. Finally, New York is a sea-level-rise hot spot. Because of changes in ocean dynamics, as well as the fact that the ground beneath the city is sinking as the continent recovers from the last ice age, seas are now rising about 50 percent faster in the New York area than the global average."[90]

Those who ring alarm bells are condemned as pessimists. The current administration—which removed Barack Obama's Climate Action Plan from the White House website as soon as Trump took office—and the Republican Party are filled with happy climate deniers. They have adopted a response to climate change similar to that of the Virginia legislature: ban discussion of climate change and replace the term with the less ominous "recurrent flooding." This denial of reality—one also employed by those who assure us we can adapt—is driven by the fossil

fuel and animal agriculture industries, the two industries most responsible for global warming. They fear that a rational, effective response to
climate change will impede profits. The media, dependent on advertising dollars, contributes to the conspiracy of silence. It ignores the patterns and effects of climate change, focusing instead on feel-good stories
about heroic rescues or dramatic coverage of flooded city centers and
storm refugee caravans fleeing up the coast of Florida.

Droughts, floods, famines, and disease will eventually see the collapse of social cohesion in large parts of the globe, including U.S.
coastal areas. The insecurity, hunger, and desperation among the dispossessed of the earth will give rise to ad hoc militias, crime, and increased acts of terrorism. The Pentagon report "An Abrupt Climate
Change Scenario and Its Implications for United States Security" is
blunt. "Disruption and conflict will be endemic features of life," it
grimly concludes.[91]

But as Goodell points out, "In today's political climate, open discussion of the security risks of climate change is viewed as practically
treasonous." When in 2014 then–Secretary of State John Kerry called
climate change "perhaps the world's most fearsome weapon of mass destruction" and compared it to the effects of terrorism, epidemics, and
poverty, the right-wing, from John McCain to Newt Gingrich, went into
a frenzy. Gingrich called for Kerry's resignation because "a delusional secretary of state is dangerous to our safety."[92]

James Woolsey, the former head of the CIA, wrote in a climate change
report for the Pentagon titled *The Age of Consequences: The Foreign-Policy
National Security Implications of Global Climate Change*:

> If Americans have difficulty reaching a reasonable compromise
> on immigration legislation today, consider what such a debate
> would be like if we were struggling to resettle millions of our
> own citizens—driven by high water from the Gulf of Mexico,
> South Florida, and much of the East Coast reaching nearly to
> New England—even as we witnessed the northward migration
> of large populations from Latin America and the Caribbean.
> Such migration will likely be one of the Western Hemisphere's

early social consequences of climate change and sea level rise of these orders of magnitude. Issues deriving from inundation of a large amount of our own territory, together with migration towards our borders by millions of our hungry and thirsty southern neighbors, are likely to dominate U.S. security and humanitarian concerns. Globally as well, populations will migrate from increasingly hot and dry climates to more temperate ones.[93]

The end is too horrible to contemplate. The tangible signs of our demise may be obvious, but this only accelerates our retreat into the delusional thinking fostered by crisis cults. We will believe, ever more fervently, that the secular gods of science and technology will save us or trust our fate to Jesus and biblical prophecies.

As Goodell writes, "People will notice higher tides that roll in more and more frequently. Water will pool longer in streets and parking lots. Trees will turn brown and die as they suck up salt water." We will retreat to higher ground, cover our roofs with solar panels, finally stop using plastic, and go vegan, but it will be too late. As he writes, "even in rich neighborhoods, abandoned houses will linger like ghosts, filling with feral cats and other refugees looking for their own higher ground."

The damage recently suffered by Houston, Tampa, Miami, and Puerto Rico is not an anomaly. It is the beginning of the end.

The ruling elites grasp that the twin forces of deindustrialization and climate change make the future precarious. They sweep up our email correspondence, tweets, web searches, phone records, file transfers, live chats, financial data, medical data, criminal and civil court records, and information on dissident movements. They store this information in sophisticated computer systems. Surveillance cameras, biosensors, scanners, and face recognition technologies track our movements. When a government watches you twenty-four hours a day you cannot use the word "liberty." This is the relationship between a master and a slave. Full surveillance, as political philosopher Hannah Arendt wrote, is not a means to discover or prevent crimes, but a device to have "on hand when the government decides to arrest a certain category of the population."[94]

We have been stripped of due process and habeas corpus and run the largest prison system in the world. Police are militarized and authorized to kill unarmed citizens, especially poor people of color, with impunity. The 1878 Posse Comitatus Act, which once prohibited the military from acting as a domestic police force, was overturned with the passing of Section 1021 of the National Defense Authorization Act. Section 1021 permits the state to carry out "extraordinary rendition"[95] on the streets of American cities and hold citizens indefinitely in military detention centers without due process—in essence disappearing them as in any totalitarian state. The executive branch of government can assassinate U.S. citizens.[96] Corporate loyalists in the courts treat corporations as people and people as noisome impediments to corporate profit.

THE CITY CENTER OF SCRANTON, nicknamed the Electric City for introducing electric streetcars in 1886, resembles a forlorn outpost in the old Austro-Hungarian Empire. It has imposing, stone buildings: the Romanesque Lackawanna County Courthouse; the Scottish Rite Cathedral—a huge Masonic temple with a 1,856-seat theater and a grand ballroom that can hold 2,300 people—and an ornate neo-Gothic municipal building.[97] There are large churches such as the neoclassical St. Peter's Cathedral and St. Luke's, with its Tiffany mosaic panel behind the font showing the ascension of Christ. These majestic buildings are surrounded by empty storefronts, shuttered movie theaters, potholed streets, boarded-up warehouses, decayed clapboard and stucco row houses, along with doughnut shops, tattoo parlors, and vacant lots. The city's population has declined from 140,000[98] to 77,000[99] over the past eight decades.

Above the city, in the Hill and Green Ridge sections of Scranton, sit the moldering Victorian mansions of the old coal barons, many of them cut up into apartments, some given over to the elements. The city, which around 1900 had the second-highest per capita income in the country, made its money first in iron and then in anthracite coal.[100] All of the rails in the country were once forged in its iron furnaces. Scranton was a mecca for Welsh, German, Irish, Italian, Polish, Russian, and Lithuanian immigrants. And it was in these mines and on the streets of this city that the United Mine Workers of America (UMWA) was born.

The workers paid in blood for their rights and their union. There were strikes in 1877 in Scranton, part of a nationwide railroad strike, over wage cuts and poor working conditions.[101] Striking miners and railroad employees were shot and several were killed by private militias and armed vigilantes hired by the coal and railroad barons. Martial law was declared.[102] Five thousand federal troops occupied the city after members of the state militia, which had been sent in to quell the strike, refused to open fire on the strikers. But the miners persisted, striking in 1900 for a wage increase, and two years later shutting down the mines again for higher pay and better conditions.

I stood outside the county courthouse in front of a statue of John Mitchell, president of the United Mine Workers of America from 1898 to 1908.[103] Mitchell led the 1902 strike.[104] He worked closely in the Pennsylvania coalfields with the radical agitator Mary Harris "Mother" Jones. Mitchell grew the union from 34,000 members to 300,000.[105] A strike in 1923 instituted the eight-hour workday (miners had been putting in up to fourteen hours a day).[106] In 1925 and 1926, 83,000 anthracite miners walked off the job for 170 days.

The city gradually diversified its industry, especially after 1902 when the Lackawanna Iron and Steel Company, founded by the Scranton family, moved its plant to a site outside Buffalo. The company was once the second-largest steel producer in the world.[107] Factories in Scranton began to produce cotton, silk, woolens, plastics, buttons, leather, shoes, furniture, mattresses, and apparel. The miners continued to dig coal.

The city became a fierce union town. The Brotherhood of Locomotive Engineers. The Knights of Labor. The American Federation of Labor. The International Ladies' Garment Workers' Union. The United Mine Workers of America. The Industrial Workers of the World, known as the Wobblies. All gone today. Of the last fifty firms to move into the county, only one, Verizon Communications, was organized, and that was because of a national contract. The only unions left, as in much of America, are the state, federal, and municipal employees unions. Less than 7 percent of workers in the private sector are unionized, a level not seen since 1932.[108]

Most of the factories are abandoned. A few serve as warehouses. I visited what was once the Capitol Records plant on the edge of Scranton, where, from 1946 until it closed in 1970, it pressed records for artists such as Frank Sinatra and the Beatles. The company name painted in large white letters, rimmed with blue, was still faintly visible on the brick facade.

Jim DiGiacoma from Olde Good Things, a New York–based company, was in the city hunting for merchandise. His company retrieves items from buildings slated for demolition, including light fixtures, bathtubs, mahogany fireplace mantels, decorative iron, and heavy oak doors. He ships some of his salvage overseas, especially to Japan. It is part of the physical cannibalization, the harvesting, of the carcass of industrial America. His company stripped Scranton's eleven-story, 250-room Hotel Casey before the building was torn down in 2001. Opened in 1911, the hotel had mahogany doors, huge terra-cotta lion heads, and ornate domed ceilings. It was replaced by a parking garage.

"We can fill forty-foot containers," said the gray-bearded DiGiacoma, standing near a large blue metal sign that once spelled out "Capitol Records" in neon lights. "We ship all over the world."

Scranton was where the playwright Jason Miller, who grew up in the city, set his 1973 Pulitzer Prize–winning play, *That Championship Season*. Four middle-aged players from a Catholic high school basketball team meet in the home of their terminally ill coach to celebrate the twentieth anniversary of their state championship. The fifth member of the starting lineup, Martin, who made the game-winning shot, refuses to attend.

"State Champions!" the coach says to his old players. "They said we couldn't do it, boys. We beat a school three times our size. We beat them in Philadelphia. We performed the impossible, boys, never forget that, never. Jesus, remember they had an eight-foot nigger, jumped like a kangaroo." [109]

The heady dreams and promises of youth in postindustrial America have shattered. The mantra, preached by the coach, of hard work, teamwork, a positive attitude, success, and the mythical values of America has been exposed as a fraud. The coach's heroes—Senator Joe McCarthy and the right-wing demagogue Father Charles Coughlin—are discredited relics of anticommunism. The world has not turned out to be the one painted for the young men in the coach's locker room in 1952.

Tom Daley, a cynical, failed writer, is an alcoholic. Phil Romano, who has become a millionaire from strip mining, is greedy and corrupt.

James Daley, Tom's brother, is an embittered school principal. George Sikowski, the mayor, is buffoonish, inept, and unpopular. He is facing the prospect of being defeated in the next election and needs Romano's financial support, something Romano gives because the mayor grants him mining permits. Romano is also having an affair with the mayor's wife. Their lives are not defined by virtues but by bribery, dishonesty, cheating, graft, political patronage, and racism.

Miller writes:

TOM: Stop lying to us. Stop telling us how good we were.

COACH (to Tom): We never had a losing season and we're not starting now . . .

TOM: That's not what Martin said.

COACH: What?

TOM: Martin? Remember him?

COACH: Yeah

TOM: But he's not here. You know why he left, why he never came back to a reunion.

COACH (Pause): Do I?

TOM: He told us the truth, twenty years ago.

COACH: Did he?

TOM: He wanted you to publicly refuse the trophy, remember? You told him in the third quarter to get that nigger center, the kangaroo, remember? He did. He went out and broke the guy's ribs.

COACH: I told him to stop him. That nigger was playing him off the court, and I told him to get tough under the boards and stop him.

TOM: He came to you a week after the game.

COACH: That's right, he did. He came to me . . . he walked in here. He came babbling something about the truth. What truth, I said, we won. That trophy is the truth, the only truth. I told him to get mean, punish some people, put some fear into them, you have to hate to win, it takes hate to win. I didn't tell him to break anybody's ribs.

(Pause). You don't believe me boys? (Appeal to majority)

GEORGE: I believe you, Coach.

TOM: We have gone through this phony ritual, champions? Shit! We stole it.

COACH: I told him there is no such thing as second place.[110]

Miller captures in the play the darkest pathology of white America—the inability to accept who we are, where we came from, acknowledge and take responsibility for the crimes we committed and with that understanding access where we are going and who we want to become. The danger of self-delusion is the central point of Miller's play.

Daniel Boorstin in *The Image: A Guide to Pseudo-Events in America* notes that in contemporary culture the fabricated, the inauthentic, and the theatrical have displaced the natural, the genuine, and the spontaneous. Reality has been converted into image and stagecraft. Americans, he writes, increasingly live in a "world where fantasy is more real than reality."[111]

"We risk being the first people in history to have been able to make their illusions so vivid, so persuasive, so 'realistic' that they can live in them," he writes. "We are the most illusioned people on earth. Yet we dare not become disillusioned, because our illusions are the very house in which we live; they are our news, our heroes, our adventure, our forms of art, our very experience."[112]

Societies and individuals, however, that make decisions about themselves and the future based on illusions, as Miller understood, self-destruct.

I WENT LATE ONE AFTERNOON to the Northern Light Espresso Bar on Courthouse Square in the center of the city. The clients there were divided into two groups: those who could leave Scranton and those who could not.

Megan Collelo, twenty-seven, was a lawyer who, for the past year, had clerked for a civil judge. She grew up in Scranton. She and her boyfriend planned to leave in a month. She said she did not want to raise children here.

"Independent businesses, except maybe restaurants, don't survive," she said. "They start up, and in less than two years they are gone. You see the conditions of the city right now economically. There is nowhere to go but up. We pretty much hit rock bottom.

"You wonder if we are going to have cops anymore," she added. "Can the city government function when there is nothing to fund it?"

At another table sat a victim of the economic collapse. Andrea McGuigan—who grew up in a nearby farm town and graduated with a degree in English literature from Mount Holyoke College, in Massachusetts—ran Anthology, the city's only bookstore at the time. It went out of business in 2011 after four and a half years. The local Electric Theatre Company, hit by the downturn in 2008, also folded due to lack of funds. The city zoo was shut down in 2009 after national attention was focused on the poor condition of its animals. McGuigan, thirty-one, now worked for the public library branch at the mall at Steamtown, in the city center. Half of the shops in the mall were empty. *smells of capitalism*

"Everyone loved the idea of supporting a local bookstore, but no one was actually buying books," she said. "They were still shopping on Amazon and [buying downloads for their] Kindles. People would say, 'I would love to buy books from you, but it is just so much cheaper to go online.' Amazon could sell books at the discount price I was paying to buy them wholesale. I knew that going in, but I thought having events, having a unique space that was tremendously gorgeous and architecturally rich and historical—I thought it would be a place where people would want to meet. I had great sideline items, so I wasn't just relying on books. I sold new and used, mostly used, so I could sell cheaper books. I wasn't trying to compete in the new hardcover market—and it still didn't work."

"When a city doesn't have a bookstore, what does it lose?" I asked.

"It loses its soul," she said. "It loses a major part of its cultural offering. I would never move to a city that didn't have a bookstore. I don't even want to live in a city that doesn't have one."

"Do you live here now?" I asked.

"I do," she said. "And I do love Scranton very much."

Apart from work in hospitals and universities, the roughly 100,000 jobs[113] in Lackawanna County are mostly in service industries—call centers, warehouse loading and unloading, trucking, and staffing administrative centers for banks and insurance companies. Bank of America, for example, employs eight hundred people. Prudential Retirement has about nine hundred workers, and MetLife around five hundred. Most of these jobs start at about $13.50 an hour. The service center personnel include accountants, IT specialists, and systems analysts, often recruited from countries such as India, who can make $45,000 or $50,000 a year. There is a growing South Asian population in the city.

Maximus, a service provider to America's for-profit health care industry, employs attorneys and doctors, and is contracted by the federal government to hear appeals from patients who seek medical procedures but have been turned down by Medicare. The attorneys and doctors at Maximus can make as much as six figures. A customer service representative at the Scranton call center makes about $25,000 a year.

In Scranton, as in the rest of the country, a widening economic divide exists between elite professionals and the working class. Those who earn middle-class salaries with pension plans and benefits have largely vanished. And those who do pull in middle-class incomes of $50,000 or $60,000 a year put in staggering hours and usually have more than one job.

I found Pat Langan, a janitor, in the basement of George Bancroft Elementary School, which was built in 1928 and named for the scholar who promoted secondary education throughout the United States. Langan, with graying stubble, a mustache, and broad, powerful shoulders, was the father of five children. He was wearing a T-shirt with a red, white, and blue guitar that read "Freedom Rocks." He had a degree in psychology and a year toward a master's in social work that he never finished. He had spent his life as a manual laborer.

"I get up twenty after six in the morning," he said, seated in a child's chair in the school library, where an air conditioner battled the summer heat. "I get here by ten to seven. I work until two-thirty or quarter to three. I go home and take a shower, maybe eat. During the summer, I usually cut lawns. I come back home. I shower again, watch TV, and go to bed, usually around midnight. On Sunday, Monday, and Wednesday, I clean a laundromat from about nine at night to eleven or eleven-thirty.

On Thursday, Friday, and Saturday nights, I work overnight at Walmart. I stock shelves. Customer service. Cashier. You name it."

He worked seventy to seventy-five hours a week. He made $15 an hour at Walmart and about the same as a janitor. He was paid $25 a night to clean the laundromat. This gave him and his family about $50,000 after taxes. He was in the middle class, but the effort he made to get there was Herculean. And if his health goes, he is finished, as are those who depend on him, including a daughter struggling to raise three children alone, and a son with Asperger's syndrome who lives at home. He hoped to keep his janitor's job at the school for another seven years, when he would be sixty-eight. If he can hang on, he can retire on an adequate pension, but with the city's persistent layoffs he might not make it.

"I try to do everything for my children," he said. "I know I neglect myself, a lot. I should be slowing down.

"The country's gone downhill, no doubt about it," he went on. "It's like a snowball going downhill. It's getting worse. Everybody seems to know what is wrong with the country, what is wrong with the city, but nobody has any answers. Leaders? We don't have much choice. When they get in there, it is like that Who song: 'Meet the new boss, the same as the old boss. We won't get fooled again.' It's the same wherever you go.

"We are not the superpower we were," he continued softly. "I don't know that in this day and age you can overthrow the government."

His daughter Kelly, twenty-six, worked behind the counter of the Northern Light Espresso Bar. She had been there for four years and made $9 an hour. She finished one semester of college but dropped out.

"We've had a lot of troubles," she said, "bad luck with everything. One of my brothers, Kevin, is mentally disabled. He lives at home. He gets Social Security. I have a sister raising three kids alone. She works as a waitress at Marvelous Muggs. One of the fathers is in jail. The other should be. They don't help her out. We take care of the kids a lot. I have no health insurance."

Kelly lived with her parents, she was trying to pay off a $5,000 student loan. Her brother Kevin went into a rage two years ago and held a knife to their mother's throat for seven hours. Kelly called the police. A SWAT team, an ambulance, and snipers surrounded the house before

Kevin was talked into giving himself up. He spent a month in jail, on suicide watch part of the time.

"My mom was more upset because we had to press charges, since the cops witnessed it," she said.

"Kevin tried to work at McDonald's," she went on, "but he has really bad anxiety. He doesn't do well in social situations. Our next goal is to get him to start learning how to drive and be independent."

She trailed off.

"It breaks my heart to see my father work so hard and not get ahead," she sighed.

Sitting next to her, her friend Danielle Rinaldi, who worked at Men's Wearhouse, started to cry. Danielle, twenty-nine, had her grandmother's birth and death dates and a hummingbird tattooed on her back. On her left wrist, she had a black puzzle piece, on her right rib cage a feather. She had an elephant on the back of her neck and the name of a man, who moved to Australia, on the inside of her lip. Kelly had an ice cream sundae tattooed on the inside of her left forearm, a bubble gum machine inside her right forearm, and a cupcake on her upper right arm.

"I hope I'm not working at a coffee shop in however many more years," she said.

That night I went to The Bog, a bar where local artists and musicians hang out. It was trivia night. The Todd Rundgren song "Hello It's Me" was playing. Conor McGuigan, who a few weeks earlier married Andrea, the former bookstore owner, read off the twenty questions.

"How many provinces are in Canada?" he shouted out.

Conor worked in regional theater. Next to the bar was an abandoned hardware store, once owned by his family.

"My grandfather died in that store in 1963 from a heart attack," he said as we stood on the sidewalk in front of the old hardware store afterward. He pointed to the blacked-out windows. "Over there, in the third bay, up above it is an abandoned six-hundred-seat theater," he said. "Frank Sinatra and Louis Armstrong played there."

Brian Reese, who joined us, had a job until a few days earlier, at a restaurant called Farley's. It closed after thirty years. He was standing on the sidewalk with the smokers. He had gone back to college to finish his degree. His wife taught public school.

"So much has happened to us," he said. "There should be such profound anger. But everyone seems docile, although many people around here are stockpiling weapons. You hear a lot of talk about guns."

I ask him what he wanted to do next.

"An MFA in creative writing," he said. "Act. Enrich my life. I've done a lot of drudgery, blue-collar jobs.

"We celebrate mining here, although it left the area environmentally devastated," he said. "Yet we see it as part of our heritage. No one is questioning why it is happening again, why a new breed of robber barons is allowed to pump poison into the ground with fracking."

One of the last functioning factories in the city makes Avanti Cigars. It has operated in Scranton for a century. Along with brands such as De Nobili and Petri, it produces Parodi cigars, nicknamed "the little stinkers" by coal miners who, forbidden to smoke on the job, chewed the tightly wound, long, dark cigars as they worked. There are also bourbon- and anise-flavored versions.

The factory employs twenty-eight people. It has a dozen rolling machines. A couple of decades ago, there were seventy workers operating sixteen machines. Built in 1954, the rollers clanked and hummed with activity on the cement floor. The cigars are dipped into a mixture of water, cornstarch, and sugar and laid out on racks to dry. Many of the employees, wearing rubber gloves and smocks as they attended to the machines, had been here for years. They started at $9.25 an hour.

Workers no longer stemmed the leaves. That work is done in Sri Lanka. But the pride of artisanship and the sense of place that come with longevity, and in some cases family ties, were palpable.

"My father is the head mechanic," said Chris Ayers, thirty-one, who kept the racks loaded and filled the rolling machines' paste boxes. "My mother worked here. My grandmother worked here. My father has been here over twenty years. Barb, who I work with, has been here almost forty, and Kathy, the supervisor, has been here over thirty. This company has been in the same family for a hundred years. That makes a big difference."

Austin J. Burke, who for thirty-one years was the president of the Greater Scranton Chamber of Commerce, met me in his office. He paints pictures of local buildings and landscapes. His work lined the walls. He lost his grandfather, crushed between two coal cars, and three uncles in mining accidents. His parents were teachers. The coal industry was already in decline when he was a boy. He worked summers driving a truck for the apparel factories.

"I spent one summer driving a dress truck," he said, speaking of 1964. "We had a central plant where we would cut all of this stuff. Then you would take it out to all these outlying plants, little mom-and-pop shops, like sweatshops. You would drop off the cut material and pick up the finished pieces and take it back to the central. It was going down at that point. It was really declining in the eighties and nearly gone by the nineties."

"Where did they go?" I asked.

"Haiti," he answered.

"We were doing cut and sew," he said. "We were primarily serving the New York houses. We made some great high-fashion stuff. See these pants?"

He put his leg up on the desk and tugged at the khaki.

"These are Brooks Brothers pants," he said. "I bought them at Pawnee Pants in Olyphant, Pennsylvania. They were retailing for seventy bucks at the time. I got them for $12 or $15. We did quality stuff. We did stuff that needed quick turnaround."

Down the street, Michael Frenchko, the owner of Electric City Tattoo Gallery, stood over twenty-two-year-old Manny Masankay, who lay on his table. Frenchko was inking a Martin Luther King quote onto Masankay's torso. Masankay said he picked it because of "not having a dad and stuff." It read, "The ultimate measure of a man is not where he stands in moments of comfort and convenience, but where he stands at times of challenge and controversy."

When Plato wrote *The Republic*, his lament for the lost Athenian democracy, he did not believe democracy could be resurrected in Athens. The classical world, unlike our own, did not see time as linear. Life was cyclical. It entailed birth, growth, maturation, decay, and death. The concept of inevitable human progress was foreign to ancient societies.

What was true for individuals was true for societies. In *The Republic*, Plato proposed that those who attempt to create the ideal state should carry out a series of draconian measures, including banning drama and music and removing children from their parents to indoctrinate them. These were Plato's desperate attempts to slow what he saw as the inevitable process of decay. But that decay and death would come, even in the ideal state, was inevitable. The Greek goddesses of fate—the Moirai—held an unalterable and tragic control over human destiny.

Plato began *The Republic* with Socrates visiting the Athenian port of Piraeus. Piraeus was filled with taverns and brothels. It was populated by beggars, thieves, galley slaves, soldiers, mercenaries, criminal gangs, and a riotous collection of Egyptian, Persian, Mede, Celt, Germanic, Phoenician, and Carthaginian sailors whose mix of discordant native tongues to the Greeks saw them lumped together as *barbarous*, barbarians. Piraeus was where elaborate spectacles and bawdy entertainment diverted the population from the sober vocation of citizenship. It was what the arena was to ancient Rome, what electronic screens and huge sporting events and concerts are to modernity.

Socrates arrived at the port as it was preparing for an all-night festival that would include a "torch race on horseback for the goddess."[114] The port was also where the Athenian war fleet, the black, trireme ships with their bronze-sheathed rams on the prow, was housed in rows of military boathouses. These warships turned Athens from a democratic city-state into an empire in the fifth century BC. And, as Plato and his pupil Aristotle understood, the building of empire, any empire, extinguishes democracy. Empire requires a centralized bureaucracy. Its complexity mandates a permanent caste of bureaucrats and military leaders who strip the citizenry of power.

Aristotle warned that in a democracy, there always existed the potential for the poor to seize the property of the rich. Democracy, Aristotle wrote, could not coexist with huge levels of inequality. Everyone had to have a stake in society. There were other responses to Aristotle's understanding, including from Athenian tyrants and later James Madison, who urged government to reduce democracy and cripple the political power of the working class.

Plato saw Piraeus as a physical manifestation of the decay and corruption that accompanied the death of democracy. These symptoms of morbidity, as the Greeks and later Sigmund Freud knew, had a seductive allure. They offered an escape from the forces of life through historical amnesia, illusions, hedonism, dreams of grandeur, nihilistic violence, a perverted sexuality, spectacle, a vain quest for eternal youth, and the persecution of truth-tellers such as Socrates.

[margin note: again ignoring reality]

The ruling elites who had abandoned civic virtue and the common good, Plato wrote, manipulated illusions flickering on the wall of a cave to distract and beguile the public. These distorted images of reality—our array of electronic images were beyond Plato's imagination—provoked irrational desires. It was a visionless life. And those who attempted to puncture the comforting illusions were, as Socrates warned, swiftly silenced or killed by the mob. Epicureanism, the belief that we should free ourselves from the prison of affairs and politics to focus our lives on pursuits independent of political association, arose to mock the Socratic call for civic engagement. Cynicism ruled. The community broke down, and "all goes wrong when, starved for lack of anything good in their own lives, men turn to public affairs hoping to snatch from thence the happiness they hunger for. They set about fighting for power, and their internecine conflict ruins them and their country."[115]

Collapse created a dreamworld "where men live fighting one another about elaborate shadows and quarreling for power, as if that were a great prize."[116] Once caught up in the frenzied Danse Macabre, it became impossible to escape until, as it always does, death worked its dark magic, dooming a once vibrant civilization to extinction.

TAKE SCRANTON AND MULTIPLY IT by a few thousand, and you have contemporary America. In nearly all of the country's nineteen thousand municipalities,[117] declining or stagnant property tax revenues, along with mounting costs, have reached crisis proportions.

The opioid crisis, the mass shootings, the rising rates of suicide, especially among middle-aged white males, the morbid obesity, the obsession with gambling, the investment of our emotional and intellectual life in tawdry spectacles, and the allure of magical thinking, from the

[handwritten: false reality that as Americans we accept as the norm. ↓]

absurd promises of the Christian right to the belief that reality is never an impediment to our desires, are the pathologies of a diseased culture. They have risen from a decayed world where opportunity, which confers status, self-esteem, and dignity, has dried up for most Americans. They are expressions of morbidity.

A loss of adequate income and social stagnation causes more than financial distress. It severs, as the sociologist Émile Durkheim pointed out in *The Division of Labour in Society*, the vital social bonds that give us meaning. A decline in status and power, an inability to advance, a lack of education and health care, and a loss of hope are crippling forms of humiliation. This humiliation fuels loneliness, frustration, anger, and feelings of worthlessness. In short, when you are marginalized and rejected by society, life often has little meaning. There arises a yearning among the disempowered to become as omnipotent as the gods. The impossibility of omnipotence leads, as the cultural anthropologist Ernest Becker wrote in *The Denial of Death*, to its dark alternative—destroying like the gods. *[handwritten: and unavoidable to this point.]*

In *Hitler and the Germans* the political philosopher Eric Voegelin dismissed the myth that Hitler—an uneducated mediocrity whose only strengths were oratory and an ability to exploit political opportunities—mesmerized and seduced the German people. The Germans, he wrote, voted for Hitler and the "grotesque, marginal figures"[118] surrounding him because he embodied the pathologies of a diseased society, one beset by economic collapse, hopelessness, and violence.

Voegelin defined stupidity as a "loss of reality."[119] This loss of reality meant a "stupid" person could not "rightly orient his action in the world, in which he lives."[120] The demagogue, who is always an *idiote*, is not a freak or a social mutation. The demagogue expresses the society's zeitgeist.

"The fool in Hebrew, the *nabal*, who because of his folly, *nebala*, creates disorder in the society, is the man who is not a believer, in the Israelite terms of revelation," Voegelin wrote. "The *amathes*, the irrationally ignorant man, is for Plato the man who just does not have the authority of reason or who cannot bow to it. The *stultus* for Thomas [Aquinas] is the fool, in the same sense as the *amathia* of Plato and the *nebala* of the Israelite prophets. This *stultus* now has suffered loss of reality and acts on the basis of a defective image of reality and thereby creates disorder . . .

If I have lost certain sectors of reality from my range of experience, I will also be lacking the language for appropriately characterizing them. That means that parallel to the loss of reality and to stupidity there is always the phenomenon of illiteracy." [121]

A society convulsed by disorder and chaos, as Voegelin pointed out, elevates and even celebrates the morally degenerate, those who are cunning, manipulative, deceitful, and violent. In an open society these attributes are despised and criminalized. Those who exhibit them are condemned as stupid—"a man [or woman] who behaves in this way," Voegelin notes, "will be socially boycotted." [122] But the social, cultural, and moral norms in a diseased society are inverted. The attributes that sustain an open society—truth, honesty, trust, and self-sacrifice—are detrimental to existence in a diseased society.

The idiots take over in the final days of crumbling civilizations. Idiot generals wage endless, unwinnable wars that bankrupt the nation. Idiot economists call for reducing taxes for corporation and the rich and cutting social service programs for the poor. They project economic growth on the basis of myth. Idiot industrialists poison the water, the soil, and the air, slash jobs and depress wages. Idiot bankers gamble on self-created financial bubbles. Idiot journalists and public intellectuals pretend despotism is democracy. Idiot intelligence operatives orchestrate the overthrow of foreign governments to create lawless enclaves that give rise to enraged fanatics. Idiot professors, "experts," and "specialists" busy themselves with unintelligible jargon and arcane theory that buttresses the policies of the rulers. Idiot entertainers and producers create lurid spectacles of sex, gore, and fantasy.

There is a familiar checklist for extinction. We are ticking off every item on it.

The idiots know only one word—"more." They are unencumbered by common sense. They hoard wealth and resources until workers cannot make a living and the infrastructure collapses. They live in privileged compounds. They see the state as a projection of their vanity. The Roman, Mayan, French, Habsburg, Ottoman, Romanov, Wilhelmine, Pahlavi, and Soviet dynasties crumbled because the whims and obsessions of ruling idiots were law.

Trump is the face of our collective idiocy. He is what lies behind the mask of our professed civility and rationality—a sputtering, narcissistic, imbecilic megalomaniac. He wields armies and fleets against the wretched of the earth, blithely ignores the catastrophic human misery caused by global warming, pillages on behalf of global oligarchs, and at night sits slack-jawed in front of a television set before opening his "beautiful"[123] Twitter app. He is our version of the Roman emperor Nero, who allocated vast state expenditures to attain magical powers, the Chinese emperor Qin Shi Huang, who funded repeated expeditions to a mythical island of immortals in search of a potion for eternal life, and a delusional Russian royalty that sat in their palaces reading tarot cards and holding séances as war decimated their nation and revolution brewed in the streets.

This moment in history marks the end of a long, sad tale of greed and murder by the white races. It is inevitable that for the final show we vomited up a figure like Trump. Europeans and Americans have spent five centuries conquering, plundering, exploiting, and polluting the earth in the name of human progress. They used their technological superiority to create the most efficient killing machines on the planet, directed against anyone and anything, especially indigenous cultures, which stood in their way. They stole and hoarded the planet's wealth and resources. They believed that this orgy of blood and gold would never end, and they still believe it. They do not understand that the dark ethic of ceaseless capitalist and imperialist expansion is dooming the exploiters as well as the exploited. But even as we stand on the cusp of extinction we lack the intelligence and imagination to break free from our evolutionary past. As the warning signs become more palpable—rising temperatures, global financial meltdowns, mass human migrations, endless wars, poisoned ecosystems, rampant corruption among the ruling class—we turn to those who chant, either through idiocy or cynicism, the mantra that what worked in the past will work in the future. Factual evidence, since it is an impediment to what we desire, is banished.

Walter Benjamin wrote in 1940 amid the rise of European fascism and looming world war:

A Klee painting named *Angelus Novus* shows an angel looking as though he is about to move away from something he is fixedly contemplating. His eyes are staring, his mouth is open, his wings are spread. This is how one pictures the angel of history. His face is turned towards the past. Where we perceive a chain of events, he sees one single catastrophe, which keeps piling wreckage upon wreckage and hurls it in front of his feet. The angel would like to stay, awaken the dead, and make whole what has been smashed. But a storm is blowing from Paradise; it has got caught in his wings with such violence that the angel can no longer close them. The storm irresistibly propels him into the future to which his back is turned, while the pile of debris before him grows skyward. This storm is what we call progress.[124]

Magical thinking is not limited to the beliefs and practices of premodern cultures. It defines the ideology of capitalism. Quotas and projected sales can always be met. Profits can always be raised. Growth is inevitable. The impossible is always possible. Human societies, if they bow before the dictates of the marketplace, will be ushered into capitalist paradise. It is only a question of having the right attitude and the right technique. When capitalism thrives, we are assured, we thrive. The merging of the self with the capitalist collective has robbed us of our agency, creativity, capacity for self-reflection, and moral autonomy. We define our worth not by our independence or our character but by the material standards set by capitalism—personal wealth, brands, status, and career advancement. We are molded into a compliant and repressed collective. This mass conformity is characteristic of totalitarian and authoritarian states. It is the Disneyfication of America, the land of eternally happy thoughts and positive attitudes. And when magical thinking does not work, we are told, and often accept, that we are the problem. We must adjust. We must have more faith. We must be positive. We must envision what we want. We must try harder. The system is never to blame. We failed it. It did not fail us.

All of our systems of information, from self-help gurus and Hollywood to political monstrosities such as Trump, sell us this snake oil. Our retreat into self-delusion is a career opportunity for charlatans who tell us what we want to hear. The magical thinking they espouse is a form of infantilism. It discredits facts and realities that mock slogans such as "Make America Great Again."

The profound alienation experienced by most Americans, the loss of self-esteem and hope, has engendered what Durkheim referred to as a collective state of *anomie*.[125] *Anomie* is a psychological imbalance that leads to prolonged despair, lethargy, and yearnings for self-annihilation. It is caused by a collapse of societal norms, ideals, values, and standards. It is, in short, a loss of faith in the structures and beliefs that define a functioning democracy. The result is an obliteration of purpose and direction, what Friedrich Nietzsche saw as the core malady of modernity: its aggressive despiritualized nihilism. This nihilism, in its most radical form, is impervious to ethical critique and must be fought, as Nietzsche understood, with a matching religious fevor.

Trump's ideological vacuum, the more he is isolated and attacked, is filled by the proto-fascist forces of the Christian right. This Christianized fascism, with its network of megachurches, schools, universities, and law schools and its vast radio and television empire, is a potent ally for a beleaguered White House. The Christian right has been organizing and preparing to take power for decades. If the nation suffers another economic collapse, which is probably inevitable, another catastrophic domestic terrorist attack, or a new war, Trump's ability to force the Christian right's agenda on the public and shut down dissent will be dramatically enhanced. In the presidential election, Trump had 81 percent of white evangelicals behind him.[126] If he leaves or is removed from office, Mike Pence, a creature of the Christian Right, will be worse.

Trump's moves to restrict abortion, defund Planned Parenthood, permit discrimination against LGBT people in the name of "religious liberty,"[127] and allow churches to become active in politics by gutting the Johnson Amendment, along with his nominations of judges championed by the Federalist Society and his call for a ban on Muslim immigrants, have endeared him to the Christian right. He has rolled back civil rights legislation and business and environmental regulations. He has elevated several stalwarts of the Christian right into power—Pence to the vice presidency, Jeff Sessions to the Justice Department, Neil Gorsuch to the Supreme Court, Betsy DeVos to the Department of Education, Tom Price to Health and Human Services (from which he was forced to resign), and Ben Carson to Housing and Urban Development. He embraces the white supremacy, bigotry, American chauvinism, greed, religious intolerance, anger, and racism that define the Christian right.

Trump's disdain for facts and his penchant for magical thinking and conspiracy theories mesh well with the worldview of the Christian right, which sees itself as under attack by the satanic forces of secular humanism embodied in the media, academia, the liberal establishment, Hollywood, and the Democratic Party. In this worldview, climate change is not real, Barack Obama is a Muslim, and millions of people voted illegally in the 2016 election.

The followers of the Christian right are Manichaeans. They see the world in black and white, good and evil, them and us. Trump's call in his speech in Poland for a crusade against the godless hordes of Muslims fleeing from the wars and chaos we created replicates the view of the Christian right. Christian right leaders in a sign of support went to the White House on July 10, 2017, to pray over Trump. Two days later Pat Robertson showed up there to interview the president for his Christian Broadcasting Network. If the alliance between these zealots and the government succeeds, it will snuff out the last vestiges of American democracy.

On the surface it appears to be incongruous that the Christian right would rally behind a slick New York real estate developer who is a public serial philanderer and adulterer, has no regard for the truth, is consumed by greed, does not appear to read or know the Bible, routinely defrauds and cheats his investors and contractors, expresses a crude misogyny and an even cruder narcissism, and appears to yearn for despotism. In fact, these are the very characteristics that define many of the leaders of the Christian right.

Trump has preyed on desperate people through the thousands of slot machines in his casinos, his sham university, and his real estate deals. Megachurch pastors prey on their followers by extracting "seed offerings," "love gifts," tithes, and donations and by selling miracle healings along with "prayer cloths," self-help books, audio and video recordings,

[handwritten marginalia: This doesn't mean all rel. it means the ppl who do not separate Church & State, using religion as a power not faith]

and even protein shakes.[128] Pastors have established within their mega-churches, as Trump did in his businesses, despotic fiefdoms. They cannot be challenged or questioned any more than an omnipotent Trump could be challenged on the reality television show *The Apprentice*. And they seek to replicate their little tyrannies on a national scale, with white men in charge.

The personal piety of many of the ministers who lead the Christian right is a facade. Their private lives are usually marked by hedonistic squalor that includes mansions, private jets, limousines, retinues of body-guards, personal assistants and servants, shopping sprees, lavish vacations, and sexual escapades that rival those carried out by Trump. They use the church's tax-exempt status to fund their extravagant lifestyles. They also engage in the nepotism found in the Trump organization, elevating family members to prominent or highly paid positions and passing on the businesses to their children.

The Christian right's scandals, which give a glimpse into the sordid lives of these multimillionaire pastors, are legion. Jim and Tammy Faye Bakker's Praise the Lord Club, for example, raked in as much as $1 million a week before Jim Bakker went to prison for nearly five years. He was convicted of fraud and other charges in 1989 because of a $158 million scheme in which followers paid for vacations that never materialized.[129] As the Bakker empire came apart, there also were accusations of drug use and rape.[130] Tammy Faye died in 2007, and now Jim Bakker is back, peddling survival food for the end days[131] and telling his significantly reduced television audience that anyone who opposes Trump is the Antichrist.[132]

Paul and Jan Crouch, who gave the Bakkers their start, founded Trinity Broadcasting Network (TBN), the world's largest televangelist network, now run by their son Matt and his wife, Laurie. Viewers were encouraged to call prayer counselors at the toll-free number shown at the bottom of the TV screen. It was a short step from talking with a prayer counselor to making a "love gift" and becoming a "partner" in Trinity Broadcasting and then sending in more money during one of the frequent Praise-a-Thons.

The Crouches reveled in tasteless kitsch, as does Trump. They sat during their evening broadcast in Louis XVI–inspired sets replete with gold rococo and red velvet, glittering chandeliers, and a gold-painted piano. Stained glass windows loomed overhead. The network's emblem, which Paul Crouch wore on the pocket of his blue double-breasted blazer, featured a crown, a lion, a horse, a white dove, a cross, and Latin phrases among other elements. The Crouches would have been at home in Trump Tower, where the president has a faux "Trump crest"—allegedly plagiarized—and has decorated his penthouse as if it were also part of Versailles.[133]

The Crouches were masters of manipulation. They exhorted viewers to send in checks for $1,000, even if they could not afford it.[134] Write the check anyway, Paul Crouch, who died in 2013, told them, as a "step of faith"[135] and the Lord would repay them many times over. "Do you think God would have any trouble getting $1,000 extra to you somehow?" he asked during one Praise-a-Thon broadcast.[136] Viewers, many of whom struggled with despair and believed that miracles and magic alone held them back from the abyss, often found it impossible to resist the emotional pressure.

When I reported on the Crouches for my 2006 book, *American Fascists: The Christian Right and the War on America*, they earned nearly $1 million a year in salary from the network, had the use of thirty ministry-owned houses, including two multimillion-dollar oceanfront mansions in the resort town of Newport Beach, California, a mountain retreat near Lake Arrowhead, and a ranch in Texas.[137] They traveled on a $7.2 million, nineteen-seat Canadair turbojet, had access to fleets of luxury vehicles, and charged most of their expenses, from meals and hotel rooms to the purchasing of antiques, on company credit cards, according to former employees.[138]

Trinity Broadcasting Network is home to many of the worst charlatans in the Christian right, including the popular healer Benny Hinn, who says Jesus will appear at one of his crusades, Adam was a superhero who could fly to the moon, and one day the dead will be raised by watching the network from inside their coffins. Hinn claims his "anointings" have cured cancer, AIDS, deafness, blindness, and numerous other ailments and physical injuries. Those who have not been cured, he says, did not send in enough money.[139]

Jesus heals free of charge so...
make it make sense.

These religious hucksters are some of the most accomplished con artists in the country, a trait they share with the current occupant of the Oval Office.

I did not use the word "fascist" lightly when I wrote about the Christian right. I spent several hours, at the end of two years of reporting, with two of the country's foremost scholars on fascism—Fritz Stern and Robert O. Paxton. Did this "Christian" ideology fit the parameters of classic fascism? Was it virulent enough and organized enough to seize power? Would it go to the ruthless extremes of previous fascist movements to persecute and silence dissent? Has our deindustrialized society replicated the crippling despair, alienation, and rage that always feed fascist movements?

The evangelicalism promoted by the Christian right is very different from the evangelicalism and fundamentalism of a century ago. The emphasis on personal piety that defined the old movement, the call to avoid the contamination of politics, has been replaced by Christian Reconstructionism, also called Dominionism. This new ideology is about taking control of all institutions, including the government, to build a "Christian" nation. Rousas John Rushdoony, in his 1973 book, *The Institutes of Biblical Law*, first articulated it. Rushdoony argued that God gives the elect, just as he gave Adam and Noah, dominion over the earth to build a Christian society. Their state will come about with the physical eradication of the forces of Satan. It is the duty of the church and the elect to "rescue" the world so Christ can return.[140]

The secular, humanist society must be eradicated. The Ten Commandments will form the basis of our legal system. Creationism or "intelligent design" will be taught in public schools. People they consider social deviants, including homosexuals, immigrants, secular humanists, feminists, Jews, Muslims, criminals, and those dismissed as "nominal Christians"—meaning Christians who do not embrace the Christian right's perverted and heretical interpretation of the Bible—will be silenced, imprisoned, or killed. The role of the federal government will be reduced to protecting property rights, "homeland" security, and waging war. Church organizations will be funded and empowered by the government to run social welfare agencies. The poor, condemned for sloth, indolence, and sinfulness, will be denied government assistance. The death penalty will be expanded to include "moral crimes," including apostasy, blasphemy, sodomy, and witchcraft, as well as abortion, which will be treated as murder. Women will be subordinate to men. Those who practice other faiths will become, at best, second-class citizens or outcasts. The wars in the Middle East will be defined as religious crusades against Muslims. There will be no separation of church and state. The only legitimate voices will be "Christian." America, they believe, will become an agent of God. Those who defy the "Christian" authorities will be agents of Satan.

Tens of millions of Americans are already hermetically sealed within this bizarre worldview. They are fed a steady diet of conspiracy theories and lies on the Internet, in their churches, in Christian schools and colleges, and on Christian television and radio. Elizabeth Dilling, who wrote *The Red Network* and was a Nazi sympathizer, is required reading.[141] Thomas Jefferson, who favored separation of church and state, is ignored. This Christian propaganda hails the "significant contributions" of the Confederacy. Senator Joseph McCarthy, who led the anticommunist witch hunts in the 1950s, is rehabilitated as an American hero. The Israeli-Palestinian conflict along with the wars in Iraq, Afghanistan, Yemen, Somalia, and Libya are defined as part of the worldwide battle against satanic Islamic terror. Presently, 42 percent of the U.S. public believes in creationism or "intelligent design." [142] And nearly a third of the population, 94 million people, consider themselves evangelical.[143]

Those who remain in a reality-based universe often dismiss these malcontents as buffoons. They do not take seriously the huge segment of the public, mostly white and working-class, who because of economic distress have primal yearnings for vengeance, new glory, and moral renewal and are easily seduced by magical thinking. These are the yearnings and emotions Trump has exploited.

Those who embrace this movement feel they are being persecuted by dark and sinister groups bent on their destruction. They elevate themselves to the role of holy warriors with a noble calling and purpose. They sanctify the rage and hypermasculinity that are the core of fascism. The rigidity and simplicity of their belief, which includes being anointed for a special purpose in life by God, are potent weapons in the fight against their own demons and desire for meaning.

"Evil when we are in its power is not felt as evil but as a necessity, or even a duty," Simone Weil wrote.[144]

These believers, like all fascists, condemn the reality-based world as contaminated, decayed, and immoral. This world took their jobs. It destroyed their future. It ruined their communities. It doomed their children. It flooded their lives with alcohol, opioids, pornography, sexual abuse, jail sentences, domestic violence, deprivation, and despair. And then, from the depths of suicidal despair, they discovered that God has a plan for them. God will save them. God will intervene in their lives to promote and protect them. God has called them to carry out his holy mission in the world and to be rich, powerful, and happy.

The rational, secular forces, those that speak in the language of fact and reason, are hated and feared, for they seek to pull believers back into "the culture of death" that nearly destroyed them. The magical belief system, as it was for impoverished German workers who flocked to the Nazi Party, is an emotional life raft. It is all that supports them. The *only* way to blunt this movement is to reintegrate these people into the economy, to give them economic stability through good wages and benefits, to restore their self-esteem.

The decision by the ruling elites in ancient Rome—dominated by a bloated military and a corrupt oligarchy, much like the United States—to strangle the vain and idiotic Emperor Commodus in his bath in the year 192 did not halt the growing chaos and precipitous decline of the Roman Empire. Commodus, like a number of late-Roman emperors, and like Trump, was incompetent and consumed by his own vanity. He commissioned innumerable statues of himself as Hercules and had little interest in governance. He used his position as head of state to make himself the star of his own ongoing public show. He fought victoriously as a gladiator in the arena in fixed bouts. Power for Commodus, as it is for Trump, was primarily about catering to his bottomless narcissism. He sold public offices to the ancient equivalents of Betsy DeVos and Steven Mnuchin.

Commodus was replaced by the reformer Pertinax, the Bernie Sanders of his day, who attempted in vain to curb the power of the Praetorian

Guards, the ancient version of the military-industrial complex. The Praetorian Guards assassinated Pertinax three months after he became emperor. The Guards then auctioned off his position to the highest bidder. The next emperor, Didius Julianus, lasted sixty-six days. There would be five emperors in AD 193, the year after the assassination of Commodus.

Trump and our decaying empire have ominous historical precedents. If the deep state, comprised of the military, intelligence agencies, government bureaucrats, and the heads of corporations, replaces Trump, whose ineptitude and imbecility are embarrassing to the empire, his removal will not restore democracy any more than replacing Commodus restored democracy in Rome.

The ruling elites, with or without Trump, will continue to force a subservient population to work harder for less, squander capital in grandiose projects such as border walls, fracking, and war. Trump's decision to increase military spending by $54 billion and take the needed funds out of domestic programs typifies the behavior of terminally ill civilizations.[145] When the Roman Empire fell, it was trying to sustain an army of half a million soldiers that was a parasitic drain on state resources.

Sigmund Freud wrote that societies, along with individuals, are driven by two primary instincts. One is the instinct for life—Eros, the quest to love, nurture, protect, and preserve. The second is the death instinct. The death instinct, called Thanatos by post-Freudians, is driven by fear, hatred, and violence. It seeks the dissolution of all living things, including our own beings. One of these two forces, Freud wrote, is always ascendant. Societies in decline are seduced by the death instinct, as Freud observed in *Civilization and Its Discontents*, written on the eve of the rise of European fascism and World War II.[146]

"It is in sadism, where the death instinct twists the erotic aim in its own sense and yet at the same time fully satisfies the erotic urge, that we succeed in obtaining the clearest insight into its nature and its relation to *Eros*," Freud wrote. "But even where it emerges without any sexual purpose, in the blindest fury of destructiveness, we cannot fail to recognize that the satisfaction of the instinct is accompanied by an extraordinary high degree of narcissistic enjoyment, owing to its presenting the ego with a fulfillment of the latter's old wishes for omnipotence."[147]

The lust for death, as Freud understood, is not, at first, repellent. I saw this in the wars I covered. A godlike power and adrenaline-driven fury, even euphoria, sweep over armed units and ethnic or religious groups given the license to destroy anything and anyone around them. Ernst Jünger captured this "monstrous desire for annihilation" in his World War I memoir *Storm of Steel.*[148]

A population beset by despair and hopelessness finds an intoxicating empowerment and pleasure in an orgy of annihilation that soon morphs into self-annihilation. It has no interest in nurturing a world that has betrayed it and thwarted its dreams. It seeks to eradicate this world and replace it with a mythical one. It turns against institutions, as well as ethnic and religious groups, that are scapegoated for its misery. It plunders diminishing natural resources. It retreats into self-adulation fed by <u>historical amnesia.</u>

[margin note: Those who fail to learn from history → are doomed to repeat it.]

Raoul Peck's documentary *I Am Not Your Negro* illustrates, through James Baldwin's prophetic work, that the disparity now gripping the United States is an inevitable consequence of white Americans' steadfast failure to confront where they came from, who they are, and the lies and myths they use to mask past and present crimes.

History "is not the past," the film quotes Baldwin as saying. "History is the present. We carry our history with us. To think otherwise is criminal."[149]

The script is taken from Baldwin's notes, essays, interviews, and letters, with some of the words delivered in Baldwin's voice from audio recordings and televised footage, some of them in readings by actor Samuel L. Jackson. Whiteness is a dangerous concept. It is not about skin color. It is not even about race. It is about the self-delusion used to justify white supremacy. It is about using moral rhetoric to defend exploitation, racism, mass murder, reigns of terror, and the crimes of empire.

"The American Negro has the great advantage of having never believed the collection of myths to which white Americans cling: that their ancestors were all freedom-loving heroes, that they were born in the greatest country the world has ever seen, or that Americans are invincible in battle and wise in peace, that Americans have always dealt honorably with Mexicans and Indians and all other neighbors or inferiors, that American men are the world's most direct and virile, that American women are pure," Baldwin wrote.

> Negroes know far more about white Americans than that; it can almost be said, in fact, that they know about white Americans what parents—or, anyway, mothers—know about their children, and that they very often regard white Americans that way. And perhaps this attitude, held in spite of what they know and have endured, helps to explain why Negroes, on the whole, and until lately, have allowed themselves to feel so little hatred. The tendency has really been, insofar as this was possible, to dismiss white people as the slightly mad victims of their own brainwashing.[150]

living outside ↗ of reality

America was founded on an imagined moral superiority and purity. The fact that dominance of others came, and still comes, from unrestrained acts of violence is washed out of the national narrative. The steadfast failure to face the truth, Baldwin warned, perpetuates a kind of collective psychosis. Unable to face the truth, white Americans stunt and destroy their capacity for self-reflection and self-criticism. They construct a world of self-serving fantasy. Those who imbibe the myth of whiteness externalize evil—their own evil—onto their victims. Racism, Baldwin understood, is driven by an inner loneliness and latent guilt.

"If Americans were not so terrified of their private selves, they would never have needed to invent and could never have become so dependent on what they still call 'the Negro problem,'" Baldwin wrote. "This problem, which they invented in order to safeguard their purity, has made of them criminals and monsters, and it is destroying them; and this not from anything blacks may or may not be doing but because of the role a guilty and constricted white imagination has assigned to the blacks."[151]

"People pay for what they do, and, still more for what they allowed themselves to become," Baldwin wrote in another essay. "And they pay for it very simply by the lives they lead. The crucial thing, here, is that the sum of these individual abdications menaces life all over the world. For, in the generality, as social and moral and political and sexual entities,

white Americans are probably the sickest and certainly the most dangerous people, of any color, to be found in the world today."[152]

Footage in the Peck documentary of past murder cases including the
1955 murder of the fourteen-year-old Emmett Till is interspersed with
the modern-day killing of young black men such as Michael Brown and
Freddie Gray. Images of white supremacist parades from the 1960s, with
young men carrying signs proclaiming "Keep America White," shift directly to footage of the unrest in Ferguson, Missouri, following the police
killing of eighteen-year-old Michael Brown on August 9, 2014. This jux-
taposition is almost too much to bear.

The film begins with Baldwin's 1957 return from France, where he
had been living for almost a decade. He comes back to join the nascent
civil rights movement. He was deeply disturbed by a photograph of Dorothy Counts, fifteen, surrounded by a mob of whites spitting and screaming racial slurs as she walked into a newly desegregated high school in
Charlotte, North Carolina.

"I could simply no longer sit around Paris discussing the Algerian
and the black American problem," he said. "Everybody was paying their
dues, and it was time I went home and paid mine."[153]

In short, he returned to the United States so that black children like
Dorothy Counts would not have to walk alone through a sea of racial
hatred. He spoke and participated in hundreds of events for the Congress
of Racial Equality and the Student Nonviolent Coordinating Committee. Martin Luther King Jr.'s Southern Christian Leadership Conference,
however, largely held him at arm's length. Baldwin was too independent
and outspoken. His words made King's Northern white liberal supporters
uncomfortable. Baldwin was scheduled to speak at the 1963 March on
Washington, but King and the other leaders of the march replaced him
with the actor Burt Lancaster. Baldwin refused to be anyone's "negro."

Baldwin was, like George Orwell, an astute critic of modern culture
and how it justifies the crimes of racism and imperialism. In his book *The
Devil Finds Work* he pits Hollywood's vision of race against the reality.[154]
The Peck documentary shows clips from films Baldwin critiqued in the
book including *The Birth of a Nation* (a 1915 movie Baldwin called "an
elaborate justification of mass murder"), *Dance, Fools, Dance* (1931), *The*

Monster Walks (1932), *King Kong* (1933), *Imitation of Life* (1934), *They Won't Forget* (1937), *Stagecoach* (1939), *The Defiant Ones* (1958), *Lover Come Back* (1961), *A Raisin in the Sun* (1961), and *Guess Who's Coming to Dinner* (1967). In film after film Baldwin pointed to the ingrained racial stereotypes of African Americans in popular culture that sustain the lie of whiteness.

Blacks were, and often still are, portrayed by mass culture as lazy and childlike, therefore needing white parental supervision and domination, or as menacing and violent sexual predators who need to be eliminated. These Hollywood stereotypes, Baldwin knew, existed as foils for an imagined white purity, decency, and innocence. They buttressed the myth of a nation devoted to the ideals of justice, liberty, and democracy. The oppressed, because of their supposed character defects, were the architects of their own oppression. Oppression was for their own good. Racism was a form of benevolence. Baldwin warned that America will consume itself if it did not face the truth.

In *The Devil Finds Work* Baldwin also wrote about the film *A Tale of Two Cities* (1935). He had read the novel by Charles Dickens "obsessively" as a boy to understand "the question of what it meant to be a nigger."[155] This novel and other novels he consumed, such as Dostoyevsky's *Crime and Punishment*, spoke of the oppressed. He knew that the oppression of the characters in these stories had "something to do with my own."[156] The books "had something to tell me."[157] He wrote:

> I was haunted, for example, by Alexandre Manette's document, in *A Tale of Two Cities*, describing the murder of a peasant boy— who, dying, speaks: "I say, we were so robbed, and hunted, and were made so poor, that our father told us it was a dreadful thing to bring a child into this world, and that what we should most pray for was that our women might be barren and our miserable race die out!" ("I had never before," observes Dr. Manette, "seen the sense of being oppressed, bursting forth like a fire.")
>
> Dickens has not seen it all. The wretched of the earth do not decide to become extinct, they resolve, on the contrary, to multiply: life is their only weapon against life, life is all that they

have. This is why the dispossessed and starving will never be convinced (though some may be coerced) by the population-control programs of the civilized. I have watched the dispossessed and starving laboring in the fields which others own with their transistor radios at their ear, all day long: so they learn, for example, along with equally weighty matters, that the Pope, one of the heads of the civilized world, forbids to the civilized that abortion which is being, literally, forced on them, the wretched. The civilized have created the wretched quite coldly, and deliberately, and do not intend to change the *status quo*; are responsible for their slaughter and enslavement; rain down bombs on defenseless children whenever and wherever they decide that their "vital interests" are menaced, and think nothing of torturing a man to death; these people are not to be taken seriously when they speak of the "sanctity" of human life, or the "conscience" of the civilized world. There is a "sanctity" involved with bringing a child into this world: it is better than bombing one out of it. Dreadful indeed it is to see a starving child, but the answer to that is not to prevent the child's arrival but to restructure the world so that the child can live in it: so that the "vital interest" of the world becomes nothing less than the life of the child.[158]

Nearly all African Americans carry within them white blood, usually the result of white rape. White slaveholders routinely sold mixed-race children—their own children—into slavery. Baldwin knew the failure to acknowledge the melding of the black and white races that can be seen in nearly every African American face, a melding that makes African Americans literally the brothers and sisters of whites. African Americans, Baldwin wrote, are the "bastard" children of white America. They constitute a peculiarly and uniquely American race.

"The truth is this country does not know what to do with its black population," he said. "Americans can't face the fact that I am flesh of their flesh."[159]

White supremacy is not defined, he wrote, by intelligence or virtue. The white race continues to dominate other races because it has always controlled the most efficient killing mechanisms on the planet. It used, and uses, its industrial weapons to carry out mass murder, genocide, subjugation, and exploitation, whether on slave plantations, on the Trail of Tears, at Wounded Knee, in the Philippines and Vietnam, in cities such as Baltimore and Ferguson, or in our endless wars across the Middle East.

The true credo of the white race is *we have everything, and if you try to take any of it from us we will kill you.* This is the essential meaning of whiteness. As the white race turns on itself in an age of diminishing resources, it is in the vital interest of the white underclass to understand what its elites and its empire are actually about.

"There are days, this is one of them, when you wonder what your role is in this country and what your future is in it," Baldwin said. "How precisely you're going to reconcile yourself to your situation here and how you are going to communicate to the vast, heedless, unthinking, cruel white majority that you are here. I'm terrified at the moral apathy—the death of the heart—which is happening in my country. These people have deluded themselves for so long that *they really don't think I'm human.*"[160]

2

HEROIN

—and then you're in serious trouble, very serious trouble, and you know it, finally, deadly serious trouble, because this Substance you thought was your one true friend, that you gave up all for, gladly, that for so long gave you relief from the pain of the Losses your love of that relief caused, your mother and lover and god and compadre, has finally removed its smily-face mask to reveal centerless eyes and a ravening maw, and canines down to here, it's the Face In The Floor, the grinning root-white face of your worst nightmares, and the face is your own face in the mirror, now, it's you, the Substance has devoured or replaced and become you, and the puke-, drool- and Substance-crusted T-shirt you've both worn for weeks now gets torn off and you stand there looking and in the root-white chest where your heart (given away to It) should be beating, in its exposed chest's center and centerless eyes is just a lightless hole, more teeth, and a beckoning taloned hand dangling something irresistible, and now you see you've been had, screwed royal, stripped and fucked and tossed to the side like some stuffed toy to lie for all time in the posture you land in. You see now that It's your enemy and your worst personal nightmare and the trouble It's gotten you into is undeniable and you still can't stop. Doing the Substance now is like attending Black Mass but you still can't stop, even though the Substance no longer gets you high. You are, as they say, Finished. You cannot get drunk and you cannot get sober; you cannot get high and you cannot get straight. You are behind bars; you are in a cage and can see only bars in every direction. You are in the kind of a hell of a mess that either ends lives or turns them around.

DAVID FOSTER WALLACE, *Infinite Jest* [1]

I was sitting in the Red Oak Diner outside Princeton, New Jersey, with Christine Pagano and her friend Jeannette. They had just finished attending an Alcoholics Anonymous meeting in a small room in the strip mall behind us. Many at the meeting said they struggled to make rent or car payments. Those with jobs worried about having their hours cut or being laid off. Some lived in terror that creditors, or the state, would electronically empty their meager bank accounts for past debts or fines. Others feared that outstanding warrants would land them in jail. One small tremor and the fragile stability they achieved could crumble to dust. A few admitted they wanted to blunt the pain again, at least for a moment, by getting drunk or high. They told each other to do their best and trust in God or a "higher power." They repeated the mantra that they had to accept that there was much in life they would never control and should always practice "acceptance." They reminded each other to "keep their side of the street clean" and not judge others or "take other people's inventory." Many in the room had come a long way, getting out of jail or prison, kicking a crippling addiction, finding a job, regaining custody of their children, reconciling with their families or partners, and falling in love. They reminded each other that to deal with adversity they had to "show up" for what they must face, however unpleasant, rather than flee back into the world of narcotics. And when the meeting was over, everyone stood up, held hands, and said the Lord's Prayer.

The rain was lashing the window next to our booth. The diner was nearly empty. Trucks on Route 206 roared past, their headlights a blur in the rainstorm. Pagano, thirty-one, had worked all day in a deli and bakery. She was up at 6:30 a.m. Her hands cupped a glass of unsweetened ice tea. Her dark, auburn hair was pulled up in a neat bun. Her eyes were accented by carefully drawn eyeliner.

Her drug use began when she was sixteen years old, after a school counselor learned Pagano's stepfather was sleeping with one of Pagano's classmates. Her mother's marriage, and whatever stability it provided in Pagano's life, imploded. The story about the classmate and Pagano's stepfather became public in her rural north Jersey community. She felt humiliated. She began to snort heroin. She dropped out of school. She worked to feed her habit. She enrolled in a drug treatment program in

2007. She got sober. She lived in a group house in Brick, New Jersey, where all the residents promised not to use drugs or alcohol. She met a man who had just got out of prison and was also in recovery. They set out to make a life together.

She worked in a diner and got a cosmetology certificate. She and her boyfriend rented a house and bought a car. She became pregnant. After she gave birth, she stayed home with her son.

"I was a new mom," she said. "I had no idea what I was doing. I was really overwhelmed. I don't remember ever really thinking about using or drinking, but I was never all right. I was never really okay with who I was. I always felt not good enough. And even as a mom, with . . . this beautiful child, I never felt okay. I used to bite my nails all the time. I was very anxiety-ridden."

She and her boyfriend attended meetings for those in recovery. They stayed clean for four years.

Pagano suspected that her boyfriend, who was working for a tree service company and was a member of the electricians union, was secretly taking the opiate OxyContin. He eventually suggested they go "doctor shopping" to get pills to sell. Her boyfriend's family had a history of addictions. His father had died in jail on Rikers Island in New York. His sister was a heroin addict and a prostitute who worked for a well-known New Jersey pimp called "Prince." Prince drove a Rolls-Royce or a white Cadillac with flashy rims and white carpeting. "He would walk into this bar in Jersey City called Ringside," Pagano said. "He would go, 'The champ is here.' "

She and her boyfriend started taking pills together. They switched to heroin a month later. It was cheaper. She snorted it for a week. Then her boyfriend shot her up. It was her first time with a needle.

"He called his sister and his sister told us where we could get heroin," she said. "And she lived in the heart of Jersey City. So we went down there and in the beginning we were selling the pills to support the heroin habit. And then our heroin habit got too big for the money. This was the first time my son's father told me that I should go out on the street with his sister."

She accompanied her boyfriend's sister, known by the street name

"Baby," to Jersey City's Tonnelle Avenue, where there is a string of cheap motels. Pagano, who is white, wore a short, shimmering gold skirt and adopted the street name "Gucci." Prostitutes on Tonnelle Avenue, which is close to the Holland Tunnel connecting Jersey City and Manhattan, made $50 for oral sex and $100 for vaginal intercourse, "but if it goes any longer than ten minutes you're charging them more." An hour cost $250 and a full night cost $1,500. To the Wall Street traders, business executives, and bankers who were the prostitutes' main customers, money never seemed to be an issue. On her first night Pagano got into cars and burst into tears or pushed the men away.

"I think the first night I actually never went through with it, but I ended up making money because I was a sobbing mess in these cars and guys just gave me money," she says. "Most of them had a lot of money 'cause they were coming from the city. So then my son's father got the idea that if I couldn't do it I would . . . make them get a room, act like I was gonna do it—and he would kick the door in—and rob them. We did that a couple times until I couldn't keep track of who I was robbing. And the last time I went to do it I had already robbed the guy [on an earlier night] and he started beating me up in the room."

It took her two weeks to have sex with the "tricks." She began to build a regular clientele and mastered survival skills.

"A couple times I got to stay in this really nice suite that overlooked Newark Airport," she said. "Some of them had a lot of money."

She would buy heroin after a night's work—she and her boyfriend together had a $500-a-day habit—from a dealer named "Kiss."

"Kiss would come out no matter when I called 'cause he knew he was getting his $500 from me," she said. She would drive home, often around 4:30 in the morning, and shoot up with her boyfriend. Her relationship with him deteriorated into that of "drug partners" and little else. They fought frequently, something they had not done while sober.

"He would throw it in my face a lot," she said of her prostitution, "but he had no problem doing my drugs. We were no longer parents. We were no longer anything."

But she still had her son, Liam.

"There were times where Kristen [Baby] would go out and I would sit in the car with my son," she said. "I would have him out in my car on Tonnelle Avenue. I thought I was a good mom 'cause I would wait in the car. She would go out and she would come back and wait in the car for me to come back with money."

She began to leave Liam with his father at night.

Cops, she said, were regular customers, although most refused to pay. Some threatened to arrest her if she did not give them unpaid sex.

"The first time I ever got raped actually was by a cop in Elizabeth," she said. "He wanted to trick off which is normal for cops. We were in the back of the police car. He had paid me. Then he punched me in the face and he took the money back. He pulled out his gun and told me I was gonna do whatever he told me to do. He stuck his gun up my vagina. He told me he was gonna pull the trigger if I didn't do what he said. He wanted to treat me like a piece of shit. Ya know, he called me a bunch of names. He made me call myself a bunch of names—a dirty prostitute. At one point he made me say that I had AIDS. Yeah.

"[Cops] would get you in the car because they would act like they were arresting you," she said, "and then once they got you in the car they would tell you, 'Oh well, if you blow me I'll let you go.' And you get smart after a while. I mean after a while I would let them take me to jail because they can't—what are they gonna say? There's nothing on video-tape. What are they gonna say? They can't. It takes you a while to learn this type of stuff."

She often opened the glove compartment to get the name and address of the driver when she entered a vehicle. She increased her rates by threatening to call the customer's wife.

Pagano also learned what to avoid. "In Jersey City there's a street when you go down Tonnelle Avenue," she said. "I think it's called Industrial Way [probably Industrial Drive]. It's industrial parks. You never, ever, ever want to go down there. And you always knew you were in trouble if you got in a car with a guy and he started driving that way. I've jumped out of many cars. 'Cause as soon as you saw you were driving down that street, you knew you were gonna get raped.

"The only cop I remember his name from down there was a Jersey City cop, we called him Barney, I don't know his real name," she said.

"He looked like Barney [Rubble, the *Flintstones* cartoon character]. He was my first prostitution arrest. And the only reason he arrested me was that I was standing next to Kristen. And she was known. When they brought us in it was her thirty-ninth prostitution arrest. They [police officers] were clapping when they brought her in. Everybody knew who she was."

On a good night Pagano made $600 to $700. On a bad night she made $100. "I made the best money in snow and rain," she said.

Some customers wanted to indulge in fetishes. "I've put diapers on guys," she said. Others wanted to put on makeup and women's clothes.

She often injected herself with heroin or smoked crack as soon as she and a client got into a hotel room. "A lot of them would do it [take drugs] with you," she said. "A lot of them pay you to get their drugs for them."

She endured for nine months. She begged her boyfriend to help her get off the streets. He decided to rob a bank. He entered a bank in Jersey City in June 2010 with a backpack and a note that said he had a bomb. He did not cover his face. He took $578 from a teller.

"I was driving on the Turnpike from our house down to Jersey City and I saw a big sign, 'FBI wanted,' with a picture of my son's father," she said. "And I pulled over on the side of the road and lost my mind."

He was arrested a month later when the FBI, the state police, and U.S. marshals kicked down the door of their house at 5:30 in the morning. He is now serving a nine-year sentence in the maximum-security federal prison at Lewisburg, Pennsylvania.

"That's when I really went off the deep end," Pagano said. "I gave up on everything."

She sent her son to live with her mother, a teacher. She moved in for a while with Baby in Jersey City. She eventually became homeless, sleeping in an abandoned flower shop. Her drug use soared. She would be awake for six or seven days at a time. She had as many as twenty clients a day. Finally, nearly broken, she got back into rehab. She became sober again. She met a man in the program. He relapsed two weeks later and went to jail. She began drinking heavily with her mother-in-law.

She started taking the bus from Williamstown, New Jersey, where she was living, to Atlantic City to trick and buy drugs. She got arrested.

When she got out of jail she decided to go to Camden. Camden was where many Atlantic City dealers got their drugs. Heroin costs $10 a bag in Camden and $6 a bag in Jersey City, but the Camden heroin was far more potent and provided a much longer high. And Camden was only twenty minutes from where she was living.

Camden is among the country's poorest and most crime-ridden cities. Once a center of industry, its entire manufacturing base has disappeared. Its population has dwindled from 120,000 in the 1950s to less than 80,000 today. Whole blocks lie abandoned. There are an estimated 1,500 derelict buildings. The roofs of many empty row houses, gas stations, stores, and warehouses have collapsed and trees poke up from them. Basements in derelict buildings are flooded. Scavengers have ripped out copper wiring, metal doors, radiators, and piping to sell to the huge scrap yard along the Delaware River. Some 175 open-air drug markets exist in the city.[2] Hookers, often white female addicts, congregate on street corners and near the main exit ramp of the multilane highway that runs overhead through the center of Camden to service truckers.

The first time Pagano took the bus to Camden, she walked up to the first person she saw upon her arrival at Walter Rand Transportation Center and asked, "Where do you sell your ass around here?" She was told to go to Broadway. She never went home. Camden, however, was not Jersey City or Atlantic City. Her clients were not wealthy businessmen or Wall Street managers. They were fellow addicts. She could not make the same kind of money. There were women on the street that would give oral sex for as little as $5.

"They'd suck your dick for a hit of crack," Pagano said. "Camden was like nothing I had ever seen before. The poverty is so bad. People rob you for $5, literally for $5. They would pull a gun on you for no money. I would get out of cars, I would walk five feet up the road and get held up. And they would take all my money. The first time it happened to me I cried an hour. You degrade yourself."

She scaled down her charges, eventually giving oral sex for $20. And she found that her clients refused to let her use condoms.

"I gave up on everything at that point, I wanted to die," she said. "I didn't care anymore. All the guilt and the shame and leaving my son, not talking to my son, not talking to my family."

Pagano met a man named "E-frie" who had just finished an eighteen-year prison sentence. He gave her drugs in return for sex. He drank heavily and smoked marijuana. He taunted her for being a junkie and frequently beat her, once pushing her down a flight of stairs.

"I was still living on the streets," she said. "I was living everywhere. Abandoned buildings. Most of my stuff was hidden all over downtown Camden. I would dig holes and bury stuff in backyards."

She fingered a ring dangling from her necklace.

"My mother gave this to me from my son," she said. "I never take it off my neck. It's a mother-and-son ring. It's made it through everything with me. Someone ripped it off my neck one time. I flipped out. It was the only thing that made me feel like I had my son with me. I found the ring afterward. I used to wear it on my hand. But I would get nervous that someone would rob me over a ring. I would dig holes and bury it. I would bury it with my money."

She put her profile on an Internet site to solicit clients. By then she had been raped as many as twenty times.

"The last time was the most brutal," she said. "It was on Pine Street near the Off Broadway [Lounge]. There's weeds on the side. I never took tricks off the street. They had to be in cars. But I was sick. I was tired."

A man on the street had offered her $20 for oral sex. Once they were alone in the weed-choked lot he pulled out a knife. He told her if she screamed he would kill her. When she resisted, he stabbed her. "He was trying to stab me in my vagina," she said. He stabbed her thigh. "It ended up turning into a big infection," she said.

"I had seen this episode of *Oprah* years ago and this girl had been raped—her survival skills kicked in and she told the guy he didn't have to do that to her, that he could do better," she said. "I got outta this guy who just stabbed me that he and his girlfriend had gotten into a fight and that she wouldn't have sex with him and that somebody was gonna have sex with him that night. He made me hold his phone that had porn on it [so he could see it as he raped her]. He never really pulled his pants all the way down. And at this point I'm bleeding pretty badly. I'm lying on glass outside of this bar. I had little bits of glass in my back. I was really scared. Then I was just numb. I asked him if he could stop at one point so I could smoke a cigarette. He let me. I got him to put the knife down because I was being good and listening to him. He stabbed the knife in the dirt. He said, 'Just so you know I can pick it up at any point.' I think in his head he thought that I was scared enough. In my head I was trying to figure out how the hell I was going to get outta there. And it occurred to me one of the things he kept asking me to do was lick his butt. And he was getting off on this. The last time he turned around and asked me to do this I pushed him. I had myself set up to get up."

She ran naked into the street. The commotion attracted the police. A passerby gave her his shirt. At five feet five inches she weighed only eighty-six pounds. Her skin was gray. Her feet were so swollen she was wearing size 12 men's slippers.

She would last four more weeks on the Camden streets, until a private investigator hired by her mother found her in September 2012. He called her mother and handed the phone to Pagano. "I told her to leave me the fuck alone, just let me die," she said. "And she told me that she was not going to let me die out there. She said, 'You will not be sleeping on the streets of Camden tonight.' "

Because Pagano had a raft of outstanding warrants, the investigator took her to jail, but her physical condition was so bad the jail refused to accept her. She was hospitalized for two weeks. She went into a methadone program that cost her mother $20,000.

"I was so hurt and so broken," she said. "I was in shock. When it all wore off I would wake up at night screaming, sweating, I had peed myself a couple times in the middle of the night. I still have nightmares. A lot of it goes back to that last rape. A lot of it has to do with E-frie.

"I live in a shitty little apartment, at thirty-one years old, with a roommate, who used to be sober and is now a stripper," she said. "I have a crappy car. I will never have a prestigious job. I've never been more happy in my life."

She was scheduled to regain custody of her son next summer.

She told me about her new boyfriend, José. She spoke his name as if his existence was a miracle.

"He knows everything there is to ever know about me and has never judged me, never," she said. "If I'm in a funk, he says, 'Just go to the 5:30 meeting,' " referring to a daily Alcoholics Anonymous session. "He doesn't even know what the 5:30 AA meeting is."

"I struggle with God," she said. "I have to believe that I haven't been put through this to give up. And there've been a lot of times when I wanted to do just that. I sat through Camden County jail [on an old warrant] sober. I was looking at all the same people I used to be out on the street with—being called Gucci again.

"I think the one thing I am most grateful for is that I am scared today," she said. "I'm scared of the law. I never was. I'm scared to lose what little I have. Not the material things—but I look at my son now. I remember the day that I had him and thinking this was it. And looking back I think I thought that this was gonna fix me. But it didn't. And I learned that nothing is going to fix me. [My son] Liam's not going to fix me. Those [AA] meetings are not going to fix me. They're going to help. [My friend] Jeannette's going to help. All these people in my life are going to help. But the only person that can fix me is me. And that's a hard pill to swallow when you've done nothing your whole life but fuck it up. And one of the biggest things I still can't get over is that even when I'm doing something right, I still feel like I'm doing something wrong. I always have that feeling that it's not good enough. That I'm not good enough. And now here I am at thirty-one. I have a huge criminal record. I have horrible credit. I lost a house. I lost a car. It amazes me that my mother still looks at me knowing what I've done—and she doesn't look at me any differently. And [when I go wrong] she'll be the first to tell you, 'That's not my daughter, that's what my daughter does when she's not thinking straight.' "

Liam, five, recently learned where his dad is. Before, when he asked, Pagano had answered by saying only, "Your dad loves you very much." But eventually she had to tell him the truth. The boy cried for more than an hour. He asked his mother to play a game in which she is a cop who arrests him so he can go to prison and talk to his father. It is a game they play often.

"He's going to be eleven when [his father] gets out," she said. "Liam wants to know if he's going to be in his life. I can't give him an answer.

It's really sad that for $578 [the father is] sitting in prison for nine years. I'm not condoning what he did. He did it. He's guilty, but nine years?

"The system is set up for us to fail," she said. "Ten years from now I'm still just going to be a number. I'm always going to have an SBI [State Bureau of Identification] number. I'm always going to have mug shots all over the Internet. Liam's father is going to be out when he's forty-two years old. And what the fuck is he going to do? And they expect people not to go back. What's he going to do? I realize everyone's got a choice, but the state won't even help me. They're not going to help him. I'm not saying people shouldn't pay for what they do. Most people don't change. I'm not going to say that they do. But some change. I fight every day to be a better person. I fight to fit into society."

The manager of the diner came over to tell us he was closing in fifteen minutes. He looked at Pagano. He saw she was distraught. "Take your time," he said gently. She was drinking coffee, pouring in little containers of creamer and stirring it continuously.

"I never thought this would be my story," Pagano said. "You couldn't have told me this. Now I cry a lot. I'm very compassionate. I never used to be. They used to call me the ice queen."

She paused and looked down at the table, trying to recover her composure. "I look in the mirror. Half the time I still see that girl again," she said, referring to her former self. "The other half of the time I see me."

We left the diner, darting through the rain to our cars.

THE POOR IN AMERICA GET only one chance. Then it is over. Those who were on the street with Pagano in Jersey City or Camden will most likely never have a private investigator rescue them, or have a mother pay for their drug rehabilitation. Most will live, suffer, and die within the space of a few squalid city blocks. No jobs. No hope. No help. They blunt their despair through alcohol or drugs. And if they do get out, as did Pagano, they carry the chains of their past wrapped around them. Employers do not want them. Landlords will not rent them an apartment. Real estate agents will not deal with them if they seek to buy a house. Banks and credit card companies will not give them credit. They never have enough money. They probably never will. They live one step away from hell. And they know what hell feels like. This is how the Wall Street gamblers, bankers, bond traders, and financial speculators, the ones with the packed wallets, the ones with the fancy cars and the multimillion-dollar homes in New Jersey's suburbs of Mendham, Chatham, and Short Hills, the ones who paid Pagano for sex during their nightly journeys home to their wives and girlfriends, want it. The hell of the poor is their playground.

And then there are all those who do not make it. Opioid overdoses are the leading cause of death in this country for those under the age of fifty.[3] Fifty-nine thousand people died in 2016 from overdoses, or 161 people a day.[4] The United States consumes 80 percent of the global opioids.[5] There are 300 million prescriptions written, and $24 billion spent annually on painkillers. The United States, Canada, and Western Europe account for 95 percent of the world's opioid consumption.[6] The United States consumes 83 percent of the world's oxycodone[7] and 99 percent of one specific opioid, hydrocodone, a powerful painkiller that provides the opioid component in Vicodin and Lortab.[8] The country supplements this "legal" addiction with over $100 billion a year on illicit marijuana, cocaine, methamphetamine, and heroin.[9]

Unscrupulous doctors dispense OxyContin (oxycodone), which is in essence prescription heroin, like candy in "pill mills" masquerading as pain clinics. These pill mills proliferated across the United States in the late 1990s after Purdue Pharma launched the drug in 1996. Doctors usually charged $200 or $250 in cash for visits. The visits lasted the few minutes it took to write new opioid prescriptions. Many doctors became very wealthy as they created a nation of addicts. And once addicted to OxyContin, addicts made an easy transition into the much cheaper heroin sold in the streets, especially since many of them chewed the tablets or crushed them to snort or inject them to get a heroin high. As many as 80 percent of heroin users started out with prescription opioids.[10] Insurance companies, which did not want to reimburse for lengthy therapy to deal with pain, paid for the pills.

The drug was pushed by legions of aggressive salespeople sent to doctors' offices and medical conferences by Purdue, a Connecticut opioid manufacturer owned by the Sackler family. Purdue and its marketing partner, Abbott Laboratories, peddled the lie that less than one percent of users become addicted. Doctors, often given gifts or taken out for lavish meals, were issued coupons for free one-time Oxy-Contin prescriptions, a common tactic to get patients hooked. Purdue spent "hundreds of millions of dollars" flying medical practitioners to resorts. "There," Sam Quinones writes in *Dreamland: The True Tale of America's Opioid Epidemic*, "the company plied them with dinners, golf outings, and spa treatments while sending them to seminars on a medical issue, led by specialists that the companies often suggested."[11] Oxy-Contin sales reached $3 billion a year.[12] Purdue was eventually hit in 2007 with federal misbranding charges that resulted in a $600 million judgment against the company. By then the damage was done.[13]

Sales of OxyContin in the U.S. have fallen by 40 percent since 2010 with public awareness of the addictive qualities of the drug.[14] Purdue, in response to the decline in sales, is building international markets through the same deceptive advertising and tactics, much as the U.S. tobacco industry did when its American market declined.

A dozen members of Congress, on May 3, 2017, sent a letter to Dr. Margaret Chan, then the director-general of the World Health Organization (WHO), "to warn the international community of the deceptive and dangerous practices of Mundipharma International—an arm of Purdue Pharmaceuticals." The Congress members charged that "the greed and recklessness of one company and its partners helped spark a public health crisis in the United States that will take generations to fully repair." They urged the WHO "to do everything in its power to avoid allowing the same people to begin a worldwide opioid epidemic."[15]

IT WAS A RAINY AFTERNOON on February 1, 2017, when I arrived at the Gosselin Funeral Home on New Dover Road in Edison, New Jersey. Outside the closed wooden double doors in the lobby that led into the viewing room were Bob and Sue Miller, their daughters Megan and Camarie, and Boris Rorer, along with about a dozen friends and Boris's relatives. The funeral director slowly opened the doors. Shannon Miller, twenty-three, who was Boris's fiance, and who had died of a heroin overdose on January 27, lay in an open casket. A small Donald Duck toy was beside her body. Her casket was surrounded by flower arrangements and helium balloons.

Shannon's mother, Sue, collapsed when she entered the room. Grief rent the air like an electric current. Sue had to be helped by her husband and sister to kneel before her daughter's coffin. She sobbed and repeated, "Shannon, Shannon, I love you."

The funeral director, standing in the back of the room, told me Miller was the tenth young overdose victim he had buried in the last two years. By the time the viewing ended six hours later, over one thousand people, many of them young, had walked past her body.

Miller grew up in Parlin, New Jersey, a small section of Sayreville, a town of 42,000 on the banks of the Raritan River. Her mother was a teacher. Bob worked as a security guard. She was the middle of two sisters, between Megan, the oldest, and Camarie, or Cam, the youngest.

"Shannon was a very funny kid," Sue remembered. "She had compassion for everybody."

Shannon was diagnosed with Chiari malformation at the age of thirteen, a condition that caused her brain tissue to extend into her spinal cord, resulting in crippling headaches.

"She was debilitated with severe migraines to the point where she could not walk," Sue told me a few weeks after the funeral. "When she did, it was a staggering walk, as if she were drunk. She could not think. She could not be in a room with lights on."

Her parents took her to see a neurologist, who prescribed a medication that inadvertently worsened her pain. They later discovered she was allergic to the medication.

The neurologist told Shannon to drink sixty-four ounces of water a day to keep her brain afloat. Aspirin and Diet Mountain Dew were supposed to help alleviate her headaches. The aspirin and Mountain Dew concoction did not always work.

"In the beginning, [the migraines] were happening more frequently. Two times a week, three times a week," Sue said. "There was a time when she was lying on my bed crying. It was going on for five days . . . I took her to the emergency room.

"She played soccer as long as she could. Soccer was her life," Sue said. "We got to the point where she just couldn't do it anymore. The migraines consumed her life."

Shannon's reliance on pain medication given to her by doctors, including Percocet, a combination of acetaminophen and oxycodone, became habitual. She turned to heroin sometime in high school, after she was no longer able to play soccer.

"Mom, I think I am an addict," Shannon said to her one day after school.

"What?" Sue said.

"Heroin," Shannon said.

"How? Why? When? What did we do? Was it us? Did we drive you to this?" Sue said.

"Mom, it was never your fault," Shannon said. "It was never Daddy's fault. Or anybody's fault."

"A parent doesn't understand that," Sue told me.

Bob and Sue signed up for a support group for family members of addicts. They attended one meeting. They were unable to face the reality of their daughter's addiction.

"I remember the first time I went to a meeting," Bob said. "A fellow told me this is the seventeenth time his son or daughter relapsed. We were only at our first time. I thought, 'Seventeen times, oh my God.' He said, 'You'll be there, you'll be there.' A couple years later, he was right."

Shannon wandered around the house at three or four in the morning, often eating in the kitchen, or went into the yard and talked on the cell phone. She hoarded possessions. She would switch from her normal voice to a childlike voice, often a sign that someone is high.

Heroin addicts crave the drug several times a day and often need it to function. "The morphine molecule exerts an analogous brainwashing on humans, pushing them to act contrary to their self-interest in pursuit of the molecule," writes Quinones in *Dreamland.* "Addicts betray loved ones, steal, live under freeways in harsh weather, and run similarly horrific risks to use the molecule.

"It became the poster molecule for an age of excess," Quinones writes. "No amount of it was ever enough. The molecule created ever-higher tolerance. Plus, it had a way of railing on when the body gathered the courage to throw it out. This wasn't only during withdrawals. Most drugs are easily reduced to water-soluble glucose in the human body, which then expels them. Alone in nature, the morphine molecule rebelled. It resisted being turned into glucose and it stayed in the body."[16]

Shannon's parents enrolled her into a treatment program.

"The costs were astronomical," Sue said. "Just to get her in a program was $6,000. Just to get her into one program. After the detox, they shipped her down to another place. That was another $5,600."

A week later she relapsed.

Running out of options, her father went to AT&T and put a tracker on her phone. But the tracking device only provided her location. There was nothing her parents could do to prevent Shannon from buying heroin. Bob saw on the tracker one night that Shannon was at the riverfront, a popular place for buying and selling drugs. He drove down there at eleven to confront her.

"What are you doing here?" Bob recalled Shannon saying.

"What are *you* doing here? Never mind what *I'm* doing here," Bob said.

The surveillance was useless.

"She got smart and wised up," Bob said. "You can leave your phone somewhere and go out with somebody else. Then I put a tracker on her car so I'd know where her car would be. Then after a while—these kids are not stupid. They figure it out. Then they'd leave the car and the phone somewhere and drive off with somebody else."

"It's easy to get," Sue said of heroin. "Every street corner in Sayreville. . . . You see someone on a street corner, any time of day, they're probably dealing. They're in the stores. They're in your restaurants. They're in your supermarkets."

Her parents reported the drug dealing to two police departments in Middlesex County. "They didn't do nothing," her father said. "They're waiting for the big investigation to make the big hero bust. Meanwhile, these people are dealing out of our houses, dealing out of ShopRite, dealing all over the place. And the local police really have no interest in it. I think they'd rather stop someone trying to go to work, give them a ticket to raise revenue in the town, than to do their job and try to get these kids help."

In a desperate attempt to cut Shannon off from her drug network, her family sent her to a rehabilitation clinic in Delray, Florida, for three months of treatment.[17]

"We didn't know [heroin] is everywhere," her mother said.

The Florida rehab program cost the family $10,000. She seemed to be recovering.

"I told my mom I want her at my Sweet Sixteen. I won't have it unless she's there," Cam said. "So we flew her in for a couple of days. It was the best thing ever."

Shannon was sent to a halfway house in Florida after she completed rehab. She repeatedly called her parents to tell them she didn't want to finish the program. Her father relented and drove to Delray Beach to get her. A week later she relapsed.

Bob and Sue found Shannon a therapist. The therapist prescribed Abilify to treat her bipolar disorder.

"When she was on [Abilify] she was fine," Sue said. "Normal talk. Rational. Everything. You'd never know anything was happening. The minute she was off it, she was right back to it. The therapist was giving Shannon samples of Abilify. She said you need to go to your doctor to get more. When we went to the doctor we found out the Abilify would cost $1,000 a month."

The insurance did not cover the medication.

"They put her on Topamax," Sue said. "But it wasn't the same—when she was on Abilify it made her feel normal. All she wanted was to feel normal. But the insurance wouldn't pay for it."

The costs of treating Shannon's addiction mounted. Their insurance coverage ended after thirty days of treatment. The family, using money inherited from Bob's aunt, spent $8,000 to $10,000 a month on out-of-pocket expenses, medications, and insurance premiums. By the time Shannon died, her family had spent $100,000 trying to save her.

"You should be in rehab or some facility for a minimum of six months to try to get any treatment," Bob said.

"The average American cannot go to the Beverly Hills treatment center," he said. "Where you go is where your money can take you. . . . People are losing houses, losing everything they've worked up for to try to save their child."

Shannon's addiction inflicted more than a financial toll on the family.

"I felt like me and my sister Megan were on the outside, growing up by ourselves," Cam said. "Our parents devoted all their time to make sure Shannon was okay. It got us mad. . . . But I knew that Shannon needed all the time. It basically ruined my family a little bit."

"I was hurt because it was all about Shannon," Megan said. "How are we going to get her better. I resorted to talking to other people instead of my parents. . . . I know now, had they not done what they did with Shannon, she probably would have been gone long before."

Then, like most addicts consumed by powerful cravings, Shannon began to steal. ShopRite banned her for shoplifting. She stole money from her family. She stole her father's collection of old milk jars. A necklace and a pair of earrings given to Megan by their grandmother disappeared.

"One day when she wasn't home, I raided her room," Megan said. "I tore up everything in her room. And I found my missing jewelry underneath her mattress. When I confronted her about it she didn't even know what to say."

"Trust is a big issue for any human being," Megan said. "Once trust was broken, which she was known to do numerous times, there's a point where you can't mentally do it anymore."

"I was sleeping with my pocketbook under my pillow," Sue said.

One day Sue, cleaning the dishes, removed her wedding ring. When she went to retrieve it the ring was gone.

"After three hours of tearing the house apart, I find her upstairs curled in a fetal position on the floor, crying. "I said, 'Shannon do you know where my ring is,' 'Yes, Mommy, I took it and hocked it.' "

"Let's go," Sue said to Shannon. "Get in the car. We're getting your father. We're going to the place. Luckily, the guy thought something was not right. He saved all the jewelry that she hocked. I had to buy it back. . . . I had a hard time forgiving her for that and she knew it. She cried the whole time, 'Please forgive me mommy.' Naturally, I did in the end."

Her parents started to throw her out of the house when she came back high.

"I'm crying on the front porch as she gets kicked out," Cam recalled. "Cops at the house. Crying."

"The screaming, the yelling, the fighting that went on in our house," Sue said. "The driving away in the car with her friend, not knowing if I was going to ever see her again . . . She was maybe nineteen, twenty."

Shannon could be gone for as long as two weeks.

"No calls. No idea where she went," Sue said. "She was out in this world of addiction. We were home, pacing the floor, wondering if I'm going to get a knock on the door from a police officer . . . 'Come identify your child.' "

Shannon's life seemed to stabilize when she met Boris Rorer, a recovering addict who worked with her at McCaffrey's supermarket in Princeton, New Jersey. Boris, who was working on his associate's degree at a community college, is a muscular, gregarious weightlifter who consumes books from the novels of Fyodor Dostoyevsky, which he reads in his native Russian, to Friedrich Nietzsche, Jack London, and Thomas Hardy.

"I was using heroin for thirteen years," he said. "I'm still an addict. I've been sober for nine years."

Boris and Shannon spent their lunch breaks together. Boris went to McCaffrey's to see her on his day off. They had their first kiss on October 13, 2015. They celebrated the kiss anniversary every month.

"We were completely different," Boris said. "That was the magical thing . . . I'd show her the weirdest foreign movies and she watched them . . . She made me promise to sit and watch the entire Harry Potter series."

Shannon moved in with Boris in an apartment complex in Hamilton, New Jersey. She decorated the apartment for holidays. Boris gave her a bracelet with the words: "I promise to marry you." The couple played mini-golf, went hiking and apple picking. They visited a wolf sanctuary. They saved money in a jar for a wedding ring. Shannon, who got a job as a teller in a bank, showered her friends with presents.

The relationship with Boris gave her family hope. Boris paid for her Abilify and Topamax. Shannon faithfully attended Alcoholics Anonymous meetings. She was in regular contact with her sponsor.

In May 2016, Boris found a wax bag that Shannon had unsuccessfully tried to flush down the toilet. She was using again.

"If it had been anybody else but her, I would have known," Boris said, "because usually it's pretty obvious to another addict. But I was in denial. With her, I had no idea. Looking back, there were times when she was high or withdrawing in front of me. I just thought maybe she wasn't feeling good."

Shannon overdosed in June 2016.

"Luckily it was on my day off," Boris said. "I found her within ten minutes of when it happened. She wasn't breathing but her heart was still beating. So the lady on the phone told me how to do CPR and everything. By that time the medics came and gave her Narcan. So she survived that. She was in the hospital that night."

Boris took her from the hospital to a rehab clinic.

By the fall of 2016 Shannon was having a harder and harder time staying clean.

"I used again," Megan recalled Shannon telling her one day. "I'm not going to do it again. I don't know why I did it. I got it from someone in Trenton."

"Here we go again. It's your life, Shannon," Megan said.

"I remember my mom and I were fighting about it afterward," Megan said, struggling to hold back tears. "I said, 'I'm not doing this crap with her again' . . . I was so disappointed."

Shannon's friends were dying from overdoses. The losses exacerbated her depression.

"Every friend that she lost, she went to every one of their funerals," her mother said. "She'd never talk too much about it. I know in her head she was thinking that could be me. . . . There was a time back in November or so, it was at least one overdose a day, for a week or so, to the point where you're afraid to go on Facebook because that's all you're hearing."

"Look at all your friends who are dying," Cam said to Shannon. "I don't want you to be like that."

"Cam, I am sick," Shannon told her sister. "I'm going to die soon."

Shannon told Cam never to use drugs. Shannon promised to send Boris to extract Cam from any parties where Cam felt uncomfortable.

"You're not going to last forever doing that kind of stuff," Megan said. "It was a waiting game. When's it going to happen?"

Shannon was most vulnerable to relapsing when she was depressed.

"Heroin temporarily treats depression and physical pain, even though she was well aware that it would make it worse," Boris said. "There are more painkillers now than there used to be. When I was starting out getting high, the progression was from snorting to shooting heroin. But most kids didn't do heroin. That was extreme. They smoked weed and drank beer. But now there's so many painkillers that kids who might otherwise get high on weed or from drinking, find painkillers in their parents' cabinets. Painkillers are the same thing as heroin. Heroin is cheaper. Heroin is stronger. Eventually, kids who would never have thought of themselves as junkies end up doing heroin."

She was clean again, for a while, but her self-esteem plummeted.

"She was always beating herself up," Sue said. " 'Oh, no one's going to hire an addict.' "

At Christmas Shannon bought stockings and put gifts in them for women in Crawford House, a halfway house where she had once been a resident. She worried the women at the house would not receive presents.

"There was definitely a part of her that wanted to stop taking heroin, who didn't want to die," Boris said. "But it was just too strong for her. There was another part of her that wanted to get high, who wanted to not do anything. Closer to the end, she was using more and more. Staying clean for shorter and shorter periods of time. Relapsing more often. In the end, it was getting harder and harder for her to control herself.

"I had the sense that something bad was going to happen," Boris said. "I didn't know what. But it was obvious. She'd either get in an accident, arrested, overdose, or something. It was spinning out of control. I was scared to death. I was hoping that something would shake her up, maybe scare her enough to stay clean."

Shannon agreed to get a Vivitrol shot, which reduces cravings. She needed to be clean for at least seven days in order for the shot to work. She relapsed the day before the treatment.

"I never stopped trying," he said as we sat in his living room. "But I felt powerless."

Boris, who by this time had a job working nights at a sober living home for recovering addicts, left the apartment at 10:20 p.m. for his shift on Thursday. Shannon stood on the balcony and waved goodbye.

"I love you," she said.

"I had a couple friends who had keys to this place just in case I couldn't get here in time," Boris recalled. "In case anything happened. Because I was just so scared from the last time she overdosed. Most nights I worry. But that night I just thought it should be fine for some reason."

She was scheduled to go to her outpatient program the next morning. Boris called her from work but there was no answer. He assumed she forgot to charge her phone. He walked into the bedroom and found Shannon lying on the carpeted floor. Her jacket and a pack of cigarettes lay next to her body. Her face was blue. Fluids dripped from her mouth. Boris grabbed the Narcan shot and administered it. He frantically gave her CPR. It didn't have any effect. He called 911. The medics came for a few minutes and left. She had been dead for too long.

The police arrived and asked Boris to leave the bedroom to prevent the body from being disturbed. They waited for the coroner. Boris screamed and sobbed in the living room. The police allowed him to say a final farewell before the coroner removed the body.

"I held her as tight as I could," he said. "I cried and begged forgiveness. I asked her to marry me. I told her I loved her. Then they took her away like some *thing* and I was alone."

Cam was the only one at home when the police rang the bell at the house in Sayreville. "They asked if anyone in the house was sick," she said. "I'm like no. 'Where are your parents?' 'My mom's at school. My dad's in Hamilton with my grandparents.' They wanted to know the address of my grandparents. I said, 'Come back when my mom comes home later.' They wouldn't tell me anything that was going on.

"I drove around for a bit," Cam said. "Came back. And my mom's coming out of a cop's car. They're back. I'm like, 'Oh my God, what's going on.' Screaming to the police. Screaming to my mom. They brought me inside. Sat me down. My mom looks at me and says, 'We lost her.' I just went berserk. I curled up into a ball and started screaming, 'No.' I didn't know what to fathom, what to think of it. I didn't want to believe it. Shannon was my best friend."

"I was at work [teaching]," Megan remembered. "My principal came into my room and said, 'I need you to come into my office real quick.' She said, 'Someone's on the phone for you.' I didn't think it was about Shannon. I was just with her two weeks ago. We went to Palmer Square [in Princeton] to grab pizza. I thought it was my grandparents honestly. My aunt's like, 'Um, Shannon passed away,'" Megan said. "I literally went numb. 'What did you say?' She said, 'Shannon's not with us anymore.' She [the principal] told me not to leave. I sat there in the office. I kept saying, 'No, no, no. I was just with her. She was fine. Everything was fine. This isn't happening.'"

Two days later, Boris called Shannon's parents to ask for her ring size. He wanted to put a wedding ring on Shannon's finger in the funeral home. Megan, furious that Shannon had lost out on a life with Boris, kicked the wall and broke her toe.

The funeral cost the family $26,000 on top of the $100,000 they had paid for Shannon's treatments.

"Kids are dying every day," Bob said. "We're not talking one or two kids. Kids are dying all over the United States. And for parents, it's a living hell trying to live through this."

Boris said heroin was less lethal when he was an addict.

"I've had three overdoses. . . . People go to the hospital and sometimes survive," Boris said. "Nowadays, the overdoses are because of the fentanyl. It's much stronger. The dealers put it in there to make it stronger. It's expensive for them to put it in. They do it for a few bags, maybe one in every how many bags will have it. It makes the brand more attractive."

It is impossible to tell by looking if fentanyl is in the bags. Addicts usually buy ten bags at a time, which is called a "bun," for bundle. A bun costs between $40 and $90.

"Even in the bags that they put fentanyl in, it's uneven," said Carly Gleason, a twenty-year-old recovering heroin addict who was close friends with Shannon. "Someone might try a piece of the bag and it's fine. Then when they do the whole bag they end up dead."

Users instantly know if there's fentanyl in heroin.

"They put it in because they want people to overdose," Boris said. "They want people to think their brand is more potent. It's a marketing strategy. Maybe one guy will die. But a lot of other people will come and start buying from them."

The marketing through murder works. Carly, who said she had been feeling dope sick for the past few weeks although she was clean, reflexively asked Boris for Shannon's bags.

"It was an addict's response," Carly said. "When people are using heroin, most of the time they try to find out who overdosed on them because usually those bags are really good. So in my mind, it was like, 'Okay, I have to get those bags.' "

Boris had flushed the heroin down the toilet.

"In the past few months, everyone's been dying . . ." Carly said. "I stopped counting after twenty-four."

THE $1 TRILLION THE U.S. government has spent since Richard Nixon declared the war on drugs has, by every measure, been a colossal failure.[18] The federal government allocates $36 billion a year for law enforcement and social services and spends $80 billion a year on the prison system, where half of all prisoners are incarcerated for drug-related crimes. This comes to about $76 billion a year.[19] And yet, decades later, more Americans under the age of 50 die from overdoses than from heart disease, cancer, suicide, or traffic accidents. The number of deaths from overdoses has quadrupled since 1999.[20]

The premise of the War on Drugs is to criminalize the addicts and the dealers and blame the pharmaceutical companies and the doctors who run pill mills. A vast industry that profits off addictions, from rehab centers and methadone clinics to police and prisons, drains huge sums from the state, addicts, and their families without ever focusing on the root causes that lead people, especially young people, to play Russian roulette with their lives. The corporate state has cast many aside, but especially the young. It has thwarted their dreams and condemned them to a life where the best many can hope for is a low-wage, mind-numbing job in the service industry. It has left them financially unable to access the counselors and therapists who could help them deal with child, sexual, and domestic abuse, as well as bullying and the emotional wounds that often plague families in economic distress. The despair, the stress, the sense of failure and loss of self-esteem, the constant anxiety of being laid off, the pressure of debt repayment, often from medical bills, is amplified in a society that has splintered and atomized to render real relationships and community difficult and often impossible. Many people, especially young people, sit far too long in front of screens seeking friendship, romance, affirmation, hope, and emotional support. This futile attempt to achieve a human connection electronically, a connection vital to our emotional and psychological well-being, especially in a society that condemns so many to the margins, exacerbates the alienation, loneliness, and despair that make opioids attractive.

"You get opioids from your own brain stem when you get a hug," writes Marc Lewis in *The Guardian.* "Mother's milk is rich with opioids, which says a lot about the chemical foundation of mother-child attachment. When rats get an extra dose of opioids, they increase their play with each other, even tickle each other. And when rodents are allowed to socialize freely (rather than remain in isolated steel cages) they voluntarily avoid the opiate-laden bottle hanging from the bars of their cage. They've already got enough."[21]

Portugal has decriminalized drugs, including heroin and cocaine. It treats the epidemic as a mental health and medical problem. Portugal has reduced heroin addiction from 100,000 when its program was initiated to 25,000. Its drug mortality rate is now the lowest in Europe. It is one-fiftieth what it is in the United States. As Nicholas Kristof wrote in his *New York Times* article "How to Win a War on Drugs: Portugal treats addiction as a disease, not a crime," if the U.S. could replicate Portugal's death rate from drug overdoses "we would save one life every ten minutes," nearly as many lives as are lost to gun violence and car accidents combined.[22]

Methadone, often distributed by roving vans, along with rehabilitation programs in Portugal, are funded by the government and are free. The prohibitive costs of treatment in the United States means that only 10 percent of Americans are able to access these services, and even then the high cost means treatment is episodic, usually too short and often useless.[23] Drug-dealing is still a crime in Portugal, but the purchase or possession of small quantities of drugs results in a fine, not a criminal charge. Those charged are ordered before a "Dissuasion Commission" where they are connected with social workers. The decriminalization of drugs, Kristof notes, has also had a huge impact on communicable diseases. "In 1999, Portugal had the highest rate of drug-related AIDS in the European Union; since then, HIV diagnoses attributed to injections have fallen by more than 90 percent and Portugal is no longer at the high end in Europe," he writes.[24]

Those who seek to anesthetize themselves, to retreat into the underworld of the Lotus-eaters, are attempting to flee from pain, despair, and dislocation. They seek in opioids the affirmation, warmth, and solidarity that should come from families, friends, and communities where they can find purpose and dignity. Decriminalizing drugs is a step. But in itself it is not enough. Corporate capitalism has made war on the communal and the sacred, on those forces that allow us to connect and transcend our temporal condition to bond with others. These bonds will be reestablished or we will slip further into a world where death is more attractive than life.

☆ Focusing on hypernationalism + the decline in middle classes power/ opportunity that directly correlates to failings in politics + community culture → leads to the rise of elites 3 ruling selfishly.

≡≡≡

WORK

When life is not worth living, everything becomes a pretext for ridding ourselves of it. . . . There is a collective mood, as there is an individual mood, that inclines nations to sadness. . . . For individuals are too closely involved in the life of society for it to be sick without their being affected. Its suffering inevitably becomes theirs.

ÉMILE DURKHEIM, *On Suicide* [1]

Dale Gustafson, sixty-one, used a gun to kill himself on May 14, 2015. He was a self-employed house painter in Rockford, Illinois, for more than thirty-five years.

"My brother liked to organize sports games," said his sister Lori of their childhood in Rockford in the 1950s and 1960s. "Baseball. We'd build forts. He was always compassionate and wanted everyone to have fun. I don't think it was popular at the time, to include people with disabilities. We had one kid in the neighborhood who was missing an arm. He made sure to include him. That was just the kind of guy he was."

Their father was a traveling salesman for companies that made nuts and bolts, pots and pans, and picnic baskets. He died from a heart attack in 1970, when Dale was sixteen. Their mother took a job as a seamstress for an upholstery shop.

Dale went to college in Oregon to study horticulture. He did not graduate. He came back to Rockford in 1980. He began to work as a house painter. He got married in 1981. He and his wife had two daughters. He bought a small bungalow.

This was when the Rockford economy began to go into a tailspin. Lori did design work in the late 1980s for the Nylint Toy Corporation. The company made metal toy trucks, cars, and construction vehicles. The company sent more and more of its work to China. Lori soon found herself out of work. The company filed for bankruptcy in January 2001, its workforce reduced from a high of about four hundred, in the 1970s, to about eighty.[2]

Lori and her husband took out bank loans to buy apartments.

"We bought buildings pretty cheap and renovated them," she said. "We remortgaged the building. You'd usually remortgage for a percentage of the value of the building. The banker said, 'Just tell us how much you want.' It didn't matter what the value of the building was. It was way underwater. They just didn't care. They were ready to write the mortgage no matter what."

They charged about $400 for a one- or two-bedroom apartment. They had twenty-seven units.

"We had a lot of blue-collar workers as tenants," she said. "As they would lose their jobs, they'd try to hang on as long as they could. We'd try to work with them as long as we could. I don't even know where they ended up. Every time a factory closed, a batch of tenants would have to leave because they couldn't afford rent."

She and her husband began to bargain with their tenants, allowing them to pay in installments.

"But they would just fall further and further behind," she said. "They sometimes fell behind three or four months before we had to evict them. They knew they couldn't catch up. Sometimes they left on their own.

"We ran the applicants through a service to check their credit history, criminal records," she said. "Pretty soon, we didn't have much to choose from, so we took the best we could find. We started getting tenants who sold drugs. Prostitutes. Some of them would do a lot of damage to the building. We got out of the business. Anything on the West Side, we sold that first. There were a few tenants we evicted. The eviction court was so crowded. The landlords say, 'They ruined the carpet, they ruined this, and here's the amount of damages.' But they were never going to be paid those damages. So when I'd go up there I'd say, 'All I want is my property back. I won't sign off on any damages because I know I'm not going to get it. Just give me the key back. Just to stop further damage.' We had to use a power washer to wash apartments that were stained with animal feces and urine." *ew.*

They sold their units before the 2008 crash.

"He was frugal," Lori said of her brother. "He only shopped at Goodwill. He wouldn't buy people gifts for Christmas. He'd make these wooden animals and paint them all and give them funny names that he'd paint on the bottom. He made birdhouses. He made doll houses for his children and his niece."

"He basically painted everything—his golf clubs, faucets, bathtubs. He even painted his driveway," Dale's best friend, Bob Barker, said.

"My daughter played soccer and he was the coach," Barker said. "My daughter played on different teams. But she decided she wanted to be with Dale again and be on his team. He always loved kids. He'd be out running with the girls during practice up and down on the field."

Dale hired people who had developmental disorders, often bringing them home with him for Thanksgiving.

"He'd do anything to lift other people up," Lori said.

Dale hiked, in sections, the Cascade Mountain range. He ran marathons. He competed in the Birkebeiner cross-country ski race. He kayaked.

"Dale worked six days a week," said Art Wiss, his former neighbor and friend for more than twenty years. "He'd have side jobs cleaning lawns, landscaping, trimming bushes. He'd spend Saturdays or Sundays landscaping."

Dale was able to pay off the mortgage on his house. He saved money in IRAs for his retirement. Dale and his wife, however, began to cash them out, wiping out the funds and provoking penalties from the IRS. The couple divorced. The divorce settlement cost Dale $50,000. It wiped him out financially. He was forced to remortgage his house for $45,000. The house was valued at $90,000. He raised his younger daughter alone. His older daughter had already left home. He slowly paid down the second mortgage.

He met a woman, Sara, who worked for the state. They married. She had medical insurance. Her insurance allowed Dale to have a knee surgery that he had been delaying.

Dale continued to work hard. He paid off the house a second time. Sara, however, ran up $30,000 in credit card debt and had large student loans.

Dale remortgaged his house again to pay off his wife's debt. When the housing market crashed in 2008, his house was underwater. Rockford had the highest rate of underwater mortgages in the United States in 2013.[3]

Dale and Sara separated. Dale realized that he would never get out of debt. He would never pay off the mortgage. He was having problems with his knees again. It was becoming increasingly more painful and difficult to paint houses. He had not paid much into Social Security.

And then he had a car accident.

He was charged for the ambulance ride to the hospital and about $800 for the hospital visit. His mother, by this time, had dementia. Dale took turns taking care of her with his sister Lori. The world seemed to close in on him.

"On the last day I saw him, he was talking a lot about family stuff," Lori said. "We have a sister who was not very nice . . . He told me she said, 'Oh you're the only one who never graduated college and you're the only one who never went to Europe.' Her words had hurt him."

A few days later, Lori, who had been unable to reach her brother, found his body at his house. He left a note saying he had been suicidal for the past six months. He told his daughters, Kelcy and Megan, that he loved them. And he asked that someone take care of his dog Buddy.

Lori began seeing a medium to talk to Dale.

"This way it doesn't really feel like he's completely gone," she said. "If I couldn't talk to him, I don't know where I'd be right now."

A WHITE MALE IN ROCKFORD committed suicide, on average, every ten days in 2016.[4]

One hundred and twenty-one Americans commit suicide daily, according to the American Association of Suicidology.[5] The overwhelming majority—93 of the 121—are men. Seven out of ten of these men are white and between the ages of forty-five and sixty-five.[6] Around 44,193

Americans commit suicide every year[7] and another 1.1 million Americans attempt suicide annually.[8]

Princeton economists Anne Case and Angus Deaton blame the suicide rates among white males on what they term a "cumulative disadvantage," meaning a combination of unemployment or underemployment, the failure of marriages, the loss of social cohesion, and declining health. They argue that the "collapse of the white, high school educated, working class after its heyday in the 1970s" led to a variety of "pathologies" that fostered a potentially fatal despair.[9]

"These slow-acting and cumulative social forces seem to us to be plausible candidates to explain rising morbidity and mortality, particularly their role in suicide, and with the other deaths of despair, which share much with suicides," they wrote. They continued:

> Traditional structures of social and economic support slowly weakened; no longer was it possible for a man to follow his father and grandfather into a manufacturing job, or to join the union and start on the union ladder of wages. Marriage was no longer the only socially acceptable way to form intimate partnerships, or to rear children. People moved away from the security of legacy religions or the churches of their parents and grandparents, toward churches that emphasized seeking an identity, or replaced membership with the search for connection or economic success (Wuthnow, 1988). These changes left people with less structure when they came to choose their careers, their religion, and the nature of their family lives. When such choices succeed, they are liberating; when they fail, the individual can only hold himself or herself responsible. In the worst cases of failure, this is a Durkheim-like recipe for suicide. We can see this as a failure to meet early expectations or, more fundamentally, as a loss of the structures that give life a meaning.[10]

Durkheim, in his book *On Suicide*, wrote:

It is sometimes said that, by virtue of his psychological make-up, man cannot live unless he attaches himself to an object that is greater than himself and outlives him, and this necessity has been attributed to a supposedly common need not to perish entirely. Life, they say, is only tolerable if one can see some purpose in it, if it has a goal and one that is worth pursuing. But the individual in himself is not sufficient as an end for himself. He is too small a thing. Not only is he confined in space, he is also narrowly limited in time. So when we have no other objective than ourselves, we cannot escape from the feeling our efforts are finally destined to vanish into nothing, since that is where we must return. But we recoil from the idea of annihilation. In such a state, we should not have the strength to live, that is to say to act and struggle, since nothing is to remain of all the trouble that we take. In a word, the state of egoism is in contradiction with human nature and hence too precarious to endure.[11]

General Motors in Anderson, Indiana, fifty miles from Indianapolis and four hours from Rockford, once had plants that employed more than 25,000 workers.[12] One in every three people in the city worked for GM five decades ago. The auto plants had to stagger their shifts so the city streets would not be jammed with workers trying to leave or get to work.[13] GM closed down its plants, relocating much of its production to Mexico, following the passage of the North American Free Trade Agreement (NAFTA). GM was gone by 2006.[14]

Anderson, like Rockford, went into a death spiral. The population fell from 70,800 to 55,000.[15] Schools, churches, supermarkets, restaurants, dry cleaners, and furniture stores were closed and boarded up. Parts of Anderson resemble a ghost town. With economic and physical decay came Durkheim's *anomie* and a powerful nostalgia to go back in time, to magically make the city whole again, to recover hope.

Pope John Paul II in 1981 issued an encyclical called *Laborem exercens*, or "Through Work." He attacked the idea, fundamental to capitalism, that work was merely an exchange of money for labor. Work, he wrote, could not be reduced to the commodification of human beings. Workers were not impersonal instruments. They were not inanimate objects. Work was about more than wages and profit. It was essential to human dignity and self-fulfillment. It imparted a sense of purpose, empowerment, and identity. It allowed workers to bond with society and contribute to social harmony and cohesion.

The pope castigated unemployment, underemployment, inadequate wages, automation, and a lack of job security as violations of human dignity. These conditions, he wrote, were forces that destroy self-esteem, personal satisfaction, responsibility, and creativity. The exaltation of the machine, he warned, reduced human beings to the status of slaves. He called for full employment and a minimum wage large enough to support a family. He called for women who stay home with children and for the disabled to receive a living wage. He advocated for universal health insurance, pensions, accident insurance, and work schedules that permitted free time and vacations to build strong families. He wrote that every profession should be represented by unions with the right to strike.

The encyclical reads:

And yet, in spite of all this toil—perhaps, in a sense, because of it—work is a good thing for man. Even though it bears the mark of a *bonum arduum* [a difficult good], in the terminology of Saint Thomas, this does not take away the fact that, as such, it is a good thing for man. It is not only good in the sense that it is useful or something to enjoy; it is also good as being something worthy, that is to say, something that corresponds to man's dignity, that expresses this dignity and increases it.[16]

Work, the pope pointed out, also "constitutes a foundation for the formation of *family life*, which is a natural right and something that man is called to."[17] Work and industriousness, he wrote, influence the whole *process of education* in the family, for the very reason that everyone "becomes a human being" through, among other things, work, and becoming a human being is precisely the main purpose of the whole process of education.

DENNY CHASER WORKED FOR GM for forty-two years. He is a member of United Automobile Workers 662, which once had 14,700 members. We drove through Anderson. He pulled over and parked on the side of the road. He peered through a cyclone fence toward a huge, boxy white building that used to be GM Plant 20. The plant, bought by Sutong, a Chinese tire company, is now a warehouse that employs forty people.

I asked him how he felt, looking at the old plant where he used to work in "production control."

"I get sick," he said. "When I go by Plant 20 I want to turn in. I've been out of the plant eleven years."

When GM left it also drove out of business auxiliary companies, from trucking firms to repair shops that depended on GM for contracts. Those fortunate enough to have GM pensions suddenly became the few people in Anderson with disposable incomes.

"The next generation is going to have it tough," Denny said in his gravelly voice. "You can't raise a family on $9, $10, $12 an hour. You can't put money in savings."

Denny joined his first labor union when he was fourteen years old.

"The day we signed the first agreement in the late fifties, I went from 90 cents an hour to a buck and a quarter," he recalled. "That 35 cents is what made me where I'm at today, still union.

"If you really grasp unionism, you are a socialist," he said. "Because we're for the little people. Fair representation. Antidiscrimination. Wages. Benefits. It all comes hand in hand. There's strength in numbers.

"When I was hired, there were 117 people in a line," he said. "And we produced an alternator every five seconds. Four lines, each with 117. Later in my career, I had job rights in that department. They had automated with robots. My assignment on the line was [to] service thirteen robots and no people. And robots don't buy cars."

We got back in the car. We passed another former factory, Magnequench, which once produced sintered magnets and was a subsidiary of GM.

Jeffrey St. Clair wrote about the plant in his book *Grand Theft Pentagon*.[18]

Sintered magnets are made from rare earth minerals pulverized into a fine powder. These magnets are key components in electronics, especially in aviation. The firm's biggest client was the Pentagon, which uses the magnets in the guidance system of cruise missiles and the Joint Direct Attack Munition or JDAM bomb. Magnequench made 85 percent of magnets bought by the Pentagon. The plant, however, was bought in 2004 by the Chinese, who shipped the machinery to China.

The Chinese appeared to have acquired Magnequench to obtain sintered magnets for their long-range missiles and for the firm's computers used to facilitate the enrichment of uranium for nuclear warheads. The 450 workers lost their jobs. The only rare earth mine is in Baotou, China. China now has control of both the technology and rare earth minerals to produce the magnets, something, as St. Clair noted, that should have been prohibited by the Committee on Foreign Investment in the United States, which regulates the sale of high-tech and defense industries to foreign firms.[19]

Chaser and I drove past a Honda dealership and a gas station where there was once a Holiday Inn and a Sheraton. We passed a Kmart store—once one of three in Anderson—that had been closed for twenty years. There was one car parked in the vast, weed-choked asphalt lot. We drove by a shuttered gas station and a guns and ammo store.

"Guns and ammo. You've got to have that," Chaser said sarcastically. "When the city starts losing jobs, one of the first things to go is schools. Property taxes. You don't have as many people paying. Because of the unemployment."

We drove by several abandoned houses that were surrounded by overgrown grass and had windows boarded over with plywood. The chipped and peeling paint was covered with graffiti.

"The grocery stores have been closed," he said. "They still got one on the West Side in the black community. They closed one or two in this area. Now, we've got big black areas that don't have access to grocery stores. That doesn't mean they don't have five convenience stores. It means they don't have a grocery store to go buy their weekly groceries."

We stop on a street with dilapidated or abandoned row houses.

"They try to make drug houses out of them," he said of the abandoned houses. "Drugs and pain pills.

"Up here on the corner used to be a TV shop," he said, pointing toward a boarded-up store. "You don't need a TV repairman anymore. If it goes out, you buy a new one.

"There's homeless [people]," he said, pointing at a group of forlorn older men and women on a street corner.

We passed a shuttered dry cleaners.

like scranton

"This town was booming," Denny said. "We had the population. We had strong schools. We had both hospitals. We had the union."

We drove by a Marsh supermarket. Red signs in the windows announced it would close in ten days. A church on the corner had a "For Sale" sign on the lawn. Not far away was a boarded-up public school.

"This is where the Guide Lamp union hall was," he said, pointing to an old factory building. "This was one of the original sit-down locations in the thirties."

The 11,500 workers in GM's Guide Lamp plant in Anderson joined the GM sit-down strikes held in Flint, Michigan, in 1936 to protest the grueling conditions, substandard wages, work schedules that left them unemployed for weeks, and GM's policy of firing workers when they turned forty.[20] Most GM workers lived in hovels and shacks at the time that lacked heating and indoor plumbing.[21]

The UAW, inspired by nationwide French sit-down strikes in May and June of 1936, demanded that GM recognize the union, agree to a minimum wage, establish a grievance system, and improve safety to reduce assembly line injuries.[22] The strike lasted forty-four days.[23]

GM obtained a court order to evict the workers from the plants[24] and when the temperature in Flint fell to 16 degrees on January 11, 1937, the heating system in Fisher Body No. 2 was mysteriously shut down.[25] A hundred workers huddled inside the freezing plant. Twenty-two policemen armed with clubs arrived at the factory. They cut off the strikers' food supply.[26] A fight erupted. Sixteen workers and eleven policemen were injured. The police lobbed tear gas bombs at the workers outside the plant. A police captain broke a glass panel above some double doors and fired his tear gas gun twice into the factory.[27]

The assault saw the UAW expand its sit-down strike to the Flint Chevrolet No. 4 engine factory in February. It was the sole producer of Chevrolet engines.[28] The takeover of the Chevrolet No. 4 plant dwindled GM's monthly car production capacity from 50,000 to 125 cars.[29]

GM was finally forced to sign its first union agreement on February

11, 1937. It recognized the union's rights to engage in collective bargaining. It recognized strikers as employees. It promised not to carry out retribution. Workers received a 5 percent pay increase. And they were permitted to talk to one another during lunch breaks.[30]

The success in Flint inspired sit-down strikes across the country. Eighty-seven sit-down strikes took place in Detroit.[31] Nine thousand shoe workers walked out of factories in New England.[32] Busboys, garment workers, longshoremen, and people in occupations that had never experienced any union activity began organizing.[33] United States Steel, the largest steel company in the world, signed a contract with the Steel Workers' Organizing Committee, a CIO-sponsored union, without a strike.[34]

The GM sit-down strike of 1936–37 was the most significant American labor conflict in the twentieth century. The UAW triumphed over one of the most powerful corporations in the nation. UAW membership grew from 30,000 to 500,000 within a year.[35] Autoworkers' wages increased by as much as 300 percent. The UAW wrote agreements with four thousand automobile and automobile parts companies.[36] Packard, Goodyear, and Goodrich announced immediate wage increases.[37]

The clout wielded by unions on behalf of workers is now a distant memory.

Denny pulled into the parking lot of a Christian school.

"This used to be Local 662," he said of the school. "It was twenty-two acres. This is what we had when we had 14,700 members. See them railroad ties? I sold them to them. I used to landscape on the outside. We used to have a Labor Day picnic here. I used to run it. I had eleven thousand hot dogs that I'd purchase. At four o'clock I had to buy another thousand to get by."

GM, at the end, demolished most of its buildings.

"It was gut-wrenching," Denny said, remembering the demolitions. "Our stuff was used all over the world. It's more than you can ever think. If you worked somewhere thirty years or more, you've got to have a certain heartfelt fondness."

I WENT TO A SPARSELY attended job fair held at the Madison Park Church of God, an African American church, in Anderson. A few companies, including Amazon, a private prison contractor, and a trucking company, had set up tables.

Michael Hill, thirty-four and unemployed, stood holding some flyers and looking blankly at the tables. He was wearing a white sleeveless T-shirt. He had a wispy black goatee. The tattoos on his arms were copies of tattoos that his father, who was a plumber and died of a heart attack when Michael was fourteen, had on his arms. Michael lived with his wife, who was disabled, and six children in Muncie, Indiana. His last job was at a company called Thursday Pools that made fiberglass pools. He was laid off two and a half months ago. He did not have enough time on the job to qualify for unemployment. Before working for Thursday Pools, he worked on his own doing home remodeling. He made $10 an hour at both the pool company and doing remodeling. He had dropped out of high school at sixteen. He didn't vote in the 2016 presidential election because there "wasn't anything worth voting for."

"Bills are piling up faster than I can get the money together to pay them," he said wearily. "Ever since the economy crashed, people are pretty much working for pennies. It's been a hard road. I make sure my kids eat. It's stressful. Depressing at times. A lot of the people I grew up with took an alternate route. A lot of them are in jail. A lot of them are in prison. A lot of them got into drugs really bad. A lot of meth and cocaine." - pandemic

Ever since Michael was laid off, he has been "constantly moving, like trying to find the next job."

"Because I was self-employed for so long, McDonald's told me I was overqualified to work there," he said. "I've had three jobs in the last month. I had to drywall the lower floor of a house. I had to lay a floor for somebody. And I had to replace the plumbing in a bathroom."

He said he made $450 last month.

"They're not wearing Abercrombie," he said of his children. "I feel bad. They want this. They want that. And Dad can't give it to them right this minute."

Judy Streeter, who grew up in Anderson, is president of the Anderson Chapter of the Indiana Black Expo. She helped organize the job fair. About 15 percent of the city is African American. Most live in West Anderson.

no longer able to make healthy and affordable meals.

"We lost our one and only grocery store," she lamented. "We seem to get dollar stores. But we don't have any real businesses on the West Side. Food restaurants, we have two. Taco Bell and Wendy's. — *fast food instead*

"We had W. T. Grants [a variety store]," Judy said of the city she knew as a girl. "We had a lot of places where individuals could go to find jobs. We had automotive stores. With the closure of General Motors, then you can see things start to deteriorate.

"The youth have nowhere to go," she said. "They have no hope. They have no desires to do anything." — *depression seeps in w/ a lack of motivation or self worth*

The economic decline has been especially hard on African Americans.

"Young black men and women have to work twice as hard in order for them to be able to do what other kids are doing," she said.

"I lost a son because of drugs," she said. "He was killed by another boy. Then I had [another son] incarcerated. They came from a good family. They come from a different upbringing. [Drugs weren't] something that was encouraged. It wasn't an atmosphere that they were exposed to. It was a part of being out there and making some bad choices. Our kids are making bad choices. But at the same time, there's just no hope. They don't have any motivation to do the things that need to get done. Why is the motivation so low? I can't answer that. My one son who was incarcerated, he spent two years going to college. In the end he still got in trouble."

She said her son could not find steady employment after he was released from prison.

"If you're going to incarcerate them, then help rehabilitate them," she said. "Help them learn how to do trades and other things . . . I have an uncle who was a Supreme Court judge. One of the things that he talked about is the fact that when they come out, they still have to put on the application they were incarcerated, which keeps them from getting employment. If we always leave that stumbling block there for them and they can't get past it, then you're not helping them. You're hurting them."

Lieutenant Larry Taylor, a heavyset corrections officer, sat at a job fair table with a colleague, Sergeant Williams. They wore blue uniforms. Taylor had spent twenty-eight years as a corrections officer.

equivalent to slave labor though. less than min wage

"We're in a position to make a job offer today," he said. "We brought applications with us. We can give them an interview today."

There was little interest from the job seekers, although Taylor said in his prison there were one hundred job openings. By late afternoon only three people had filled out applications. This may be because applicants must submit to "a background check, a clear urine analysis, drug screen, a check of the references they submit, and also a check to see if there's any back taxes they owe that they haven't made arrangements to take care of," he said.

The starting salary was $14.16 an hour. Veterans could get an extra 50 cents an hour.

"Benefits are from day one," he said. "As soon as the person receives a phone call saying, 'Report at six o'clock on Monday over here.' It will start right then. They'll have health insurance, vision, dental. They will start accumulating their leave time. They have paid military leave. We have a lot of people in the National Guard or Army Reserves."

"Why is it hard to fill these jobs?" I asked.

"My personal opinion: the work ethic is just not what it used to be," he said. "A job used to really mean something. You felt an obligation to your job. When you agreed to take a job from your employer, you worked for that employer. You don't call off sick when you weren't sick. You came to work. You felt an obligation towards them, towards the other people you work with. You knew what your job duties entailed. You know if you weren't there somebody else had to pick up that slack for you. That caliber of individuals is really hard to find now."

He admitted the job had its downsides.

"The old-school bullying type things—real hard stares, negative comments," he said. "To a female, they could say something really rude about their personal hygiene, things that a woman would take to heart. To a male, they might say something about how soft he is. It's almost a high school mentality.

"One of the hardest things for me was to tell someone my father's age, 'No,' " he went on. "But that is a part of my job."

The guards were unionized when Taylor first began working at the prison. But Indiana governor Mitch Daniels signed an executive order in 2005 that eliminated collective bargaining for all state employees, essentially outlawing their unions, stripping them of unionized rights, and voiding their union contracts.[38] The order obliterated the unions for corrections officers, highway police, hospital workers, and other state employees. Daniels also privatized state functions, including the food service in the state's twenty-eight prisons. The governor claimed the state had saved over $100 million from 2005 to 2011, although the privatization cost hundreds of jobs.[39] Daniels signed a "right to work" provision in 2012 to the state's labor laws that bars union contracts from requiring nonunion members to pay fees for representation. The provision is used by unionized companies to employ nonunion labor.

"We had at least seven unions," Taylor said. "You had your pick. Now they're all gone. Now if an officer has a complaint or felt like he wasn't done fairly, he has the SEAC, the State Employees' Appeals Commission. It's his right to turn around and file paperwork. Of course, they always try to settle everything at the lowest level of the facility.

"It used to be the state ran everything that goes on inside the facility," he said. "Everything. The kitchens. The states were in charge of that. Aramark [a private contractor] runs our food service [now]. PEN Products runs our laundry. Grace College runs our education. Medical is always a contract now. The state used to run their own medical department. The state does [still] run commissary [a store within a correctional facility]."

Taylor said the quality of the food plummeted once food service was outsourced to Aramark. He brings his own meals.

"Back when I hired in, we had an officers dining room," he said. "A lot of facilities [that have] been around still have officers dining rooms. Nobody, to my knowledge, staffs them or runs them anymore. A long time ago, you would buy a meal ticket. The meal cost you 50 cents. And it was really good food. The offenders did prepare it. But it was prepared in the officers dining room and they had a man who was in charge of watching them."

The prisoners work in a variety of prison industries that pay about 25 cents an hour.

"There is a lot of industry there," he said. "Our facility, the Correctional Industrial Facility, we have a Meritor brake service, a PEN Products shop that runs an upholstery shop. Those are both different companies. PEN Products is tied in with the state. Meritor is a private industry.

"The state pays on four different pay scales—A, B, C, and D. 'A' would be, for instance, 35 cents an hour," he said. " 'B,' a dime less. 'C,' a dime less. A [prisoner] that goes to work for Meritor, a private company, might start off with that 'A' pay. Every ninety days they get a dime raise. That continues for over a year. Then it gets up over a dollar."

Meritor refurbishes old brakes and sells them.

"They look like they're brand-new when they go back out," he said.

"The only population that has dropped is the staffing population," he said. "At these job fairs, we tell people this is a job that they make into a career. Hopefully, we'll find career people and not just job people. Ideally, it's a younger person who has worked a little while and has their head screwed on straight. Someone who will say, 'I need a career. I need a future. I need something that will always be there.' It's sad to say but prisons will always be there."

Taylor, who was white, said he worried about the nation's moral decline. He and his wife, a bus driver, homeschool their children. The deciding factor was "evolution versus creation."

"We believe in the Bible," he said. "We believe the world was created by God just like the Bible says.

"Abstinence isn't taught in school," he went on. " 'We're just going to give you all the condoms and different things to prevent children. Here's the different diseases you could get.' But all that can be prevented if you just abstain. - unrealistic

"Bullying is always a factor," he said. "There's bullying everywhere. People commit suicide because of bullying. I think we felt [homeschooling] was a safer environment to raise our kids in.

"I used to wonder [about the prisoners] initially when I was first hired by the department, 'How many of these guys were just in the wrong place at the wrong time?' " he said. "Then after I was there for a little while, I got to know them. It changed to, 'How many of these gentlemen have had break after break after break?' And the judge finally got tired of looking at him."

He said he voted for Trump, as did most of his neighbors.

"I think people were ready for somebody to put their fist down and say, 'You know what, it's stopping right here,'" he said. "I think we should have circled the wagon as a country a long time ago. You know what, world, we're going to focus on ourselves the next year. So nothing is coming out. We're not exporting nothing and we're not importing nothing. Good luck to you. We'll see you in a year. Let the whole world rise up and say, 'Oh my gosh. What are we going to do without the United States?' I'm tired of not focusing on us. We have to focus on ourselves."

— not totally wrong but intense nationalism is very dangerous

IN INDIANAPOLIS, AN HOUR FROM Anderson, the Carrier plant was being downsized—another in a long series of hammer blows to Indiana's workers. Carrier had announced in February 2016 that the facility would close, putting over a thousand people out of work, and move to Mexico, where workers earn $3 an hour without benefits. Workers in the U.S. earn about $20 an hour and have pensions, health insurance, and paid vacation.

I drove to the Steelworkers Local 1999 to speak with the former president Chuck Jones.

"We met with the company to see what we could do to keep the facility here in Indianapolis," Jones said. "We identified about $22 million, according to the company's figures, in concessionary givebacks per year. The company costed it out. Came back and said, 'Well, we're saving $65 million a year [by moving to Mexico].'

"They said, 'Well, the only way that you guys can achieve $65 million is if everyone worked for $5 an hour and you can't do that because that's below minimum wage,'" he said. "'And nobody would have any benefits at all. So it's a noble gesture, seeing what you can do. But you can't get there.'"

"If I were in office right now Carrier would not be leaving Indiana," Trump announced on April 20, 2016.[40]

Trump and Mike Pence, the former governor of Indiana, came back to Indianapolis on December 1, 2016, to announce they had negotiated a deal with Carrier to save 1,100 jobs. Carrier is part of UTC Climate, Controls & Security, a unit of United Technologies Corp.

This "was an out-and-out lie," Jones said.

"The state of Indiana was going to offer $7 million in tax abatements [to UTC to keep Carrier jobs in-state], at taxpayers' expense," he said. "We sit there. There's a handful of us who'd been told two hours before that 550 jobs were going to Monterrey, Mexico. Trump and Pence and UTC never mentioned anything about losing 550 jobs.

"People assumed at that point in time that their jobs were safe," he went on. "Well, we know part of them were. But people thought the whole facility was safe.

"We got a company like Carrier, a corporation like UTC, who is making record-breaking profits," he said. "It's corporate greed. They don't care about what they're doing to their employees, our members, their families, the communities, the schools, the businesses. They don't care because the bottom line is, it's $65 million a year that they're going to be saving. It's all about making sure the CEOs and the people who have stock in UTC make a little more money.

"In Carrier's situation, the state of Indiana rewarded Carrier and UTC, at the taxpayers' expense, $7 million, over ten years, to move 550 jobs out of the city of Indianapolis," he said. "And then [losing] another 700 [jobs], in Huntington, Indiana, which is a UTC plant. Also, the federal government has rewarded UTC with more military contracts. They're involved with helicopters. They got close to $6 billion in military contracts. So you've got a company that takes jobs out of this country. Then we got our political people who reward them with military contracts. Something is wrong with that story.

"We couldn't sell Hillary," he said. "I wasn't even going to try to sell Hillary to them. The only thing I would ask them is, 'If you're going to vote for Trump'—he was going to win Indiana anyway—'Please vote for our Democratic nominee for governor in the down ticket.' And that didn't work out either.

"The Democratic Party got lazy," he said. "The working-class people, instead of coming out and voting, they stayed home. A lot of our people, labor people, get caught up too much on guns and stuff like that instead of looking at who has got their best interest in mind, as far as the economic part.

"The Democrats have let us down," he said. "They forgot about the working-class people."

I DROVE TO TERRE HAUTE to visit the home of Eugene Victor Debs, now a museum on the campus of Indiana State University.

Debs burst onto the national stage when he organized a railroad strike in 1894 after the Pullman Company cut wages by up to one third but did not lower rents in company housing or reduce dividend payments to its stockholders.[41] Over a hundred thousand workers staged what became the biggest strike in U.S. history on trains carrying Pullman cars.[42]

The response was swift and brutal.

"Mobilizing all the powers of capital, the owners, representing twenty-four railroads with combined capital of $818,000,000, fought back with the courts and the armed forces of the Federal government behind them," Barbara W. Tuchman writes in *The Proud Tower: A Portrait of the World Before the War, 1890–1914*.[43] "Three thousand police in the Chicago area were mobilized against the strikers, five thousand professional strikebreakers were sworn in as Federal deputy marshals and given firearms; ultimately six thousand Federal and State troops were brought in, less for the protection of property and the public than to break the strike and crush the union."[44]

Attorney General Richard Olney, who, as Tuchman writes, "had been a lawyer for railroads before entering the Cabinet and was still a director of several lines involved in the strike,"[45] issued an injunction rendering the strike illegal. The conflict, as Debs would write, was a battle between "the producing classes and the money power of the country."[46]

Debs and the union leaders defied the injunction. They were arrested, denied bail, and sent to jail for six months. The strike was broken. Thirty workers had been killed. Sixty had been injured. Over seven hundred had been arrested. The Pullman Company hired new workers under "yellow dog contracts," agreements that forbade them to unionize.[47]

When he was in jail, Debs read the works of socialist writers Edward Bellamy and Karl Kautsky, as well as Karl Marx's *Das Kapital*. The books, especially Marx's three volumes, set the "wires humming in my system."[48]

"I was to be baptized in Socialism in the roar of the conflict. . . . In the gleam of every bayonet and the flash of every rifle the class struggle was revealed," he writes. "This was my first practical lesson in Socialism."[49]

Debs came to the conclusion that no strike or labor movement could ultimately be successful as long as the government was controlled by the capitalist class. Any advances made by an organized working class would later be reversed by the capitalists when they regained absolute power, often by temporarily mollifying workers with reforms. Working men and women had to achieve political power, a goal of Britain's Labour Party at the time, or they would forever be at the mercy of the bosses.[50]

Debs especially feared the rise of the monolithic corporate state. He foresaw that corporations, unchecked, would expand to "continental proportions and swallow up the national resources and the means of production and distribution."[51] If that happened, he warned, the long "night of capitalism will be dark."[52] — *which it is.*

This was a period in U.S. history when many American Christians were socialists. Walter Rauschenbusch, a Christian theologian, Baptist minister, and leader of the Social Gospel movement, thundered against capitalism.

Debs turned to the Bible as often as to Marx, arguing, "Cain was the author of the competitive theory" and the "cross of Jesus stands as its eternal denial."[53] Debs's fiery speeches, replete with words like "sin" and "redemption," were often thinly disguised sermons. He equated the crucified Christ with the abolitionist John Brown.[54] He insisted that Jesus came "to destroy class rule and set up the common people as the sole and rightful inheritors of the earth."[55] "What is Socialism?" he once asked. "Merely Christianity in action."[56] He was fond of quoting poet James Russell Lowell,[57] who wrote:

> He's true to God who's true to man;
> Whenever wrong is done.
> To the humblest and the weakest,
> 'neath the all-beholding sun.
> That wrong is also done to us,

And they are slaves most base,
Whose love of right is for themselves
And not for all the race[58]

It was also a period beset with violence, including anarchist bombings and assassinations. An anarchist killed President William McKinley in 1901, unleashing a wave of state repression against social and radical movements. Striking workers engaged in periodic gun battles, especially in the coalfields of southern West Virginia, with company militias, National Guard units, paramilitary groups such as the Coal and Iron Police, and the U.S. Army. Hundreds of workers were killed. Debs adamantly opposed violence and sabotage, arguing that these actions allowed the state to demonize the socialist movement and legitimize violence by the state. The conflict with the capitalist class, Debs argued, was at its core about competing values. *rich v everyone else.*

Debs turned to politics when he was released from jail in 1895. He was one of the founders of the Socialist Party of America and, in 1905, the Wobblies, along with Mother Jones and William "Big Bill" Haywood.[59] He was the Socialist Party candidate for the U.S. presidency five times in the period 1900 through 1920—once when he was in prison—and ran for Congress in 1916.[60]

The Socialist Party in 1912 had 126,000 members, 1,200 office-holders in 340 municipalities, and 29 English and 22 foreign-language weeklies, along with three English and six foreign-language dailies. It included in its ranks tenant farmers, garment workers, railroad workers, coal miners, hotel and restaurant workers, dockworkers, and lumberjacks. Debs traveled from New York to California during the 1912 presidential campaign on a train called the Red Special. He spoke to tens of thousands.[61] He helped elect socialist mayors in some seventy cities, including Milwaukee.[62] He propelled two socialists into Congress.[63] In the elections of 1912 he received nearly a million votes, 6 percent of the electorate.[64] Eighteen thousand people went to see him in Philadelphia and in New York City fifteen thousand people paid 15 cents to a dollar to hear him speak in Madison Square Garden.[65]

The socialist and radical parties and unions terrified the ruling elites, who instituted tepid reforms in an attempt to stanch the support for these groups. At the same time the state began a campaign to crush the movement. Department of Justice agents in 1912 made simultaneous raids on forty-eight IWW meeting halls across the country and arrested 165 IWW union leaders. One hundred and one went to trial, including Haywood, who testified for three days. One of the IWW leaders told the court:

> You ask me why the I.W.W. is not patriotic to the United States. If you were a bum without a blanket; if you had left your wife and kids when you went west for a job, and had never located them since; if your job had never kept you long enough in a place to qualify you to vote; if you slept in a lousy, sour bunkhouse, and ate food just as rotten as they could give you and get by with it; if deputy sheriffs shot your cooking cans full of holes and spilled your grub on the ground; if your wages were lowered on you when the bosses thought they had you down; if there was one law for Ford, Suhr, and Mooney [I.W.W. leaders] and another for Harry Thaw [heir to a multimillion-dollar mine and railroad fortune who used his wealth to avoid prison time for murder]: if every person who represented law and order and the nation beat you up, railroaded you to jail, and the good Christian people cheered and told them to go to it, how in hell do you expect a man to be patriotic? _RELEVANT TODAY._
> This war [World War I] is a business man's war and we don't see why we should go out and get shot in order to save the lovely state of affairs that we now enjoy.[66]

Debs demanded an end to child labor,[67] and denounced Jim Crow and lynching.[68] He called for women's suffrage, a graduated income tax, unemployment compensation, the direct election of senators, employer liability laws, national departments of education and health, guaranteed pensions for the elderly, nationalization of the banking and transport systems, and replacing "wage slavery" with cooperative industries.[69]

On June 18, 1918, in Canton, Ohio, Debs, as he had often done in the past, decried the unholy alliance between capitalism and war, the use of the working class by the capitalists as cannon fodder in World War I, and the Wilson administration's persecution of antiwar activists, unionists, anarchists, socialists, and communists.[70] Wilson, who had a deep animus toward Debs, had him arrested under the Sedition Act, which made it a crime to "willfully utter, print, write, or publish any disloyal, profane, scurrilous, or abusive language about the form of the Government of the United States,"[71] or to "willfully urge, incite, or advocate any curtailment of the production" of anything "necessary or essential to the prosecution of [a U.S. war, in this case against Germany and its allies].[72]

Debs did not contest the charges. At his trial, he declared: "Washington, Paine, Adams—these were the rebels of their day. At first they were opposed by the people and denounced by the press . . . And if the Revolution had failed, the revolutionary fathers would have been executed as felons. But it did not fail. Revolutions have a habit of succeeding when the time comes for them."[73] On September 18, 1918, minutes before he was sentenced to a ten-year prison term and stripped of his citizenship, the sixty-two-year-old Debs rose and told the court:

Your Honor, years ago I recognized my kinship with all living beings, and I made up my mind that I was not one bit better than the meanest on earth. I said then, and I say now, that while there is a lower class, I am in it, and while there is a criminal element I am of it, and while there is a soul in prison, I am not free.

I listened to all that was said in this court in support and justification of this prosecution, but my mind remains unchanged. I look upon the Espionage Law as a despotic enactment in flagrant conflict with democratic principles and with the spirit of free institutions. . . . Your Honor, I have stated in this court that I am opposed to the social system in which we live; that I believe in a fundamental change—but if possible by peaceable and orderly means. . . .

I am thinking this morning of the men in the mills and the factories; of the men in the mines and on the railroads. I am thinking of the women who for a paltry wage are compelled to work out their barren lives; of the little children who in this system are robbed of their childhood and in their tender years are seized in the remorseless grasp of Mammon and forced into the industrial dungeons, there to feed the monster machines while they themselves are being starved and stunted, body and soul. I see them dwarfed and diseased and their little lives broken and blasted because in this high noon of Christian civilization money is still so much more important than the flesh and blood of childhood. In very truth gold is god today and rules with pitiless sway in the affairs of men.

In this country—the most favored beneath the bending skies—we have vast areas of the richest and most fertile soil, material resources in inexhaustible abundance, the most marvelous productive machinery on earth, and millions of eager workers ready to apply their labor to that machinery to produce in abundance for every man, woman, and child—and if there are still vast numbers of our people who are the victims of poverty and whose lives are an unceasing struggle all the way from youth to old age, until at last death comes to their rescue and lulls these hapless victims to dreamless sleep, it is not the fault of the Almighty: it cannot be charged to nature, but it is due entirely to the outgrown social system in which we live that ought to be abolished not only in the interest of the toiling masses but in the higher interest of all humanity. . . .

I believe, Your Honor, in common with all Socialists, that this nation ought to own and control its own industries. I believe, as all Socialists do, that all things that are jointly needed and used ought to be jointly owned—that industry, the basis of our social life, instead of being the private property of a few and operated for their enrichment, ought to be the common property of all, democratically administered in the interest of all. . . .

I am opposing a social order in which it is possible for one man who does absolutely nothing that is useful to amass a fortune of hundreds of millions of dollars, while millions of men and women who work all the days of their lives secure barely enough for a wretched existence.

This order of things cannot always endure. I have registered my protest against it. I recognize the feebleness of my effort, but, fortunately, I am not alone. There are multiplied thousands of others who, like myself, have come to realize that before we may truly enjoy the blessings of civilized life, we must reorganize society upon a mutual and cooperative basis; and to this end we have organized a great economic and political movement that spreads over the face of all the earth. . . .

Your Honor, I ask no mercy and I plead for no immunity. I realize that finally the right must prevail. I never so clearly comprehended as now the great struggle between the powers of greed and exploitation on the one hand and upon the other the rising hosts of industrial freedom and social justice.[74]

Three years later, Debs's sentence was commuted by President Warren Harding to time served. He was released from prison in December of 1921 in poor health.[75] His citizenship was not restored until five decades after his death in 1926.[76] The labor movement and Socialist Party had been broken by the time he died.

The breakdown of capitalism saw a short-lived revival of organized labor during the 1930s, often led by the Communist Party. This resurgence triggered yet another prolonged assault by the capitalist class, one that accelerated after the social unrest of the 1960s.

The social, political, and civil rights won by workers in long and bloody struggles have been stripped away. Government regulations have been rolled back to permit corporations to engage in abuse and fraud. Unions are moribund.

We have to begin all over again. We must do so understanding that we can only pit power against power. Our power only comes when we organize.

I walked through the Debs museum in Terre Haute with its curator, Allison Duerk. It has about seven hundred visitors a year. School groups rarely come. The valiant struggle by radical socialists and workers has been consciously erased from history and replaced with the vacuity of celebrity culture and the cult of the self.

The walls of the two-story frame house, built by Debs and his wife in 1890, are covered with photos and posters, including pictures of Debs's funeral on the porch and five thousand mourners in the front yard. There is the key to the cell in which he was held when he was jailed the first time. There is a photo of Convict No. 9653—Debs—holding a bouquet at the entrance to the federal penitentiary in Atlanta as he accepts the nomination from leaders of the Socialist Party to be their 1920 presidential candidate. There are gifts including an intricately inlaid wooden table and an ornately carved cane that prisoners sent to Debs, who was a tireless advocate for prisoners' rights.

I opened the glass panel of a cherry wood bookshelf and pulled out one of Debs's books, running my fingers lightly over his signature on the inside flap. I read a passage from a speech he gave in 1905 in Chicago:

The capitalist who does no useful work has the economic power to take from a thousand or ten thousand workingmen all they produce, over and above what is required to keep them in working and producing order, and he becomes a millionaire, perhaps a multi-millionaire. He lives in a palace in which there is music and singing and dancing and the luxuries of all climes. He sails the high seas in his private yacht. He is the reputed "captain of industry" who privately owns a social utility, has great economic power, and commands the political power of the nation to protect his economic interests. He is the gentleman who furnishes the "political boss" and his swarm of mercenaries with the funds with which the politics of the nation are corrupted and debauched. He is the economic master and the political ruler and you workingmen are almost as completely at his mercy as if you were his property under the law.

I leafed through copies of *Appeal to Reason*, the Socialist Party newspaper Debs edited, which once had almost 800,000 readers and the fourth highest circulation in the country. It was shut down in 1922, a victim as well of the purges carried out against populist movements in the name of anticommunism.

Debs, like many of his generation, was literate. He read and reread Victor Hugo's *Les Misérables* in French. It was his father's bible. It became his own. His parents, émigrés from Alsace, named him after the French novelists Eugène Sue and Victor Hugo. His father read Sue, Hugo, Voltaire, Rousseau, Dumas, and other French authors at night to his six children.

Debs found in Hugo's novel the pathos of the struggle by the wretched of the earth for dignity and freedom. He was well aware, like Hugo, that good people were usually relentlessly persecuted, were rarely rewarded for virtue, and that those who held fast to truth and justice often found the way to their own cross. But there was no other choice. The kingdom of evil had to be fought. It was a moral imperative. The stripping away of what is human, the loss of dignity and self-worth, negated all that was precious and sacred in life.

"Intellectual and moral growth is no less indispensable than material improvement," Hugo wrote in an appendix to *Les Misérables*. "Knowledge is a viaticum [the Eucharist given to those near death]; thought is a prime necessity; truth is nourishment, like wheat. A reasoning faculty, deprived of knowledge and wisdom, pines away. We should feel the same pity for minds that do not eat as for stomachs. If there be anything sadder than a body perishing for want of bread, it is a mind dying of hunger for lack of light."[77]

4

SADISM

Fascism countenances that religiosity that stems from sexual perversion, and it transforms the masochistic character of the old patriarchal religion of suffering into a sadistic religion. In short, it transposes religion from the "other-worldliness" of the philosophy of suffering to the "this worldliness" of sadistic murder.

WILHELM REICH, *The Mass Psychology of Fascism* [1]

A beefy security guard, dressed in black and holding a clipboard, greeted me outside the old San Francisco Armory on Market Street in the Mission District. A "leather pride" flag was flying from the top of one of the Moorish revival turrets above us.

"Are you here for the Mindfuckery class?" he asked.

"Yes," I said.

"Name and identification," he demanded.

I give him my New Jersey driver's license. He held it up to the list of names and checked me off.

"Wait here," he said. "Someone will escort you down."

On the sidewalk outside the armory there were a few dozen homeless men and women, part of the army of three thousand people [2] who sleep each night on the streets of San Francisco. Many were seated in front of blankets covered with an assortment of tattered books, old clothing, dented toasters, lamps, and used watches for sale.

The British businessman Peter Acworth bought the armory and

former National Guard training facility in 2006 for $14.5 million.[3] It had been closed in 1976 and sat largely vacant for three decades.[4] Acworth made it the headquarters of Kink.com, one of the world's largest websites for BDSM films and live streams. BDSM stands for a combination of the abbreviations B/D (Bondage and Discipline), D/s (Dominance and submission), and S/M (Sadism and Masochism). Kink.com once produced as many as 100 films a month but shut down its film operations in early 2017, unable to compete with free online porn.[5]

A perky woman in a short skirt came out of the building after a few of us had gathered on the steps. She escorted us downstairs to a basement room with no windows. The walls were chipped and cracked, exposing dark, greenish paint beneath the beige overcoat. A few bare neon bulbs cast an uneven light over the floor, leaving the corners in shadows. There were four rows of folding chairs facing a raised cement platform.

I entered the gloomy basement room with about two dozen people, mostly men dressed in black. We were here for a six-hour course called "Creative Mindfuckery & Authentic Interrogation for BDSM Intensive." The instructor went by the name Danarama.

The room, where we would spend most of the day, was, according to the escort, once used as a weightlifting room by the National Guard. I had been in the room two days earlier attending another seminar called "Hot, Healthy Humiliation." That course taught techniques for verbally degrading and insulting your partner. The instructor, the psychologist Liz Powell, told us verbal abuse would make your partner feel "empowered."

"I am a polyamorous, medisexual slut," Powell said shortly after we had entered the room. "Medisexual is a term my friend and I coined. It's the opposite of demisexual. A demisexual has to have a romantic relationship to feel sexual attraction and desire. A medisexual is a 'fun first' person. We need to have a sexual connection in order to develop romantic feelings. I also identify as a slut. I like to have a lot of sex with a lot of different people in a lot of different ways. I'm a variety person."

She said she had been doing "humiliation play" for over a decade.

"The psychological aspects of BDSM have always been some of the most interesting and engaging for me," she said. "Like it's really fun to hit people with heavy things. It's really fun to tie people up. But getting deep inside someone's head, like really getting in there and seeing their little dark secrets in their dark corners—that to me is the biggest, juiciest part of it. Let's hear about you."

She asked the group if anyone had questions.

"I'm B.J.," a man said. "What is the psychology behind healthy humiliation? What makes it healthy? What's healthy about it?"

"I'm Julia," said a woman. "I want to know why different people find humiliation sexy."

"My name is Marcus," said a man with a German accent. "I have fetish. I like sex and smell. But I am a romantic. For me, in the end it is about the relationship and good connection."

I said nothing.

Evoking "embarrassment," Powell said, was the lowest level of play followed by "humiliation" and then "degradation." She said she hoped to shatter our "taboos" and teach us how to take our partners to the parts of their psyche they were "most afraid of." She insisted humiliating and degrading our partner would be "empowering" and "healing" for them.

"There are a lot of people who are black who enjoy race play, who enjoy playing a Civil War era slave," she said. "There are women who have been sexually assaulted who really enjoy rape fantasies. There are people who have experienced fat shaming who would want their partner in the context of that scene to replicate those kinds of things.

"If I'm playing with my lover, and he tells me I'm a fat, ugly, worthless bitch, and as soon as I'm done, he says 'oh my God, baby, you looked so good in that moment, I loved how those tears were streaming down your face, I loved the curve of your hip as you turned over, it was so beautiful,' I get to experience that same emotion but I get a very different closure on it. Instead of it sticking to me as a little tiny scar, I get to open it back up and heal it.

"There's nothing quite so hot as that moment where I'm telling them what a filthy mess they are with their tears all over their face and their spit all over their face and that I just need to show them what a filthy little slut they are, right?" she said.

She asked us to give her words we could use in "humiliation play."

She volunteered "Slut. Whore. Bitch. Sissy. Cock-sucker. Fuck kid. Fuck toy."

The other students shouted out, *worthless, dirty, useless, cunt, anal whore, cum dumpster, stupid, dumb, fat,* and *bad.*

"I find it hot to call someone a stupid, dumb used-up cum dumpster," Powell said.

She said words should be cleared with a partner. Powell, who was heavyset, said she does not, for example, allow her partner to call her fat.

"But if someone calls me a fuck pig I'm totally into that," she said, smiling.

She told us to think of words that work for us.

"You might be totally into this slut whore cunt thing," she said. "But sissy and cocksucker do not work for you. Or you might super be into cum dumpster but anything about animals doesn't work for you."

She said that women can allow themselves to be called "a worthless cunt" and still be a feminist.

"I had done a fantastic humiliation play with this dom [short for the dominant partner in a sexual relationship] of mine," she said. "[In] the scene that we had been doing I was so worthless and terrible that I couldn't even make him cum. So he was fucking me in all the ways and I couldn't make him cum. He kept talking about how awful it was that I can't make him cum. As soon as it was over, he gave me a hug and said 'you have no idea how hard it was to not cum. The second you slipped out of me I was on the edge fighting the entire scene. You were so hot. It was so amazing.'

"If they said something that sticks with you, like you're too stupid to even figure out how to suck their dick," she advised, "you can ask them—I worry sometimes that I'm not very good at cock sucking. Can you tell them they did a good job? That's okay. It's your job, as a top, to say you are amazing at sucking my cock."

She told us military veterans gravitated to BDSM. Powell spent five years in the army.

"In terms of stuff like humiliation and Kink, people in the military are real kinky," she said. "Deployment is the biggest adrenaline rush you can imagine. When folks come home, they're looking for ways to get that adrenaline rush again. A lot of them will explore Kink and BDSM. A lot of them will drink heavily, use drugs, drive motorcycles way too fast. You see a lot of people who are experimenting with it, not often in the best ways. It's a part of what happens."

She handed out flyers advertising her services for private counseling.

"My next class will be Nasty Naughty Negotiation," she said.

Powell, it turned out, was a benign warm-up act for "Creative Mindfuckery & Authentic Interrogation for BDSM Intensive." The men in the room wore the black outfits of doms. The three or four women in the class looked morose, as if they had been dragged there by their partners. One woman sat apart from the group. She appeared from her avid note taking to have a clinical or professional interest in BDSM techniques. There was one lesbian couple.

Danarama, rail thin with a chalky complexion, told us his class would teach us how to combine verbal humiliation and degradation with "torture." The use of the word "torture" surprised me.

He urged us to secretly gather as much personal information on our subjects and use it to spook them during the interrogation. If a partner has a favorite stuffed animal named Bonko, "then you can say maybe I won't hurt you, but *bam* take out Bonko here. You can drop something and say this is a nice yellow. This is like the yellow in your bedroom. When you drop useless things like that, two things happen. First, they feel betrayal. How did you know that? Who have you been talking to?

"Mention a job they used to have that they never told you about," he says. "When you drop it in there it becomes creepy. I'm all about being creepy. If you're creeped out by certain things, note that. The chances are other people are creeped out by them too. You want to use this information to build your scenario."

Danarama introduced a young woman who was a "model" at Kink. She would be used to demonstrate techniques.

"Everything we do here is just play," he says to her softly. "I still respect you. The people in the room still respect you as well."

The woman smiled weakly as her eyes darted back and forth.

"Make sure when you get consent you get it immediately," he said. "Just because someone gave you consent before, it doesn't mean that consent is universal. Consent is a very transient thing. Some people may want to get fucked up in the ass last week. But not today. Make sure you're always checking in. Another thing you want to do is assure them of repeated, continuous aftercare. Aftercare is one of the most important parts of this workshop. You want to make sure they're able to calm down. They're not shocked by what you've done to them. Say, 'You have my number. I'll be around. We can talk about anything anytime.' You don't want to just call them the day after like you do with normal BDSM scenes. Tell them to contact a therapist now before our scene. So they don't have to do it afterward. Then they'll go, 'Oh my God, what are you going to do to me?' "

BDSM, like porn and prostitution, is defended by its proponents because of "consent."

This concept of consent, however, outrages feminists. Domestic violence, they argue, is excused because women "consented" to stay with an abusive partner. Rape and sexual violence are excused because the woman "consented" to invite the man into her home or was wearing provocative clothing. A woman "consents" to sell her body as a prostitute or in a porn film because she needs money.

Danarama said we should create feelings of "anxiety" in our partner. We must "stress them out." He told us to "build expectations" before the session. He suggested we leave notes telling those who will become our victims to cancel the mail delivery or make sure to bring a safety pin or a rubber band.

"You can mail them Band-Aids," he said. "Then fuck with them. Did you not get that in the mail? What did you do with that thing?"

He recommended building a "dead man switch" that required a victim to hold on to it. The "dead man switch" would go off if the victim fainted or was incapacitated and was unable to keep pressing the button.

"If they pass out then the light comes on or the bells go off," he said laughing.

He placed a metal box with a small window over the woman's head.

"What are you doing?" he said in a high voice, imitating a victim.

"I'm making a dead man's switch," he answered in his mock dialogue.

"What's that?" he said, his voice raised again in alarm as if he were the victim.

"Look it up," he answered, lowering his voice to be the dom.

"Please don't do this," he screams in a falsetto. "Why are you doing this?"

"I need a safety because with what I'm going to do to you I can't visibly see you or hear you," he said in his mock dialogue. "So this is for your safety. I want something to alert me in case you pass out or die."

The class laughed throughout his performance.

He told us a good way to create anxiety in the victim is to "pretend you're incompetent." That, he said, is a "fun game."

He suggested we carry out mock interrogations with tables that have "scary instruments" and stage secret society initiations and kidnapping.

"How many Catholics are here?" he asked. A couple of men raised their hands.

"Thank you Catholicism for your contribution to BDSM," he intoned. "The whole doctrine of punishment leading to forgiveness. Catholicism has done so much for BDSM. The humiliation. The Catholic school skirts."

He told us to make our victim change into a hospital gown or get them to put on "other people's clothing" that "feels dirty and smells." He recommended removing all furniture from the interrogation room and covering windows with newspapers.

"The more uncomfortable they'll be, the better," he said. "You can use a burlap sack. It's unattractive and it's itchy. You're adding constant stress to them."

He projected an image on his computer of prisoners kneeling in orange jumpsuits at Guantánamo Bay.

"You can tell how uncomfortable they are because they're wearing a polyester jumpsuit thing with a separate shirt and pants," he said. "They have a hat on. This is torture. They're stuck for hours in a place where you can't control the feeling of your clothing. It's hot. It's sweaty. It's a very uncomfortable situation. The more uncomfortable they are the more you can get them to do things for you."

He joked that we should "spank our slave once a day for a beautiful life."

"Give them opportunities to fuck up," he went on. "It gives you opportunities to fuck with them even more."

He described techniques he enjoyed inflicting on his victims, including the "coffee grind" where the dom pushes the victim against a wall, slaps the wall next to the victim's head, and whispers "something very sexual into their ear." He told us to push them backward while they are blindfolded and have someone catch them as they are about to hit the floor.

"Put them in a hood," he said. "You can put them in a gas mask. Not only can you control their breath and isolation, you can block the lenses so they can't see out. At the Kink store we have this mask where you can see in but they can't see out because of a special mirror. It's called the One Lane Magic blindfold. We sell it on Kink.com. It's really neat. I highly recommend it. I'm dying to try it on myself."

He showed us a video of a blindfolded female victim in a coffin. The coffin was filled with dirt. Danarama poured water on the dirt so the woman was encased in mud. He placed a lid on the coffin. He pounded nails into a piece of wood on top of the coffin to make the woman think the lid was being nailed shut. The muffled screams of the frightened woman come from inside the coffin.

"We left her there for about fifteen minutes," he said smiling. "She thought it was like an hour. She thought she was nailed in the coffin."

He turned to the model seated on a stool. She had been told to cover her naked body with a plastic garbage bag, her head poking out of a hole. This was part of the humiliation. He held up a box of cellophane wrap.

"This is a very dangerous thing to do actually," he said. "You have to make sure the plastic doesn't asphyxiate her. If a piece goes in while they're breathing it's very, very dangerous."

"Are you okay to continue?" he asked her.

She nodded and shifted uncomfortably.

"Take a breath in," he said. "Out. Breathe in. Take a long slow breath out."

He then swiftly wrapped the cellophane three times around her head. Her face was squeezed and distorted. Her mouth was agape. He waited about a minute before poking a hole through the cellophane. She gasped for air. He repeated this several times. Once, after telling her to exhale, he immediately covered her face with cellophane, forcing her to gag for air.

The class burst into laughter.

"Criticize them all the way," he intoned.

He said we should tell victims to take dictation.

"Write 'Dan has a huge cock,'" he said. "Let me see that? Not good enough. Try it again. No, you fucked up already. What are you doing wrong? Do you know what you're doing wrong? Try it again. Go figure it out. I can't even read that. Just stop. This is inexcusable."

The men in the room erupted again in laughter.

He recommended we purchase an online speech-jamming app. The app prevents a victim from speaking in coherent sentences because of the slight delay in auditory feedback of the user's own voice. He put headphones on the model to demonstrate.

"Say the Pledge of Allegiance," he said.

"I pledge . . ." she mumbled.

"How long have you been saying this?" he asked in mock anger. "Why do you hate America?"

The class laughed.

"This is a really fun game to play with people who have a lot of pride and are bratty," he said.

He told us to pretend we were going to put rubbing alcohol on our victim's vagina and light it.

"She knew I had rubbing alcohol," he said. "I also had a spray bottle of water. I sprayed her cunt with water. And I had an ice pack. During the interrogation, I kept saying, you're not answering my question. I'm going to set your cunt on fire."

Slamming the ice pack on her vagina would make her think he had lit the rubbing alcohol, he said.

"She was convinced I had set her cunt on fire," he said. "I said I'm going to do it again. Tell me your secret. Tell me your secret. She told me her secret."

He told us to push a woman's breast down a blender and turn it on.

"Make sure they have a small breast," he recommended.

One of the men in the class asked Danarama how he got into BDSM.

"I was raised very shy," he said. "I was teased a lot in school. I was really insecure. We moved around a lot, being in the military as a family. I didn't form a lot of attachments to people in my classes. I felt very unattractive. I felt like I had nothing to offer. What I did have was some creativity. I was a good actor. One of the reasons I got into bondage was I had this fetish for girls wearing shiny clothes, shiny skirts. I had a bondage instructor. I had some rope at home. I was so amazed at how thrilled she was by getting tied up and fucked as opposed to just fucked. It made me feel, 'Oh my gosh. I can do something. I'm special.' "

THE SADISM CELEBRATED IN THIS basement room has become an accepted part of mass culture. *Fifty Shades of Grey*, like the movie *American Sniper*, expresses the ethos of a predatory world where the weak and the vulnerable are objects to exploit. The powerful are narcissistic and violent demigods. Our pleasure comes at the expense of another. An array of amusements and spectacles, including TV "reality" shows, huge sporting events, social media, porn, alluring luxury products, drugs, alcohol, and magic Jesus, offers enticing exit doors from reality. We yearn to be rich and powerful. We want to be celebrities. Those we humiliate and crush are as deserving of their fate.

I met Gail Dines in a small café in Boston. She is the author of *Pornland: How Porn Has Hijacked Our Sexuality* and a professor of sociology and women's studies at Wheelock College.

"The porn industry has hijacked the sexuality of an entire culture and is laying waste to a whole generation of boys," she warned. "And when you lay waste to a generation of boys, you lay waste to a generation of girls.

"When you fight porn, you fight global capitalism," she said. "The venture capitalists, the banks, the credit card companies are all in this feeding chain. This is why you never see anti-porn stories. The media is implicated. It is financially in bed with these companies. Porn is part of this. Porn tells us we have nothing left as human beings—boundaries, integrity, desire, creativity, and authenticity. Women are reduced to three orifices and two hands. Porn is woven into the corporate destruction of intimacy and connectedness, and this includes connectedness to the earth. If we were a society where we were whole, connected human beings in real communities, then we would not be able to look at porn. We would not be able to watch another human being tortured.

"If you are going to give a tiny percent of the world the vast majority of the goodies, you better make sure you have a good ideological system in place that legitimizes why everyone else is suffering economically," she said. "This is what porn does. Porn tells you that material inequality between women and men is not the result of an economic system. It is biologically based. And women, being whores and bitches and only good for sex, don't deserve full equality. Porn is the ideological mouthpiece that legitimizes our material system of inequality."

To keep the legions of easily bored male viewers aroused, porn makers produce increasingly violent and debasing videos. Kink.com was the cutting edge of porn. It, like Extreme Associates, specialized in graphic rape scenes, and, along with JM Productions, promoted the very real pain inflicted on women on its sets. JM Productions pioneered "aggressive throat fucking" or "face fucking" videos such as the "Gag Factor" series, in which women gag and often vomit. It ushered in "swirlies," in which the male performer dunks the woman's head into a toilet after sex and flushes. The company promised, "Every whore gets the swirlies treatment. Fuck her, then flush her."

"Women are told in our society they have two choices," Dines said. "They are either fuckable or invisible. To be fuckable means to conform to the porn culture, to look hot, be submissive and do what the man wants. That's the only way you get visibility. You cannot ask adolescent girls, who are dying for visibility, to choose invisibility."

None of this, Dines pointed out, was by accident. Porn grew out of the commodity culture, the need by corporate capitalists to sell products.

"In post–Second World War America, you have the emergence of a middle class with a disposable income," she said. "The only trouble is that this group was born to parents who had been through a depression and a war. They did not know how to spend. They only knew how to save. What [the capitalists] needed to jump-start the economy was to get people to spend money on stuff they did not need. For women they brought in the television soaps. One of the reasons the ranch house was developed was because [families] only had one television. The television was in the living room and women spent a lot of time in the kitchen. You had to devise a house where she could watch television from the kitchen. She was being taught.

"But who was teaching the men how to spend money?" she went on. "It was *Playboy*. This was the brilliance of Hugh Hefner. He understood that you don't just commodify sexuality, you sexualize commodities. The promise that *Playboy* held out was not the girls or the women, it was that if you buy at this level, if you consume at the level *Playboy* tells you to, then you will get the prize, which is the women. The step that was crucial to getting the prize was the consumption of commodities. He wrapped porn, which sexualized and commoditized women's bodies, in an upper-middle-class blanket. He gave it a veneer of respectability."

The VCR, the DVD, and, later, the Internet allowed porn to be pumped into individual homes. The glossy, still images of *Playboy*, *Penthouse*, and *Hustler* became tame, even quaint. America, and much of the rest of the world, became pornified. The income of the global porn industry is estimated at $96 billion, with the United States market worth about $13 billion.[6] There are, Dines writes, "420 million Internet porn pages, 4.2 million porn Web sites, and 68 million search engine requests for porn daily."[7]

Along with the rise of pornography there has been an explosion in sex-related violence, including domestic abuse, rape, and gang rape. A rape is reported every 6.2 minutes in the United States, but the estimated total, taking into account unreported assaults, is perhaps five times higher, as Rebecca Solnit points out in her book *Men Explain Things to Me*.[8]

"So many men murder their partners and former partners that we have well over a thousand homicides of that kind a year—meaning that every three years the death toll tops 9/11's casualties, though no one declares a war on this particular kind of terror," Solnit writes.[9]

Porn, meanwhile, is ever more accessible.

"With a mobile phone you can deliver porn to men who live in highly concentrated neighborhoods in Brazil and India," Dines said. "If you have one laptop in the family, the man can't sit in the middle of the room and jerk off to it. With a phone, porn becomes portable. The average kid gets his porn through the mobile phone."

The old porn industry, which found its profits in movies, is dead. The points of production no longer generate profits. The distributors of porn make the money. And one distributor, MindGeek, a global IT company, dominates porn distribution. Most users are adolescent boys. It is, Dines said, "like handing out cigarettes outside of a middle school. You get them addicted.

"Around the ages of twelve to fifteen you are developing your sexual template," she said. "You get [the boys] when they are beginning to construct their sexual identity. You get them for life. If you begin by jerking off to cruel, hardcore, violent porn then you are not going to want intimacy and connection. Studies are showing that boys are losing interest in sex with real women. They can't sustain erections with real women. In porn there is no making love. It is about making hate. He despises her. He is revolted and disgusted by her. If you bleed out the love you have to fill it with something to make it interesting. They fill it with violence, degradation, cruelty, and hate. And that also gets boring. So you have to keep ratcheting it up. Men get off in porn from women being submissive. Who is more submissive than children? The inevitable route of all porn is child porn. And this is why organizations that fight child porn and do not fight adult porn are making a huge mistake.

"Pornography has socialized a generation of men into watching sexual torture," Dines said. "You are not born with that capacity. You have to be trained into it. Just like you train soldiers to kill. If you are going to carry out violence against a group you have to dehumanize them. It is an old method. Jews become kikes. Blacks become niggers. Women become cunts. And no one turns women into cunts better than porn."

I DROVE AN HOUR THE day after the Mindfuckery workshop from San Francisco to a town where I met Robin, a petite woman without the large artificial breasts common in porn, at a table outside a Starbucks. Robin was thirty-two and had performed in about forty porn films. She was willing to use her real first name. But she asked that the name she used as a porn actress not be revealed. Type her porn name into Google and there are 1,260,000 results.

She had a troubled childhood, like most women who enter prostitution and porn, which included being gang raped when she was fifteen.

"At fifteen I was harbored," she says. "I was kept in a house and was there for sexual use. It was an exchange [sex for drugs]. They would hide me from my family and the police at their disposal. We were drug dealers."

Her parents, hoping to get her back into school, sent her to a "specialty boarding school" for "behavior modification" for thirteen months outside Ensenada, Mexico, called Casa by the Sea. The school, run by World Wide Association of Specialty Programs and Schools (WWASPS), practiced corporal punishment.

She and other students were hog-tied, a practice that she would repeat on Kink film sets. Administrators forced them to face a wall for three days or run laps barefoot for infractions. The worst punishment was being sent a few miles down the road to a site called "High Impact."

"Kids came back very skinny and dirty from there," she said.

The students were forbidden from complaining to their parents.

"If we started to cry on the phone they would hang it up," she said.

She wrote her parents an eleven-page letter.

"I knew it was Mexican people who were reading the letters so I knew they wouldn't read eleven pages of English," she said. "In the middle I put what I really wanted to say, what was going on, please take me home. If you take me home here's a home contract. I'll follow these rules. And they came and got me. Otherwise, I would have been there until I was eighteen."

She arrived home with an eating disorder. She began to drink heavily and use drugs. She took jobs at strip clubs.

"I found myself in L.A.," she said. "I was going to do hair. I couldn't make ends meet. I looked into the porn thing. I believe the porn agent manipulated me. It was Lisa Ann."

Lisa Ann is the porn actor who was "Serra Paylin" in the 2008 film *Who's Nailin' Paylin: Adventures of a Hockey MILF.* Paylin in the film has sex with Russian soldiers, and screams as she is having intercourse, "Drill, baby drill!" *Who's Nailin' Paylin* sold four times more than most of Hustler's porn videos. Five more were produced, including *Obama Is Nailin' Paylin.* Nina Harley played Hillary Clinton in a 2015 film where, as Clinton, she "fucks black guys for votes," and Jada Fire plays Condoleezza Rice. The film ends with a lesbian ménage à trois between "Serra," "Hilly," and "Condi."

"I think they take $200–$300 [of what we are paid by porn studio]," she said of Lisa Ann's agency. "I'm not sure. They're basically traffickers."

"She basically told me you can keep your hair dressing job," Robin said. " 'Just try girl-girl. We won't schedule you during your other job. Just see if this is for you. You're very beautiful. You can make it as a star. Go at your own pace.' I think it was all bull crap."

Robin earned minimum wage as an assistant at a hair salon. She made $70 after a twelve-hour shift. "I was living in a sober living home," she said. "I was just really struggling. It was so stressful. I had never worked so hard. Plus, I had all these emotional problems. I couldn't accept criticism. I didn't know how to navigate social skills. I would leave crying.

"I'd want to go back to the strip club every time," she said. "Stripping was on and off throughout my life. I'd go back for a couple of weeks to survive. I could never make that work because of the alcoholism. I couldn't make normal jobs work because of the emotional stuff.

"My first shoot was on a day I had to go to work," she went on. "So I had to make the decision. Am I going to give this a shot?"

The porn studio offered her $1,000 for forty-five minutes to one hour.

"Am I going to this job to work twelve hours and make $70 and blow my chance with this woman who is willing to take me under her wings?" she recalled thinking. "Maybe this is my shot in life. . . . Having $1,000 is worth finding out. That was my frame of mind. I was twenty-one years old.

"They made me feel like a movie star," Robin said. "They did my hair and makeup. Right when I got there they said, 'Oh, you're not Asian. You looked Asian in your pictures.' I felt so scared. It started that weird self-esteem panic. Survival panic. I just left my job to try this. Now they don't even like me because I'm not Asian. They said, 'Well, what else can you do?' I didn't even know what my options were. I had never done prostitution. I don't even know. They started listing these things. Will you do this? Will you do that? I picked the least disgusting thing on the list. It was swallow. It was the least aggressive and scary thing. One of them was a cream pie where they cum inside you. It was for the Bang Bros.

"Luckily, the guy on set was really nice and tried to make me feel comfortable," she went on. "He knew it was my first time. He told me not to get involved with the party girls. He was making me feel more human. I was so scared the whole time that my legs were shaking. I got through it. It wasn't so bad. I didn't feel so harmed. I was probably disassociating the whole time. What made it better was that the guy was really nice to me and seemed human. I walked away with a check. The money makes the shock of everything go away. Okay, I'm safe now. I can get through the next few weeks."

She accepted more work. Her boundaries swiftly evaporated under the pressure of producers.

"When you're someone who has already experienced rape and all kinds of weird stuff, you don't even know where those boundaries are," she said. "Now you're pushing farther and farther and farther. It was an issue of cognitive dissonance. To survive, you have to convince yourself that you like it and this is sexual exploration. In some ways it is a sexual exploration. But the lines of sexual autonomy and degradation are so blurred. Do I want to do this because I'm curious? But I'm also making money and being watched? It's very confusing. Both on set and for the people watching in the world.

"I was hired there for one type of shoot," she said. "Boy-girl. Actually, I think it was with two men. This woman told me we were going to start off slow. We did not start off slow. I'm thrown into swallowing. Now I'm with two guys. I've never done that in my life. I get on set and the porn director is propositioning me to do anal. I don't even do anal in my personal life. He offered me double the money. I found out later women in the porn industry don't do that until the end of their careers. Once you do that, that's all they want. The life of your career is over. He did that to me on my second day. I was just thinking I don't know when I'm going to get hired again. I really need that money. . . . One thing led to another. I said maybe if I have some alcohol. They said we don't normally do this but get her some alcohol. Then all of a sudden I'm tricked into him [the director] doing it to me first.

"He's the director and he has to do it to me first to warm me up or whatever," she said. "By the end of the day I had done three guys anally.

And I did not want to. I don't even remember. I was not drunk. I had one shot. But I completely dissociated it. Later in life, I've had ex-boyfriends use this film against me. Every time they make me look at it, I feel, I feel it now . . ."

She stopped speaking and choked back tears.

"I shouldn't even go there," she whispered.

"They make me watch it," she began again of former boyfriends. "Sometimes the porn [films] will come out [with] a new [release] date . . . so it looks like I had just done it."

She said there are times when she can't cope with her past, when she is unable to eat or drink and has to "curl up in a ball and scream for hours."

She lived in Los Angeles when she first worked for Kink in 2007. Kink paid her plane ticket to San Francisco. A van picked her up at the airport. She said Kink was the first time she did "fetish."

"They pay you on the rate of sexual act," she said. "If it's boy-girl, which means there's a penis in a vagina, they pay $900 to a $1,000. It's less [money] for girl-girl. Kink's website has prices. Look at the talent application.

"Kink is one of the better companies," she admitted. "They have a lot more professionalism. They have more women workers, in terms of the regular staff who do the makeup and paperwork. They're more progressive. They provide lunch for you as well. They used to have a hot tub on the roof so you could relax after the scene. They provide products. For people in the industry, it's really important to have sanitary and hygiene products. They were always stocked with that. Tylenol. Tampons. Wipes. Lotions. Enema. Towels. Shampoo. You use enema before an anal shoot. In that sense, it helped me relax before I got there. But I was really scared because I had never done this."

She was hired to take part in a series of Kink films called "Hog Tied."

"It's a five-hour shoot," she said. "You're being tortured for five hours. I was trying to look at it like an experimentation. He [the director] set it up that way too: 'There's a safe word. We're going to go slow. I'm going to watch how you feel. We're not going to push you too far.' They try to frame it as if you're in charge. You want to be hired again. They're treating you really nice. . . . You're so lost in the process that by the end of it you're like, 'Oh my God, what just happened? What did I just do? How did I do these god-awful things for five hours?'

"There was no sex involved in this scene," she said. "It was him doing things to me. . . . What I really didn't like was the suction [plastic cups placed on the vagina to enlarge it]. I didn't like the vaginal torture."

She was electrocuted with a cattle prod.

"They tied me up and hung me from the ceiling," she said. "The board broke. I fell to the ground.

"They put a hook in my ass," she said. "They tied my ponytail to it. They tied my arms to a barrel. They tied my legs to a barrel. He put a vibrator on me. That's all I remember. Five hours is a long time. For $900. Was it worth it?"

She walked away from the five-hour shoot bruised and in shock. In the bathroom she saw women from other shoots, bleeding.

Later, I watched the film. It begins with a short interview between Robin, identified by her porn name, and a man the audience cannot see. Robin sits on a wooden box in the center of the screen. She is wearing silver heels, a fitted, dark gray T-shirt, and a short pink skirt. Her hair is pinned back with a pink flower-clip. Her face is caked with makeup. The unseen man, named Matt, asks how she is doing and her age. She tells him twenty-two. He wants to know how long she has been in the "industry." She says six months. She says she has done thirty porn shoots. The man wants to know her favorite male performer. She says Derrick Pierce "because he choked me out while the camera wasn't looking." She laughs.

"Aaah!" Matt says. "So you like to do things behind the scenes huh? So you're just a dirty little whore all the time, not just . . . ? "

She laughs again and interjects, "Yeah."

Matt asks about her sexual history and if she likes "sucking cock."

Matt enters the screen, revealing himself for the first time. He is tall with a large build, short gray hair, and is dressed in black. He stands behind Robin, grabs her by her arms. He fastens a muzzle tightly around her head as she winces.

"This is a new thing I've found . . ." Matt says. "I think you're going to like it."

He lifts her skirt up revealing black panties and shoves his fingers inside her vagina. Robin groans. He pushes her to the side and walks offscreen.

"Take your shoes off!" Matt commands.

Robin, seated on the floor, removes her shoes.

"Come on! Come on! Come on!" he shouts. "You keep guys waiting all the time, don't you! Taking forever to get ready . . . Stand up!"

She stands up. Matt pulls down a hook attached to a rope hanging from the ceiling. He attaches it to a hook on the front of Robin's face muzzle. He raises her head so it is facing the ceiling. He ties her hands behind her back.

"Very nice," he says.

He pulls up her skirt and reveals her backside to the camera.

"Oh . . . look at this big ass!" he says, striking her there. "I like it! It's amazing, this ass!"

She spreads her legs. He keeps hitting her on her rear. He pulls her skirt and bra above her breasts. He turns her around to face the camera. He pinches her nipples as she winces in pain. Her cries are muffled by the mask.

"I can do whatever I want, right?" he says.

He forcefully grabs her left nipple. She cries out.

Matt pulls down her panties.

"I tell you what, this pussy better be shaved when I take a look or I'm going to punch you," he says.

He walks off camera and returns with a black leather flogger. He beats her across the side of her naked body. Robin groans in pain. Scenes like this dominate the film. She is yanked upward by the rope attached to her face muzzle. Matt pushes a vibrator attached to a stick into her vagina. He then inserts his fingers from his free hand into her vagina along with the vibrator.

"Nothing's going to stop you baby . . . this is what it's like to feel helpless . . . your body is going to cum whether you like it or not," he tells her.

Robin groans and has an orgasm, or at least simulates one.

"What do you say?" he asks.

"Thank you," she says, her voice muffled by the muzzle.

In another scene she is lying facedown in the center of the room. Her wrists and ankles are tied together behind her back. The rope is attached to a wooden plank inches above her body. The plank is hanging from a rope attached to the ceiling.

"I think it's time for one of these, little girl," Matt says, as he shoves a ball gag into her mouth and fastens it tightly at the back of her head. He produces two floggers and asks her which flogger he should use to whip her. He beats her with one flogger and then the other. He then beats her feet with a cane. He attaches little silver weight-balls to the metal clips on her nipples. Her nipples are pulled downward. He begins to flog Robin again, this time on her vagina.

"Bad pussy!" he shouts as he repeatedly hits her vagina.

He brings in a suction device, shaped like a test tube. He places it on her clitoris. She twists and writhes in pain.

"It hurts . . . OWWW . . . NO it hurts," she shouts. "I don't like it!"

Matt flogs her breasts. He switches from torture device to torture device. At one point he masturbates.

"You're a little fucking whore and I like it," he says.

Robin, who occasionally tries to speak, mutters words that are incomprehensible. Matt uses his hand to block her nose and mouth so she cannot breathe.

"I'm just going to hold your breath until you die," he says as she struggles to get air.

He flogs her breasts, vagina, and ass. "Fuck!" she screams.

He puts a hook into her vagina. He removes the hook and places it in her anus. He grabs a rope attached to the back of her head and ties that around the hook in her anus, so that her head arches backward. He continues to flog her. She cries in pain when she is hit. He shoves a dildo in her mouth.

"NO MOOOORE . . ." she pleads.

He produces a cattle prod and shocks her breasts and vagina. He resumes the flogging.

"I was raised on porn. We're all indoctrinated to be stimulated by porn," Robin said, when we spoke, echoing Dines. "It was sexual education. It's on TV. The men I've been with are expecting what I saw on TV. From music. It's glorified as the highest potential of a woman. If I don't have self-esteem this is my only way to gain self-esteem and to have a sense of identity. It's my only survival—mentally, physically, spiritually. I'm really pissed off we don't have sexual autonomy. I'm now wired to be attracted to certain things. I no longer have control over my body to say when and where I can be present in my body. Maybe I want to be fulfilled with just one person. But because I have all these images in my mind I have to go to these images for enjoyment. Where does this come from? As adolescents, instead of learning sex education in a holistic, healthy, nonrepressive way, we're sneaking to those video channels and we're seeing choking and degradation.

"I was around strippers," she said. "I was seeing what men were glorifying on a daily basis. I now am attracted to what men glorify. I can't undo it. I can't make myself attracted to a different thing. I am programmed that way now. Even in an intimate relationship I have to think these certain thoughts to be able to enjoy it. I have had some intimate relationships that were so safe I was able to enjoy it. . . . In my head I'm thinking of a threesome. I have to see him being with another woman to feel anything. I don't know why that is."

She said these fantasies are probably the result of "doing porn and growing up in a pornified culture. Women in general have a really hard time orgasming. We find tricks to do it. Those tricks come in through what we see, what we're exposed to.

"I can't feel my body," she said. "So I have to see him do it with someone else. Even though in real life I wouldn't be comfortable with that. I would feel degraded. I would feel unimportant. I would feel a sense of loss. Sometimes it's weirder. Sometimes I have to see degradation in my fantasy. The degradation of the man to the woman, sometimes me."

"Is this verbal?" I asked.

"No," she answered. "Physical. Forcefulness. Choking. Sometimes rape. I'm working on it in therapy.

"I've been indoctrinated," she said. "I'm not the only one. All the little boys who are watching it. Partners that I've been with. They can't cum unless they're doing it really, really hard and forceful. Us women feel like we have to pretend we like it so that they're happy. It's a cycle of people not being happy."

She worked on Kink's webcam site. Kink hired about forty "models" a week for its films and nineteen websites. Website shoots were held once a week and uploaded once a week.

"You can interact with customers [through webcams]," she said. "You get the sickest of the sickest people. You can't see them. But they ask you to do certain things that are very painful. Like gagging yourself to the point of vomit. Blasphemy about Jesus. Pinching nipples with weights and putting more and more weights on. They like to see you drink your pee."

"Women do this?" I asked.

"They pretend," she said. "They trick the camera. They put apple juice in a bucket next to a bucket that they see."

"I gagged myself with a dildo," she said. "The more messy it is the more they like it. The more saliva. The more makeup that's streaming down your face. The more horrible you look the better they like it."

She said one customer paid a woman who worked with Robin "thousands of dollars extra to eat a bunch of Taco Bell and then throw it up as she masturbated. They gag themselves to throw up while they're masturbating naked. That's the only way the guy can orgasm. These men are paying tons of money to make you torture yourself on camera. It's really sick things. They pay the most money."

"I've had a lot of rape ones," she said. "They wanted me to tie myself up and pretend I was getting raped. Tape myself and struggle on webcam. But you're alone. It's really weird. The better you can act the more they like it.

"The girls around me who claimed they felt empowered, I was seeing them become depressed," she said. "They were tricking themselves by saying they liked these things. But it didn't seem authentic to me. I could relate to it. I had wanted it to be authentic. [But] if I was honest with myself, I would much rather be paid at a normal job. That wasn't an option. These women were outcasting themselves from society. They're saying, 'This is our identity; we are bad chicks that like all this hardcore porn.' But I saw on their off days they were not happy. One woman told me she's so sick of this, she's too old for this. She doesn't have the energy. I've struggled with suicidal thoughts throughout my life. Lots of trauma. I have three hours of therapy a week. I personally know two people who have committed suicide.

"I've done three Kink movies," she said. "One had a lot more torture. I can't tell you anything about that because I don't remember. I remember the bamboo really hurt. I did the webcam for three months in 2014 at Kink. It felt like a safer option than porn.

"You have to hustle," she said of the webcam work. "Maybe fifteen hours a week. You don't make the same amount of money as porn. But you need regular customers. I'd do two to five hours in a stretch. I can talk. They can only type. You're just there reading a computer screen. They want to see you suffer. It does matter how. They're very particular. For the most part, they want to see you in pain. But there are some people who don't want to see you in pain. They want you to degrade them. They want to be called a sissy boy. Scum. Worm. Anything mean. Talk about how small their penis is. It's very expensive. It's like $9.99 a minute if it's private.

"I did this one porn movie with Vivid Alt. It's a genre," she said. "It's alternative porn, more creative and artsy. I actually felt really proud of that movie. I felt honored I got to be creative. I was actually performing. I did a lot of acting in that movie. It didn't feel yucky to me. I really liked the people I was working with. We had relationships outside of work. It was just that one movie. It was called *The Bad Luck Betties*. It was about a girl gang that was the go-between between Hollywood and L.A. We were monitoring the drug trafficking on the money end. There was this perverted governor who was taking advantage of women and we were going to kick his butt. There was a story to it. The women were the powerful people in the movie. There were sex scenes. Mine was with Tommy Pistol. We were friends in real life.

"I feel bad for the men," she said. "A lot of the men take Viagra and it eventually stops working. One of my agents in the past had to shoot up his penis. It's also not good for your heart. It's dangerous for the heart. It's also humiliating for them. It's a lot of pressure for them to perform. They're psychologically affected by whether or not they're able to. A woman can fake it. A man can't. There are porn directors degrading them and putting pressure on them. They're paid less. I wouldn't feel bad for all of them. There are some who are mean and disgusting."

I asked her if she has relationships with men who watch porn.

"That's a big issue for me," she said. "He'd have to be willing to give it up. I think in general porn feeds a sick part of us. It's that desensitized part. When we leave it alone, you're able to cultivate a healthier, more vibrant sexual arousal. What bothers me would be him buying into the degradation of women. I don't want to be with someone who thinks that is okay.

"I was invited to Kink's Christmas party," she remembered. "The owner, Peter, had his friends doing coke in his basement. Peter was dancing behind me, grabbing me and touching me. I had never talked to him before. For somebody who has trauma—I have been sex trafficked—I have alarms on my body. The only thing that can disarm those alarms is money. I shoved him off of me.

"The career of a porn star is usually one to one and a half years," she said. "I know some people who have been in it for ten. You get shot out. Once you've done everything then you're garbage to them unless you have built a following and a name for yourself."

"So the agent just stops calling you?" I asked.

"Yeah," she said. "That's when they turn you on to high-end escorting if they haven't done that already. Prostitution, trafficking, and porn are interrelated. I have no idea why porn agents are not considered pimps under the trafficking law. They're absolutely manipulating and trafficking and coercing.

"I really want to sue this porn producer," she said of a producer who made her have sex with him before the film. "I had never done prostitution. You're in the privacy of someone's room. No one is watching. You could be dead at any moment. Nobody would care or know. This porn producer in L.A. hires me and takes me to a back room. He propositions me $500 to go into his back room and to have sex with him first. He said, 'This is what all the girls do. We call it privates. This is how all the girls get jobs.' I didn't know what he was talking about. I go into the room. There's a bed. There's a television. It's a small room in the house we're supposed to be shooting in. He pressures me and convinces me this is where the money's really at. The porn is just the facade. I blacked out and did it."

IT IS DIFFICULT TO CHALLENGE the lies disseminated about "sex work" just as it is to challenge the lies about "military virtues." Those who counter the dominant narrative, even if they speak from long personal experience, are silenced or attacked. Speaking the truth about war, or the truth about prostitution, is lonely and often futile.

Rachel Moran, who was a prostituted woman in Ireland for seven years, accomplished in her book *Paid For: My Journey Through Prostitution* what I attempted to do in my book *War Is a Force That Gives Us Meaning*—reveal, respectively, the reality of prostitution and war. And she has endured very similar responses. Women and girls who are being prostituted have often dismissed her, just as many war correspondents, soldiers, and marines addicted to the rush of battle, the hypermasculinity and the adrenaline highs that come with war, dismissed my book. They are unable to examine the darkness and tragedy of their own lives. Mass culture has largely shut Moran out, just as it shuts out those who speak the truth about war. The manufactured illusion of heroes or glamorous call girls plays to a culture that celebrates the objectification of "weaker" human beings. And since those who have escaped the clutches of prostitution or war, often struggling to cope with trauma, guilt, and shame, are reticent to resurrect in public the nightmare that will hound them for the rest of their lives, there are few public voices that dare name these illusions.

"People who depict prostitution as glamorous usually view prostitutes against the backdrop of expensive hotel foyers," Moran wrote in her book.[10]

They imagine prostitutes as entering or leaving five-star hotels, wearing sharp designer suits and high heels, and the look set off with vivid red lipstick. I've walked into more hotels more times than I could count, wearing sharp suits, high heels, and every shade of lipstick. None of that changed what was going on in my heart or in my mind, and none of it made any difference to the bodily experience involved here. None of it was of any practical benefit to my mouth, breasts, or vagina. What was going on was the very same thing that was going on when I was lifting my skirt in the backstreet alley. The nature of prostitution does not change with its surrounds. It does not morph into something else because your ass is rubbing against white linen as opposed to roughed concrete.

She blasted, when we met, the notion that prostitution is in any way a form of sex. "The nature of sex is mutuality," she said. "And where you don't have mutuality, you have sexual abuse."

The war industry, like the prostitution industry, feeds off the despair, poverty, and hopelessness that afflict the lives of many of the young, especially young men and women of color. In a world of closed doors and few opportunities, the military, like prostitution, appears to offer a way out. Military recruiters are little more than uniformed human traffickers, targeting the vulnerable, making promises that are usually never kept, and handing out cash payments to the desperate.[11] Once they have their prey trapped, like all pimps and traffickers, they force them into a life that bears no resemblance to the fantasy they peddled.

Moran, like many other girls and women forced into prostitution, was desperate and homeless. Her home life, dominated by mentally unstable parents who raised her and her siblings in crippling poverty, had been a disaster. And the state, preoccupied with imposing austerity and budget cuts, had abandoned her. She started working the streets at fifteen. She soon discovered that announcing her age to her clients was useful because "they get off faster and I got out of the car faster."

"I was in indoor prostitution for quite a few years, and for every ten times that phone rang, eight or nine times you would be asked, 'How old is the youngest girl on today?' " she said. "It was always that, the youngest girl, the youngest girl, the youngest girl. Never stopped. And it was a particularly creepy question to have to listen to, because I usually was the youngest girl," she said.

"I have never seen anyone come to prostitution out of a circumstance that wasn't in some way, shape, or form negative," she told me.

She scoffed at the idea that prostitution offers girls and women a "choice," since, as she wrote, "It is *others* who use the bodies of prostituted women as *they* so choose. That is the intention and the purpose and the *function* of prostitution." [12] Prostituted women have no real freedom of choice, and even less control over their bodies than do Marine Corps recruits on Parris Island. Once you sign on for war or prostitution you become someone else's property. Fear becomes your dominant emotion. "If anything is more pervasive than violence itself it is the threat of it," Moran writes of being prostituted. [13]

To endure war or prostitution, it is better not to think or feel. Spend long enough in war or prostitution and you will, as Moran and I eventually did, become numb, dominated by paranoia and deeply distrustful. You lash out, sometimes physically, at whatever or whoever you perceive to be a threat. You become a hunted animal. You divide the world between predators and prey.

"You have to dissociate," Moran told me. "You have to split yourself off from the reality of what's currently happening. If you are having your body used by—it was up to ten men a day when I was on the streets—you've got to be able to shut off from that. You just couldn't keep on doing it unless you could pretend that it's not happening. That's what I always did. I just shut it out."

"It is difficult to describe how hollow a woman feels after she has been used sexually by ten different men," Moran wrote. "Of course, the experience rarely stopped at the agreed-upon hand relief or oral sex. Even when a man has accepted that he will not be putting his penis in you, he often has no compunction about shoving his fingers or other objects in you and mauling you and biting you and trying to shove his tongue down your throat and everywhere else. I know by the rabid, doglike behavior of one particular client that he'd have liked nothing better than if he'd bit and sucked my nipples till they gushed blood." [14]

Moran estimated that about 30 percent of her clients "actively get off on hurting you and watching you being hurt."

"Prostitution is violence in and of itself," she said. "To put your hands on another person when you know they don't want your hands there, and to put your penis into the orifices of somebody's body when you know that they don't want your penis inside them or near them, that is pathological behavior. And money doesn't erase that. Money does not have some kind of magical quality that can take away the essence of a person's behavior or an exchange between two people.

"If sex work is work, what are its primary qualifications?" Moran asked. She answered her own question: "The ability to resist your urge to vomit, to cry, and to pretend that your current reality wasn't happening."

Armed combatants in war, who surrender their individuality and usually their capacity for moral choice, become part of a herd of dehumanized killers. Sex in wartime is reduced to its crudest biological function. It is referred to in marching cadences and ribald small talk like defecation. Pornography, prostitution, and rape are ubiquitous in war zones. In war, empathy, compassion, and love are banished. Human beings, especially women, become objects, to exploit or kill.

The violence and commodification of human beings for profit are the quintessential expressions of global capitalism. Our corporate masters are pimps. We are all being debased and degraded, rendered impoverished and powerless, to service the cruel and lascivious demands of the corporate elite. And when they tire of us, or when we are no longer of use, we are discarded. If the United States accepts prostitution as legal and permissible in a civil society, as Germany has done, we will take one more collective step toward the global plantation being built by the powerful. The fight against prostitution is the fight against a dehumanizing corporate capitalism that begins, but will not end, with the subjugation of impoverished girls and women.

Poverty is not an aphrodisiac. Those who sell their bodies for sex do so out of desperation. They often end up physically injured, with a variety of diseases and medical conditions, and suffering from severe emotional trauma. Selling your body for sex is not a choice. It is not about freedom. It is an act of economic slavery.

ACWORTH, WHO APPEARED IN HIS own BDSM videos, also ran sites such as Fucking Machines and Hogtied. "Fucking machines"—one was housed in a glass case at the entrance—have mechanized, thrusting metal dildos. The armory's gift shop sold the Fucking Machine for $2,827.99. Also available were Buckle Collars, Slave Ankle Bracelets, Slave Wrist Cuffs, Slave Collars, the Ultra Cock Bot Machine Stroker, Red-Rubber-Tip Clamps, Kensie Taylor Ball Gags, the ThudStinger Flogger, Shredder Nipple Clamps, the Leather Head Harness with Gag, Electro Genital Clamps, and black shirts, hats, and hoodies with words "gangbang" and "submission" on them.

I took a tour of the armory on my first night in San Francisco. While we were on the upper floor, the walls of which were adorned with paintings of women in physical bondage, Peter Acworth walked past us with a woman.

"And there is the man who made all this possible," the woman giving us the tour said, as Acworth glanced back at us. He gave us a slight smile. The tour group applauded.

"Another component that we have here, which is totally unique to us as a porn production studio: we have a huge educational component," the tour guide said. "We have online education. We have on-site education. We have KinkUniversity.com. It's full of tutorials on any BDSM activity. If you go outside and buy yourself a strap-on, and you're, like, 'What do I do with this thing?' you can go to KinkUniversity.com and look up a tutorial on how to use a strap-on and then go to town. . . . We have workshops here two, three times a week on so many different topics. I myself am a Japanese rope bondage instructor here. I've been teaching for almost four years now. We teach total beginners all the way to advanced suspension.

"There's a really good class on rough sex taught by Danarama that we offer regularly," she went on. "There was a class recently on pussy play. There was a class on how to fuck like a porn star. There's a class on role play and fantasy play. If anybody is in town tomorrow, Dan is an amazing educator. His class is on creative mindfuckery, an authentic interrogation. There are some spots left in this class. There was a class recently on squashing. It's sensation play with food. Just hose everyone down in the end."

She criticized California's Prop 60 that was on the November 8, 2016, ballot. It would have required porn actors to use condoms.

"It will drive the industry out of the state and see a loss of tax revenues," she said. "It will allow adult film performers and producers to be sued. It threatens privacy. It is the start of an effort to shut down the industry completely. Make sure you vote against it." The measure was defeated.

The upper floor of the armory was a series of Victorian period rooms. Actors, or "models," as Peter Acworth, the founder and CEO of Kink.com and occasional Kink performer, likes to call them, since the pain is not simulated, dressed in period costumes. They played various hierarchical roles from maids to masters. Hooks and chains dangled from the ceiling. In one of the rooms, the walls covered with red velvet, was an old oak post office desk where various collars, clamps, chains, rope, and rubber ball gags were stored. The models must act for the cameras, Acworth told the *San Francisco Bay Guardian* in 2008, "according to the rules of domination and submission."[15] Films were shot here and on lower floors. Sets on other floors included mock bedrooms, an interrogation room, a padded cell, a bar, and a doctor's office.

One of Kink's films featuring Acworth is titled *Fresh Meat on the Upper Floor*, with "Peter Acworth, Mellanie Monroe & Cherry Torn." In the film, "Big Tit Mellanie Monroe is reviewed by Master Acworth in the film as a potential house slut." A character referred to as Mr. Mogul, who rarely appears on-screen, is the master of the house with the authority to decide which women stay and which women leave.

"Mogul thinks she's not, er, she's not sufficiently experienced in BDSM, hasn't thought it through sufficiently. Err, I'd like to see her up here on account of her obvious attributes," Acworth says in the film, clearing his throat. "So we are here today to figure that out and to persuade Mogul into training her. She's quite heavily bound here. I'm different from Mr. Mogul in that I tend to keep my slaves bound up when they're getting tested.

"Stand up," Acworth says to Monroe.

Monroe stands up. She is blond, naked, and wearing a blindfold. Behind her is Cherry Torn, who is referred to as the "head slave." She has short black hair and is wearing black suspenders, black heels, and a black dog collar. Acworth, dressed in black pants, a white shirt, and a purple tie, places gold clamps on Monroe's nipples. Acworth holds some papers in his hands. He removes the blindfold and warns Monroe "not to look the master or the mistress in the eye."

She glances up at Acworth. He slaps her. He places his hand over her face.

"DO NOT," he says forcefully, "look me in the eye."

Acworth orders her to look forward. He slaps her four times on her rear. He is carrying a wooden cane.

"So, get down into a squatting position," Cherry Torn orders, "all the way down, up on your toes, good."

Cherry Torn orders Monroe to get on all fours. She pushes her chest to the ground and tells her to put her arms behind her back. The scene is set in what looks like a Victorian study. The torture implements are laid out on the sofa. The camera focuses on Monroe's backside and vagina as Acworth grabs her buttocks. Her "ass is a fine, fine thing," he says. He asks her if she has been working out at the gym.

"Yes sir," she says.

Acworth licks his finger and thrusts it into her vagina. He slaps her rear nine times.

Acworth, in the next scene, sucks on Monroe's breasts and then yanks her head back by her hair. He watches as her wrists are tied behind her back. He places a gold clamp on her vagina to keep it open. Cherry Torn fingers Monroe's vagina as Acworth ties rope tightly around Monroe's breasts.

"It's definitely moist," Cherry Torn says. "I wouldn't say it's dripping."

Cherry Torn separates the clamp on Monroe's vagina and spreads it apart to reveal Monroe's clitoris.

"I see this pussy has been fucked by a few people," she says to Monroe, adding, "a public disgrace."

Cherry Torn asks if she squirts or has ever taken a fist.

"No, Ms. Torn," she answers.

Acworth continues to tie rope around Monroe's limbs. He pulls one leg behind her and ties it up. The camera shows a full frontal view of her vagina with the clamps separating it. Monroe has quick, shallow breaths. She appears to be in pain. Ackworth inserts a dildo into her vagina. Cherry Torn says to Monroe, "You don't like being told what to do."

"No," Monroe protests. "I like being a slave."

"How do you feel about being called names?" Cherry Torn asks.

"I like it, Ms. Torn."

"Is there anything you don't like being called?"

"No," she says. "Can I cum please, sir?"

"Can she cum?" Acworth asks as he looks at the camera, addressing those watching online. "Has she earned any kind of right to cum this afternoon? We want to hear from you, the members."

Cherry Torn looks at the screen on a laptop where members online are apparently voting on whether Monroe can cum or not. The members by a vote of five to two say she cannot cum. Acworth removes the dildo and smacks her vagina as he tells her, "You have not earned it."

Clamps are attached to Monroe's nipples. Cherry Torn places a little weight-ball on the chain between the clamps so that it pulls Monroe's nipples down. Acworth is tying her arms up behind her shoulders and head with the rope. Monroe is placed on a very short stool.

"So this is going to be tight for a short period of time," Acworth says. "We're going to test your endurance."

Cherry Torn has her vagina close to Monroe's face. She spreads her vagina so Monroe can see her clitoris, then she turns around and sticks her rear into Monroe's face.

"So, you want to do your ass, nice," Acworth says.

Monroe thrusts her tongue into Cherry Torn's rear.

"That's nice!" Acworth says.

Monroe groans. Acworth comes up behind Monroe and grabs her breasts, which still have the gold clamps on. Monroe continues to use her tongue on Cherry Torn's rear. Acworth unties the rope holding Monroe's arms behind her. He removes the clamps from Monroe's nipples. She shrieks in pain. Acworth aggressively grabs her breasts. Monroe looks as if she's about to cry. Acworth begins kissing her on the face while grabbing her breasts. Monroe is crying. Monroe eventually performs oral sex on Acworth as he sits on a couch.

"I'm going to fuck you for a bit," Acworth says. Acworth has sex with her from behind, only unzipping his pants.

"Thank you, sir," she says.

"Touch your own clit," he demands. She complies. Cherry Torn is shown staring at the screen of the laptop in the background. Acworth ejaculates on Monroe's back.

"Oh, thank you sir," Monroe says.

"There's my seal of approval!" Acworth says as he flicks semen from his hands onto her back.

The insistence by Acworth that his "models" have unprotected sex led two men and one woman to sue Acworth in 2014 after they apparently contracted HIV on one of his shoots. One "model," John Doe, said he was blindfolded and made to perform oral sex on dozens of "untested, unidentified members of the general public." The three "models" said they were told they would be "out of a job" if they attempted to use condoms.[16]

Porn is a throwback to another era, one of masculine and imperial domination, racism, slavery, baronial splendor, and unchallenged, white male supremacy. It is the darkest fantasy of white males. The evocation of the past is the evocation of a world where all women knew their place, where the "lesser" races of the earth are subjugated and exploited and, when they resist, slaughtered. This celebration of the past is not accidental. Edward Said explained the appeal of sexual stereotypes for white male elites in his book *Orientalism*.

"[The local] women are usually the creatures of a male power-fantasy," Said wrote of white colonizers. "They express unlimited sensuality, they are more or less stupid, and above all they are willing." Moreover, he went on, "when women's sexuality is surrendered, the nation is more or less conquered."[17] The sexual conquest of indigenous women, Said pointed out, correlates with the conquest of the land itself. It is a sexual representation of the power dynamic between master and slave.

"IN PORNOGRAPHY AND PROSTITUTION THERE'S a racial hierarchy, just like racism," said Alice Lee, one of the founders of Asian Women Coalition Ending Prostitution in Vancouver, when we met. "Asian women are most depicted with torture. Black women are often depicted with a lot of violence. Each race has a way of being depicted. That's how men choose. It's like a pizza menu. Men can choose the race and stereotypes that go along with the race. . . . This racism is not acknowledged by those in First World countries, including the left. Sexualized racism renders us invisible and irrelevant. It makes it impossible for us to be considered human.

"The global trade, particularly of Asian women, has been steadily worsened by the neoliberal policies of First World countries," said Lee. "These policies are grounded in social disparities of race, class, and gender. They create conditions that force poor women to migrate. Those who support legalizing prostitution often argue that trafficking is bad, but prostitution is acceptable. But trafficking and prostitution are inseparable.

"Asian women are trafficked primarily to earn money in prostitution to support their families," she said. "And we are developing generations of women who are prostituted and are abandoned to exploitation. When we were in Cambodia we went to a neighborhood where women aged out as prostitutes in their twenties, and where 90 percent of the women became prostitutes. Communism in China stamped out prostitution, at least visible prostitution. But with Chinese capitalism, prostitution is everywhere.

"Women in China work for a dollar a day in factories," Lee said. "Traffickers trick these women into prostitution by offering an escape from their despair with a promise of better jobs and improved working conditions. In mining towns and centers of resource extraction, women are recruited and brought in as prostitutes to service the men. They are brought into military bases and to tourist sites. Where there is economic exploitation, militarism, and ecological destruction, women are being prostituted and exploited."

One rainy evening I walked through the Downtown Eastside ghetto in Vancouver. I passed prostituted women, most of them aboriginals, on the desolate street corners. The cruelty and despair that mark their lives will soon become familiar to many if the architects of corporate capitalism remain in power. Downtown Eastside has the highest HIV infection rate in North America. It is filled with addicts, the broken, the homeless, the old, and the mentally ill, all callously tossed onto the street.

Prostituted women on the streets in the Downtown Eastside are often beaten, tortured, or murdered. Many have disappeared. The Royal Canadian Mounted Police reported that 1,017 indigenous women and girls in Canada were murdered between 1980 and 2012,[18] a figure aboriginal women's groups contend is too conservative. As prostitution and pornography become normalized, so does male violence against women.

Lee Lakeman, one of Canada's best-known feminists, met with me and several members of the Vancouver Rape Relief & Women's Shelter one morning in their storefront office in Vancouver.

Lakeman opened her home in Ontario in the 1970s to abused women and their children. By 1977 she was in Vancouver working with the Rape Relief & Women's Shelter, founded in 1973, and now the oldest rape crisis center in Canada. She has been at the forefront of the fight in Canada against the abuse of women, building alliances with groups such as the Aboriginal Women's Action Network and the Asian Women Coalition Ending Prostitution.

Lakeman and the shelter refused to give the provincial government access to victims' files in order to protect the anonymity of the women. They also denied this information to the courts, in which, Lakeman said, "defense attorneys try to discredit or bully women complainants in criminal cases of male violence against women." This defiance caused the shelter to lose government funding. "It is still impossible to work effectively in a rape crisis center or a transition house and not be breaking the Canadian law on a regular basis," said Lakeman.

Lakeman, along with the radical feminists allied with the shelter, is the bête noire not only of the state but of many liberals who think physical abuse of a woman is abhorrent if it occurs in a sweatshop but somehow acceptable in a porn studio, a hotel room, an alley, a brothel, a massage parlor, or a car. Lakeman is fighting a world that has gone numb, a world that seeks to banish empathy, a world where solidarity with the oppressed is a foreign concept. And, with upheavals ahead caused by climate change and the breakdown of global capitalism, she fears that if legal mechanisms are not in place to protect poor girls and women, the exploitation and abuse will increase.

"We have never stopped having to deal with misogyny among activists," she said. "It is a serious problem. How do we talk to each other as movements? We want to talk about coalition building. But we want new formations to take women's leadership seriously, to use what has been learned in the last forty or fifty years. We deal with the most dispossessed among women. And it is clear to us that every sloppy uprising, or every unplanned, chaotic uprising, devastates poor women. We need to have thoughtfulness built into our practices of revolt. We do not want the traditional right-wing version of law and order. We work against it. We do not call for a reduction in men's rights. But, without an organized community, without state responsibility, every woman is on her own against a man with more power.

"We are seeing a range of violence against women that generations before us never saw—incest, wife abuse, prostitution, trafficking, and violence against lesbians," she went on. "It has become normal. But in periods of chaos it gets worse. We are trying to hang on to what we know about how to care for people, what we know about working democratically, about nonviolence, yet not be subsumed by the state. Yet we have to insist on a woman's right not to face every man alone. We have to demand the rule of law.

"Globalization and neoliberalism have accelerated a process in which women are being sold wholesale, as if it is okay to prostitute Asian women because they are sending money home to poor families," Lakeman said. "This is the neoliberal model proposed to us. It is an industry. It is [considered] okay . . . just a job like any other job. This model says people are allowed to own factories where prostitution is done. They can own distribution systems [for prostitution]. They can use public relations to promote it. They can make profits. Men who pay for prostitution support this machinery. The state that permits prostitution supports this machinery. The only way to protect women, and fight capitalism and racism, is to stop men from buying prostitutes. And once that happens we can mobilize against the industry and the state to benefit the whole antiracist and anticapitalist struggle. But men will have to accept feminist leadership. They will have to listen to us. And they will have to give up the self-indulgence of prostitution.

"The left broke apart in the 1970s over the failure to contend with racism, imperialism, and women's freedom," she said. "These are still the fault lines. We have to build alliances across these gaps. But there are deal breakers. You can't buy women. You can't beat women. You can't expect us to coalesce on the 'wider' issues unless you accept this. The problem with the left is it is afraid of words like 'morality.' The left does not know how to distinguish between right and wrong. It does not understand what constitutes unethical behavior."

Even though many radical feminists are hostile to the policies of the corporate state, they call for laws to protect women and the police to intervene to halt the exploitation of women.

"In the progressive left it is popular to be antistate," she said. "It is not popular to say we have to press the state to carry out particular policies. But all resistance has to be precise. It has to reshape society step by step. We can't abandon people. This is hard for the left to get. It is not, for us, a rhetorical position. It comes from our answering the crisis line every day. There is cheap, thin rhetoric from the left about compassion for the prostituted, without ever doing anything concrete for the prostituted."

The legalization of prostitution in Germany and the Netherlands has expanded trafficking and led to an explosion in child prostitution in those two countries.[19] Poor girls and women from Asia, Eastern Europe, and Africa have been shipped to legal brothels there. The wretched of the earth, part of the globalized capitalist model, are imported to serve the desires, sadism, and fetishes of those in the industrialized world.

Forced labor in the global private economy generates illegal profits of $150 billion, according to a report by the International Labour Organization.[20] The ILO estimated that almost two thirds of the profits, $99 billion, came from commercial sexual exploitation. More than half of the 21 million people the ILO estimates as having been coerced into forced labor and modern-day slavery are girls and women trafficked for sex.[21] They are moved from poor countries to rich countries, like livestock. The report does not cover internal trafficking in which women are transported from rural to urban areas or from neighborhood to neighborhood. Traffickers hold out promises of legitimate, well-paying jobs to poor women, but when the victims show up, the traffickers or the pimps strip them of their documents and throw them into a crippling debt peonage, by imposing trumped-up fees or lending them money to maintain drug addictions. The average age at which a woman enters prostitution is between twelve and sixteen.[22] In one study the average age at which prostitutes died was thirty-four.[23] Each woman forced into sexual slavery in Europe, the ILO estimated, can generate a profit of $34,800 a year for those who hold them in bondage.[24]

Lakeman called what has happened in countries such as Germany and the Netherlands "the industrialization of prostitution."

Sweden in 1999 criminalized the purchasing of sex. Norway, Iceland, and recently Ireland have done the same. The two responses—the German model and the so-called Nordic model—have had dramatically different effects. The German and Dutch approach normalizes and expands human trafficking and prostitution. The Nordic approach contains it. Sweden has cut street prostitution by half and freed many women from sexual slavery. Lakeman, citing the Nordic model, calls for criminalizing the buying, rather than the offering, of sexual services. Those whose bodies are being sold should not be punished.

"Third World women are used in the developed world for domestic labor, the care of the old and the undisciplined sexuality of the men," Lakeman said. "Our liberty as women cannot rest on this deal."

"When some women are bought and sold," said Hilla Kerner, an Israeli woman who has worked at the Vancouver shelter for ten years, "all women can be bought and sold."

5

HATE

The ideal subject of totalitarian rule is not the convinced Nazi or the dedicated communist, but people for whom the distinction between fact and fiction (i.e., the reality of experience) true and false (i.e., the standards of thought) no longer exists.

HANNAH ARENDT, *The Origins of Totalitarianism*[1]

[As] he listened to the cries of joy rising from the town, Rieux remembered that such joy is always imperiled. He knew what those jubilant crowds did not know but could have learned from books: that the plague bacillus never dies or disappears for good; that it can lie dormant for years and years in furniture and linen chests; that it bides its time in bedrooms, cellars, trunks, and bookshelves; and that perhaps the day would come when, for the bane and the enlightening of men, it would rouse up its rats again and send them forth to die in a happy city.

ALBERT CAMUS, *The Plague*[2]

Dylann Roof fired seventy-seven shots[3] from his .45-caliber Glock pistol at parishioners attending a Bible study at the black Emanuel A.M.E. Church in Charleston, South Carolina, on June 17, 2015. He murdered nine of them. Roof, twenty-one at the time, was an alienated, poor, uneducated white man who dropped out of school in ninth grade.[4] He was groomed on racist conspiracy theories on the Internet, social media, in white supremacist chat rooms, and at Confederate heritage sites and slavery monuments to become a killer.[5]

"The event that truly awakened me was the Trayvon Martin case," he wrote in his 2,500-word manifesto about the unarmed 17-year-old boy shot in Florida by George Zimmerman that was posted on his website, TheLastRhodesian.com.[6] The site also had some sixty pictures, a few of which showed him wearing a No. 88 T-shirt.[7] H is the eighth letter of the alphabet and two Hs, or 8s, are shorthand among neo-Nazis for "Heil Hitler."[8]

"I kept hearing and seeing his name, and eventually I decided to look him up," he wrote of Martin. "I read the Wikipedia article and right away I was unable to understand what the big deal was. It was obvious that Zimmerman was in the right. But more importantly this prompted me to type in the words 'black on White crime' into Google, and I have never been the same since that day. The first website I came to was the Council of Conservative Citizens. There were pages upon pages of these brutal black on White murders. I was in disbelief. At this moment I realized that something was very wrong. How could the news be blowing up the Trayvon Martin case while hundreds of these black on White murders got ignored?"[9]

He explained, his grammar, syntax, and spelling sometimes incorrect, that he "researched deeper" and "found out what was happening in Europe," which he called "the homeland of White people." He wrote:

I think it is fitting to start off with the group I have the most real life experience with, and the group that is the biggest problem for Americans.

Niggers are stupid and violent. At the same time they have the capacity to be very slick. Black people view everything through a racial lense. Thats what racial awareness is, its viewing everything that happens through a racial lense. They are always thinking about the fact that they are black. This is part of the reason they get offended so easily, and think that some thing are intended to be racist towards them, even when a White person wouldn't be thinking about race. The other reason is the Jewish agitation of the black race.

He expounded on the neo-Confederate rewriting of history that pervades much of the South, including in school textbooks. He went on:

I wish with a passion that niggers were treated terribly throughout history by Whites, that every White person had an ancestor who owned slaves, that segregation was an evil an oppressive institution, and so on. Because if it was all it true, it would make it so much easier for me to accept our current situation. But it isn't true. None of it is. We are told to accept what is happening to us because of ancestors wrong doing, but it is all based on historical lies, exaggerations and myths. I have tried endlessly to think of reasons we deserve this, and I have only come back more irritated because there are no reasons.

Only a fourth to a third of people in the South owned even one slave. Yet every White person is treated as if they had a slave owning ancestor. This applies to in the state where slavery never existed, as well as people whose families immigrated after slavery was abolished. I have read hundreds of slaves narratives from my state. And almost all of them were positive. One sticks out in my mind where an old ex-slave recounted how the day his mistress died was one of the saddest days of his life. And in many of these narratives the slaves told of how their masters didnt even allowing whipping on his plantation.

"In modern history class it is always emphasized that, when talking about 'bad' things Whites have done in history, they were White," he wrote. "But when we lern about the numerous, almost countless wonderful things Whites have done, it is never pointed out that these people were White. Yet when we learn about anything important done by a black person in history, it is always pointed out repeatedly that they were black. For example when we learn about how George Washington carver was the first nigger smart enough to open a peanut."

He decried the censorship of "honest" scientists and sociologists who dared to name the hierarchy of races. "How could our faces, skin, hair, and body structure all be different, but our brains be exactly the same," he asked. "This is nonsense we are led to believe."

"Negroes have lower Iqs, lower impulse control, and higher testosterone levels in generals," he wrote. "These three things alone are a recipe for violent behavior. If a scientist publishes a paper on the differences between races in Western Europe or Americans, he can expect to lose his job."

He had sections titled "Jews," "Hispanics," and "East Asians," noting that "the majority of American and European jews are White," that "there is good White blood worth saving in Uruguay, Argentina, Chile and even Brasil," although he added "they are still our enemies." He wrote that he had "great respect for the East Asian races" because "they are by nature very racist and could be great allies of the White race.

"I hate the sight of the American flag," he wrote. "Modern American patriotism is an absolute joke. People pretending like they have something to be proud while White people are being murdered daily in the streets. Many veterans believe we owe them something for 'protecting our way of life' or 'protecting our freedom.' But im not sure what way of life they are talking about. How about we protect the White race and stop fighting for the jews.

"Even if my life is worth less than a speck of dirt, I want to use it for the good of society," he wrote toward the end, quoting his "favorite film," *Himizu*.

Himizu is a dark, dystopian 2011 Japanese film, with graphic and unsettling scenes of violence. It follows the lives of two teenagers struggling to survive in a country ravaged by an earthquake and tsunami and consumed by anarchy and chaos. One of the boys, Sumida, murders his father and goes on a killing spree with a knife. The line that follows the quote Roof cites is: "I'll kill idiots who trouble citizens." [10]

"I have no choice," Roof concluded. "I am not in the position to, alone, go into the ghetto and fight. I chose Charleston because it is most historic city in my state, and at one time had the highest ratio of blacks to Whites in the country. We have no skinheads, no real KKK, no one doing anything but talking on the internet. Well someone has to have the bravery to take it to the real world, and I guess that has to be me." [11]

When he walked into the church's basement Fellowship hall at about 8:15 p.m. he was carrying eighty-eight hollow-point bullets he had purchased at Walmart.[12] Hollow-point bullets increase in diameter when they enter human flesh to maximize tissue damage, blood loss, and shock. He sat with the twelve members of the Bible study class.[13] He had prepared for what he hoped would be the start of a race war by making pilgrimages to Confederate heritage sites, including the Museum and Library of Confederate History in Greenville, with its display of Civil War weapons, Confederate uniforms, and framed portraits of South Carolina's forty-eight Confederate generals; the Boone Hall plantation with its half-mile row of majestic oaks, its big house, and nine remaining slave quarters; and Sullivan's Island, the largest slave port in the United States.[14] African men, women, and children were placed in quarantine on the island before being transported to Charleston for sale. Nearly half of all of the ancestors of African Americans are estimated to have passed through Sullivan's Island.[15]

"You blacks are killing White people on the streets everyday and raping White women everyday," he shouted at his victims when he was shooting, according to the journal he kept in jail.[16]

Roof is currently in the United States Penitentiary in Terre Haute, Indiana, where federal death row inmates are housed and executed.

"White people are pretending," he wrote in his journal, decorated with Nazi crosses and Klan runes, which was confiscated and used in his trial. "Grown adults waiting around playing pretend. Pretending we are all the same and equal, pretending that nothing bad is happening, and pretending like they have a future. Well unless we take real, possibly violent action, we have no future, literally. I am 21 years old and I don't play pretend."[17]

"I would rather live imprisoned knowing I took action for my race than to live with the torture of sitting idle," he went on. "It isn't up to me anymore. I did what I could do, I've done all I can do. I did what I thought would make the biggest wave. And now the fate of our race sits in the hands of my brothers who continue to live freely."

"I do not regret what I did," he wrote. "I am not sorry. I have not shed a tear for the innocent people I killed. I do feel sorry for the innocent

White children forced to live in this sick country, and I do feel sorry for the innocent White people that are killed daily at the hands of the lower races. I have shed a tear of self pity for myself. I feel pity that I had to do what I did in the first place. I feel pity that I had to give up my life because of a situation that should never have existed."

During his trial, he sought to represent himself and fire his defense attorney, David Isaac Bruck, because he was Jewish.[18] He later demanded that the public defense lawyers assigned to handle his appeal also be replaced because one was of Indian descent and the other was Jewish.[19] He appeared in court dressed in cheap polyester pants and wearing scuffed shoes decorated with neo-Nazi codes and Klan runes.[20] He had few friends, had apparently never had a girlfriend, regularly abused drugs and alcohol. He had held only one job, cutting grass for Clark's Termite & Pest Control for a few months, on and off, in Irmo, South Carolina. He either lived with his mother or drifted aimlessly from couch to couch.[21]

He had gone on Craigslist anonymously four months before the murders looking for companions, as long as they were not "Jews, queers, or niggers," to take a historic tour of Charleston.[22] He imagined that in the future a grateful president would pardon him.[23]

Roof represents the symbiotic and deadly relationship between the alt-right and the so-called alt-lite. The alt-lite, represented by figures such as Milo Yiannopoulos, frame their arguments around the protection of "Western civilization" and "Western culture" that are under assault from globalization seeking to erode "traditional" values. Many of the alt-lite disavow the overt racism and anti-Semitism of the alt-right, although they embrace the rabid Islamophobia and demonization of immigrants. The views of the alt-lite dominate sites such as Breitbart or Prison Planet, which have millions of readers. The softer tone of the alt-lite gives racism and bigotry a foothold and acceptability in the mainstream, especially with the election of Trump. It is attractive to disaffected white men like Roof who often suffer from economic, social, and sexual frustration. They believe they are the "forgotten victims" of deindustrialization. They seek comradeship and meaning, and perhaps most importantly, they long for a cause that allows them, first on the Internet and then later in physical acts of racist violence, to vent their anger and become self-anointed warriors in a noble crusade. Alt-lite figures serve as conduits that funnel disaffected followers into the arms of the rabid alt-right. The uptick of hate crimes seems to bear this theory out. Hate crimes in Chicago rose 20 percent in 2016, 24 percent in New York City, 50 percent in Philadelphia, and 62 percent in Washington, D.C., according to "Hate Crime Analysis & Forecast" published by the Center for the Study of Hate and Extremism.[24]

Jesse Singal in a *New York Times* article wrote of Patrick Hermansson, a twenty-five-year-old graduate student from Sweden who went undercover within the alt-right for the British antiracist group Hope Not Hate:

> The newly initiated are offered many opportunities to participate directly. A teenager in a suburban basement can join a coordinated global effort to spread misinformation about Emmanuel Macron, France's centrist president, in the hopes of helping far-right leader Marine Le Pen. Anyone who wants to do so can help spread the word about supposed mainstream media censorship of the Muslim "crime wave" the far right says is ravaging Europe.
>
> These efforts—a click, a retweet, a YouTube comment—come to feel like important parts of an epochal struggle. The far right, once hemmed in by its own parochialism, has manufactured a worldwide online battlefield anyone with internet access can step into.
>
> And if you're one of those newcomers happily playing the part of infantryman in the "meme wars" that rage daily, maybe, along the way, one of your new online Twitter buddies will say to you, "Milo's O.K., but have you checked out this guy Greg Johnson?" Or maybe they'll invite you to a closed online forum where ideas about how to protect Europe from Muslim migrants are discussed a bit more, well, frankly. Maybe, if you're really lucky, you'll eventually discover a whole new political movement to join.
>
> All of which can explain why members of the hard-core alt-right are watching the explosive success of their more moderate

counterparts with open glee, unable to believe their good luck. "I'm just fighting less and less opposition to our sorts of ideas when they're spoken," Mr. Johnson, the Counter-Currents [a publishing arm of the alt-right] editor, told Mr. Hermansson. His optimism, unfortunately, appears to be well founded.[25]

The stagnation, lack of opportunity, and hopelessness afflicting young men and women provides fertile soil for hate groups.

"How can people blame young White people for having no ambition, when they have been given nothing, and have nothing, to look forward to?" Roof wrote in his journal. "Even your most brain-dead White person can see that there is nothing good on the horizon."[26]

IT WAS A SWELTERING JULY afternoon when fifty protesters, many dressed in fatigues and wearing shirts that identified them with groups such as Proud Boys, Oath Keepers, Bikers for Trump, the Alt Knights, and a militia group called American Patriot the III%, gathered in a gravel parking lot in Deposit, New York. They had come for the "Second Annual Ride for Homeland Security." Pickup trucks, cars, and motorcycles were adorned with American flags. Deposit, a depressed rural community in upstate New York with a population of 1,577, is located at the confluence of the Oguaga Creek and the West Branch of the Delaware River near the border with Pennsylvania.[27]

The protesters, several driving all night, planned to ride past a small community called Islamberg, an enclave of two hundred mostly black Muslims in nearby Hanover, with seventy acres of farmland and woods.[28] The community, with its modest homes of wood and cinder blocks along dirt roads, is a punching bag for right-wing conspiracy theorists.

The protesters milled about in the parking lot under the gaze of nearby State Police. Three counter-protesters stood near a car and filmed the group. The event opened with a short prayer. A stocky man handed me a flyer titled, "Islam: A religion of peace?" It read:

KORAN 2:191 "Slay the unbelievers wherever you find them."
KORAN 3:28 "Muslims must not take the infidels as friends."

KORAN 3:85 "Any religion other than Islam is not acceptable."

KORAN 5:33 "Maim and crucify the infidels if they criticize Islam."

KORAN 8:12 "Terrorize and behead those who believe in scriptures other than the Koran."

KORAN 8:60 "Muslims must muster all weapons to terrorize the infidels."

KORAN 8:65 "The unbelievers are stupid; urge the Muslims to fight them."

KORAN 9:5 "When opportunity arises kill the infidels wherever you find them."

KORAN 9:30 "The Jews and Christians are perverts, fight them."

KORAN 9:123 "Make war on the infidels living in your neighborhood."

KORAN 22:19 "Punish the unbelievers with garments of fire, hooked iron rods, boiling water, melt their skin and bellies."

KORAN 47:4 "Do not hanker for peace with the infidels; behead them when you catch them."

There are far more calls by the God of the Hebrew Bible and Christian Book of Revelation for holy war, genocide, and savage ethnic cleansing than in the Koran, from the killing of the firstborns in Egypt to the wholesale annihilation of the Canaanites. God repeatedly demands the Israelites wage wars of annihilation against unbelievers in Numbers, Deuteronomy, Joshua, and the Book of Revelation. Everyone, including women, children, and the elderly, along with their livestock, are to be killed. Moses ordered the Israelites to carry out the "complete destruction" of all cities in the Promised Land and slaughter all the inhabitants, making sure to show "no mercy." From Joshua's capture of the city of Ai to King Saul's decimation of the Amalekites—Saul methodically dismembers the Amalekite king—God sanctifies bloodbath after bloodbath. "You shall not leave alive anything that breathes," God thunders in the Book of Joshua, "But you shall utterly destroy them." Joshua "struck all the land, the hill country and the Negev and the lowland and the slopes and all their kings. He left no survivor, but he utterly destroyed all who breathed, just as the Lord, the God of Israel had commanded" (Joshua

10:40, 11:15). And while the Koran urges believers to fight, it is also emphatic about showing mercy to captured enemies, something almost always scorned in the Bible, where, according to Psalm 137, those who smash the heads of Babylonian infants on the rocks are blessed. Whole books of the Bible celebrate divinely sanctioned genocide. The Koran doesn't come close. The willful blindness by these self-proclaimed Christian warriors about their own holy book is breathtaking.

Islamberg was founded in 1980 by African American followers of the Pakistani Sufi cleric Mubarik Ali Shah Gilani.[29] Gilani, who lives in Pakistan, urged his followers to leave urban areas and form religious communities in rural parts of the country.[30] There are about a dozen communities across the United States adhering to Gilani's teachings.[31] There is no evidence of criminal activity taking place in Islamberg according to local law enforcement.[32]

This does not prevent Fox News and other right-wing outlets from referring to Islamberg as the center of homegrown American jihadism.[33] Gilani is routinely linked to the murder of *Wall Street Journal* reporter Daniel Pearl, who was in Pakistan writing a story about the British national Richard Reid, known as the "shoe bomber," and his possible links to al Qaeda. Pearl believed he was being taken to meet Gilani at a restaurant in downtown Karachi on the evening of January 23, 2002, when he was abducted. A radical Islamic group beheaded Pearl in a gruesome video nine days later. Gilani was cleared of all involvement in Pearl's death.[34]

The Clarion Project posted a YouTube video in 2014 titled "Guerilla Training of Women at Islamberg, Hancock, N.Y., Headquarters of Muslims of the Americas." The video showed blurry clips of women wearing fatigues and headscarves doing marching drills along a road and scrambling through underbrush carrying assault rifles.[35] The Christian Action Network calls Islamberg "America's first Islamic government."[36] It charges that the children in the community are being groomed to be terrorists, that girls are denied an education, and those who break the community's rules "are often tied to trees and whipped for disobeying."[37]

The demonization of the rural community of Muslims eventually promoted racists to act, illustrating the deadly convergence of the alt-lite and the alt-right. The FBI aborted a firebombing and armed assault on the community planned by Robert Doggart, a former congressional candidate from Tennessee in 2015. He was sentenced to twenty years in prison.[38] On June 2, 2017, Johnson City police arrested Ramadan Abdullah, forty miles from Islamberg, and seized multiple pistols, assault weapons, and about ten thousand rounds of ammunition ranging from .38-caliber to armor-piercing incendiary rounds.[39] Law enforcement officials did not link Abdullah with Islamberg. The Clarion Project, however, claimed Abdullah was one of the founders and that his weapons were for the "guerilla training compound."[40]

Proud Boys, which the Southern Poverty Law Center describes as a "fight-club 'fraternity' of young, white, pro-Trump men to defend free speech rights by 'alt-right' leaders and engage in street fighting,"[41] publicized the Clarion Project's report.

"This past month there was an arms bust in Johnson City, New York down the road from the compound," the Proud Boys wrote. "It was later confirmed that the man in question was indeed headed to Islamberg, and the weapons were needed to 'protect themselves' against an upcoming 'biker rally' (that would be us)."[42]

The prospect of a gun battle with radical Muslims may have discouraged supporters from attending, according to Konstantine Dee from Queens, a thirty-two-year-old Proud Boy at the protest.

Still, the some three dozen people who appeared for "Second Annual Ride for Homeland Security" was an improvement over the previous year, when only five members of the American Bikers United Against Jihad showed up.[43]

These rallies and events acculturate and groom white racists to carry out acts of violence.

Daniel Peters drove nearly four hours to join the ride past Islamberg. He works six days a week from home in New York City as a computer network manager, starting at 7:00 a.m. and sometimes not finishing until 11:00 p.m.

When Peters joined the Oath Keepers last year, it was a relief to finally "not feel alone," he said. He called Islam "an evil cult" and denounced the prophet Muhammad as "a very bloodthirsty, sadistic killer."

"Historically, either they kill you or you kill them," he said.

He conceded that the Muslim population in the United States was small but noted that when the Europeans came to America they were also numerically a minority.

"Look," he said, glancing at the State Police who flanked the road toward Islamberg. "They're setting aside the traffic for us and everything. I feel like I'm in a Bill Clinton convoy.

"History is filled with collapses of civilizations," he went on. "What happens in America, is the price of food will skyrocket. There's going to be some kind of long-term disaster. For long-term survival after a disaster, it requires a community for security."

He said the impending collapse was a major reason he joined Oath Keepers.

The alt-right and militia groups say they are preparing for societal collapse. Once the electric grid goes out, they warn, it will trigger a race war. They are stockpiling food, water, supplies, weapons and ammunition to fight off the black and brown people that will flee the chaos of urban areas and roam the countryside like packs of wild animals.

A few months earlier, I had traveled to Logan, Utah, to a "prepper" convention where those awaiting the impending collapse heard talks and purchased survival gear and supplies.

Suzanne Freeman, a portly grandmother, stood in a livestock pen in the Logan fairgrounds. She held a microphone attached to a portable speaker that rested on a small folding table. I sat in the bleachers with about two dozen white middle-aged men and women. She said she was the mother of ten children, with three grandchildren. She described her near-death experience in 1999 after suffering an ectopic pregnancy.

She said she felt her spirit rise up out of her body during surgery, and hover in the left, upper corner of the hospital room. She was able to look down on her body and the working surgeons.

"I thought, 'I had to get back,' " she said. "I had seven children and three grandchildren. I thought, 'I am not going to leave my body. It just isn't time for me.' My youngest was a year old. Maybe he was two. I started to go back. I felt this grip on my arm. It was like a bungee chord. It stopped me cold."

"I've always wondered, would I recognize Jesus?" she asked. "I knew exactly who he was. I wasn't exactly thrilled to see him either," she said smiling.

"I panicked when I saw Jesus," she said. "I didn't want to go with him. I have seven kids, I can't go. He says 'Come with me.' I'm like, 'No, I have to go back.'

"I remember I could feel his feelings and hear his thoughts," she said. "I felt his love for me. But it didn't matter. I said, 'I'm not going with you.' He says, 'But there's people who want to meet you.' "

I looked at those in the bleachers to gauge their reactions. The onlookers did not move or speak. The millennialist or chiliastic belief—the doctrine that Christ will return to earth and rule for a thousand years—has a firm grip on the imaginations of many in Utah.

Jesus, she explained, "busted out laughing. With his laugh, it stopped me cold from the temper tantrum I was having. It was so wonderful. We always hear the Lord is perfect. He has the perfect laugh. It was so beautiful I stopped what I was doing. I was in awe. He laughed for a while."

Jesus promised her she would be able to return. He floated with her up to heaven. They entered the gates that were adorned with a "cameo" of Jesus. She saw family members and ancestors who had died.

"I saw this man dressed in 1800 clothes," she said to the audience. "His arms were like this," she said stretching out her arms, "and he was walking fast. He came up to me. I knew exactly who he was. It was Joseph Smith [the founder of Mormonism]. He shakes my hand really excitedly. He says, 'I have to shake hands with the lady who actually told Christ no.' He jumped over and did a back flip. Joseph Smith really did do that in those days. I'm sure he was a hyperactive child. Good thing he lived on a farm. It must have got the wiggles out of him. I distinctly remember thinking his pants doesn't match his jacket. Later on, two or three years later, David Lindsay's paintings, he painted a picture of Joseph Smith with a blue jacket and brown pants. I told him he got it wrong. He had a brown jacket."

She also saw Brigham Young "behind him with a top hat." Brigham, she said, told Smith "Now is not the time!" for back flips.

The audience laughed. Most appeared well versed in the histories of

Joseph Smith, the founder of the Church of Jesus Christ of Latter-day Saints or Mormons, and Brigham Young, the second president of the church.

Those in heaven lined up to shake her hand. Jesus commanded her to write about her near-death experience and her visit to heaven when she returned to earth. She saw angels. She saw Jesus's life pass before her from his birth to his crucifixion.

"His arm is around my shoulder," she said. "He loved me so much. I could feel his pure love aiming towards me and I didn't feel like I deserved it.

"I was shown the last days," she said. "At first I did not see any particular areas of the damage. I saw a flood. I saw infant babies floating down the river. We're picking dead bodies up and this infant was alive. I really hope I'll never be at a flood scene picking dead bodies from a freezing river. I'm hoping it was just to show that there are disasters and Heavenly Father does take people home. There's always miracles. Some beautiful, wonderful miracles that are meant to happen for people who are meant to survive it. It doesn't matter where you live, God will protect you if that's what's meant to be. In the end you will hear the spirit to be led away. We're all human. We all need to learn that. It's vital. I'll just say this. There's a lot of miracles in the last days. He has a plan. No one knows the plan but Heavenly Father. We just have to take it step by step.

"I saw the founding fathers," she said. "I met with them. Thomas Jefferson really struck me as a really good man. . . . He was the first one to have a church in the White House. They claimed he cut up scriptures but he actually made a scrapbook of what the Lord said. He cut up the Bible and posted it on some other paper only of what the Lord said. I saw him write the Declaration of Independence. I saw Moses standing next to him whispering in his ear.

"Do you guys have any questions?" she asked when she finished.

A woman raised her hand.

"What did Jesus look like?" she asked.

"His hair was brown with auburn and blond highlights," Freeman answered. "He had a Jewish nose and deep blue eyes. Joseph Smith had blue eyes. The blue eyes intrigued me."

"Did you see the Second Coming?" someone asked.

"It's not as clear for me," she answered.

"I do have gifts [for seeing the dead]," she said. "I went to a funeral . . . this person comes to me. He sits on top of his flowers on his casket and just looks at me and, la-di-da! Finally I had to tell him, 'You behave, it's your funeral.' "

She chuckled.

"Did you have a question?" she said pointing to a man. "I swear I thought I saw you had your hand up. It was your spirit I guess? Just kidding.

"I talked to Mary, Mother of Christ," she told us. "She was a very lovely lady. Very small. No Jewish features. Blue eyes. She said there is a place—she had to get permission from Jesus—and she took us there, a place called the reassigned children area. Aborted babies go there. If someone who is pregnant makes a choice not to have the child, those children have a choice to come back and have a body."

Freeman's talk ended. The audience filed out respectfully. A few stayed behind to chat and ask more questions.

There was no debate in the Logan fairgrounds about the looming end times. The shorthand they use for what is coming is TEOTWAW-KI—"The End Of The World As We Know It."

Stacks of the magazine *American Survival Guide* were scattered around the fairgrounds. On the cover, a man with a pistol tucked into the front pocket of his cargo pants held up a compass in front of a huge military-style truck. Articles included, "On the Move: How to Build an Alcohol Stove," "How to Hunt Ethically," "Can You Really Trust Your City's Resources?," "How to Get off the Grid Now," and "Dental Distress: How to Deal with Mouth Pain When a Dentist Is Nowhere to Be Found." Inside were ads for water filtration systems, survival knives, and weapons such as Del-Ton's AR-15. There were also ads for pills to treat erectile dysfunction, including Viagra, Levitra, and Cialis, all marketed as "Men's Lifestyle Medications." These "lifestyle" ads featured the head of a bald eagle and an American flag above three plastic pill containers.

One article was headlined "Discovery Channel's 'Naked and Afraid' Star, E. J. Snyder, Shares His Top 10 Tips for Staying Alive." Snyder, whose nickname is "Skullcrusher," was shown naked with a burlap bag slung over his shoulder and covering his genitals. A KA-BAR military knife dangled from a rope around his neck. He had a salt-and-pepper beard and held what looked like a burned-out torch in his right hand. The tips offered by the former soldier included "Find Water," "Create Your Weapons," and "Keep That Iron Will." A box at the end of the article gave his contact information for his survival courses.

One of the survival trucks, known as the "Plan B EMP-Proof 1986 Expandable 6x6 Command Center," was parked inside the building. I walked up a metal ramp and stood in the back. The truck was customized from the frame of an old military truck. The survival trucks, which can cost as much as $500,000 depending on the amenities, usually come with a stove and refrigerator that are hooked up to solar panels and batteries. The trucks are called "bug out" vehicles with the assumption that in an emergency a family can climb into one and "bug out"—flee into the wilderness to survive.

Many of those in the fairgrounds speculated that North Korea, or perhaps China, Russia, or Iran, was building a satellite that would be used to detonate a nuclear weapon over the United States to trigger what they called an EMP, or electromagnetic pulse, that will kill millions and wipe out much of the country's electric grid. The electrical grid could, they say, be down for a decade. Chaos and anarchy will swiftly envelop the country. Roving gangs of predators, desperate for food, will terrorize rural white America. Those who do not retreat into fortified bunkers with crates of food, water, weapons, and stockpiles of ammunition will be attacked and probably killed.

A popular item at the fairground stalls was the "Faraday bag" which would protect electronic items such as cell phones from the crippling electromagnetic pulses.

There is no evidence that such a weapon exists. But proponents, who have drawn elaborate diagrams and charts, buttress their dark predictions with the Book of Revelation, the Book of Mormon, dizzying numerical sequences, and astrological charts. They also peddle the "Blood Moon Prophecy"—the belief that four consecutive lunar eclipses and six full moons in between that began with the April 2014 lunar eclipse and ended with the lunar eclipse on September 2015 is divine proof that the apocalypse is approaching. The leaders of the Mormon Church denounced the "Blood Moon Prophecy" but it finds wide acceptance among survivalists.

I found Brandon Mysliwiec, thirty, and his sister, Telly, twenty-seven, sitting in camp chairs in a corner of the fairgrounds building. Mysliwiec was the organizer of the weekend. He was from Evanston, Wyoming, and ran a store that catered to survivalists. He had six children. He said he had stockpiled enough supplies, including thirty thousand pounds of wheat and "hundreds of blankets," for his extended family of thirty-six, to survive for seven years.

"I have solar panels and generators for everybody," he said. "Walkie-talkies for everybody. Toilet paper alternatives. We've got first-aid. You name it, we have it."

He told me all of his relatives, including his older children, owned weapons and practiced shooting.

"My father's AR-15 doesn't do more than my 30-30 does," he said. "There's no difference. The AR-15 is a .223, so there's much smaller bullets, which makes it less lethal but more accurate."

Mysliwiec, like nearly everyone I spoke to at the fairgrounds, said God spoke to him directly.

"I literally had words thrown in my head," he said. "It was a few years ago. I was probably twenty-eight. I am Mormon. I had a dream, I won't go into that, but after the dream I woke up and sat there and pondered a few things from my dream. And then I literally had words coming into my head. I don't know if I can say it exactly word for word. It was inspirational. But basically it said I needed to find a way to help people get prepared."

Mormons are instructed by the church to stockpile food and supplies for the Second Coming.

He said he tells survivalists to buy three hundred pounds of wheat. It is less than $100 and it can keep someone alive for a year, he told me, if they eat a pound a day.

"It's the cheapest way," he said, "although you'll hate it."

"The best thing to do for water is just keep two weeks of water," he said. "A gallon a day per person. Get yourself a good filter."

He had Faraday bags made by Tech Protect for sale on a folding table along with products he manufactured, including essential oils for medicinal use and fluoride-free toothpaste.

"You should have seeds in your storage," he went on. "If our infrastructure is knocked out, you'll need a way to survive until the infrastructure is rebuilt. What if your year supply of food runs out? You need to have something to do. Eat off your storage while you plant your first garden."

He said survivalists should form groups of about a hundred people to defend and sustain themselves.

"I'm happy about a collapse coming," he said. "I see the way the world is now. I'd rather have it collapse now and start over."

"We do believe tribulations is a cleansing time," he went on. "There are plenty of people who will die specifically to be cleansed from the earth."

Telly, who has two small daughters, had to cope as a girl with the anxiety that comes growing up in a household preparing for the apocalypse.

"I grew up with my dad talking about it," she said. "I felt my whole life I was living in a state of crisis. I developed a lot of anxiety . . . I was scared. I had panic attacks. I had anger problems."

I walked outside the fairgrounds building. Dan Weatbrook, a Mormon truck driver from Garland, Utah, who started work each day at 4:30 a.m., was cooking pancakes on a wood-burning "rocket stove." The seven-hundred-pound stove had a four-foot griddle and a three-foot oven. It sold for $5,850. He was handing out small pancakes on white paper plates.

"I was driving up one morning and this spirit said to me to feed a lot of people with no electricity," he said. "That's the only instruction I got. Certainly before that I had never heard of a rocket stove. I became interested in it. It was no accident."

"I believe what the prophets say," he said. "I believe what the Bible says. There's going to be hard times. The Book of Revelation is very specific."

He looked at the stove, which resembled a black box with two vertical pipes at the back.

"What makes it sound like a rocket is the roar," he said. "They use a lot of air and a little bit of fuel. Rocket stoves are all over the Internet."

He handed me a paper plate with a warm pancake on it. He first constructed his stoves for a few hundred dollars apiece.

"We have eight children," he said. "We lost twin boys. We have six married. And eighteen grandchildren. So I make ten stoves. Then I pat myself on the back and say, 'Ah, I've done it.' The spirit comes back and says 'No, go bigger.'

"At the end of one year, when we lose electricity nationwide, ninety percent of Americans will be dead," he said. "How many people in New York City? They've got no food. They've got no way to cook. You need to get away from big populations as quickly as possible. Just read some Revelations. That happened in Katrina in New Orleans. Three days and you got cops in Walmart looting."

He said he grew his own food and raised chickens.

"I will tell you when it is time to flee and when it is time to arm for war," he said, reciting from Chapter 46 of the Book of Mormon.

"Then in Chapter 48," he went on, "it says you protect your land, property, and people. So I spent the last two and a half years, and many, many thousands of dollars, and [I'm] armed for war. I buy lots of guns and bullets. They are AR-15s. Pistols. My neighbor is a big hunter. He has lots of guns."

James Vierra, in another animal pen inside the building, described the aftermath of an EMP attack. He said that within twelve months following a nationwide blackout, "up to 90 percent of the U.S. population could perish from starvation, disease, and societal breakdown." Urban areas, he predicted, would descend swiftly into barbarity with the collapse of law and order, the loss of drinking water, refrigeration, heat, air-conditioning, and telecommunication. Food stores would be looted and emptied within a few days. Gas stations, fire stations, and hospitals would cease to function. There would be no telephone service or radio and television broadcasts. Credit cards would be useless. The destroyed electrical transformers, most made by foreign companies, would take years to replace.

"When it comes down, it creates the Compton effect," he said, as he showed the crowd a slide of what the EMP attack would look like. "The photon gamma rays released from the nuclear device come into contact and knock a free electron loose. The loose free electron gets charged and magnetized at the same time. That's what makes it so deadly. It attaches to our natural magnetic fields on the earth. It starts to spin.

"If the blast happens at night and it's a clear night we'll see the blast," he said. "By the time we see the light it's already done. The lights won't work anymore in the house."

A man asked if an EMP weapon had ever been used by the U.S. military.

"It's classified," Vierra answered curtly. "There's nothing that's been released to the public. I have tried to acquire some information on this. I have been denied access.

"Include Heavenly Father in your plan," he advised. "If I'm in a situation where I need to protect my family with physical force, the Lord is behind me."

He warned that "gangs" from cities with "military-grade weapons" would roam the countryside.

"I have a rifle that I can shoot at 1,200 yards," he said. "I might be spending a lot of time on my roof. Unless they have a drone and can see my laying there, I can reach them."

"So the main threat will be foreign, from China or Korea?" a man asked.

"No," he answered. "I believe it will be domestic because we are at a turning point for a revolution."

When the American populace rises up in revolt, he said, the U.S. military will be ordered by Washington to use EMP weapons to shut down the nation's power grid.

Survivalists are not limited to white nativists but, as *The New Yorker* reported, include the wealthy on the East and West Coasts who pay $3 million and more for luxury post-apocalypse apartments in a decommissioned nuclear missile silo in Kansas. Silicon Valley billionaires have bought up thousands of acres of land in the Midwest and in remote parts of the globe such as New Zealand where they plan to hole up and wait out the apocalypse.[44]

The common denominator of this fusion between survivalists and the alt-right is nationalism, xenophobia, and racism.

THE CONVOY OF CARS, TRUCKS, and motorcycles left the parking lot in Deposit and drove down the highway. They turned onto a dirt road that led past Islamberg. State Police were standing in front of the entrance to Islamberg. A few of the Muslims from the community filmed the vehicles as they passed. The caravan of cars and motorcycles pulled into a parking lot a few miles away. Many then drove to a house outside Binghamton where there was beer, food, and a bonfire.

I sat at a table in the barren dining room of the house, which was for sale, with the owner, Kat, who recently lost her job, and Scott Seddon, the founder of the militia group American Patriot the III%, or AP3. Its name was inspired by the belief that only 3 percent of the population actively fought the British during the American Revolution.

Seddon founded AP3 when Barack Obama took office in 2009. His initial focus was to connect survivalists for the coming collapse. But the militia soon took on a political coloring. It has expanded to multiple chapters nationwide, he said, each involved with organizing protests, training militia, and teaching survival skills to prepare for an imminent natural or man-made calamity. He estimates AP3 currently has thirty thousand to fifty thousand members. It also provides security for right-wing protests and rallies.

"I founded it out of fear, to be honest with you," he said. "I saw a change starting to occur in this country that really made me scared. It started with Obama."

He launched into an attack on the Reverend Jeremiah Wright, Barack Obama's former pastor in Chicago who delivered fiery sermons on the evils of empire and white supremacy. He called Wright "anti-American."

"Black Lives Matter went to the freaking White House," he said of a July 2016 meeting at the White House with Obama. "Everybody is a victim in America today.

"The majority of antifa have that victim mentality," he went on, referring to antifascists who advocate property destruction and violence. "There's no excuse for them to be in rallies every other week insulting people and not holding a job. Most of these kids, 90 percent of antifa, don't have jobs."

Michael Mosher, a former marine who is in charge of AP3's statewide security, joined us at the table. He had a tattoo of crossed rifles, another read "My Fight," and a third was the 3 percenter symbol of the militia. He also had a tattoo of the head of a buck.

"They're a bunch of immature kids," Mosher said of antifa. "They're disrespectful. If you don't agree with them, they spit on people. They throw urine at people."

"They throw bottles at people," Seddon said.

"How do they throw urine?" I asked.

"In little balloons," Mosher said.

"Every event I've been to where there has been antifa, there's always one heavyset ethnic chick that does nothing but scream the entire time," he went on.

"They're paid actually," Kat said, joining the conversation. "They have paid organizers that come and recruit these kids online from Craigslist or what-not. They do pay them like fifteen bucks an hour to come out."

"When we were at the rally point this morning, there was a red Cadillac across the street," Mosher said. "An older woman was sitting in the driver's seat. A heavyset lady was outside of the car recording. They were filming the entire time."

He said antifa was "funded by George Soros."

"They're socialists," Seddon said. "They're communists. They're the troubled youth of America who don't want to work. They think the upper one percent should hand them everything.

"The antifas are supposedly reaching out to the Muslim communities as well to get their backing," he said, "which doesn't make sense to me. Muslims are against homosexuality."

"A lot of antifa members are ambiguous homosexuals," Kat said. "They're definitely not alpha men or alpha women."

"They're the misfits," Mosher said.

"They're misguided," Seddon said. "The patriot community, thank God, has a growing number of homosexual men and women. I'm a straight male, 110 percent. But some of our best, most patriotic men and women in America are gay. There's definitely no discrimination against gay people. But antifa supports a group—Muslims—that thinks gay people are an abomination."

"And we don't," Kat said. "We're trying to stick up for all these people who don't understand what they're bringing into the country, by bringing in all these Muslim refugees who are actually just migrants bringing in Sharia law and believe that homosexuality is an abomination. They're going to kill all of us."

"That's what they do in the Middle East," Seddon said.

"The rise in terrorism across Europe and England, we don't want that to happen here," Seddon said. "It's not going to be accepted if it starts. That's why we wanted to show up today. Just to let them know we're here. We're aware. We're Americans. We love our country."

"We're not going to give up our country the way England and London has," Mosher said.

"I'm quite sure Europe is going to be one big Islamic state, probably in the next twenty to thirty years," Kat said.

"Yeah," Seddon said, "except Eastern Europe. Eastern Europe is standing their ground."

"France, U.K., Germany, I think Finland was having a problem," Kat said. "Sweden, they're all having problems. Poland is going to resist. Look up the rape capitals of the world. They're all going to be where these large immigrant populations are. And also, missing people. Look it up. It's going to be where all these refugees are. They're number one in the slave trade, the sex slave trade, too. I just want to protect my family. I don't want that here."

"I've spent six years in the Marine Corps," Mosher said. "I've been overseas to Iraq, Afghanistan. I've fought them. I don't want them here. I've met people who I guess you would call moderate Muslims. They were normal people. I never had any issues with them. When I went over there, it was a whole lot different—they hate us so bad."

"Why?" I ask.

"To be honest with you, I think part of it comes from the United States getting involved in a lot of conflict overseas," he said. "But it also is in the Koran, anybody that doesn't follow them is supposed to be beheaded or whatever. I've seen their book. Their job is to kill us unless we convert to Islam."

"They're already inside our federal government," Seddon said. "Homeland Security has some people who are deeply entrenched. What's the name of the [Palestinian American] female speaker that [New York City] mayor [Bill] de Blasio loves? [Linda] Sarsour. She's right there next to de Blasio when he makes speeches at events. She's put up on a pedestal. Listen, in this country, Sharia law just ain't happening. It violates our entire Constitution. We're a free country. Anytime you start implementing a law that tells you, 'You have to do this, you have to abide by this,' you're going against the Constitution of the United States."

"Why are there so few African Americans in militias?" I asked.

"Because the left spins us as being racist bigots, when [actually] we allow anybody into the group," Seddon said. "Like I said, we have homosexuals in the group. We have a lot of Mexicans, believe it or not. Veterans. The media spins us as racist KKK members. Listen, we accept almost anybody into AP [American Patrol]. The only people I'd scrutinize a little more, unfortunately, would be the Muslim community. And no felons."

"Do you have any Muslims?" I asked.

"They have no interest in the group," Seddon said.

"Our country is divided completely," Mosher said. "Some people think it's going to lead to a civil war or a revolutionary war. I hope it happens during my time and not my son's."

Mosher said about 85 percent of the militia's members were veterans. Mosher and Seddon left the house to join the other militia members standing around the bonfire in the backyard. The light was fading.

Kat, recently divorced, lost her job in February 2017 as the cheer coach at Ithaca College. She had been there only a year. She is the mother of three boys and a girl, ages twenty-two, twenty-one, fourteen, and twelve.

"This [losing her job] was for my views of being a Christian Trump supporter," she said. "That's all it was."

"We went on break right after the election because the school shuts down from December to January after finals," she said. "We came back after inauguration. A couple of my girls [on the cheer team] seemed to be upset all the time. One of them was a Muslim refugee from Afghanistan. The other one was of Asian descent. I'm pretty sure she was a lesbian."

A few of the girls she coached confronted her about the pro-Trump opinions she had posted on Facebook, including a photo she had put up after the Women's March in Washington of a veteran woman captioned, "The real women who marched for us."

"They were fired up, started calling me a racist," she explained. "I said listen, I understand you're upset about the election. I understand these things. But it is what it is. This is how democracy works. This is your president now. You can't keep missing practices and getting up and calling me names.

"They weren't having it," she said. "This went on for over an hour. I was so tired. I couldn't even talk anymore." The verbal altercation ended when two girls stormed out of the cheerleading practice. " 'We're not coming back if you're still here,' " she recalled one of the girls saying.

When she was fired the next day—she received a terse email saying her contract had been terminated—her world disintegrated. She was still trying to cope from a recently dissolved marriage.

"This was my life," she said. "This was all I ever knew. I cheered for fourteen [years] myself. And I've been coaching for six [years]. I was so heartbroken. I guess my life is going to be different now. . . . I didn't know what to do. . . . I have to figure it out."

She was planning on moving to Ithaca after she sold the house she had shared with her ex-husband. Now she had nowhere to go. She began spending more time on the Internet.

"I didn't understand why these girls hated me so much. . . . I've been crying all week about what happened at school," she said. "I started reaching out on Facebook. Told everyone what happened. I put out publicly what happened to me at Ithaca College in a long post. I was embarrassed. I just lost my job. My career is over. My career is over! All of a sudden I started getting all these shares, 'I'm so sorry about what happened to you.' I heard about . . . the refugee crisis in Europe. People started talking to me about Islam."

Then it hit her. One of the cheerleaders who argued with her was Muslim.

"At the time I was really not all that familiar with Islam," she said. "I thought it was a real religion. I did not know why that Muslim girl didn't like me . . . because on the news you don't get correct information. You're getting very one-sided biases. On Facebook, we share real information with each other.

"A lot of us were afraid to say anything during the Obama administration because you'll be called a racist," she said. "Then all of a sudden, when we felt comfortable when Trump got in, I think everyone started waking up and started to be vocal, and learning more, and sharing information."

She came to believe, after reading posts on Facebook, that Islam is "a death cult basically started by a Satan-worshipper who came from a tribe that sacrificed children." She was mortified. The newfound fear and need to resist gave her a mission in life. She had to help save America from Muslims.

"I feel a very big threat to our humanity now. . . . I had done so much research on Islam," she said. "I basically made it my job. . . . I was as passionate about cheer as I am about this patriot movement," she said. "There's a lot of Muslim organizations that are behind the scenes putting people in offices, just like they did in Europe. You've got a Muslim mayor in London.

"Obama was the Manchurian candidate, wouldn't you agree?" she asked. "He was a plant. He was in the Muslim Brotherhood's back pocket. He was placed there on purpose. They're going to kill all of us.

"I got very vocal on Facebook," she said. "I'm sharing information. Next thing I know, I went from 1,200 followers to 5,000. They're Friending me. Basically, people are listening. They're waking up. I'm really, really excited about it. We're all coming out and starting to fight back. We are the resistance.

"I want to keep people safe," she said. "I want to fight for women. Not have their genitals cut off. Not be stoned to death. Or shamed or honor-killed."

These sentiments, revolving around a perceived assault by Muslims, African-Americans, Latinos, feminists, gays, liberals, and intellectuals against national identities, dominate the ideology of right-wing hate groups.

Stefan Meyer, twenty-five, a four-year Marine Corps veteran, sat in a bar in Parkville, Maryland. He was a member of the Maryland Chapter of Proud Boys. He joined after the riots in Baltimore following the death of Freddie Gray. He wanted to fight Black Lives Matter and antifa.

"[Freddie Gray] rammed his head into the walls of the police van so that it would look like police brutality," he said. "He hit himself against a bolt. So he killed himself trying to frame the cops. And people started destroying my city. I was furious."

Meyer was a commercial driver who was going through a divorce. He went to work at 4:30 in the morning and got home at 4:30 in the afternoon.

"I break my back at work for $20 an hour," he said. "Out of the $800 a week that I make, I see maybe almost $500 of it. Which for all intents and purposes isn't bad. But most of it is going to rent. Rent is not cheap. Rent is $1,040 for one bed, one bath. And a tiny kitchen.

"These days, I just sit at home and sleep," he said. "That's about it. [Being a part of the Proud Boys,] it gets me out more. I got to see the White House. I've never seen it before."

Meyer said he was bullied and excluded at school.

"I was tiny," he said. "I barely broke a hundred [pounds] in high school."

When he began dating a girl in high school, they agreed to keep their relationship secret so she wouldn't be teased. He once tried to give her a bracelet in front of her friends.

"She had this horrified look on her face," Meyer recalled. "So I said, 'Hey, I forgot to give this back to you, I'm so sorry.' I didn't want to embarrass her."

Meyer joined the Marines after high school.

"I would have liked to go when Afghanistan was still going on," he said. "There were a lot of men out there that are a lot better than I am. It upsets me a lot of people died that I didn't get to take that bullet for.

"Since day one," he said of Marine Corps boot camp, "you're just screaming, 'Kill!' There's nothing behind it. There's no 'Kill this.' There's no 'Kill that.' It's just, 'Kill.' Which is why we're such an effective fighting force. That's our job. To go in and win battles and win wars. At least it used to be. That's how wars were won. Now [the battle] happens on the news. I'm not sure which is worse."

Meyer described how he and other militia members, also veterans, casually spoke of killing people when they gathered at events such as the Freedom of Speech rally in Washington, D.C., in June 2017.

"Everyone will just say, 'I just want to fucking kill someone,'" Meyer said.

"It's not out of hate or rage," he went on. "It's just what was drilled into them for so long, for so many years."

The Democratic Party blamed its 2016 election defeat on Russian interference in the election, the leaked emails of Hillary Clinton's campaign manager John Podesta, and FBI director James Comey's decision, shortly before the vote, to send a letter to Congress related to Hillary Clinton's private email server. It refused to acknowledge the root cause of its defeat, the abandonment of workers, deindustrialization, the wars in the Middle East, and vast social inequality. The party's rhetoric about watching out for the working and middle class worked for three decades. But it has lost credibility among those it has betrayed. The idea that tens of thousands, or hundreds of thousands, of Clinton supporters read the Podesta emails and switched their votes to Trump, or were swayed by the Comey announcement to abandon Clinton, is absurd. The failure to confront reality is ominous, not only for the Democratic Party, but for American democracy.

The malaise that infects Americans is global. Hundreds of millions of people have been severed by modernity from traditions, beliefs, and rituals, as well as communal structures, which kept them rooted. They have been callously cast aside by global capitalism as superfluous. This has engendered an atavistic rage against the technocratic world that condemns them. This rage is expressed in many forms—nativism, neofascism, jihadism, the Christian right, alt-right militias, and the anarchic violence of antifa. The resentment springs from the same deep wells of despair. This despair exacerbates racism, bigotry, and xenophobia. It poisons civil discourse. It celebrates hypermasculinity, violence, and chauvinism. It promises the return to the mythical past.

Corporate elites, rather than accept their responsibility for the global anarchy, define the clash as one between Western civilization and racist thugs and medieval barbarians. They see in the extreme nationalists, anarchists, religious fundamentalists, and jihadists a baffling irrationality that can be quelled only with force. They have yet to grasp that the disenfranchised do not hate them for their values. They hate them because of their duplicity, greed, use of indiscriminate industrial violence, and hypocrisy.

The more the ruling elites are attacked, the more they too retreat into an idealized past, self-glorification, and willful ignorance. Pankaj Mishra writes in *Age of Anger: A History of the Present*:

> Thus, in the very places [in the West] where secular modernity arose, with ideas that were then universally established—individualism (against the significance of social relations), the cult of efficiency and utility (against the ethic of honour), and the normalization of self-interest—the mythic Volk has reappeared as a spur to solidarity and action against real and imagined enemies.
>
> But nationalism is, more than ever before, a mystification, if not a dangerous fraud with its promise of making a country "great again" and its demonization of the "other"; it conceals the real conditions of existence, and the true origins of suffering, even as it seeks to replicate the comforting balm of transcendental ideals within a bleak earthly horizon. Its political resurgence shows that *ressentiment*—in this case, of people who feel left behind by the globalized economy or contemptuously ignored by its slick overlords and cheerleaders in politics, business and the media—remains the default metaphysics of the modern world since [Jean-Jacques] Rousseau first defined it. And its most menacing expression in the age of individualism may well be the violent anarchism of the disinherited and the superfluous.[45]

The proponents of globalization promised to lift workers across the planet into the middle class and instill democratic values and scientific rationalism. Religious and ethnic tensions would, they insisted, be alleviated or eradicated. This global marketplace would create a peaceful, prosperous community of nations. All we had to do was get government out of the way and kneel before market demands, held up as the ultimate form of progress and rationality.

What we were never told was that the game was fixed. We were always condemned to lose. Our cities were deindustrialized and fell into decay. Wages declined. Our working class became impoverished. The rapacious appetite of capitalists and imperialists never considered "such constraining factors," Mishra wrote, "as finite geographical space, degradable natural resources and fragile ecosystems."[46]

In carrying out this project of global expansion, no form of coercion or violence was off-limits. The conflicts in Egypt, Libya, Mali, Syria, and many other places, Mishra notes, are fueled by "extreme weather events, the emptying of rivers and seas of their fish stocks, or the desertification of entire regions on the planet."[47] The refugees being driven by their homelands' chaos into Europe are creating political instability and empowering right-wing nationalists. Mishra warns that "the two ways in which humankind can self-destruct—civil war on a global scale, or destruction of the natural environment—are rapidly converging."[48]

Shorn of traditional patterns of existence, we are knit together "by commerce and technology,"[49] forces that Hannah Arendt called "negative solidarity."[50]

The backlash resembles the anarchist, fascist, and communist violence and terrorism that took place at the end of the nineteenth century and in the early twentieth century. Nowhere is this truer than with the calls for jihad by Islamic radicals, most of whom have no religious training and who often come out of the criminal underworld. The jihadist leader Abu Musab al-Zarqawi, nicknamed "the sheikh of slaughterers" in Iraq, had, as Mishra writes, "a long past of pimping, drug-dealing and heavy drinking."[51] The Afghan-American Omar Mateen reportedly was a frequenter of the nightclub in Orlando, Florida, where he massacred forty-nine people, and had been seen there drunk.[52] Anwar al-Awlaki, who preached jihad and was eventually assassinated by the United States, had a penchant for prostitutes.[53] Abu Muhammad al-Adnani, a senior leader of Islamic State before he was killed, called on Muslims in the West to kill any non-Muslim they encountered. "Smash his head with *narrative of violence*

a rock, or slaughter him with a knife, or run him over with your car, or throw him down from a high place, or choke him, or poison him," Adnani told followers.[54]

The Russian revolutionary anarchist Mikhail Bakunin's "propaganda by deed" is, Mishra writes, "now manifest universally in video-taped, live-streamed and Facebooked massacres."[55] It grew, he writes, "naturally from the suspicion that only acts of extreme violence could reveal to the world a desperate social situation and the moral integrity of those determined to change it."[56] These imported ideas filled the void left by the destruction of indigenous beliefs, traditions, and rituals. As Mishra says, these jihadists "represent the death of traditional Islam rather than its resurrection."[57]

"As it turned out," he writes, "the autocratic modernizers failed to usher a majority of their wards into the modern world, and their abortive revolutions from above paved the way for more radical ones from below, followed, as we have seen in recent years, by anarchy."[58]

The terrorist attacks in Paris and London were driven by the same resentment as that which led Timothy McVeigh to bomb the Alfred P. Murrah Federal Building in Oklahoma City in 1995, killing 168, including 19 children, and injuring 684.[59] And when he was imprisoned in Florence, Colorado, the prisoner in the adjacent cell was Ramzi Ahmed Yousef, the mastermind of the first attack on the World Trade Center, in 1993. After McVeigh was executed, Yousef commented, "I never have [known] anyone in my life who has so similar a personality to my own as his."[60]

Mishra writes, "Malignant zealots have emerged in the very heart of the democratic West after a decade of political and economic tumult; the simple explanatory paradigm set in stone soon after the attacks of 9/11—Islam-inspired terrorism versus modernity—lies in ruins."[61] The United States, aside from suffering periodic mass killings in schools, malls, and movie theaters, has seen homegrown terrorists strike the Boston Marathon, a South Carolina church, Tennessee military facilities, a Texas Army base, and elsewhere.

"The modern West can no longer be distinguished from its apparent enemies," Mishra notes.[62] The hagiography of the U.S. Navy sniper Chris

→ east

Kyle in Clint Eastwood's movie *American Sniper* celebrates the binary worldview also adopted by jihadists who deify their suicide bombers.

American Sniper lionizes the most despicable aspects of U.S. society—the gun culture, the blind adoration of the military, the belief that we have an innate right as a "Christian" nation to exterminate the "lesser breeds" of the earth, a grotesque hypermasculinity that banishes compassion and pity, a denial of inconvenient facts and historical truth, and a belittling of critical thinking and artistic expression. ← humanities, arts

"Savage, despicable evil," Kyle wrote of those he was killing from rooftops and windows.[63] "That's what we were fighting in Iraq. That's why a lot of people, myself included, called the enemy 'savages.' . . . I only wish I had killed more."[64] At another point he writes: "I loved killing bad guys[65]. . . . I loved what I did. I still do . . . it was fun. I had the time of my life being a SEAL."[66] He labels Iraqis "fanatics" and writes "they hated us because we weren't Muslim."[67] He claims "the fanatics we fought valued nothing but their twisted interpretation of religion."[68]

"I never once fought for the Iraqis," he wrote of our Iraqi allies. "I could give a flying fuck about them."[69]

He and his fellow platoon members spray-painted the white skull of the Punisher from Marvel Comics on their vehicles, body armor, weapons, and helmets. The motto they painted in a circle around the skull read, "Despite what your momma told you . . . violence does solve problems."

"And we spray-painted it on every building and wall we could," Kyle wrote in his memoir. "We wanted people to know, *we're here and we want to fuck with you. . . . You see us? We're the people kicking your ass. Fear us because we will kill you, motherfucker.*"[70]

Kyle was given the nickname "Legend." He got a tattoo of a Crusader cross on his arm. "I wanted everyone to know I was a Christian. I had it put in red, for blood. I hated the damn savages I'd been fighting," he wrote. "I always will."[71]

Following a day of sniping, after killing perhaps as many as six people, he would go back to his barracks to smoke Cuban Romeo y Julieta No. 3 cigars, play video games, watch porn, and work out.[72] On leave, something omitted in the movie, he was frequently arrested for drunken bar fights.[73] He dismissed politicians, hated the press, and disdained superior officers, exalting only the comradeship of warriors. His memoir glorifies white, "Christian" supremacy and war.[74] It is an angry tirade directed against anyone who questions the military's elite, professional killers. It is a mirror of the warped ideology of the jihadists he hates.

Kyle was shot dead at a shooting range near Dallas on February 2, 2013, along with a friend, Chad Littlefield.[75] A former marine, Eddie Ray Routh, who had been suffering from PTSD and severe psychological episodes, killed the two men and stole Kyle's pickup truck. Routh was sentenced to life in prison.[76]

"The xenophobic frenzy unleashed by Clint Eastwood's film of Kyle's book suggested the most vehement partisans of holy war flourish not only in the ravaged landscape of South and West Asia," Mishra writes.[77] "Such fanatics, who can be atheists as well as crusaders and jihadists, also lurk among America's best and brightest, emboldened by an endless support of money, arms, and even 'ideas' supplied by terrorism experts and clash-of-civilization theorists."[78]

Mishra finds a similar situation in his own country, India. "In their indifference to the common good, single-minded pursuit of private happiness, and narcissistic identification with an apparently ruthless strongman and uninhibited loudmouth, [Indian prime minister Narendra] Modi's angry voters mirror many electorates around the world—people gratified rather than appalled by trash-talk and the slaughter of old conventions,"[79] he writes. "The new horizons of individual desire and fear opened up by the neoliberal world economy do not favour democracy or human rights."[80] Mishra goes on:

ISIS, born during the implosion of Iraq, owes its existence more to Operation Infinite Justice and Enduring Freedom than to any Islamic theology. It is the quintessential product of a radical process of globalization in which governments, unable to protect their citizens from foreign invaders, brutal police, or economic turbulence, lose their moral and ideological legitimacy, creating a space for such non-state actors as armed gangs, mafia, vigilante groups, warlords and private revenge-seekers.

ISIS aims to create a Caliphate, but, like American re-
gime-changers, it cannot organize a political space, as distinct
from privatizing violence. Motivated by a selfie individualism,
the adepts of ISIS are better at destroying Valhalla than building
it. Ultimately, a passion for grand politics, manifest in ISIS's
Wagnerian-style annihilation, is what drives the Caliphate,
as much as it did [Gabriele] D'Annunzio's utopia [the short-
lived Italian Regency of Carnaro led by D'Annunzio, a self-
proclaimed Duce]. The will to power and craving for violence
as existential experience reconciles, as [philosopher and social
theorist Georges] Sorel prophesized, the varying religious and
ideological commitments of its adherents. The attempts to place
them in a long Islamic tradition miss how much these militants,
feverishly stylizing their murders and rapes on Instagram, reflect
an ultimate stage in the radicalization of the modern principle
of individual autonomy and equality: a form of strenuous self-
assertion that acknowledges no limits, and requires descent into
a moral abyss.[81]

The left is no more immune to these pathologies than the right.
Late one afternoon, about two dozen black-clad members of antifa
gathered in front of the Time Warner Center in New York City's Columbus Circle to protest the statue of Christopher Columbus. Many covered
their faces. Most of the protesters appeared to be in their twenties and
thirties. The event was called "NYC Says: Do It Like Durham!" It was
hosted by Hoods4Justice, Workers World Party, People's Power Assem-
blies, and NYC Shut It Down. Antifa is split on the issue of violence.
Those who champion violence align themselves with the black bloc.

A woman shouted rhythmically into a megaphone: "No Trump! No
KKK! No fascist USA!"

The group chanted her words back to her.

After about an hour they started marching south. Police told protest-
ers to get off the street. One young man refused to move to the sidewalk.
An officer grabbed him. Several more protesters grabbed his other arm.
The tug-of-war lasted about thirty seconds. The man's eyes were shut

as the protesters shouted. The police finally tackled and handcuffed the man. Soon the protesters continued marching, chanting, "No Trump, no KKK, no fascist USA!"

Antifa, like the black bloc—so named because they dress in black, obscure their faces, move as a unified mass, seek physical confrontations with police and opposing protesters, and destroy property—seems more established on the West Coast, where their presence at protests can grow to a few hundred in cities such as Portland, Seattle, and Berkeley.

It is more difficult to interview members of antifa and the black bloc than the alt-right. Members of the alt-right usually give their legal names, will endure an hour or more of questions, and, despite their diatribes against the press and "fake news," appear to revel in media attention. Alt-right organizations are hierarchical, with delineated lines of authority that often replicate the military. Groups have their own websites, will appoint spokespeople, and hold public meetings. None of this is true for antifa. The members of antifa are very wary of outsiders, with some justification. Most cover their faces and demand anonymity because of concerns about being identified by law enforcement.

Jeff—not his real name—was a thirty-one-year-old Hispanic. He was dressed in black. A red scarf covered the bottom half of his face. He had a master's degree in theater from Pace University. He owed $100,000 in student loans. He worked odd jobs, handing out coupons in Times Square or doing construction. He usually earned about $10 an hour.

"Antifa is not a group," he explained. "It's a tactic to protest against something. We do it anonymously to protect ourselves from the state. There's no real group to speak of. We should all be antifascists theoretically. It's just that we put our bodies on the line because sometimes you need to in order to protect the more marginalized and vulnerable.

"I've experienced exploitation," he said. "I've been not paid for my labor. I've been jobless. I've had to skip meals. I've had to go to Food Not Bombs for meals. Poverty is not a joke here. That's the core of our struggle: class struggle. I've been beaten up and arrested by the police. I've been stopped and frisked. I've felt the capacity and the power of the state, and I don't like it. As a Latino, [seeing] this war against Latinos, this genocide against black people, basically trying to finish off the genocide of indigenous people, I think it's important that people of color take a stand against white supremacists and this hetero-patriarchal, imperialist, capitalist power structure. If we don't do this no one else is going to.

"It's the responsibility of white people to dismantle white supremacy and they're failing pretty miserably at it," he said. "So the best thing we can do is survive and try to bring that system down by any means necessary. If our white allies want to join us, they're welcome. But we're not waiting around for them."

"The system is like a cancer," said Michael. He is of Filipino descent and was also dressed in black. "There's the disease. Then there's chemotherapy. They're both aggressive. But one is going to kill you. And one is going to save you. That's how I've always looked at antifa. The fight against the system is chemotherapy. The system is rooted in violence. The justification of nonviolence comes from some weird higher morality, and not understanding that violence is inherently part of the system. Self-defense is necessary. It's like dealing with domestic abuse. If someone is beating you up, you have the right to defend your body. We have a relationship with the system. And that relationship, unfortunately, is abusive. When people are like—'Oh, why are they breaking windows?' It's about addressing the nature of violence. We are trying to stop the system's violence.

"My mother came to this country as a caregiver," he said. "She worked for $5 an hour in some rich person's house. Being a single mom, who had to leave her child in the Philippines, that was a big sacrifice to be a part of the American dream. Who are you to suddenly tell a person who made so much of an effort to try to be here, 'By the way, you can't fucking be here because you're an immigrant'?"

Antifa and the black bloc oppose organized movements. This ensures their powerlessness. They call for preemptive violence—what adherents call "collective self-defense"—and insist that those whom they, and they alone, define as "fascists" deserve to be violently attacked and silenced. It is one thing to defend yourself from attack. It is quite another to go hunting for those you hate, armed with bats, bricks, rocks, clubs, and balloons filled with urine. The absolutism, which posits that the ends always justify the means, is the same disease that infects the alt-right. The surrendering of moral capital by the left will make any uprising against the corporate state impossible. These absolutists brand any critic, even one opposed to the corporate state and the empire, as a fascist apologist who deserves to be physically assaulted and silenced. My criticisms of antifa and the black bloc have resulted in protests outside lecture halls where I was speaking. The protesters, their faces covered, held signs that read "Fuck You! Chris Hedges." My address and phone number were posted on their websites and followers were told to "mess" with me. Death threats were called into some of my events. I arrived to give a talk in Los Angeles and the organizers, because of the threats, had hired three bodyguards. This binary vision of the world—you are with us or against us—characterizes all forms of fundamentalism.

"There are two kinds of Fascists," the Italian writer Ennio Flaiano said, "Fascists and anti-fascists." [82]

Antifa is another example of the country's expanding cults of violence, products of our decadent, militarized culture. "The masked militants of Antifa seem to be more inspired by Batman than by Marx or even by Bakunin," the political writer Diana Johnstone [83] wrote.

"The idea that the way to shut someone up is to punch him in the jaw is as American as Hollywood movies," Johnstone went on. "It is also typical of the gang war that prevails in certain parts of Los Angeles. Banding together with others 'like us' to fight against gangs of 'them' for control of turf is characteristic of young men in uncertain circumstances. The search for a cause can involve endowing such conduct with a political purpose: either fascist or antifascist. For disoriented youth, this is an alternative to joining the U.S. Marines.

"That is also the logic of U.S. imperialism," she wrote, "which habitually declares of its chosen enemies: 'All they understand is force.' Although antifa claim to be radical revolutionaries, their mindset is perfectly typical of the atmosphere of violence which prevails in militarized America. In another vein, antifa follows the trend of current Identity Politics excesses that are squelching free speech in what should be its citadel, academia. Words are considered so dangerous that 'safe spaces' must be established to protect people from them. This extreme vulnerability to injury from words is strangely linked to tolerance of real physical violence." [84]

Antifa seeks to justify its violence by arguing that the rise of fascism in Europe in the 1920s and 1930s could have been halted if antifascist groups had attacked fascist groups when they were first forming. This is a huge distortion of history.

"The argument that militant anti-fascists put forward, is that if you look at the historical fascism in the '20's and '30's, small groups often grow large," Mark Bray, the author of *Antifa: The Anti-Fascist Handbook*, said when we met in New York. "Parliamentary politics and debates can't consistently be counted upon to stop their advance. So the idea is to organize against small and medium-sized fascist groups as if they could be the germs, the seeds of future fascist movements and machines, essentially not allowing them to articulate their politics in a collective way or become mainstream in society."

"People talk about the store windows that are broken," said a twenty-one-year-old woman and antifa member who used the pseudonym "Nargis." "Usually, expensive cars are also targets. Yeah, it's private property. But it's private property that inevitably comes from oppression. Why does that person have a limo? The workers in his factory are not getting the money they need. Link those two things. The targets of antifa's violence are intrinsically linked to the symbols of exploitation. That moment of violence is nothing in comparison to the [violence that the] person who is burning the car has faced on a daily basis.

"I'm from India," she went on. "A lot of people in India would say, 'But Gandhi wouldn't have wanted this.' He also didn't do much for the anticolonial movement. There were millions of citizens on the ground, burning up police stations, throwing bombs at British administration buildings. Nobody talks about that."

Nazis and communists in Germany in the 1920s and 1930s aggressively sought out street violence. Confrontations mobilized and energized their base, many of whom lived on unemployment insurance and were filled with collective humiliation and rage. The Nazis organized marches through working-class neighborhoods where the Communist Party had a strong following to provoke clashes, while communists infiltrated Nazi meetings and rallies to instigate brawls.

Ian Kershaw, in his biography of Hitler, and Richard Evans in *The Coming of the Third Reich*, like most historians of the period, saw the widespread violence as polarizing the society. It wasn't, as Bray argues, that there wasn't enough violence perpetrated by the left. It was that there was too much. Violent confrontations were a daily part of life in late Weimar Germany. This chaos stoked the fears among the ruling elites and the middle class of a communist seizure of power. The Nazis may have been repugnant and even buffoonish, but they pledged, like the alt-right, to uphold traditional values and law and order. The Russian Revolution was only fifteen years old in 1932, a year before the Nazis came to power. It had already inspired the armed Spartacist Uprising of January 1919 in Berlin and a violent communist uprising in 1923 in Hamburg.

The left in Germany should have learned from the abortive uprisings that answering fascist violence with violence was political suicide. The ruling Social Democratic Party of Germany, which held power during the revolts in 1919 and 1923, created the Freikorps, a militia of demobilized soldiers, which became the antecedent to the Nazi Party, to quell the disturbances. The socialists turned to the right-wing militias and the military when it felt threatened from the left. Rosa Luxemburg's murder after the failed Spartacist Uprising illustrated the ultimate loyalties of liberal elites in a capitalist society: when threatened from the left, when the face of socialism showed itself in the streets, elites would—and will—make alliances with the most retrograde elements of society, including fascists, to crush the aspirations of the working class.

Liberalism, which Luxemburg called by its more appropriate name—"opportunism"—is an integral component of capitalism. When the citizens grow restive, it will soften and decry capitalism's excesses. But capitalism, Luxemburg argued, is an enemy that can never be appeased. Liberal reforms are used to stymie resistance and then later, when things grow quiet, revoked. The last century of labor struggles in the United States is an example of Luxemburg's observation.

"Social reform," Luxemburg wrote, "does not constitute an invasion into capitalist exploitation, but a regulating, an ordering of this exploitation in the interest of capitalist society itself."[85]

The fascists successfully used the specter of left-wing violence and a communist takeover to position themselves as the best equipped, because they were the most brutal, to save Germany in the 1920s and 1930s from communism. But they needed the communists and the socialists to play their part in the political theater, which they did.

The battle hymn of the Nazi Party, the Horst Wessel song—named for a brownshirt murdered by a member of the communist Red Front-Fighters' League who was swiftly elevated by the Nazis to a cult figure—celebrated the importance brute force played in the Nazi mystique. The song, as Evans wrote, "speaks volumes for the central role that violence plays in its quest for power."[86]

"Cynically exploited for publicity purposes by manipulative propagandists like Goebbels, it became a way of life for the ordinary young brownshirt like Wessel, as it was for the young unemployed workers of the Red Front-Fighters' League," Evans wrote of the street violence.[87] He went on:

> This kind of aggression found its outlet in constant clashes with rival paramilitaries on the streets. In the middle period of the Republic, beginning in 1924, all sides did indeed draw back from political violence on the scale of the January uprising of 1919, the Ruhr civil war of 1920 or the multiple conflicts of 1923, but if they put away their machine guns, it was only to replace them with rubber truncheons and knuckledusters. Even in the relatively stable years of 1924–9, it was claimed that Communists had killed 29 Nazi activists, while the Communists themselves reported that 92 "workers" had been killed in clashes with "fascists" from 1924 to 1930. Twenty-six members of the Steel Helmets [the armed branch of the conservative German National People's Party] were said to have fallen in the fight against Communism and 18 members of the Reichsbanner [the paramilitary organization set up by the Social Democratic Party, the German Center Party, and the liberal German Democratic Party to fight

the Nazis and the communists] in various incidents of political violence from 1924 to 1928. These were only the most serious consequences of the continual fighting between rival paramilitary groups; the same sources counted injuries sustained in the battles in the thousands, many of them more serious than mere bruises or broken bones.

In 1930 the figures rose dramatically, with the Nazis claiming to have suffered 17 deaths, rising to 42 in 1931 and 84 in 1932. In 1932, too, the Nazis reported that nearly ten thousand of their rank-and-file had been wounded in clashes with their opponents. The Communists reported 44 deaths in fights with the Nazis in 1930, 52 in 1931 and 75 in the first six months of 1932 alone, while over 50 Reichsbanner men died in battles with the Nazis on the streets from 1929 to 1933.[88]

Evans quotes the account of a communist sailor, Richard Krebs, who led a detachment of a hundred members of the Red Front-Fighters' League to break up a Nazi meeting in Bremen addressed by Hermann Göring. His detachment entered the hall and "each man was armed with a blackjack or brass knuckles." When Krebs rose to speak, Göring ordered the brownshirts to evict him. Krebs wrote:

A terrifying melee followed. Blackjacks, brass knuckles, clubs, heavy buckled belts, glasses and bottles were the weapons used. Pieces of glass and chairs hurtled over the heads of the audience. Men from both sides broke off chair legs and used them as bludgeons. Women fainted in the crash and scream of battle. Already dozens of heads and faces were bleeding, clothes were torn as the fighters dodged about amid masses of terrified but helpless spectators. The troopers fought like lions. Systematically they pressed us towards the main exit. The band struck up a martial tune. Hermann Göring stood calmly on the stage, his fists on his hips.[89]

As Evans writes, "scenes like this were being played out all over Germany in the early 1930s."[90] The police tacitly sided with the fascists, he wrote, since they "regarded the Red Front-Fighters' League as criminals. This followed a long police tradition of conflating crime and revolution, but also reflected the fact that Communist strongholds tended to be based in poor, slum areas that were centres of organized crime."[91] By the time Hitler came to power in 1933, the country was exhausted. It yearned for the stability and "law and order" promised by the Nazi Party. The violence and chaos, much of it instigated by the Nazis, had made the fascists if not attractive at least necessary.

The violent wing of antifa and the black bloc are an example of what Theodore Roszak in *The Making of a Counter Culture* called the "progressive adolescentization"[92] of the American left. These groups, leaderless and enthralled by their collective power to inflict violence, function as a mob. They assault not only the alt-right but reporters, liberals, and anticapitalists who criticize their assaults, and police. They provoke clashes with opponents, even if they are holding nonviolent events or marches.

"Their thinking is not only nonstrategic, but actively opposed to strategy," Derrick Jensen, author of several books, including *The Culture of Make Believe*, told me of groups that use these tactics. "They are unwilling to think critically about whether one is acting appropriately in the moment. I have no problem with someone violating boundaries [when] that violation is the smart, appropriate thing to do. I have a huge problem with people violating boundaries for the sake of violating boundaries. It is a lot easier to pick up a rock and throw it through the nearest window than it is to organize, or at least figure out which window you should throw a rock through if you are going to throw a rock."

The violent left revels in the hypermasculinity that enthralls the alt-right. This hypermasculinity taps into the dark lust that lurks within us to destroy, not only things but also human beings, especially when we suffer from collective humiliation. This lust overpowered most of the combatants in the wars I covered as a foreign correspondent. The crowd, especially when it is armed, gives to its member a godlike power. Marching as an anonymous mass—in black with faces covered—overcomes alienation, feelings of inadequacy, powerlessness, and loneliness. It provides comradeship. It allows an inchoate rage to be unleashed on any target. Pity, compassion, and tenderness are banished for the intoxication of force. It is the same intoxication felt by the swarms of police who pepper-spray and beat peaceful demonstrators. It is the intoxication that energizes groups of white racists marching down a street with Confederate flags. It turns human beings into beasts.

The explosive rise of the Occupy Wall Street movement, which saw protesters in 2011 from around the country take over public spaces to decry social inequality, came when a few women, trapped behind orange mesh netting, were pepper-sprayed by NYPD deputy inspector Anthony Bologna.[93] The cruelty of the state was exposed. And the Occupy movement, through its steadfast refusal to respond to police provocation, resonated across the country. Losing this moral authority, this ability to show, through nonviolent protest, the decadence of elites, is crippling to a resistance movement. It reduces us to the moral level of the oppressors. And that is what the oppressors want.

These absolutist sects are rigid and dogmatic. They alone possess the truth. They alone understand. They alone arrogate the right, because they are enlightened and we are not, to shut down competing points of view. They hear only their own voices. They heed only their own thoughts. They believe only their own clichés. And this makes them not only deeply intolerant, but dangerous.

"Once you are hostile to organization and strategic thinking, the only thing that remains is lifestyle purity," Jensen said. " 'Lifestylism' has supplanted organization in terms of a lot of mainstream environmental thinking. Instead of opposing the corporate state, [lifestylism maintains] we should use less toilet paper and should compost. This attitude is ineffective. Once you give up on organizing or are hostile to it, all you are left with is this hyperpurity that becomes rigid dogma. You attack people who, for example, use a telephone. This is true with vegans and questions of diet. It is true with anticar activists toward those who drive cars. It is the same with the anarchists. When I called the police after I received death threats I became to bloc anarchists 'a pig lover.'

"If you live on Ogoni land and you see that Ken Saro-Wiwa [the Nigerian author and environmental activist who was hanged in 1995 by the military dictatorship of General Sani Abacha] is murdered for acts of nonviolent resistance," Jensen said, "if you see that the land is still being trashed, then you might think about escalating. I don't have a problem with that. But we have to go through the process of trying to work with the system and getting screwed. It is only then that we get to move beyond it. We can't short-circuit the process. There is a maturation process we have to go through, as individuals and as a movement. We can't say, 'Hey, I'm going to throw a flowerpot at a cop because it is fun.' "

PROTESTERS FROM ANTIFA AND THE alt-right converged in Charlottesville, Virginia, on August 12, 2017. The clash was sparked by the proposed removal of Confederate general Robert E. Lee's statue. The "Unite the Right" rally to protest the removal attracted influential white supremacists such as former KKK grand wizard David Duke and writers from the *Daily Stormer*, a neo-Nazi publication.

"When the Trayvon Martin case happened, Michael Brown, and Tamir Rice, every single case it's some little black asshole behaving like a savage and he gets himself in trouble shockingly enough," Christopher Cantwell, one of "Unite the Right" rally's white supremacist speakers, told VICE News. "Whatever problems I might have with my fellow white people, they generally are not inclined to such behavior. You gotta take that into consideration when you're thinking about how to organize your society. . . . This is a part of the reason why we want an ethnostate. The blacks are killing each other in staggering numbers from coast to coast. We don't really want to have a part in that anymore. The fact that they resist us when we say, hey, we want a homeland, it's not shocking to me. These people want violence. And the Right is just meeting market demand."[94]

"This represents a turning point for the people of this country," Duke said in Charlottesville. "We are determined to take our country back. We're going to fulfill the promises of Donald Trump."[95]

Violence erupted before the rally started. Virginia governor Terry McAuliffe declared a state of emergency by 11:30 in the morning.

At noon, when the rally was scheduled to begin, white nationalist marchers, under pressure from crowds of antifa, retreated toward the Market Street parking garage. Antifa pursued them. A group of neo-Nazis separated DeAndre Harris, a twenty-year-old member of Black Lives Matter, from the counter-protesters and chased him into the garage.

They tore down the garage's wooden barricades and attacked Harris. Some used steel poles to beat him into unconsciousness. Counter-protesters flooded in to rescue Harris. The neo-Nazis, outnumbered, let him go.

The police arrived after Harris was pulled out of the garage. A large green Virginia state armored police vehicle blocked access to the garage. The National Guard, in camouflage helmets and bulletproof vests, carrying transparent shields, entered the garage after Harris was rescued. They soon reemerged and blocked antifa from reentering the parking facility.

Harris was bleeding profusely from his head and mouth.

"Every time I went to stand up I was knocked back down," Harris wrote later on his GoFundMe page. "If it was not for my friends that I came with I would have been beaten to a pulp." [96]

He suffered a concussion, an ulnar fracture in his arm, and required eight staples in his head. [97]

Darrell Vaughn, twenty-two, was standing alone with his Confederate flag around the corner from the garage. He looked nervous. He had been separated from his friends when counter-protesters attacked them. He had a deep gash on the left side of his forehead. Vaughn's face, neck, and hands were smeared with blood.

Vaughn, tall and heavyset, had driven with three friends from New Castle, Virginia, a small town two hours away, to protest the removal of the statue. They were attacked within ten minutes of their arrival in Charlottesville.

"I was hit four or five times by a baton," he said. "Three people was hitting me with it. Then my buddy, they were all over him. I tried to get to him. I just kept getting hit. I felt a little dizziness."

Vaughn lived the first twelve years of his life in Baltimore. There were shootings nightly in his neighborhood, he said.

"Our house got shot up," he recalled. "There's ten bullet holes on the side of the house."

His best friend's dad went to prison.

"On the street corner, alleyways, you see drug deals going on," he said. "People drugged up walking the streets . . . A big thing up there was stealing cars, taking it somewhere and burning it down. There's a patch of woods, I think it's called Herring Run Park, only patch of woods in that area. Go down there and there'd be ten, fifteen cars burned down. That still goes on today. A lot of it was drug deals gone wrong. Somebody got mad at somebody else. That was a way to take it out on someone."

Vaughn's father, a cabinetmaker, struggled with drug addiction. His parents frequently fought.

"He got into drugs during the nighttime," he said. "There were times when I walked downstairs to get something to drink in the kitchen, and he's passed out on the table. He almost burned the house down one night because he left the stove on and passed out."

Most of Vaughn's childhood friends, although he is white, were African Americans. Vaughn said he would have likely supported Black Lives Matter and antifa if his mother hadn't divorced his father and moved to Virginia when he was twelve.

Vaughn and his three younger brothers found themselves in New Castle, a rural town of 120 people.[98]

"No more 5:30 in the morning sirens," he said. "I'm like, where's all that at?

"The first year of school, I kept a lot to myself. Didn't talk to nobody because I thought everyone was different," he said. "When I moved to Virginia, I was still listening to rap music. And everyone up here was like, 'Why are you listening to that?'

"A year or two after I moved here, I just grew into it," he said. "I made a few friends. They took me hunting, fishing, riding on dirt roads, stuff like that, and after I done it I just stuck to it. Country stuff. I loved it."

He started listening to country music. When he bought his first truck he flew the Confederate flag. It was what everyone else did.

"I understand why Mom took us out of that environment," he said. "I'd probably be doing drugs, gone to jail, if I stayed in Baltimore."

When people in his small town started dismissing the Black Lives Matter movement as a media conspiracy, he did too. Police brutality, he said, does not disproportionately affect black people.

"A cop shoots a black person and it's all over the news," he said.

"When they shoot a white person, you don't hear nothing about that at all. They're trying to blame everything on racism. It's sickening. A lot of cops, they have to defend themselves. [A guy with a] fake gun, waving it around and he got shot because the police didn't know it was a fake gun—what do you expect them to do? They have to defend themselves."

When asked if he was referring to Tamir Rice, the twelve-year-old whose toy air gun was mistaken for a real weapon, Vaughn said, "It might have been that one. There's a lot of them like that. I can understand why people got mad but they had to defend themselves. They deserved what they got."

Vaughn, who could not afford to go to college, works as a power line repairman. His job, which involves climbing trees, is difficult and dangerous.

"I don't make the money I want to make," he said. "Right now I'm making $13.86 [an hour]."

The shouting between protesters and counter-protesters was muffled by the roar of a Virginia State Police helicopter circling overhead. Vaughn spotted one of his friends, Bobby Bryant, a thirty-three-year-old power line repairman.

Bryant said he had come to Charlottesville to "support history."

"I'm not KKK," he said. "I'm not Hitler. I mean, I believe in some things the KKK says. But other things I don't. When the KKK first started, what I gather is, if a dude raped a woman back in the day, they got their ass whooped, house burned down, and burned on the cross. I think that should still be in place. . . . Some stuff I don't like, how they hate black lives. Black lives do matter. But so do everyone else's lives."

Bryant and Vaughn paused. A woman, trembling, slowly limped past them. Another woman was helping her. The injured woman stopped to stare at the men, each of them holding Confederate flags. Her eyes widened. Vaughn and Bryant averted their gaze. Bloodied people begin to stagger onto the street. Many were shaking.

A twenty-year-old neo-Nazi had plowed his car into a crowd of counter-protesters, injuring nineteen and killing one. The scene of the crash was blocked off with yellow police tape. A pale young woman with brown hair, later identified as Heather Heyer, was motionless, seated on the ground, her back against a building. Several people surrounded her. Her eyes were closed. Her face was expressionless. She was dead.

When Vaughn learned that a counter-protester had been killed, he said nothing.

Someone else muttered, "Good."

The "Unite the Right" organizer, Jason Kessler, later tweeted, "Heather Heyer was a fat, disgusting Communist. Communists have killed 94 million. Looks like it was payback time." [99]

Nearly two dozen members of the left-wing Redneck Revolt, with red cloth around their necks, were in the street carrying semiautomatic weapons. Some wore black bulletproof vests. They described themselves as antiracist and anticapitalism. [100] About thirty-two members of the Pennsylvania Light Foot Militia were also there. [101] They wore green bulletproof vests and also carried semiautomatic rifles. They said they were there to provide protection for both sides, although it was the white nationalist organizers who initially contacted them to attend. [102] The Light Foots' assault weapons had thirty-round magazines. [103] Members of III% Security Force were also there. The Three Percenters' National Council later denounced members who chose to protect neo-Nazis, and discouraged its members from going to future events organized by white supremacists. [104]

The radical left and the radical right, each made up of people who have been cast aside by the cruelty of corporate capitalism, have embraced holy war. Their marginalized lives, battered by economic misery, have been filled with meaning. They hold themselves up as the vanguard of the oppressed. They claim the right to use force to silence those defined as the enemy. They sanctify anger. They are consumed by the adrenaline-driven urge for confrontation. These groups are separated, as Sigmund Freud wrote of those who engage in fratricide, by the "narcissism of minor differences." [105]

It was inevitable that we would reach this point. A paralyzed government, unable and unwilling to address the rudimentary needs of its citizens, as I saw in the former Yugoslavia and as was true in the Weimar Republic and Czarist Russia, empowers extremists. Extremism, as the social critic Christopher Lasch wrote, is "a refuge from the terrors of inner life." [106]

Germany's Nazi brownshirts had their counterparts in that nation's communist Red Front-Fighters' League. The far-right anticommunist death squad Alliance of Argentina had its counterpart in the guerrilla group the People's Revolutionary Army during the "Dirty War." The Farabundo Martí National Liberation Front (FMLN) rebels during the war I covered in El Salvador had their counterparts in the right-wing death squads, whose eventual demise seriously impeded the FMLN's ability to recruit. The Serbian nationalists, or Chetniks, in Yugoslavia had their counterparts in the Croatian nationalists, or Ustaše. The killing by one side justifies the killing by the other. And the killing is always sanctified in the name of martyrs.

The violence by antifa in Charlottesville saw a surge in interest and support for the movement, especially after the murder of Heyer. Antifa was applauded by some of the counter-protesters in Boston during an alt-right rally there on August 19, 2017. In Charlottesville, antifa activists filled the vacuum left by a passive police force, holding off neo-Nazi thugs who threatened the philosopher and activist Cornel West and clergy who were protesting the white nationalist event. This was a propaganda coup for antifa, which seeks to portray its use of violence as legitimate self-defense. Protecting West and the clergy members from physical assault was admirable. But this single act no more legitimizes antifa violence than the violence of the Gambino crime family was legitimized by the turkeys, Christmas gifts, and Fourth of July fireworks that John Gotti gave to his neighbors. Antifa, like the alt-right, is the product of a diseased society.

The white racists and neo-Nazis may be unsavory, but they too are victims. They too lost jobs and often live in poverty in deindustrialized wastelands. They too are frequently plagued by debt, foreclosures, bank repossessions, and the inability to repay student loans. They too suffer from evictions, opioid addictions, domestic violence, and despair. They too face bankruptcy because of medical bills. They too have seen social services gutted, public education degraded and privatized, and the infrastructure around them decay. They too often suffer from police abuse and mass incarceration. They too are often in despair and suffer from hopelessness.

Street clashes do not distress the ruling elites. These clashes divide the underclass. They divert activists from turning on structures of power. They give the corporate state the justification to impose harsher forms of control and expand the powers of police. When antifa assumes the right to curtail free speech, it becomes a weapon in the hands of its enemies to take that freedom away from everyone, especially the anticapitalists.

The focus on street violence diverts activists from the far less glamorous work of building relationships, alternative institutions, and community organizing that alone will make effective resistance possible.

"Politics isn't made of individuals," the political commentator Sophia Burns writes in "Catharsis Is Counter-Revolutionary." "It's made of classes. Political change doesn't come from feeling individually validated. It comes from collective action and organization within the working class. That means creating new institutions that meet our needs and defend against oppression." [107]

As long as personal, violent catharsis masquerades as acts of resistance, the corporate state is secure. Indeed, the corporate state welcomes this violence because violence is a language it can speak with a proficiency and ruthlessness that none of these groups can match.

The protests by the radical left, as history professor Aviva Chomsky points out, confuse moral purity, with politics.

"Rather than organizing for change, individuals seek to enact a statement about their own righteousness," Chomsky writes in "How (Not) to Challenge Racist Violence."

> They may boycott certain products, refuse to eat certain foods, or they may show up to marches or rallies whose only purpose is to demonstrate the moral superiority of the participants. White people may loudly claim that they recognize their privilege or declare themselves allies of people of color or other marginalized groups. People may declare their communities "no place for hate." Or they may show up at counter-marches to "stand up" to white nationalists or neo-Nazis. All of these types of "activism" emphasize self-improvement or self-expression rather than

seeking concrete change in society or policy. They are deeply, and deliberately, apolitical in the sense that they do not seek to address issues of power, resources, decision making, or how to bring about change.[108]

The corporate state seeks to discredit and shut down the anticapitalist left. Its natural allies are the neo-Nazis and the Christian fascists. The alt-right is bankrolled by the most retrograde forces in American capitalism. It has huge media platforms. It has placed its ideologues and sympathizers in positions of power, including in law enforcement, the military, and the White House. And it has carried out acts of domestic terrorism that dwarf anything carried out by the left. White supremacists were responsible for forty-nine homicides in twenty-six attacks in the United States from 2006 to 2016, far more than those committed by members of any other extremist group, according to a report issued in May 2017 by the FBI and the Department of Homeland Security.[109]

There is no moral equivalency between antifa and the alt-right. But by brawling in the streets, antifa allows the corporate state, which is terrified of a popular anticapitalist uprising, to use the false argument of moral equivalency to criminalize the work of all dissidents.

As the Southern Poverty Law Center states categorically in its pamphlet *Ten Ways to Fight Hate*, "Do not attend a hate rally."[110]

"Find another outlet for anger and frustration and for people's desire to do something," it recommends. "Hold a unity rally or parade to draw media attention away from hate. Hate has a First Amendment right. Courts have routinely upheld the constitutional right of the Ku Klux Klan and other hate groups to hold rallies and say whatever they want. Communities can restrict group movements to avoid conflicts with other citizens, but hate rallies will continue. Your efforts should focus on channeling people away from hate rallies."[111]

What took place in Charlottesville, like what took place in February 2017 when antifa and black bloc protesters thwarted U.C. Berkeley's attempt to host the crypto-fascist Milo Yiannopoulos,[112] was political theater. It was about giving radicals a stage. It was about elevating their self-image. It was about appearing heroic. It was about replacing personal alienation with comradeship. Most important, it was about the ability to project fear. This newfound power is exciting and intoxicating. Many of those in Charlottesville on the left and the right were carrying weapons. A neo-Nazi fired a round from a pistol in the direction of a counter-protester.[113] Neo-Nazis carried AR-15 rifles in Charlottesville and wore quasi-military uniforms and helmets that made them blend in with police and state security. There could easily have been a bloodbath. A march held in Sacramento, California, in June 2016 by the neo-Nazi Traditionalist Worker Party to protest attacks at Trump rallies ended with a number of people stabbed.[114] Police accused counter-protesters of initiating the violence.[115] It is a short series of steps from bats and ax handles to knives to guns.

The conflict will not end until followers of the alt-right and the anti-capitalist left are given a living wage and a voice in how we are governed. Take away a person's dignity, agency, and self-esteem and this is what you get. As political power devolves into a more naked form of corporate totalitarianism, as unemployment and underemployment expand, so will extremist groups. They will attract more sympathy and support as the wider population realizes, correctly, that Americans have been stripped of all ability to influence the decisions that affect their lives—lives that are getting steadily worse.

Some in the liberal class, deeply complicit in the corporate assault on the country and embracing the dead end of identity politics, will seek to regain credibility by defending the violence by groups such as antifa. Natasha Lennard, for example, in *The Nation* calls the "video of neo-Nazi Richard Spencer getting punched in the face" an act of "kinetic beauty."[116] She writes, "if we recognize fascism in Trump's ascendance, our response must be anti-fascist in nature. The history of anti-fascist action is not one of polite protest, nor failed appeals to reasoned debate with racists, but direct, aggressive confrontation."[117]

This violence-as-beauty rhetoric is at the core of these movements. It saturates the vocabulary of the right-wing corporate oligarchs, including Trump, antifa, and the black bloc. This rhetoric poisons discourse. It dehumanizes whole segments of the population. It shuts out those who speak with nuance and compassion, especially when they attempt to acknowledge the suffering and humanity of opponents. It thrusts the society into a demented universe of them and us. It elevates violence to the highest good. It eschews self-criticism and self-reflection. It is the apotheosis of alienation, a celebration, as Walter Benjamin wrote, of our "own destruction as an aesthetic pleasure."[118]

6

GAMBLING

I played golf with my friends, and then I started to play with the hustlers.
And I learned a lot. I learned about golf; I learned about gambling. I
learned about everything.

DONALD TRUMP[1]

Ahmed's father-in-law took him to the Taj Mahal in Atlantic City on his first night in the U.S. It was 1993. The Taj Mahal had opened three years earlier. Ahmed, not his real name, was dazzled by the opulence, the glittering crystal chandeliers and gilded columns. He was told that the casino was owned by a famous American billionaire. The Taj Mahal was the emblem of everything that America was supposed to promise.

Ahmed had arrived from Syria, where he was an electrician with a college degree. He was a prudent and responsible young man who came to the U.S. to marry his fiancée, a childhood sweetheart. They were at the Taj to celebrate.

It was his first time in a casino. His senses were overwhelmed. The free alcohol, the abundance of steak and seafood in buffets, and the soothing soundtracks were alluring and seductive.

He won $100 that night playing slot machines.

"I felt great," he said. "I thought, 'Wow, I love the United States.' "

He itched to return to the casino, but he was living at his in-laws' house. It was difficult to escape their gaze. He found an excuse two weeks later. He took his wife to the Taj Mahal to celebrate the Fourth of July.

The newlyweds moved into their own house around Christmas. Ahmed was freed from his in-laws. He began visiting the Taj Mahal every other week. He started to accumulate losses but convinced himself he could win them back.

"You keep chasing it," Ahmed said. "The more you lose the more you chase. I need to catch up. I lost $1,000 at first. Now I've lost $5,000. I have to keep playing to win it back."

He would withdraw money from the ATM before going home, to give his wife the illusion that he was winning. His wife wasn't watching their finances closely. It was the 1990s—before the advent of instant online banking. Ahmed moved money back and forth between their banks to prevent her from seeing their dwindling savings. Eventually he stopped caring how much he lost. He gambled for the high, to stay in what gamblers call the "zone." He craved the lulling sounds of the slot machines and the escape from reality. He manufactured fights with his wife to give himself an excuse to go to the Taj Mahal.

"I come home," he said. "She's happy. She made me lunch or dinner. But I find something. I find any reason to have a fight with her. 'Oh she made me upset so I have to leave the house now.' So I get in my car and go straight to the casino."

Ahmed's wife confronted him in 1998 about the missing money and his long hours away from home. She suspected he was having an affair. He told her about his gambling addiction.

"She said she'd rather me be cheating than put us in all this debt," Ahmed said. "We're going to lose our home now."

His wife took him to his first Gamblers Anonymous (GA) meeting in July 1998. He continued visiting the casino behind her back. She divorced him six weeks later and left with their baby son. Ahmed started going to the Taj Mahal daily.

"That's when things got really bad," he said. "I'd stay at the casino until five in the morning. Drive to work. After work drive straight to the casino."

He owned five gas stations. He tried to limit his gambling by gambling only with the earnings he made from one of his gas stations.

"I'd spend the money within three hours or so, usually $5,000 a day," he said. He made $5,000 a day from one of his gas stations. "Then I'd drive back to another gas station. Take all the money earned from that gas station that day and go back to the casino. After that money is spent I think, 'It's only two or three o'clock in the morning, I still have time.' I'd go to the other gas station. In the same night I'd drive back and forth two or three times. Fifty miles each way."

He drove back and forth between Atlantic City and his gas stations every night.

"I never slept," he said. "I slept two hours in my car sometimes. Sometimes I take a nap in a hotel at the casino."

He lost all sense of time. He was often unsure of what day it was.

He sued a former employee for stealing money. He forgot to show up for the lawsuit. He played slot machines for as long as ten or twelve hours. He went longer and longer periods without sleep. The police pulled him over three times in the course of sixty days for reckless driving. On one night he drove a car he was supposed to be selling at his gas station. It had no registration or insurance. He got into an accident. The police impounded the car.

The police dropped him off at the Galloway Diner. It was twelve miles from the Taj Mahal. Ahmed was carrying $10,000 in cash. He could have paid for a cab to drive him to the Taj Mahal. He walked for four hours instead.

"The $20 I would have spent on the cab was going to be the $20 I was going to win with," Ahmed said.

He saved every cent to gamble with. He did not speak to his mother for six years to avoid paying for a phone card.

"I never spent $20 to call my mom but I spent $5,000 a day at the casino," he said. "It doesn't make sense. It's crazy thinking."

The court suspended Ahmed's driver's license for five years.

"I got out of court," he said. "My car was parked five blocks away. I got in my car and drove to the casino. It's crazy. The crazy things we do to gamble. Nothing could stop me from gambling."

Whenever he drove to Atlantic City, he would stop at the last gas station on the left side of White Horse Pike to fill up his tank and buy a carton of cigarettes. He knew by the time he left the casino he wouldn't have any money for gas or cigarettes. He could no longer meet his mortgage payments.

"My house was worth almost half a million dollars," he said. "I sold it for $325,000 or $330,000 or so because I couldn't afford to keep it anymore. I just accepted the first offer and sold it. I made about $68,000 from the house."

He took the $68,000 and drove to Atlantic City.

"That's the craziness," he said. "Why go to the casino with $68,000? What am I going to get out of that?"

When he signed an apartment lease, he paid the landlord $12,000 up front to cover the rent for the next thirteen months. He knew he would gamble away the rest of his money.

"Every time I sat there gambling, I knew in the back of my mind I'm going to lose my house," he said. "I'm going to end up on the streets. I'm going to kill myself. I wasn't happy. But I just couldn't stop."

He slept in his apartment for four nights out of the thirteen months he rented it. Although he rarely went inside his apartment, he would drive by to pick up his mail. He didn't want the mailman to report him missing. If the police came searching for him it might interrupt his gambling. He would toss unopened electric, phone, and car bills in the backseat and drive back to Atlantic City.

And then he had a falling-out with the Taj Mahal. The slot attendants were switching shifts early one morning. They made him wait for his winnings. It made Ahmed late for work. He erupted in anger. He started gambling at the Showboat, the casino connected to the Taj Mahal. He had, however, amassed 40,000 comp points at the Taj Mahal. He returned to trade in his points for crab, fish, and steak at the Taj Mahal buffet. He traded in the points for a pool table and two televisions: a forty-two-inch and a seventy-two-inch.

"I never even turned the TV on," he said. "I spent all of my time at the casino."

When a friend asked him how much his television cost him he joked it was worth a million dollars. Ahmed lost over a million dollars during his ten-plus years of addiction.

"My W2 form in 2001 showed I made $110,000 that year but I lost a quarter of a million dollars that same year," he said. "My accountant was pulling his hair. He said, 'How do you lose that much money if that's all you made?' Because it's all the money I won from the casinos."

He became homeless when his apartment lease ended after the thirteen months. He slept in his car for the next eighty days. The bank repossessed his car. He slept on the streets for a week. He decided to commit suicide.

"I was going to end my life then," Ahmed said. "I couldn't take it."

"How many people have killed themselves at the casino?" he asked. "A lot of people jump from the roof of casinos."

He decided to gamble one last time. He took public transportation to the closest casino—the Parx Casino in Philadelphia. He was so confused he took four buses and two trains to get to a casino that was ten minutes away. He arrived at Parx Casino after five hours.

That night he won $140,000.

"I will never forget that night," he said. "I could have walked away with that money to buy a house and a brand-new car. But it wasn't about the money. We gamble for the high. It is like a drug."

He took his winnings and gambled throughout the night. By 5:00 a.m. he was broke. He stood there, like a zombie, waiting for the clock to turn 6:00 so he could use his free slot play voucher. When players earn a certain number of points in one night, they can play one free slot game starting at 6:00 a.m.

"When I won that money I made deals with myself," he said. " 'I don't think I need $140,000. I'll be fine with $100,000.' Then, 'I think I don't need $100,000. Eighty thousand dollars will do it. Sixty thousand dollars will do it. Twenty thousand dollars will do it. You know what, all I need is $2,000. I have to pay $1,200 to get my car back. I'll still have $800 left for a hotel room that will last until I get my paycheck again.' And then—'Well, I don't really need my car, I'll just keep $500 for the hotel room.' Then after that, 'You know what, $100 will do it. I'll borrow some money from someone.' Then I thought I'm going to kill myself anyway. What do I need money for? Then the last $100 was gone. I had nothing. That was how my brain worked. We are insane."

He thought of ways he would kill himself as he waited for the free slot play. He had been having suicidal thoughts for the last ten years. When he parked on the top floor of the Taj Mahal garage he would imagine hitting the gas before slamming the brakes and flipping his Jeep Cherokee.

"I wasn't afraid of dying," Ahmed said. "I was afraid that if I didn't die I would spend the rest of my life disabled with no way to kill myself."

He was saved by a chance encounter with a Gamblers Anonymous member at the Parx. They were relieved to see each other. They left the casino together and promised to help each other recover.

Ahmed slept on the carpeted floor of his fellow GA member's apartment for three months. Then he moved in with his GA sponsor for three years. He had one relapse when he returned to the Taj Mahal for a month. But he was able to gradually free himself from his addiction. Ahmed, who is forty-nine, has a new wife and a four-year-old child. He recently bought a house and a dog. His eldest son from his first marriage is twenty-two. Ahmed often feels anger and guilt when he thinks of him. These feelings make him want to gamble. He goes to three GA meetings every week.

"Sometimes the guilt would take me back," he said. "The guilt I have towards my son, my ex-wife, my mom. We gamble to punish ourselves. I deserve to be punished. I deserve to be hungry, to be angry, to be tired all the time. I deserve any kind of punishment because I did that to my family.

"We want to gamble when we feel boredom, loneliness, grief, loss, or when we want to celebrate good fortune," he said. "We try to find any excuse to go back and gamble. That's why the meetings are very important to us. Whenever something happens—if we don't go to the meeting and talk about it—we go and gamble."

Ahmed was one of two people who attended a GA meeting in a Sunday School classroom in New Jersey on a Saturday night. The other six members had stopped coming.

"The casino gives me statements," he said. "It shows how much I won and lost. If you win over $12,000 you have to pay taxes on it. I owed the IRS thousands and thousands of dollars. I just finished paying it off.

I paid the IRS from 2000 to 2014. They were taking money every two weeks from my paycheck. Two thousand fifteen was the first year that I got money back after I filed my taxes."

"There is no cure," he said. "We never get better."

IT WAS AN OVERCAST OCTOBER afternoon in 2016, a day before the Trump Taj Mahal casino was scheduled to close at 5:59 a.m. I turned off Pacific Avenue. I drove between two huge white gates flanked by two-ton white, cast-stone elephants. The Taj Mahal entrance was topped by an array of seventy turquoise and teal fiberglass minarets and a dozen gold-tipped domes. A neon sign with red and gold lettering read, "Trump Taj Majal Casino and Resorts." A lighted fountain in front of the glass casino doors was decorated by two rows of six white and gold urns. The Trump Taj Mahal cost $1.2 billion to build. Trump called it the "eighth wonder of the world." Casino operators were instructed to answer incoming calls with the words, "Thank you for calling the Trump Taj Majal, where wonders never cease." The waitresses wore "harem girl" outfits. It would go through bankruptcy five times.

The casino was, when it was built, New Jersey's tallest building and the world's largest casino. The opulent suites, when they were opened, were named after historical personalities—Alexander the Great, Michelangelo, Napoleon, Cleopatra. The suites cost around $10,000 a day. Those in the penthouse, whether in the Egyptian suite or the cobalt blue French Emperor suite, arrived by helicopter on the roof. Charter buses, far below, unloaded gamblers from New York, Maryland, New Jersey, and as far away as Pittsburgh and Cleveland. It was possible, from the heights above, to look down on the toiling serfs, hoping through a run of luck to rise skyward. Like most of Trump's buildings, the floor numbers were inflated—and false. The second floor of the Taj Mahal hotel was labeled as the 14th on the elevator panel. The elevator climbed from there to the top, the "51st" floor, in reality the 42nd floor.

A few dozen striking casino workers in ponchos and red shirts, braving the drizzle, held "Unite Here!" signs on the sidewalk. I passed red and orange lamps flanking the road. Three thousand casino employees would be out of work within twenty-four hours.

There were 5,300 parking places in the two colossal parking decks outside the casino. A tired, middle-aged woman who looked as if she was from South Asia sat in the parking booth. She took my $10. There was a handwritten note—"tips appreciated"—taped to the booth window. About a dozen cars were parked on the dimly lit first floor. Tunnels and enclosed halls from the parking decks led directly into the casino. The twenty-two-space tour bus terminal was empty. Most of the twelve restaurants in the casino were closed. The casino's arena, seating 5,500, had shut its doors. The Trump Taj Mahal was about to die.

The spread of casinos and gambling across the Northeast, begun on Native American reservations in the 1990s, has cut gambling revenues in half in Atlantic City.[2] Gambling revenue peaked in 2006 at $5.2 billion in Atlantic City.[3] Forty states have legalized some form of gambling.[4] A casino was opened in Queens, New York, eleven opened in Pennsylvania, and others were built in Maryland and Ohio. If casinos open in northern New Jersey, as some developers are proposing, the gambling industry in Atlantic City will see several more bankruptcies and perhaps collapse. It is an economic model built on sand.

"In a postindustrial United States, casinos have become both a metaphor for a roller-coaster economy and a key service industry selling experiences and dreams," write Ellen Mutari and Deborah M. Figart in *Just One More Hand: Life in the Casino Economy.* "As various economic bubbles have burst, the U.S. economy since the start of the new millennium has seemed to be more of a casino than a factory: a place where you put down your money and cross your fingers. Buying a home, saving for retirement, getting a student loan, starting a business, or even accepting a job seem like risky ventures rather than sure bets. In such turbulent times, we all seem to be gamblers, even when we do not intend to be."[5]

There were 900 commercial casinos in the U.S., in 2017, according to the American Gaming Association.[6] Casinos make more than $37 billion annually.[7] This is more profit than the music industry ($6.8 billion) and movie industry ($10.7 billion) combined.[8] It is more than the $17.8 billion earned by the four major U.S. sports leagues.[9] Slot machines and video poker generate at least 62 percent of casino revenues, according to a 2013 American Gaming Association report.[10] Casinos in Iowa and South Dakota receive over 90 percent of their revenues from slots.[11]

When I walked inside the Taj, glittering Austrian crystal chandeliers, which cost $14 million each,[12] dangled over the softly lit interior. Many were missing strings of beads. The walls were covered with mirrors. I looked out at rows of gaming tables, blackjack tables, roulette wheels, and three thousand slot machines[13] that twinkled with colored lights. The slot machines emitted beeps, hums, and dings of various pitches. They stretched over an area the size of three football fields. The gambling floor was almost empty. The dealers stood in front of vacant, felt-covered tables. Most of the gamblers who slumped in the cushioned chairs in front of the slot machines were elderly and haggard. They robotically pulled down levers or pushed square buttons. They stared blankly at the spinning screens in front of them. One slot machine generates between $200 and $300 a day for the casino. The dedicated gamblers are given courtesy drinks. Housekeepers occasionally enter rooms to discover the corpses of elderly men or women who spent hours drinking more alcohol than their bodies could absorb. It is not uncommon for slot players to wet and soil themselves.

The seventeen computerized check-in desks near the entrance were empty. A lone clerk stood behind the long counter facing empty rope lines. Toilets in the bathrooms, adorned with Carrera marble, were covered with plastic bags and had signs reading "Out of Order."

I walked along the soiled and worn carpet through long, deserted, and poorly lit corridors on the upper floors. Semicircular beige wall sconces, some of which enclosed burned-out bulbs, were placed every few feet on either side of the hall. The sconces were dirty and cracked. The ceiling had brown water spots. The air smelled of mold. Three quarters of the 1,250 rooms had been mothballed. The casino felt like a ghost ship. It reminded me of the hulking, gutted casinos I saw in the former Yugoslavia during the war. When the Yugoslav economy collapsed in the late 1980s, huge state enterprises closed. Unemployment soared. The economy nosedived. The Yugoslav state, in desperate need of foreign currency, licensed an array of casinos to attract European tourists. Trying to build a viable economy from gambling proved futile, although it enriched and empowered organized crime.

Gambling is about creating illusions. The spinning reels on the slots, for example, are fake. They do not slowly run out of momentum. They are programmed to look that way. Computer chips determine the outcome the moment the button is pushed or the lever pulled.

"Thus it is possible for game designers to reduce the odds of hitting a big jackpot from 1 in 10,648 to 1 in 137 million," writes John Rosengren in *The Atlantic*. "Moreover, it is almost impossible for a slots player to have any idea of the actual odds of winning any jackpot, however large or small. Virtual reel mapping has also enabled a deliberately misleading feature, the 'near miss.' That's when a jackpot symbol appears directly above or below the payline. The intent is to give the player the impression of having *almost* won—when, in fact, he or she is no closer to having won than if the symbol had not appeared on the reel at all. Some slot machines are specifically programmed to offer up this near-miss result far more often than they would if they operated by sheer chance, and the psychological impact can be powerful, leading players to think, *I was so close. Maybe next time.*"[14]

The adrenaline rush of anticipation, administered in twenty-second bursts, on slot machines reconfigures the human brain over hours, days, weeks, months, and years to create a crippling addiction the industry calls "continuous gaming productivity." Heart rates and blood pressure rise with each bet. Time, space, the value of money, and human relationships dissolve. It is pure escapism and extreme social isolation. And many gamblers, like Ahmed, lose everything: marriages, families, jobs, mental health, and even their lives. One in five gambling addicts attempts suicide—the highest rate among addicts of any kind, according to the National Council on Problem Gambling.[15]

This is the new American capitalism. It is not about producing products but escapist fantasies. It is about trying to make money with money whether on Wall Street or in casinos. It is a world of glitter and noise in which social status is determined by the amount of money you are willing to spend. The more you spend, the more you are pampered. High-volume players are given free hotel rooms and gifts. They are handed passes for special "clubs" with buffets. Scantily clad female hostesses hover around them with complimentary drinks. They are invited, if they spend enough, to exclusive parties with supermodels and Hall of Fame athletes. The large colored chips convert cash into a sort of Monopoly money—as if it is all just a game.

Casinos build detailed profiles of their most dedicated gamblers. It issues them player cards that take the place of money or tickets. The player card acts like a debit card. It also allows the casino to track a gambler's bets and individual winnings and losses. It records how often a gambler pushes the buttons on the slot machines, how fast a gambler plays, the value of the bets, and how long the gambler stays at the machine. Machines are calibrated to adapt to personal gambling rates, to speed up or slow down the betting. The card also records food, drink, and hotel room preferences.

The traits and the habits of the gambler, triangulated with demographic data, are pieced together to allow the industry to build player profiles. These profiles know at what point a player accumulates too many losses and too much pain and walks away from a machine. A few moments before that pain threshold is reached, a hostess will magically appear with a voucher for a free meal, drinks, or tickets to a show. Gamblers are also tracked from above. On the ceiling are hundreds of "eyes in the sky," [16] closed circuit television cameras that allow casino security to watch for cheating or misconduct by patrons and employees. Plainclothes security personnel patrol the floor, often placing small bets to mask their presence.

"Many surveillance and marketing innovations first used in casinos were only later adapted to other domains," writes Natasha Dow Schüll in her book *Addicted by Design*, "including airports, financial trading floors, consumer shopping malls, insurance agencies, banks, and government programs like Homeland Security." [17]

"They have an algorithm that senses your pain points, your sweet spots," Schüll told me when I interviewed her in New York. "The zone is a term that I kept hearing over and over again as I went to Gamblers Anonymous meetings and spoke to gambling addicts. This really describes a state of flow where time, space, monetary value, and other people fall away. You might say a state of flow, or the zone, sounds very different from the thrills and suspense of gambling. But what the casinos have hit upon is that you actually make more money when you design a flow space into these machines. People don't even know that they're losing. They just sit there. Again, it's time on machines."

Casinos have devised formulas to calculate the "predicted lifetime value" of dedicated patrons.[18] Gamblers are assigned value rankings. The biggest losers are called "whales."[19]

A casino is able to manage twenty thousand behavioral models per second off multiple floors through player cards.[20] Casinos create what they call "crowd contouring" to lure targeted groups of gamblers into casinos by appealing to their habits, schedules, and gambling proclivities. Schüll writes:

> "Let's say we want to see the profitability of females fifty-five and older. *Who are these ladies? Where do they live? How can we target them better?*" The representative showed an animated map of an unidentified city, titled "ground floor, little old ladies, carded play time." As the clock in the upper left-hand corner spun, the city flared and pulsed with color, registering the home addresses of older women gamblers as they began and ended sessions of machine play on the ground floor of one casino over the course of a day. In the wee hours, small circles of color dotted the landscape, with red centers indicating the neighborhoods most heavily populated by current onsite players. Starting at 8 a.m., the center of the map dramatically blossomed outward into a bright red flower, reaching maximum size at 11 a.m. and shrinking back in the evening; across the city, discrete pockets of "little old ladies" continued to gamble throughout the night. Armed with this knowledge, the casino was in a position to tailor its offerings to the play schedules and affinities of the market segment in question.[21]

There was no lobby at the casino. I was funneled from the entrance directly onto the gambling floor. It felt claustrophobic. It was disconcerting not to see exits, clocks, or windows. This was by design. Casinos are open twenty-four hours a day. Once you are inside, the owners do not want reminders of the world outside. The odds over time always favor the casino. The longer you gamble the more you lose.

"The lobby that's there is really just shunting you into these other profit spaces," Schüll told me. "Carpets are not supposed to ever have right angles because this would mean casino patrons have to stop and reflect and make a conscious decision to turn into a gaming area. Instead, you want to curve their bodies around. And the places they sit are covered, enclosed, very welcoming little cocoons where they can disappear in front of these slot machines. It's a logic of convolution and confusion. These are the actual words they use. It's called space elimination. It's not like modern architecture where you have clear lines of sight. You're trying to give people perspective. They're trying to take people's perspective away and move them where they want them to go. This logic, which plays out in the carpets and even how far the ceiling comes down, is also playing out in the design of the cabinets and screens. Disorientation is a design strategy. They want to keep patrons in a zone where—and I'm quoting from a casino design manual—they remain 'open and permeable to emotional triggers.' No clocks. Clocks are like a right angle. It brings you into time and space. It locates you. They don't want you to feel located. They want to disorient you."

The goal, at least at the Taj Mahal, was to become Donald Trump. Trump, whose name and image were ubiquitous in the Taj Mahal, is the first casino magnate to become president. A casino is as enticing as it is ruthless. The moment your money is gone you are worthless. The smiles, the gifts, the attention, the harem girls with the drinks, and the free rooms vanish. You disappear down the rabbit hole and another sucker walks through the door to take your place.

AMERICANS IN 2016 LOST $116.9 billion gambling.[22] There are 404 land-based casinos, 500 tribal casinos, 327 card rooms, 54 racetracks, and 16,089 gaming devices placed in convenience stores, gas stations, bars, airports, and even supermarkets.[23] It is estimated the country spends as much as $400 billion a year illegally betting on sports.[24] Americans spend another $70 billion—or $300 for every adult in the country—on lottery tickets. Taxes on gambling—state and local governments earned $27.7 billion in 2015—are vital to budgets beset by declining tax revenue.[25] "State lotteries provided more revenue than state corporate income taxes in 11 of the 43 states where they were legal, including Delaware, Rhode Island, and South Dakota," Derek Thompson writes in *The Atlantic*. "The poorest third of households buy half of all lotto tickets."[26] This stealth tax is used to cover the taxes the rich and corporations no longer pay.

Slot machines cater, like the games on computers and phones, to the longing to flee from the oppressive world of dead-end jobs, crippling debt, social stagnation, and a dysfunctional political system. They shape our behavior with constant bursts of stimulation. We become rats in a Skinner box. We frantically pull levers until we are addicted and, finally entranced, by our adrenaline-driven compulsion to achieve fleeting and intermittent rewards. Behavioral psychologist B. F. Skinner found that when pigeons and rats did not know when or how much they would be rewarded, they pressed levers or pedals compulsively. Skinner used slot machines as a metaphor for his experiment.[27]

The engineers of America's gambling industry are as skillful at forming addiction as the country's top five opioid producers—Purdue Pharma, Johnson & Johnson, Insys Therapeutics, Mylan, and Depomed. Slot machines, which account for 85 percent of all gambling revenue,[28] replicate the effects of pharmacological opiates.

Roger Caillois, a French sociologist, wrote that the pathologies of a culture are captured in the games the culture venerates.[29] The old forms of gambling—blackjack or poker—allowed the gambler to take risks, make decisions, and even, in his or her mind, achieve a kind of individualism or heroism at the gambling table. It was a way to rise above a monochromatic existence. It was a way to assert an alternative identity.

Machine gambling, however, is an erasure of the self. Slot machines, as the sociologist Henry Lesieur wrote, are an "addiction delivery device."[30] They are electronic morphine,[31] "the crack cocaine of gambling."[32] They are about creating somnambulism, putting a player into a trancelike state that can last for hours. It is a pathway, as Schüll points out, to becoming the walking dead. It feeds "the death instinct," the overpowering drive by a depressed and traumatized person to seek pleasure in a self-destructive activity that kills the organism.

"It is not the chance of winning to which they become addicted," writes Schüll in *Addiction by Design*, "rather, what addicts them is the world-dissolving state of subjective suspension and affective calm they derive from machine play." [33]

The science of keeping people in front of slot machines—called "time of device" within the industry—has led to the creation of ergonomic consoles, appealing, warm pixilation on screens, seductive video graphics, and surround-sound acoustics. [34] The hype and glitter of a casino befits a gigantic Venus flytrap. Fields of flashing slot machines emit four hundred different sounds all in the key of C because it is supposed to be less fatiguing than other keys. [35] Gamblers, their brains numbed into submission, mechanically surrender their money. The images on the slots, often lifted from familiar television shows such as *Bonanza*, *I Love Lucy*, and *The Price Is Right* or movies like *Aladdin or The Wizard of Oz*, along with board games such as Monopoly, are used to make gamblers feel as if the machines are familiar. The red lights and fast music accelerate the rate of gambling. Pleasant scents and oxygen, to keep players awake, are pumped through the floor vents. Soft lights make the room feel like a womb.

"Gamblers would say, 'It's so weird but sometimes when I win a big jackpot I feel angry and frustrated,' " Schüll said. "What they're playing for is not to win, but to stay in the zone. Winning disrupts that because suddenly the machine is frozen, it's not letting you keep going. What are you going to do with that winning anyway? You're just going to feed it back into the machines. This is more about mood modulation. Affect modulation. Using technologies to dampen anxieties and exit the world. We don't just see it in Las Vegas. We see it in the subways every morning. The rise of all of these screen-based technologies and the little games that we've all become so absorbed in. What gamblers articulate is a desire to really lose a sense of self. They lose time, space, money value, and a sense of being in the world.

"It's the flip side to the incredible pressure, which is experienced as a burden, to self-manage, to make choices, to always be maximizing as you're living life in this entrepreneurial mode," she said.

"People have called it a mode of ludo-capitalism [the profiting from games]," she said. "In a way, you can connect that to the ludo-politics that we see. Pleasure. To get what you want. What you want is to escape into a flow, to be taken away. We see this in the political domain a lot— in the rallies, in the surging of feelings, the distraction. If you look at the way a casino is designed, and you remember that Trump is a designer of many casinos, including his non-casino properties, they follow the same design logic of disorientation and trying to sweep people away from themselves, away from rationality, away from a position where they have clear lines of sight and can act as decision-making subjects. You see that on the floors of casinos. You see that in political rhetoric today."

The casinos drove two hundred restaurants in Atlantic City out of business.

"Before the casinos, the kitchen at Curt Kugel's Luigi's restaurant had cranked out as many as 1,000 dinners a night when the Miss America Pageant or the AFL-CIO convention came to town," writes Bryant Simon in *Boardwalk of Dreams: Atlantic City and the Fate of Urban America*.[36] After the Resorts casino opened in 1978, the first legal casino built outside Nevada, Kugel's revenues swiftly fell by half.

By the time Bill Moyers aired a CBS special called *Big Gamble in Atlantic City* in 1986, Kugel's restaurant had been replaced by a parking lot. Father Dante Girolami at St. Nicholas of Tolentine Roman Catholic Church told Moyers his congregation of seven hundred families had dwindled to two. His masses were usually empty or visited by luckless gamblers practicing "the virtue of hope."[37]

Drugs and prostitutes flooded the city. Trump hired Joseph Weichselbaum, a three-time convicted felon who was eventually imprisoned for trafficking marijuana and cocaine, to manage his helicopter fleet.[38] The helicopter service ferried the rich to and from Trump casinos. The high rollers in Atlantic City could get anything they desired, from sex to cocaine. Weichselbaum's easy access to drugs was probably an asset. When Weichselbaum was waiting for his sentence, Trump wrote to the judge saying he was "a credit to the community."[39] The trafficker received three years, although he served only eighteen months. The couriers who physically delivered the drugs for Weichselbaum got up to twenty years.

Weichselbaum moved into Trump Tower with his girlfriend when he was released from prison.

The array of casino cameras and security, coupled with the city's high crime rate and poverty, subliminally send the message that gamblers are safe only on casino property. And this is probably true. When I was reporting in the Atlantic City during October and November 2016, there were twenty-four attempted robberies or armed robberies at convenience stores and two robberies of taxi drivers.

Casinos are constructed, as Mike Davis and Hal Rothman write, like all postmodern cities based on fear, anxiety, and the yearning for safety and exclusion.[40] Public spaces are unsafe and depressing.

"The Casino Reinvestment Development Authority (CRDA), the public corporation that oversaw the reinvestment of casino dollars, spent $88 million, raised from parking fees and the redevelopment tax on gambling revenues, in widening roads, bulldozing the bus station, and tearing down a couple of gloomy bars and dozens of Northside houses and apartment buildings," Simon writes in *Boardwalk of Dreams* of the project undertaken in the 1990s.[41]

Gamblers, once the project was complete, were able to reach casinos along well-groomed one-way streets with twenty thousand shrubs, eight thousand flowers, and one thousand trees planted in straight lines on either side of the road.[42] Simon quotes a local activist as describing the project as essentially a "Negro remover."[43]

Trump's lavish casino—it opened in 1990 with a concert by Michael Jackson—was an extravaganza built with $820 million in unsustainable debt, including the issuing of $675 million in junk bonds with a 14 percent interest rate.[44] Marvin B. Roffman, a casino analyst at the Philadelphia investment firm Janney Montgomery Scott, told *The Wall Street Journal* that the Taj would need to make $1.3 million a day to meet its interest payments.[45] No casino had ever brought in that much money. The Taj was doomed from the start. Trump soon had to service interest rates of $95 million a year.[46] He was able to get new loans for a while and then went bust. It was a brief and giddy moment of insane excess. But it was good for his outsized brand, even if it showed an atrocious lack of business sense. Trump had borrowed money at high interest rates and lied about the rates to regulators. Trump dumped the losses on stock and bondholders, who were fleeced for more than $1.5 billion.[47] Numerous local contractors and suppliers, never paid by Trump, went bankrupt.

"But even as his companies did poorly, Mr. Trump did well," wrote Russ Buettner and Charles V. Bagli in a *New York Times* article titled "How Donald Trump Bankrupted His Atlantic City Casinos, but Still Earned Millions." "He put up little of his own money, shifted personal debts to the casinos and collected millions of dollars in salary, bonuses and other payments. The burden of his failures fell on investors and others who had bet on his business acumen."[48]

THOSE LEFT BEHIND BY THE brief, wild excess were struggling.

Peter Battaglini, sixty, portly and jovial, worked at the Taj for twenty-six years as a bellman. He was there on the day it opened in 1990. He had worked previously as a bellman at the Showboat. He joined the union in 1987. His salary was $3.40 an hour plus tips. He usually took home $80 to $100 a day. On busy weekends he could make $150 a day. Most of the tips were around $5. Groups paid an automatic gratuity. He was married with two daughters, twenty-two and nineteen.

"When it was good, we were making $35,000 to $40,000 a year," he said. "Our health care was paid for by the hotel. We could raise a family.

"The hardest thing is when we were very busy," he went on. "We were constantly moving. We moved luggage up to the rooms. We pushed trolleys. We'd go to the rooms. We greet the guests. We explain the hotel to them. We go back down. It's a continuous thing. We used to have junkets in buses come in. We'd have two to three junkets sometimes, five cartloads of luggage that we had to deliver to the rooms. It was a very physical job. My knees, they ache. My lower back, I have problems with my shoulder. Doing that repetitively for all those years."

The glitz and the glamor, however, rubbed off on the staff. European stars, such as the Italian singer Eros Ramazzotti and the Three Tenors, performed at the casino's arena about once a month.

"It was exciting, especially in the beginning," he said. "We got to meet everybody from Elton John to Michael Jackson. All the sports stars came in. For the first few years it was just incredible working there. You'd see everybody. It was very exciting. We had a basketball tournament there. Dr. J, Kareem Abdul-Jabbar, Mickey Mantle, was there. Any star you can imagine. Britney Spears. Michael Jordan used to come by the desk and say hello to you every day. Tony Bennett."

Four decades later, five of Atlantic City's twelve casinos have closed, costing nearly eight thousand people their jobs. Huge casinos—the Revel and Showboat—were vast empty hulks on the city's boardwalk. Trump once owned three casinos in Atlantic City and one in Indiana. The Trump Plaza and the Trump Taj Mahal casinos were shut down. The Trump Marina, his third casino, was sold to Texas billionaire Tilman Fertitta. Fertitta renamed it the Golden Nugget. Trump's casino in Gary, Indiana, a 340-foot-long vessel called Trump Princess with more than 1,500 slot machines, declared bankruptcy in 2004. They all failed because of mismanagement.

The numbers of gamblers at the Taj declined. The physical plant began to deteriorate. By the time Trump disappeared, the owners did little to maintain the property. They fired the sixty-person marketing team. Managers began to be hostile, writing up complaints on employees to get them fired or harassing them into leaving. The goal was to reduce the size of the unionized workforce.

"Once he left the decline was really dramatic," Battaglini said of Trump. "If there was a leak in the ceiling they'd put a bucket under it for days. The carpet was getting worn and torn and they'd put tape. There was no paper towels in the men's or ladies' room. Faucets weren't being fixed. This was starting . . . around 2011.

"People were getting fired at a rate that was a lot higher than prior years," he said. "A lot of people just left because of the way they were being treated. It was strenuous. Every day you'd go in there wondering what was going to happen. I happened to be a shop steward. Whenever anybody in my department had an issue they'd come to me. I was constantly going back to management trying to say work it out. My department had the same management. But the pressure from above was telling them to do anything possible to get rid of the employees. They didn't want us there anymore. We knew the place. We knew how the business worked. They wanted to eliminate us. They always blamed Local 54 for all the problems. They wanted people to come in with no benefits, no pension. If they brought new hires and the union was in there, they'd start at a low scale. Hourly rate. If someone came in brand-new they start at $3.40 an hour. Whereas that person might be making $9 an hour if they've been there for a few years.

"You'd walk around leaky ceilings," he told me. "Paint was peeling. The rooms were in shambles. If something broke, say a faucet or a toilet, instead of fixing it you'd put it out of order. Now you're cutting down on people coming in. Eventually, the guests start realizing it. . . . A coffee shop that might be open twenty-four hours was now open eight hours. . . . The rooms weren't working. People called down but nothing happened. They couldn't get an extra towel. Everything you would expect wasn't happening. They cut out all entertainment. We didn't have entertainment the last few years. We had an arena that sat virtually empty for the last five years."

The loss of thousands of jobs and millions in tax revenue threw Atlantic City into bankruptcy. In December 2016 the state of New Jersey took over city management under a rescue law. It assumed the power to break union contracts, hire and fire workers, and sell off public assets.

Hedge fund vultures began to circle over the Atlantic City carcass. Carl Icahn, with an estimated worth of $18.8 billion,[49] is the prototype of the corporate raider who buys up distressed companies and "harvests" them for their assets. He and a group of investors take over a company. They demand, in the name of "shareholder activism," that the company slash wages, reduce or cut benefits, and strip itself of assets to profit the outside investors. By the time they are done the company is bankrupt. This tactic, pioneered by Icahn, fueled the stock market boom of the 1980s. It was soon copied by hedge funds that refined his terminology to call themselves "activist investors." Icahn is estimated to be responsible for the loss of more than 35,000 American jobs as well as the elimination of pensions or health benefits for more than 126,000 American families.[50]

Icahn eventually became the sole lender to Trump Entertainment.[51] He closed Trump Plaza and put a thousand people out of work.[52] He demanded that workers at Trump Taj Mahal take a 35 percent pay cut, give up their health insurance, $3 million in pension contributions, and paid lunch breaks.[53] He no longer invested in maintenance. His moves triggered a strike by the Local 54 of the Hotel Employees and Restaurant Employees International Union (HEREIU).

Al Kare worked as a waiter at Plate restaurant, one of twelve in the Taj, for twenty years.

"The mold was infesting huge portions of the hotel," he said. "They had to shut down the old tower, the Taj Tower, because of mold. They shut down parts of it, bit by bit, in the last five years. They shut down whole floors."

Entire hotel floors were out of commission. Roaches, bedbugs, mice, and rats began to proliferate, despite room costs that could reach $300 a night on weekends.

"It was crazy," Battaglini remembered. "You had to deal with them. They'd come down irate, screaming. It's the first employee they see. It's not your fault. I understood why they were mad.

"The Taj Mahal was the place to go in the city," he said sadly. "And to see it decline like that, it just sucked the wind out of you. Near the end, we didn't even want to go into work."

"We had mice in the Chairman's Club," Kare says. "It's a buffet set up with a good bar. It's a high roller's restaurant. . . . The whole building was infested with mice. They had one of those assisting dogs that went after a mouse. People were yelling at the dog. The dog got nervous and took a dump. No one saw it. Some customer slipped in it. This is how you're treating your money players?"

Icahn, whom Trump named a special adviser on regulation in his administration, went to bankruptcy court in 2014 in Delaware.[54] His reduction in staff included casino security. Four people were murdered at the Taj Mahal between 2008 and 2011.[55] There were no murders at the city's other casinos during the same period.[56] In one 2010 incident, a man kidnapped from the parking deck was murdered.[57] Sixteen months later a couple was shot and killed in a carjacking inside the casino's parking garage.[58]

Marc Scittina, fifty-four, worked at the Taj Mahal for twenty-six years as a food server in the Limited Access Players Club. The lounge offered food, priority reservations, and beverages to those carrying Trump One cards. These patrons were given gifts—coffeepots, vacuum cleaners, and Kindles. Staff often developed close relationships with gamblers.

"Unlike the quintessential proletarians who assemble objects, service workers' products are their customers' experiences," write Mutari and Figart in *Just One More Hand.* "On the job, they attempt to evoke particular emotions in their customers, but must control their own emotions in order to do this. The skill required to do both while focusing on the detailed activities that create the service is often invisible, difficult to measure and poorly compensated."[59]

The workers felt betrayed. "Since 2000, they've threatened in negotiations to take our pensions," said Scittina. "We got concessions and contracts passed back. We got compensation packages cut by approximately 33 percent. We gave back our sick days. We gave back birthdays, holidays, approximately 65 percent of our vacation pay. We didn't take a monetary paycheck raise. For the last twelve years we only got 80 cents worth of raises. All that was thrown back into the pot for us to work with the company. We started making those concessions during the last three contracts, 2011."

Rose Hall, fifty-two, worked twenty-seven years at the Taj as a room attendant.

"They changed the mattress to a heavier one," she told me. "I'd say four to five years ago. They were thick. They were pillow-top ones that you can't flip; you had to turn. Mice, bed bugs, rats, roaches. I saw it all. A lady put bedbugs in a cup and called management. We told management about it and they gave her a food coupon and said they'd exterminate the room. I come in the next day there's a new guest in the room. I'm serious. The room was never cleaned. The roaches are crawling on the door. The rats are running around. They got rats too. They were big. You see those big old traps, they were for rats. Some people checked out, some got accommodated."

"These were running around in the restaurants and even in the club where I worked," Scittina said of the rats. "I'd be talking to a customer and I'd jump. People say, 'Marc, what did you see?' I'd try to play it off. But then it runs across underneath their legs and they go nuts."

"I'm in the back cooking, one of the busboys comes back and says, 'Chuck, Chuck, you should see them,' " said Chuck Baker, fifty-seven, who worked as a cook. "I said, 'Who?' He said, 'The mice, they're running around the dining room.' People got their cell phones out."

THE COMPANY WENT INTO BANKRUPTCY on September 16, 2014.[60] Seven thousand casino workers were laid off over a two-week period from the Revel, Trump Plaza, and Showboat casinos.[61] Icahn's negotiators met with the union. The negotiators demanded the workers surrender their health insurance and pensions. They demanded the city grant the casino $150 million in tax relief.[62] A third of Atlantic City's casinos were now closed.

The jobs with health benefits existed only as long as the casinos had a monopoly on gamblers. Once gambling was legalized in other states, once revenues declined, once staff was reduced, the benefits evaporated. More was expected of workers. Those with seniority were let go. They were replaced with part-time and temporary workers who were paid less and denied benefits. Casino jobs looked like every other poorly paid and uncompensated menial job in America.

The workers, who between 2004 and 2014 had given up raises in order to maintain health benefits, were abandoned. Union benefits, including health insurance contributions to the pension plan and severance pay, cost the billionaire investor about $14 million a year. He had no intention of paying it.

The casino magnates and Wall Street speculators are the incarnation of the mob. They inherited the thuggish bodyguards, the shady business practices, and the scantily clad chorus girls, models, and beauty pageant queens. Casinos compete for fame. They build more rooms. They are adorned with more costly fixtures and materials. They have better amenities. They have the most opulent and expensive suites. It is an endless battle for bigger, glitzier, and more alluring. And when the old becomes redundant or overshadowed it is dynamited into rubble and a new miracle is erected in its place.

David Cay Johnston in his book *The Making of Donald Trump* described Trump as "a modern P. T. Barnum selling tickets to a modern variation of the Feejée Mermaid, one of the panoply of Barnum's famous fakes that people decided were worth a bit of their money."[63]

Johnston wrote how by 1990, "Trump's inability to pay his debts had put him at risk of losing his casinos."[64] The rules of the New Jersey Casino Control Commission required casino owners to have enough liquidity to pay their bills or see their ownership license revoked. Trump would either get a government rescue package or declare bankruptcy. Casino regulators, Johnston wrote, documented that Trump was down to his last $1.6 million.[65] He had obligations to make payments on more than $1 billion worth of bonds every ninety days on his three casinos in Atlantic City. Johnston wrote:

> Trump's obvious difficulty complying with the financial stability requirements of the Casino Control Act raised a glaring question: Had regulators been monitoring Trump's finances since he got his casino license in 1982? The answer was no. The regulators had been too busy with work they deemed more important. There was, for example, the predawn arrest of a cocktail waitress named Diane Pussehl, who was pulled from bed and charged with a felony for picking up a $500 chip on the floor of Harrah's casino. A judge tossed the case out, so the casino regulators filed a misdemeanor charge. It also was tossed. Then they went after Pussehl's license, arguing she was morally unfit to work in a casino. Pussehl kept her license.[66]

Trump, as Johnston wrote, "could have been swept into the dustbin of history if the DGE [Division of Gaming Enforcement] prosecuted high-level offenders with the same rigor as it did the Diane Pussehls of the industry."[67] Trump hired over one thousand lawyers to hammer out an agreement to keep the banks from collecting on the $3.2 billion he owed.[68] He was saved by government regulators. His license was not revoked. But many of his small contractors were never paid. A year later in 1991 the Trump Taj Mahal filed for Chapter 11 bankruptcy.[69] "He later sold stock in his casinos," Johnston wrote, "where investors lost their shirts (while Trump kept getting paid millions of dollars in salary, bonuses, and money to pay off his bad debts)."[70]

The economist Adam Smith wrote that profits are often highest in nations on the verge of economic collapse. These profits are obtained, he warned, by massively indebting the economy.[71] A *rentier* class, composed of managers at hedge funds, banks, financial firms, casino operators, and an entertainment industry, makes money not by manufacturing products but from the control of economic rents. To increase profits, lenders, credit card companies, and others charge higher and higher interest rates. Or they use their monopolies to gouge the public.

These profits are counted as economic growth. But this is a fiction, a sleight of hand, like unemployment statistics or the Consumer Price Index, used to mask the vast speculative shell game.

"The head of Goldman Sachs came out and said that Goldman Sachs workers are the most productive in the world," the economist Michael Hudson told me. "That's why they're paid what they are. The concept of productivity in America is income divided by labor. So if you're Goldman Sachs and you pay yourself $20 million a year in salary and bonuses, you're considered to have added $20 million to GDP, and that's enormously productive.

"We're talking with tautology," Hudson told me. "We're talking with circular reasoning here. So the issue is whether Goldman Sachs, Wall Street, and predatory pharmaceutical firms actually add product or whether they're just exploiting other people. That's why I used the word 'parasites' in my book's title [*Killing the Host: How Financial Parasites and Debt Bondage Destroy the Global Economy*]. People think of a parasite as simply taking money, taking blood out of a host or taking money out of the economy. But in nature it's much more complicated. The parasite can't simply come in and take something. First of all, it needs to numb the host. It has an enzyme so that the host doesn't realize the parasite's there. And then the parasites have another enzyme that takes over the host's brain. It makes the host imagine that the parasite is part of its own body, actually part of itself and hence to be protected. That's basically what Wall Street has done. It depicts itself as part of the economy. Not as wrapping around it, not as external to it, but actually the part that's helping the body grow, and that actually is responsible for most of the growth. But in fact it's the parasite that is taking over the growth.

"The result is an inversion of classical economics," Hudson said. "It turns Adam Smith upside down. It says what the classical economists said was unproductive parasitism actually is the real economy. And that the parasites are labor and industry that get in the way of what the parasite wants, which is to reproduce itself.

"The great Roman historians Livy and Plutarch blamed the decline of the Roman Empire on the creditor class being predatory, and the latifunda," Hudson said of the ancient Roman private estates. "The creditors took all the money, and would just buy more and more land, displacing the other people. The result in Rome was a dark age, and that can last a very long time. The dark age is what happens when the *rentiers* take over.

"If you look back in the 1930s, Leon Trotsky said that fascism was the inability of the socialist parties to come forth with an alternative," Hudson said. "If the socialist parties and media don't come forth with an alternative to this neofeudalism, you're going to have a rollback to feudalism. But instead of the military taking over the land, as occurred with the Norman Conquest, you take over the land financially. Finance has become the new mode of warfare.

"You can achieve the takeover of land and the takeover of companies by corporate raids," he said. "The Wall Street vocabulary is one of conquest and wiping out. You're having a replay in the financial sphere of what feudalism was in the military sphere."

The debauched ethics of all casino magnates, including Trump, define the dark, petulant heart of America. Our schools and libraries lack funding, our infrastructure is a wreck, drug addiction and suicide are an epidemic, and we flee toward the promise of magic, unchecked hedonism, and perpetual stimulation. There is a pathological need in America to escape the dreary and the depressing.

"When a population becomes distracted by trivia," wrote the cultural critic Neil Postman, "when cultural life is redefined as a perpetual round of entertainments, when serious public conversation becomes a form of baby-talk, when, in short, a people becomes an audience and their public business a vaudeville, then a nation finds itself at risk: cultural-death is a clear possibility."[72]

Con artists and swindlers exploit the frustrations and anger of a betrayed people. They make fantastic promises they never keep. They prey on the vulnerable. They demand godlike worship. They conjure up a world of illusions and fantasy. And then it implodes. The workers and patrons at the Trump Taj Mahal were victimized first. Now it is our turn.

7

FREEDOM

Her full nature, like that river of which Cyrus broke the strength, spent itself in channels which had no great name on the earth. But the effect of her being on those around her was incalculably diffusive: for the growing good of the world is partly dependent on unhistoric acts; and that things are not so ill with you and me as they might have been is half owing to the number who lived faithfully a hidden life, and rest in unvisited tombs.

GEORGE ELIOT, *Middlemarch* [1]

Previously I have described the prisons as a sociological community in which a large number of men must be controlled by a small number—the large number having only the potential power of their number. If ever unified, they could threaten the authority of the minority. For purposes of security it is essential that the population remain divided. To that end it is necessary that a sense of community be discouraged, that communication among prisoners be made difficult; that leaders, natural or potential, be isolated; that passivity be encouraged and assertiveness, which is too close to aggressiveness, be restricted even if it might be applied to positive ends; that self-confidence be eroded and self-doubts be engendered; that prejudices and biases which divide the community be encouraged or at least tolerated; that sources that feed pride be restricted, because pride is potential power; that lethargy be rewarded; that individuality be obliterated; that the spirit of man be broken in the service of obedience.

All of these make sense, are psychologically sound, if the purpose is to keep a large group of men under the control of a small group of men. The fact that most of this is antithetical to the concept of building strength of character or rehabilitation, which is the purported goal of imprisonment, is aside from the point, because the purported goal is not the real goal. A warden's job is not the rehabilitation of prisoners: it is the maintenance of order.

—WILLARD GAYLIN, *In the Service of Their Country: War Resisters in Prison* [2]

I t was close to midnight. I was sitting at a small campfire with Sybilla and Josh Medlin behind an old warehouse, in an impoverished section of Anderson, Indiana. The Medlins paid $20,000 for the warehouse. It came with three lots, which they use for gardens. They share the produce they grow with neighbors and the local homeless shelter. There are three people currently living in the warehouse, which the Medlins converted into living quarters. There have been as many as ten. The warehouse is called the Burdock House.

"The burdock is seen as a worthless, noxious weed," Josh, thirty-three, said. "But it has a lot of edible and medicinal value. A lot of the people we come into contact with are also not valued by our society. The burdock plant colonizes places that are abandoned. We are doing the same thing with our house."

"It was a house of hospitality," said Josh, who, like his wife, came out of the Catholic Worker Movement. "We were welcoming people who needed a place to stay, to help them get back on their feet. Or perhaps longer. That didn't work out as well as we hoped. We weren't really prepared to deal with some of the needs that people had. And perhaps [didn't have] the skills. We were taken advantage of. We weren't really helping them. We didn't have the resources to help them."

"For the Catholic Workers, the ratio of community members to people they're helping is a lot different than what we had here," Sybilla, twenty-seven, said. "We were in for a shock. At the time there were just three community members. Sometimes we had four or five homeless guests here. It got kind of chaotic. Mostly mental illness. A lot of addiction, of course. We don't know how to deal with hard drugs in our home. It got pretty crazy."

Two or three nights a month people gather, often around a fire, in back of the Burdock House. They bring food for a potluck dinner or chip in $5. Local bands play, poets read, and there is an open mic. Here they affirm what we all must affirm—the talents, passions, feelings, thoughts, and creativity that make us complete human beings. Here people are celebrated not for their jobs or status, but for their contributions to others. And in groups like this one, unseen and unheralded, lies hope.

"We are an intentional community," said Josh. "This means we are a group of people who have chosen to live together to repurpose an old building, to offer to a neighborhood and a city a place to express its creative gifts. This is an alternative model to a culture that focuses on accumulating as much money as possible and on an economic structure based on competition and taking advantage of others. We value manual labor. We value nonviolence as a tactic for resistance. We value simplicity. We believe people are not commodities. We share what we have. We are not about accumulating for ourselves. These values help us to become whole people."

The message of the consumer society, pumped out over flat screen televisions, computers, and smartphones to those trapped at the bottom of society, is shrill and unrelenting: *You are a failure.* Popular culture celebrates those who wallow in power, wealth, and self-obsession, and perpetuates the lie that if you work hard and are clever, you can become a "success," perhaps landing on *American Idol* or *Shark Tank.* You can invent Facebook. You can become LeBron James, Bill Gates, Mark Zuckerberg, Kelly Clarkson, or Jennifer Lawrence. You can rise to be a business titan. The disparity between the glittering world that people watch and the bleak world they inhabit creates a collective schizophrenia. It manifests itself in diseases of despair—suicides, addictions, mass shootings, hate crimes, and depression. We are to blame for our own misfortune.

Hope means rejecting the thirst for public adulation. It means turning away from the maniacal self-creation of a persona that defines social media. It means searching for something else—a life of meaning, purpose, and, ultimately, dignity.

We do not become autonomous and free human beings by building pathetic, tiny monuments to ourselves. It is through self-sacrifice and humility that we affirm the sanctity of others and the sanctity of ourselves. Those who fight against cultural malice, whether squatting in old warehouses, taking over Zuccotti Park, resisting in Standing Rock, or refusing to be broken by our prison system, have discovered that life is measured by infinitesimal and often unacknowledged acts of solidarity and kindness. These acts of kindness, like the nearly invisible strands of a spider's web, spin outward to connect our atomized and alienated souls to others. The good, as the radical Catholic priest Daniel Berrigan told me, draws to it the good. This belief—held although we may never see empirical proof—is profoundly transformative. But know this: when these acts are carried out on behalf of the oppressed and the demonized, when compassion defines the core of our lives, when we understand that justice is a manifestation of love, we are marginalized and condemned by our sociopathic elites.

"If you care about other people that's now a very dangerous idea," Noam Chomsky suggests. "If you care about other people you might try to organize or to undermine power and authority. That's not going to happen if you care only about yourself. Maybe you can become rich, you don't care whether other people's kids can go to school or afford food to eat or things like that. In the United States that's called libertarian for some wild reason. I mean it's actually highly authoritarian but that doctrine is extremely important for power systems as a way of atomizing and undermining the public."[3]

Those who resist effectively in the years ahead may not be able to stem the economic decline, the mounting political dysfunction, the collapse of empire, and the ecological disasters. But they will draw from acts of kindness, and the kindness of others, the strength and courage to endure. It will be from these relationships—ones formed the way all genuine relationships form: face-to-face rather than electronically—that radical organizations will rise from the ashes to resist.

Sybilla, whose father was an electrician and who is the oldest of six, did not go to college. Josh was suspended from Earlham College in Richmond, Indiana, for throwing a pie at William Kristol as the right-wing commentator was speaking on campus in 2005. He never returned. Earlham, he said, like most colleges, is a place "where intellectualism takes precedence over truth."

"When I was in high school I was really into the punk rock community," Sybilla said. "Through that I discovered anarchism."

"Emma Goldman?" I asked.

"Yeah, mostly that brand of anarchism," she said. "Not like I'm going to break car windows for fun."

She was attracted to the communal aspect of anarchism, and the understanding that power, no matter who held it, was always demonic. It fit with the values of her parents, who she said "are very antiauthoritarian" and "who always taught me to think for myself." She read a book by an anonymous author who lived outside the capitalist system for a couple of years. "That really set me on that direction even though he is a lot more extreme," she said, "only eating things from the garbage. Train hopping. As a teenager, I thought, 'Wow! The adventure. All the possible ways you could live an alternative lifestyle that's not harmful to others and isn't boring.'"

She left Anderson when she was eighteen and moved to Los Angeles to join the Catholic Worker community.

"I [too] became pretty immersed in the anarchist scene," Josh said, whose introduction to anarchism came through the writer Derrick Jensen. "I'm also a Christian. The Catholic Worker Movement is the most well known example of how to put those ideas in practice. Also, I really didn't want anything to do with money."

"A lot of my friends in high school, despite being a part of the punk rock community, went into the military," Sybilla said. "Or they're still doing exactly what they were doing in high school."

The couple live in the most depressed neighborhood of Anderson. Squatters inhabit abandoned buildings, drug use is common, the crime rate is high, and the dilapidated houses are neglected. Weeds grow in abandoned lots and yards. The police rarely appear when someone from this part of the city dials 911. When they do arrive they are often hostile.

"If you're walking down the street and you see a cop car, it doesn't make you feel safe," Josh said.

"A lot of people view them [police] as serving the rich," Sybilla said. "They're not serving us.

"Poor people are a tool for the government to make money with small drug charges," she added. "A lot of our peers are in jail or have been in jail for drugs. People are depressed. Lack of opportunity. Frustration with a job that's boring. Also, no matter how hard you want to work, you just barely scrape by. One of our neighbors who is over here quite a bit, he had a seventy-hour-a-week job. Constant overtime. And he still lives in this neighborhood in a really small one-bedroom apartment. I think Anderson has really bad self-esteem. A lot of young people, a lot of people my age I know are working for $9, $10 an hour. Moving from job to job every six months. Basically, enough money to buy alcohol, cigarettes, and pay the rent.

"My mom's generation grew up thinking they were going to have a solid job," she said. "That they were just going to be able to start a job and have a good livelihood. And that's not the case. Just because you want to work really hard it doesn't necessarily mean you're going to make it.

"I work as a cashier at the local Christian college," she said, referring to Anderson University. "It's a small school with two thousand students. I work in the cafeteria. The contract changed. The school stopped doing its own food service many years ago. Has been hiring private companies. After I worked there for a year the contract was up. It was a new company [Aramark] and they're huge. . . . I think it's the biggest food service company. They do most hospitals, schools, prisons. And the job conditions changed so dramatically. Our orientation with this new company, they had this HR guy come. He's like, 'You're going to work for the biggest company in the world. You should be so excited to be a part of our team. We're going to make you great. Anderson used to be this really powerful city full of industry. The employees demanded so much from the companies. And [the companies] all left.'

"We're just looking at him," she said. "Why is this relevant? Basically the message was, 'You guys have no other choice. So you don't choose to work with us. You have to. And we're going to do what we want you to do.' At the time I was making $7.50 an hour. They hired me at $7.50

from the old company. They hired the people beside me for $8, which I was not happy with. The old employees were making more money because they got consistent raises throughout the years. They would have them do jobs like carrying crates of heavy food up the stairs. Jobs that they knew they physically couldn't do, in hopes that they would quit, I think. They didn't want to pay that higher wage. And the students weren't happy either. We lost about half the workforce. There were a hundred employees when they came in. They had reduced down to fifty. That makes my job twice as hard. But I still make $7.50. With no hope for a raise anytime soon.

"I went up to them," she continued. "I said, 'I need to make as much as these people at least. I've been here for a year. I'm a more valuable employee.' And they were like, 'If you don't like it, quit. Maybe you can get a job at Burger King.' I was so angry. I started talking to some of my coworkers to see if they were interested in making the job better rather than quitting. And a lot of them were. Especially the people who'd been there for years and years and who were familiar with GM and UAW [the United Automobile Workers union]. And weren't scared of it. So we started having meetings. I think the campaign took two years. And we successfully organized. It's been a huge improvement. Even though it's still a low-paying job, everything is set. They can't change their mind about when we get raises. They can't change their mind about what the hiring rate is. They can't take these elderly people and make them start carrying boxes rather than run a cash register. They were also firing people for no reason. That doesn't happen anymore. . . . The employees have a voice now. If we don't like something, when our contract is up for renegotiation we can change it.

"The jobs we have are boring," she added. "My job was so boring. Having this as an outlet, also with the challenge of creating the union there, I was able to not feel so useless."

Sybilla publishes *The Heartland Underground*. The magazine, which sells for $2 a copy and comes out every four or five months, reviews local bands, publishes poets and writers, and features articles on the best techniques for Dumpster diving.

An author who used the pseudonym "Arbitrary Aardvark" wrote an article called "I Was a Guinea Pig for Big Pharma," about earning money by taking part in medical experiments. He would stay in a lab for about two weeks and take "medicine, usually a pill, and they take your blood a lot. You might be pissing in a jug or getting hooked up to an EKG machine or whatever the study design calls for, and they take your blood pressure and temperature pretty often." He made between $2,000 and $5,000 depending on how long the study lasted. Most of his fellow "lab rats" were "just out of jail or rehab." In one study he had a bullet-tipped plastic tube inserted down his nose into his intestines. "It was the most painful thing I've been through in my adult life." He said he and the other subjects did not like reporting side effects because they were "worried that they'll be sent home without a full paycheck, or banned from future studies." He admitted this probably affected the reliability of the studies. He became ill during one of the experiments. The pharmaceutical company refused to pay him, blaming his illness on a preexisting condition. He wrote:

> I signed up for one that was going to pay $5,000, but a week into it my liver enzymes were all wrong, and they took me out of the study but kept me at the site, because I was very sick. It turned out I'd come down with mono just before going into the study. And then I got shingles, not fun. . . .
>
> I'd spent 3 years trying to be a lawyer and failed. I'd worked in a warehouse, as the Dalai lama's nephew's headwaiter, as a courier and a temp. Lost money day trading and then in real estate. I was ready to try medical experiments again. I tried 3 times to get in at Eli Lilly but never did. Lilly no longer does its own clinical trials after a girl . . . killed herself during an antidepressant study.

In an essay titled "Sometimes the Voices in Your Head Are Angry Ghosts," Jared Lynch wrote:

> Death shrouded the whole spacetime of the latter half of high school, coating it in an extra vicious layer of depression. The

first night we stayed in the house I sat in the living room, writing about ghosts in a composition book. . . . I had a package of single edge blades in the back of my top desk drawer and sometimes I flirted too closely with that edge of darkness. I thought a lot about the blades at school. My daydreams were consumed by untold suicides, and countless times I came home to find one of my past selves in the tub with his forearm opened wide and grinning with his life essence surrounding him in the tub on the wrong side of his skin.

It was a strange, beautiful time. Melancholia wrapped around the edges with the golden glow of nostalgia for a time that felt like I had died before it existed. . . . I fell into an expected, but incredibly deep pool of depression and I found the single edge razors that one of my future selves had so graciously left behind in my top drawer. I bled myself because I wanted to be with the lovely, lonely ghosts. I bled myself more than I ever had, but I didn't bleed enough to capture myself in the barbs of the whirlpool of my depression.

The *cri de coeur* of this lost generation, orphans of global capitalism, rises up from deindustrialized cities across the nation. This generation has been cast aside by a society that views them as cogs, menial wage slaves who will do the drudgery that plagues the working poor in postindustrial America.

Parker Pickett, twenty-four, who works at Lowe's, is a poet and a musician. He frequently reads his work at Burdock House. He read me a few of his poems, including "This Is a Poem with No Words." It had these lines:

> . . . *I kinda forget*
> *that I go day to day looking at darkened and escaping light*
> *behind the eyes of homeless on sidewalks sometimes not*
> *cognizant and other moments the cardboard is their story but*
> *nonetheless they'll move on as I have moved on,*
> *as Jesus moved on,*
> *as Buddha moved on. . . .*

I sat on a picnic table at Burdock House next to Justin Benjamin. He cradled his guitar, one of his tuning pegs held in place by locking pliers. The fire was dying down. Justin, twenty-two, calls himself WD Benjamin, the "WD" being short for "well dressed." He wore a white shirt, a loosely knotted tie, and a suit coat. He had long, frizzy hair parted in the middle. His father was a steelworker. His mother ran a day care center and later was an insurance agent.

"Kids would talk about wanting something better or leaving," he said. "Yet they weren't doing steps to take it. You saw they were going to spend their whole lives here begrudgingly. They would talk stuff. They would never do anything about it. It was all just talk."

He paused.

"Substance [abuse] ruined a lot of lives around here," he said.

He said that by fourteen most kids in Anderson realized they were trapped.

"We had seen our parents or other people or other families not go anywhere," he said. "This business went under. Pizzerias, paint stores, they all go under. About that time in my life, as much as I was enthralled with seeing cars rushing past and all these tall buildings, we all saw, well, what was the point if none of us are happy or our parents are always worrying about something. Just not seeing any kind of progression. There had to be something more.

"I've had friends die," he said. "I had a friend named Josh. We'd say, 'He Whitney Houston-ed before Whitney Houston.' He pilled out and died in a bathtub. It happened a month before Whitney Houston died. So that was a weird thing for me. Everyone is going to remember Whitney Houston but no one will remember Josh. At the time he was sixteen.

"I see friends who are taking very minimal jobs and never thinking anywhere beyond that," he said. "I know they're going to be there forever. I don't despise them or hold anything against them. I understand. You have to make your cut to dig out some kind of a living. . . . I've done manual labor. I've done medical, partial. Food service. I've done sales. Currently I'm working on a small album. Other than that, I play for money. I sell a lot of odds and ends. I've been doing that for years. Apparently I have a knack for collecting things and they're of use for somebody.

Just paying my way with food and entertainment for somebody. I live right across from the library. Eleventh Street. I can't remember the address. I'm staying with some people. I try to bring them something nice, or make dinner, or play songs. I do make enough to pay my share of utilities. I wouldn't feel right otherwise."

He was saved, he said, by the blues—Son House, Robert Johnson, all the old greats.

"My finger got caught in a Coke bottle trying to emulate his style of slide guitar," he said of House. "I asked my dad to help me please get it out. There was just something about people being downtrodden their whole lives. I used to not understand the plight of the black community. I used to think, 'Why can't they just work harder?' I was raised by a father who was very adamant about capitalism. Then one day my sister-in-law told me, 'Well, Justin, you just don't understand generational poverty. Please understand.' People were told they were free yet they have all these problems, all these worries. . . . It's the natural voice. You listen to Lead Belly's 'Bourgeois Blues,' it's a way of expressing their culture. And their culture is sad. 'Death Don't Have No Mercy' talks about the great equalizer of death. It didn't matter if you're black or white, death will come for you."

He bent over his guitar and played Robert Johnson's "Me and the Devil Blues."

"I've seen a lot of GM people, they just live in this despair," he said of the thousands of people in the city who lost their jobs when the General Motors plants closed. "They're still afraid. I don't know what they're afraid of. It's just the generation they came out of. I worked with plenty of GM people who were older and having to work for their dollars begrudgingly. They're like, 'I was made promises.'

"I was born three pounds," he said. "I was not destined for this world. Somehow I came out. I did the best I could. That's all I've done. I'll never say I'm good at anything. At least I have the ability to think, speak, and act. Three pounds, to this now. I just can't see the use of not fighting. You always have to think about what's going to lay down in the future. What's going to happen when the factories close down? Are you going to support your fellow coworkers? Are you going to say, 'No, things will come back?' Are you going to cast everything to damnation? Cast your neighbors down, say it was their fault the jobs are gone?

"I've never seen the heights of it," he said of capitalism. "But I've seen the bottom. I've seen kids down here naked running around. I've seen parents turn on each other and kids have to suffer for that. Or neighbors. I'd just hear yelling all night. It's matters of money. It's always the kids that suffer. I always try to think from their perspective. When it comes down to kids, they feel defeated. When you grow up in a household where there's nothing but violence and squabbling and grabbing at straws, then you're going to grow up to be like that. You're going to keep doing those minimum jobs. You're fighting yourself. You're fighting a system you can't beat."

Walker Percy in his 1971 dystopian novel *Love in the Ruins* paints a picture of a morally degenerate America consumed by hedonism, wallowing in ignorance, led by kleptocrats and fools, fragmented into warring and often violent cultural extremes, and on the cusp of a nuclear war. It is a country cursed by its failure to address or atone for its original sins of genocide and slavery. The ethos of ceaseless capitalist expansion, white supremacy, and American exceptionalism, perpetuated overseas in the country's imperial wars, eventually consumes the nation itself. The accomplices, who once benefited from this evil, become its victims. How, Percy asks, does one live a life of meaning in such a predatory society? Is it even possible? And can a culture ever regain its equilibrium when it sinks into such depravity?

The novel's main character, a doctor named Tom More, is a suicidal alcoholic and a womanizer. He has invented the "Ontological Lapsometer" to measure human souls. He notes that "the dread chasm that has rent the soul of Western man" has worsened "ever since the famous philosopher Descartes ripped body loose from mind and turned the very soul into a ghost that haunts its own house."[4]

Percy, who like the Russian writer Anton Chekhov was a medical school graduate, was steeped in the classics, theology, philosophy, literature, and history. He knew the common denominators of decaying societies. The elevation of the morally degenerate in the last days was never accidental. These corrupt elites reflected back to the society, as does Trump, its spiritual emptiness. The feckless Romanovs in Russia, the megalomaniacal Kaiser Wilhelm II in Germany, and the doddering head of the Austro-Hungarian Empire, Franz Joseph I, in the last days of the European monarchies exhibited the same stupidity, self-delusion, and self-destructiveness seen in the late American Empire. The moment of terminal decline is always marked by an inability to acknowledge reality and by monstrous, ill-fated schemes, often expressed in wars, to restore a supposed golden age.

"In every civilization its most impressive period seems to precede death by only a moment," the theologian Reinhold Niebuhr wrote. "Like the woods of autumn, life defies death in a glorious pageantry of color. But the riot of this color has been distilled by an alchemy in which life has already been touched by death. Thus man claims immortality for his spiritual achievements just when their mortal fate becomes apparent; and death and mortality are strangely mixed into, and potent in, the very pretension of immortality."[5]

Our capitalist elites have used propaganda, money, and the marginalizing of their critics to erase the first three of philosopher John Locke's elements of the perfect state: liberty, equality, and freedom. They exclusively empower the fourth, property. Liberty and freedom in the corporate state mean the liberty and freedom of corporations and the rich to exploit and pillage without government interference or regulatory oversight. And the single most important characteristic of government is its willingness to use force, at home and abroad, to protect the interests of the property classes. This abject surrender of the state to the rich is illustrated in the 2017 tax code and the dismantling of environmental regulations. This degradation of basic democratic ideals—evidenced when the Supreme Court refuses to curb wholesale government surveillance of the public or defines pouring unlimited dark money into political campaigns as a form of free speech and the right to petition the government—means the society defines itself by virtues that are dead. The longer this illusion is perpetuated, the more an enraged public turns to demagogues who promise a new utopia and then, once in power, accelerate the assault.

All of our institutions are corrupted. The press, universities, the arts, the courts, and religious institutions, including the Christian church, have ingested the toxic brew of American exceptionalism, the myth of American virtues, and the conflation of freedom with unfettered capitalism. The liberal church, like the bankrupt liberal class, holds up multiculturalism and identity politics as an ethical imperative and ignores the primacy of economic and social justice. It tolerates the intolerant, giving credibility to those who peddle the heretical creed of the "prosperity gospel," a creed that says God showers divine favors in the form of wealth and power on the Christian elect. This idea makes Trump one of God's favorites. It is also an idea that is a complete inversion of the core message of the Christian Gospels.

In Percy's novel, the Roman Catholic Church has rebranded itself as the American Catholic Church, based in Cicero, Illinois. It celebrates Property Rights Sunday. The priest raises the Eucharistic host in the Mass, conducted in Latin, to the tune of "The Star-Spangled Banner." Sermons focus on how the rich in the Bible—Joseph of Arimathea and Lazarus—were specially blessed by God. Evangelical Christians stage ever more elaborate spectacles and entertainment, including nighttime golf—the Moonlight Tour of the Champs—advertised with the slogan "Jesus Christ, the Greatest Pro of Them All."[6]

Today's secularists have their own forms of hedonism, self-worship, and idolatry. Spirituality is framed by puerile questions: How is it with me? Am I in touch with myself? Have I achieved happiness and inner peace? Have I, along with my life coach, ensured that I have reached my full career potential? Am I still young-looking? What does my therapist say? It is a culture based on self-absorption, medical procedures to mask aging, and narcissism. Any form of suffering, which is always part of self-sacrifice, is to be avoided. The plight of our neighbor is irrelevant. Sexual degeneracy—narcissists are incapable of love—abounds in a society entranced by casual hook-ups and pornography. In the Percy novel's "Love Clinic," "volunteers perform sexual acts singly, in couples, and in groups, behind viewing mirrors in order that man might learn more about the human sexual response."[7]

"I believe in God and the whole business but I love women best, music and science next, whiskey next, God fourth, and my fellowman hardly at all," More says. "Generally I do as I please."[8]

The single-minded pursuit of happiness, with happiness equated with hedonism, wealth, and power, creates a population consumed by anxiety and self-loathing. Few achieve the imagined pinnacle of success, and those who do are often psychopaths. Building a society around these goals is masochistic. It shuts down any desire for self-knowledge because the truth of our lives is unpleasant. We fill the spiritual vacuum with endless activities, entertainment, and nonstop electronic hallucinations. We flee from silence and contemplation. We are determined to avoid facing what we have become.

Renegades in the novel have formed armed guerrilla bands in the swamps. These "castoffs" and "disaffected" rebels include "dropouts from Tulane and Vanderbilt, M.I.T. and Loyola; draft dodgers, deserters from the Swedish army, psychopaths and pederasts from Memphis and New Orleans whose practices were not even to be tolerated in New Orleans; antipapal Catholics, malcontented Methodists, ESPers, UFO-ers, Aquarians, ex–Ayn Randers, Choctaw Zionists who have returned to their ancestral hunting grounds, and even a few old graybeard Kerouac beats. . . ."[9]

The United States in Percy's book has been fighting a war in Ecuador for fifteen years. The old and infirm, like the poor and disabled, are abandoned by the society. The elderly are shipped off to a euthanasia facility called Happy Isles Separation Center where they are finished off with the "Euphoric Switch."[10] Those pushed aside by the corporate state live in misery and poverty and are treated as a criminal caste.

More—whose ancestor was St. Thomas More, the writer of *Utopia*—and his three paramours escape to the abandoned ruins of the local Howard Johnson's. The faded Rotary banner still adorns the banquet room. It reads: "Is it the truth? Is it fair to all concerned? Will it build goodwill and better friendships?"[11] More and one of his lovers, Moira, sit on a moldering bed. Scrawled on the wall are the words "For a free suck call room 208."[12]

"I am surrounded by the corpses of souls," says Father Rinaldo Smith, the pastor of the tiny remnant of Catholics who refuse to join the American Catholic Church. "We live in a city of the dead."[13]

"There are Left states and Knothead states," Percy writes—Knothead being the new name of the Republican Party—"Left towns and Knothead towns but no center towns. . . . Left networks and Knothead networks, Left movies and Knothead movies. The most popular Left films are dirty movies from Sweden [one depicted fellatio being performed in mid-air by two skydivers in free fall on an outdoor two-hundred-foot screen]. All-time Knothead favorites, on the other hand, include *The Sound of Music, Flubber*, and *Ice Capades 1981*, clean movies all." [14]

The Democratic Party is now the Left Party. The political agenda is captured in the acronym LEFTPAPASANE, which stands for "Liberty, Equality, Fraternity, The Pill, Atheism, Pot, Anti-Pollution, Sex, Abortion Now, Euthanasia." [15]

The elites, who live in well-protected gated communities, all get along with each other whether they are members of the Left Party or the Knothead Party. They are, like the Clintons and the Trumps, members of the same exclusive club.

"The scientists, who are mostly liberals and unbelievers, and the businessmen, who are mostly conservative and Christian, live side by side in Paradise Estates," he writes of the gated community in the novel. "Though the two make much of their differences—one speaking of 'outworn dogmas and creeds,' the other of 'atheism and immorality,' etcetera—to tell the truth, I do not notice a great deal of difference between the two." [16]

"Paradise Estates, where I live, is a paradise indeed, an oasis of concord in a troubled land," More says. "For our beloved old U.S.A. is in a bad way. Americans have turned against each other; race against race; right against left, believer against heathen, San Francisco against Los Angeles, Chicago against Cicero. Vines sprout in sections of New York where not even Negros will live. Wolves have been seen in downtown Cleveland, like Rome during the Black Plague. Some southern states have established diplomatic ties with Rhodesia. Minnesota and Oregon have their own consulates in Sweden (where so many deserters from these states dwell)." [17]

"People look and talk and smile and are nice and the abyss yawns," he writes. "The niceness is terrifying." [18]

In the novel's raging culture wars, the political triumphs of the left include removing the words "In God We Trust" from pennies. The Knotheads enacted a law that required "compulsory prayers in the black public schools and made funds available for birth control in Africa, Asia, and Alabama."[19] An exclusive private school, Valley Forge Academy—like the privatized education being implemented by Trump appointee Betsy DeVos—is "founded on religious and patriotic principles and to keep Negroes out."[20]

Students in the universities, radical multiculturalists, and moral purists "are a shaky dogmatic lot," Percy writes. "And the 'freer' they are, the more dogmatic. At heart they're totalitarians: they want either total dogmatic freedom or total dogmatic unfreedom, and the one thing that makes them unhappy is something in between."[21]

"Even now, late as it is, nobody can really believe that it didn't work after all," Percy writes.

The old U.S.A. didn't work! Is it even possible that from the beginning it never did work? That the thing always had a flaw in it, a place where it would shear, and that all this time we were not really different from Ecuador and Bosnia-Herzegovina, just richer. Moon Mullins blames it on the niggers. Hm. Was it the nigger business from the beginning? What a bad joke: God saying, here it is, the new Eden, and it is yours because you're the apple of my eye; because you the lordly Westerners, the fierce Caucasian-Gentile-Visigoths, believed in me and in the outlandish Jewish Event even though you were nowhere near it and had to hear the news of it from strangers. But you believed and so I gave it all to you, gave you Israel and Greece and science and art and the lordship of the earth, and finally even gave you the new world that I blessed for you. And all you had to do was pass one little test, which was surely child's play for you because you already had passed the big one. One little test: here's a helpless man in Africa, all you have to do is not violate him. That's all.

One little test: you flunk!

God, was it always the nigger business, now, just as in 1883, 1783, 1683, and hasn't it always been that ever since the first tough God-believing Christ-haunted cunning violent rapacious Visigoth-Western-Gentile first set foot here with the first black man, the one willing to risk everything, take all or lose all, the other willing just to wait and outlast because once he was violated all he had to do was wait because sooner or later the first would wake up and know that he had flunked, been proved a liar where he lived, and no man can live with that. And sooner or later the lordly Visigoth-Western-Gentile-Christian-Americans would have to falter, fall out, turn upon themselves like scorpions in a bottle.[22]

We will have to build new, parallel institutions that challenge the hegemony of corporate power. It will not be easy. It will take time. We cannot accept foundation money and grants from established institutions that seek to curtail the radical process of reconstituting society. Trusting in the system, and especially the Democratic Party, to carry out reform and wrest back our democracy ensures our enslavement. Communities such as Burdock House will be pivotal.

"Power is organized people and organized money," the organizer Michael Gecan told me. "Most activists stress organized people and forget organized money. As organizers, we stress both.

"We think the issues are, in a sense, the easy part," said Gecan, the codirector of the Industrial Areas Foundation, the largest network of community-based organizations in the United States and the author of *Going Public: An Organizer's Guide to Citizen Action.* "When we go to a place like East Brooklyn, or South Bronx, or the West Side of Chicago, you can take a ride around the neighborhood and see many of the issues right up front. What we can't see is—is there a fabric of relationships among institutions and leaders in those areas? We spend the first year, or two, or three, building that. Identifying leaders. Identifying institutions that are actually grounded in those communities. Doing training with leaders. Raising money so that the organization doesn't run out of money right at the start.

"We don't take government money," he said. "We want independence. We want ownership. We want people to have skin in the game.

We want people to be able to walk away from any situation they want to, to confront anyone they want to, without worrying about having their budget being slashed or eliminated. So we stress both. Organized people and organized money is essentially building the foundation of the organization first. And then, once that's fairly solid, we begin identifying issues through a real, deliberate process of house meetings, individual meetings, soliciting to people. And not just doing a poll in the community. [We find out] what do you care about? What are you concerned about? By asking people what they are concerned about and are they willing to do something about it."

This process of institution building permits organizers and activists to eventually pit power against power. Politics is a game of fear. Those who do not have the ability to frighten power elites do not succeed. All of the movements that opened up the democratic space in America—the abolitionists, the suffragists, the labor movement, the communists, the socialists, the anarchists, and the civil rights movement—developed a critical mass and militancy that forced the centers of power to respond. The platitudes about justice, equality, and democracy are just that. Only when ruling elites become worried about survival do they react. Appealing to the better nature of the powerful is useless. They don't have one.

We once had within our capitalist democracy liberal institutions— the press, labor unions, political third parties, civic and church groups, public broadcasting, well-funded public universities, and a liberal wing of the Democratic Party—that were capable of responding to outside pressure from movements. They did so imperfectly. They provided only enough reforms to save the capitalist system from widespread unrest or, with the breakdown of capitalism in the 1930s, from revolution. They never adequately addressed white supremacy and institutional racism, or the cruelty that is endemic to capitalism. But they had the ability to mitigate some of the suffering that plagued working men and women. There was never enough social mobility, but there was some. Public education, including institutions such as the City College of New York, rivaled the private institutions, including prep schools and Ivy League colleges, where the wealthy sent their sons and daughters to be groomed for plutocracy.

These liberal institutions—I spend 248 pages in my book *Death of the Liberal Class* explaining how this happened—collapsed under sustained assault during the past forty years of corporate power. They exist now only in name. They are props in the democratic facade. Liberal nonprofits, from MoveOn.org to the Sierra Club, are no better. They are feeble appendages to a corporatized Democratic Party. There are, as the political philosopher Sheldon Wolin reminded us, no institutions left in America that can authentically be called democratic.

But, even more ominously, the militant movements that were the real engines of democratic change have been obliterated by the multipronged assault of communist witch hunts and McCarthyism, along with deindustrialization, a slew of antilabor laws and deregulation, and corporate seizure of our public and private institutions. This has left us nearly defenseless, forcing us to start all over again.

"The decision making in those situations is not about merit, how nice you are, or how deep the need is," Gecan said. "It's about, 'Do you have enough power to compel a reaction from the state or a reaction from the corporate sector?' When people say, 'What are you building around?' I say, 'We're building around power.' People who understand power tend to have the patience to build a base, do the training, raise the money, so when they go into action they surprise people."

I asked Gecan what characteristics he looks for in identifying leaders.

"Anger," he shot back. "It's not hot anger. It's not rhetorical anger. It's not the ability to give a speech. It's deep anger that comes from grief. People in the community who look at their children, look at their schools, look at their blocks, and they grieve. They feel the loss of that. Often, those people are not the best speakers or the best-known people in the community. But they're very deep. They have great relationships with other people. And they can build trust with other people because they're not self-promotional. They're about what the issues are in the community. So we look for anger. We look for the pilot light of leadership. It's always there. It's always burning. Good leaders know to turn it up and down depending on the circumstance."

If we are to succeed we will have to make alliances with people and groups whose professed political stances are different from our own and, at times, unpalatable to us. We will have to shed our ideological purity. The legendary organizer Saul Alinsky, whose successor, Ed Chambers, was Gecan's mentor, argued that the ideological rigidity of the left—something epitomized in identity politics and political correctness—effectively severed the left from the lives of working men and women. This was also true during the Vietnam War when college students led the antiwar protests and the sons of the working class did the fighting and dying in Vietnam. The left often dismiss Trump supporters as irredeemable racists and bigots, ignoring their betrayal and suffering. Condemning all those who support Trump is political suicide. There are "no permanent enemies, no permanent allies, only permanent interests," [23] Saul Alinsky often said, paraphrasing the British prime minister Lord Palmerston.

"We have to listen to people unlike ourselves," Gecan said, observing that this will be achieved *not* through the Internet but through face-to-face relationships. "And once we've built a relationship we can agitate them and be willing to be agitated by them."

The decline of the local press, along with civic and church organizations, has played a large part in our disempowerment, Gecan argues. We have lost connection with those around us. We have retreated inward and do not understand the corporate structures of power that wreak havoc on our lives. This is by design.

"Over seventy-five years the process of community dissolution that took place in Back of the Yards has been mirrored in thousands of U.S. communities," Gecan wrote of Alinsky's first community organization, Back of the Yards Neighborhood Council, founded in 1939 in Chicago. "Everywhere the tightly-knit worlds of a dozen or so blocks—where workplace, church, neighborhood, recreation, tavern, and political affiliation were all deeply entwined—have given way to exurban enclaves, long commutes, gathered congregations, matchmaker websites, and fitness clubs filled with customers who don't know one another. A world where local news was critically important and closely followed—often delivered by local publishers and reporters and passed along by word of mouth—has been replaced by the constant flow of real and fake news arriving through social media. A world of physically imposing and present institutions and organizations has morphed into a culture of global economic dynamics and fitful national mobilizations built around charismatic figures."[24]

Gecan conceded that America's future under a Trump presidency, and amid democratic institutions' collapse and climate change, is bleak. But he warned against falling into despair or apathy.

"In 1980 in New York, all the liberal establishment, the entire establishment, was saying New York would never be as strong as it once was," he said. "It was called benign neglect. They wrote off parts of New York permanently in their minds."

But community groups, including Brooklyn Congregations, which built five thousand low-income homes with Gecan's help, organized to save their neighborhood.

"Our organizations and our leaders simply didn't accept that judgment from the elites," Gecan said. "Things are tough, hard, but we're going to build an organization. We're going to identify things we can correct and correct them—with government if we can, or without it. We'll raise our own money. We'll figure out our housing strategy. We'll hire our own developer and general manager. It's about being more flexible about solutions. It's not about relying on what the state or market says is possible. It's about creating your own options."

The corporate state, he said, has learned how to manipulate protests and render them impotent. He dismissed as meaningless political theater the boutique activism in which demonstrators coordinate and even choreograph protests with the police. Activists spend a few hours, maybe a night, in jail and are "credentialized" as dissidents. Gecan called these "fake arrests." "Everyone looks like they've had an action," he said. "They haven't."

These protests, he said, were sterile reenactments of the protests of the 1960s. Genuine protest, he said, has to defy the rules. It cannot be predictable. It has to disrupt power. It has to surprise those in authority. And these kinds of protests are greeted with anger by the state.

"Three things have to be happening in great organizations: people have to be relating, people have to be learning, people have to be acting," he said. "In many religious circles, there's some learning going on, there's a little bit of relating going on, but there's no action. There's no external action. And it's killed many institutions. In a lot of activism, there's a lot of acting but there's not much relating or learning, so people make the same mistakes again and again.

"I was in Wisconsin during the [Governor Scott] Walker situation and the reaction to it," he said about the 2011 protests by union members and their supporters. "They did twenty-three major demonstrations. Fifty [thousand], seventy [thousand], 100,000 people. After the second or third I said to those people, 'Why are you doing all this? Because as you do these [protests], you can't be building relationships in local communities. And you don't know what your own members are thinking about this situation.' It ended up being unfortunately the case.

"Can we rebuild unions?" Gecan asked. "We can. It takes time. And we're doing it in some parts of the country. Can we rebuild civic life in our cities? We have and will do more. Can we take these people on? I know we can. But it will take different tactics. It will take some very unconventional allies that will surprise people."

IN NOVEMBER 2016 I FLEW to Bismarck, North Dakota, and drove to the Standing Rock tribal nation encampment. The direct road into the encampment was blocked by checkpoints. On side roads I repeatedly ran into other checkpoints, manned by private, armed security forces that had no form of identification on their uniforms. They refused my request to see their identification. They demanded to see my press credentials before denying me access. It was only by taking a myriad of dirt roads and swinging in a wide loop around the encampment that I was finally able to enter.

I descended into a vast encampment of crude wooden lodges, yurts, tents, and teepees that held a few thousand people, self-described "water protectors," who were attempting to halt the development of a $3.7 billion pipeline under construction by Texas-based Energy Transfer Partners.[25] The bitter prairie wind, sending the wind chill down to near zero, whipped across the broad flatlands. I covered my face with a scarf. Wood smoke filled the air. American flags flew upside down, traditionally a sign of distress, from improvised flagpoles, along with tribal flags of the two hundred tribal nations represented at the encampment. Rows of green Porta-Potties were placed throughout the camp. Men with axes chopped logs. They stacked the wood in huge piles for fires. A plane circled lazily overhead, no doubt taking pictures of the encampment's activities for the small army of law enforcement officials that surrounded the protesters.

Trump would later sign executive actions to authorize the building of the Dakota Access Pipeline or DAPL and the Keystone XL pipeline, which had been killed by the State Department and White House in 2015.[26] The National Guard and law enforcement in late February 2017 forcibly evicted the water protectors and shut down the encampment.[27] On June 1, 2017, the pipeline began moving North Dakota oil into South Dakota and Iowa to a distribution point in Illinois.[28] The Standing Rock and three other Sioux tribes took the issue to federal court.[29]

The encampment, located at the confluence of the Cannonball and Missouri Rivers, arose spontaneously in April 2016 when a few indigenous activists set up a makeshift outpost in an attempt to physically block the construction of the 1,172-mile pipeline.[30] The pipeline was designed to pass about a mile north of the Standing Rock Sioux tribal nation. The Energy Transfer Partners engineers planned to run the 30-inch-diameter steel pipe 90 to 110 feet under the Missouri River.[31] This land was ceded to the Sioux under the 1868 Treaty of Fort Laramie, which, like some four hundred treaties the U.S. government signed with Native American communities, was promptly violated by Washington.[32] The Missouri River provides the tribe's drinking water. The area is rich in farmland, ancient burial grounds, and artifacts. The small group of water protectors were joined by dozens, hundreds, and eventually as many as ten thousand supporters from around the country. They built three more satellite camps.[33] The Standing Rock encampment established on the floodplain along the banks of the Missouri River formed a governing structure. It built communal dining rooms, a medical center, and a school; established a postal service, internal security, a press center; and setup venues for community meetings and entertainment.

"I've seen a lot of companies come into North Dakota because of the Bakken Shale," the chairman of the Standing Rock Tribal Council, Dave Archambault II, said, shivering in the icy wind. The Bakken Shale is one of the largest oil development projects in the United States in the last forty years. It is located in eastern Montana and western North Dakota, as well as parts of Saskatchewan and Manitoba in the Williston Basin.

"In 2003, they were getting leases," he said. "In 2006, they started fracking. We've seen a lot of money come into the state. You see the landscape change from what it was prior to 2000. People who live there understand what I'm talking about. There are spills where the earth still hasn't healed. In northwest North Dakota you'll find green bins filled with straining socks that collect the fracking fluid. They're just dumped.

"The way they collect tar sand, it completely destroyed Mother Earth," he said. "It's bringing something dirty into America to get refined. The energy used to refine [costs more] than it's worth. That's the will of the nation: do whatever it can to extract fossil fuels. We oppose any fracking. We had a resolution, a moratorium passed. No fracking on Standing Rock. We oppose the destruction of Mother Earth. We were never opposed to energy independence, national security, or economic development. Those are the three things [used to] justify the Dakota Access Pipeline.

"They pit the protesters against law enforcement," he said of the company. "They pit the state government against tribal government. Anytime there is aggression from water protectors, anytime there's aggression from law enforcement, there's a reaction. I don't condone violence."

I walked through the encampment with Kandi Mossett from the Mandan, Hidatsa, and Arikara tribes in North Dakota. She had been at the site since August 15. She is one of the leading voices in the fight to bring visibility to the impacts that climate change and the fossil fuel industry inflict on indigenous communities. We stood over a small fire tended by two Native elders.

"This here is one of the sacred fires," she explained. "There are two here at the camp. It's been going since the beginning. It's never allowed to be put out because of how the fire balances on the water. Men are the keepers of the fire. Women are the keepers of the water. There always has to be a balance. It was lit April 1st. It's maintained every day."

The plane passed above us. She peered into the hills where law enforcement officials with scopes were looking down on the protesters. The activists had already been brutally pushed out of satellite sites, including on October 27 when they were driven from "the treaty camp," which blocked the main road. Police from six states, a small army of private security contractors, and the National Guard confronted them. The militarized force used armored personnel carriers, rubber bullets, stun guns, Tasers, tear gas, cannons that shot water laced with chemicals, and sound cannons that cause permanent hearing loss to push the protesters back. Drones hovered overhead. Attack dogs were unleashed on the crowds. Hundreds were beaten. The 141 who were arrested were held in dank, overcrowded cells.[34] Many were charged with felonies. The press, or at least the press that attempted to report honestly, was harassed and censored. Reporters were often detained or arrested. And mixed in with the water protectors was a small army of infiltrators, spies, and agents provocateurs, who initiated vandalism and rock throwing and singled out leaders for arrest.

"It hurts," Mossett said of the sound cannon. "My ears were ringing well into the night."

An infiltrator was caught on video during the October 27 eviction pointing to Mossett, as police waded into the crowd, to identify her for arrest.

"He is also shown in the video walking and picking up rocks," she said of the infiltrator. "He starts throwing them at police. When he throws rocks, I see a few other people throw water bottles. One of our women says, 'Stop throwing shit!' So people stop. But there's instigators and infiltrators. We've had, here at this fire, two women who were called bikers because of the way they were dressed. When they lifted up their hands with everybody, people saw they had wires on. Security went to them. They said, 'We see that you're miced.' They took off running. Went over the fence. And a car came zooming, picked them up, and they took off. It's not easy to keep them out. They can roll under the fence. They can come from under the security gates. We know they're here.

"There's been around five hundred of us who have been arrested to date," she said. "Hundreds who have been sprayed in the face, shot with rubber bullets, attacked by DAPL private security dogs. I don't think [a single] one of those security guys has been arrested. Just this week, one of those guys was pointing his gun at everybody. He shot six or seven rounds into the air."

She lifted the flap of a large tent. We walked inside. It was filled with donated items from around the country including canned goods, blankets, toilet paper, deodorant, toothpaste, and soap. We walked past a yurt that served as the school for about twenty children. A huge refrigeration truck, its engine humming, was hooked up to a generator and solar panels.

Fracking devastated Mossett's tribal nation in North Dakota.

"It's been a complete change from the little community I grew up in, where you knew your neighbors and you borrowed a cup of sugar," she said, her voice breaking with emotion. "You walked without fear as children. It's not like that anymore. Literally, people try to kidnap our kids who are walking home from elementary school. All these man camps spring up around our community. There's violence. The rapes. The incidents. It wasn't just women. It's children. There were babies who were taken. Sickening things are happening.

"Hundreds and hundreds of police protecting a pipeline," she mused. "Where were you when we needed you in our community? Where were you when we needed you to protect us from predators?

"They use anywhere between five hundred to two thousand chemicals in the process of fracking," she said. "They dig around ten thousand feet. When you go that deep below the surface you get to the naturally occurring radioactive materials . . . They have technology that will drill horizontally for miles. They literally create mini-earthquakes. They crack open shale. What flows up is all the produced water, which [will] never [be] available for animal or human consumption again. They're supposed to take that water to injection sites where they pump it back, where it's supposed to stay forever. But the companies have to pay a certain amount—like $30,000—to haul it to an injection site. Whereas if they dump it, it's just a $10,000 fine. So they drive on the reservation with their nozzles pointed.

"North Dakota is a huge fossil fuel state," she said. "We have seven coal-fired power plants. As a result, every single bit of the eleven thousand miles of rivers, lakes, and streams in North Dakota is already contaminated with mercury.

"We have been seeing, even in the past summer during a fishing tournament, deformities in the mouths of the fish," she said. "We're seeing sores and pus. Fish and wildlife service are finding dissolved solids in the fish that are a result of the fracking and chemicals going into the water.

"If you're in North Dakota, natural gas is a by-product of the industry," she went on. "So the flaring came as a result. You see these huge flares on the ground. Do a 360 and that's what you see everywhere. It's like a war zone."

The children on the reservation became ill.

"When my little niece was seven we had to rush her to the hospital because she couldn't breathe," she said. "They couldn't believe it: she was breathing through the size of a pinhole, her lungs were so constricted. We said, 'Does she have asthma?' 'No.' She's going to take asthma medication for a few weeks. But we don't know what it is. This all started happening when fracking came to our community.

"Growing up on the reservation in North Dakota, it was normal to have people around me be sick all the time," she said. "Two years into my undergrad program, I was diagnosed with stage four sarcoma tumor. The first thing my mom did was break down crying. I probably would have been a lot more scared if I had understood what that meant at the time. Most people with a stage four sarcoma don't make it. It took them three weeks to diagnose it because it wasn't attached to muscle or bone like it was supposed to be. It was in my subcutaneous tissue, which is a nice way of saying fat. I found a pea-sized lump. It was really purple. It was changing colors. I knew it was bad. I went to the Indian health service because that's our insurance. I had to get a referral; it was the only way to get [off the reservation] to see a doctor. And they wouldn't give it to me. They said come back in thirty days. I was back in six days. It had gone from pea-sized to walnut-sized. In six days. He took one look at it. Gave me the referral. . . . Came back, did a wide incision, have a scar. About ten and a half inches. They took a skin graft off the back of my leg. . . . I had another surgery to take off the skin graft. Had another surgery to repair that surgery. Then another surgery because they didn't sew it up

258 AMERICA: The Farewell Tour

right. I think it was five surgeries. Then I had to get bone scans, CAT scans. After ten years, I was considered legally cured. I refused radiation. I refused chemotherapy. I knew what it did. I wanted to have kids. This was when I was younger. I knew it could hurt good cells and bad cells. So they said okay, it's your choice. I survived. But I have friends who didn't."

She started to cry.

"I have a friend who left behind two beautiful children," she said, choking back tears. "She got cancer in her uterus. They couldn't operate. She died. It's really hard. My partner's grandma has lung cancer. We're like, 'We're going to fight this.' Three months later she was gone. Person after person. We just buried my uncle this past year for prostate cancer. My other uncle has prostate cancer but they caught it soon enough. My grandpa had cancer. It makes me question, 'Why am I still here when other people lost their battle?' That's a big part of why I'm doing what I'm doing. What does environmental racism mean? What does climate justice mean? Our own people in our own communities didn't even understand the concept that we were unfairly and disproportionately targeted by the fossil fuel industry. We lacked the resources to push back.

"I have two shoe boxes full of obituaries," she said. "You know how thin a piece of paper is. Just from the people I know, the funerals that I attended. I could write on each of them what kind of cancer they died from. I use the information to put a face and a name, to say this was so-and-so. This is what they died from. Maybe get some justice that way. Instead of just being an ignored population.

"A government literally tried to terminate us," she said, her voice breaking again. "We're still here. That's what's beautiful. And we're fighting. And we're winning against all odds. We are going against them unarmed. I'm with my three-year-old daughter half the time, going against Army National Guard, police from seven different states, GS4—they're tier 1, highly militarized, just back from Afghanistan and Iraq mercenaries. Against us. It's the craziest thing in the world, to be standing there against people fully suited up in riot gear. Every single one of them had a real gun on them as well. As well as canisters—that looked like fire extinguishers—of pepper spray. Huge canisters. And Tasers.

"My grandfather was a World War II vet," she said. "He had two

Purple Hearts. He walked around with a metal plate in his head all his life. He was there when they stormed the beaches in Normandy. He was eighteen years old when he was there. He didn't fight for his country and walk around with a metal plate for his granddaughter to be attacked by people who are supposed to be protecting civilians in this country."

I walked up the hill overlooking the encampment. I pushed open the flap to a yurt to speak with Native American activist Tom B. K. Goldtooth. He invited me to sit. We warmed ourselves in front of a small, wood-burning cast iron stove.

"I was a young man during that Red Power movement," he said. "I sometimes tease and joke about it. I was recruited by some of the AIM [American Indian Movement] leadership back then.

"The role of this activism, called Red Power, the American Indian Movement, the United Indian Movement, United Native Americans, the National Indian Youth Council, the Women of All Red Nations, all these are manifestations of the prophecies of the sixth generation that try to address the issues of colonization, assimilation, acculturation," he said. "The products of industrialization that drive us away from who we are. Activism helped me identify my role. I've always been committed to nonviolence. It's a part of my teachings. I mentioned anger, frustration, rage. The foundation of that understanding of love and compassion for *Unci Maka*, that love for Mother Earth, understanding the balance of the colors in the rainbow that encompass everyone. It's always been there. It's a search to find that patience and how we utilize our mind and heart. The longest journey sometimes is between the mind and the heart.

"I talk about the need for young people to have patience, to put the prayer first, rather than just jumping out there and putting their energy into action," he said. "That's what the corporations want. That's what the government wants. They want us to react. They want us to feel that anger. When the anger escalates, our feelings, frustrations, it goes back to that rage. The rage of the machines. It feeds off the unhappiness of people.

"The prophecies say we're dealing with a monster, a predator, a black snake [the pipeline] that could eat up all life itself," he said. "That's why this is a spiritual responsibility. To bring in that light, that compassionate light. We have no other place to go. Earth is my home. Do not be fearful of change. Out of the chaos comes balance and harmony. There really is a need for us to reevaluate that relationship we have with Mother Earth.

"Economic systems continue to eat up life itself, even the heart of workers, and it's not sustainable," he said. "Mother Earth is crying out for a revolution. It's not just here with indigenous people. It's with my brothers and sisters in the Amazon. I've experienced the spiritual woman of the forest with her long black hair that goes all the way down to her ankle. She's the one who came in a dream and said we are to unite the women of the Amazon and the women of the north who are affected by oil, who live near rivers and come from families that have been resistant since day one. We brought these women to Paris, France, during the United Nations climate negotiations last year. Some of them were here, in fact, to lift up that voice as women. The women here are the foundation of the resistance.

"One of the actions held two and a half months ago came from the women," Goldtooth continued. "We saw there was a need to bring our voices, heart, to the front lines of police barricades south of Mandan, North Dakota. Those police are separated from nature. They're separated from themselves. They're separated from me. I feel sadness that we can't talk. But I feel there is hope. We took our voices to the memorial bridge, in honor of the veterans, that separates Mandan from Bismarck. Our Native people action team made a big red banner, which symbolizes that we are the red line of protection of the sacredness of water. We mobilized a one-mile caravan leaving here in prayer. The women just got through doing a ceremony along the Cannonball River. They brought water with them. They said, 'We, as your grandmother, aunties, and sisters, want to give water.' At the police line, where the North Dakota State Highway Patrol, Morton County sheriffs—I don't think the National Guard was there yet—they offered them water."

"If the pipeline is built, is that a defeat?" I asked.

"That oil is going to run dry a lot sooner than they think," he said wryly. "Maybe that corporation is going to go bankrupt. Who knows."

The resistance by the water protectors at Standing Rock provides the template for future resistance movements. It was nonviolent. It was sustained. It was highly organized. It was grounded in spiritual, historical, and cultural traditions. It grew organically out of community. And it lit the conscience of the nation. It failed in its ultimate aim to stop the pipeline, approved by Trump when he took office, but it showed us how to resist.

GEORGE LAKEY, THE EUGENE M. Lang Visiting Professor for Issues in Social Change emeritus at Swarthmore College and a sociologist who focuses on nonviolent social change, compares the response of Sweden and Norway in the 1920s and 1930s to the rise of fascism with the response in Italy and Germany. We live, Lakey argues, in a similar historical moment. Lakey was a trainer for Mississippi Freedom Summer during the civil rights movement and coauthored with Martin Oppenheimer *A Manual for Direct Action: Strategy and Tactics for Civil Rights and All Other Nonviolent Protest Movements*, one of the seminal texts of the civil rights movement. We met in New York City.

"Fascism was a definite threat," he said of Sweden and Norway. "And they were also experiencing [economic] depression. Norway's degree of depression was even worse than Germany's. It was the worst in Europe. The highest unemployment in Europe. People were literally starving. The pressure, the pro-fascist setup that the Depression brings, was very present both in Sweden and in Norway. What the Nazis did there—what they did in Germany and what the fascists did in Italy—was provocation, provocation, provocation. 'Bait the left. The left will come. And we'll have street fighting.' "

Street violence, he said, echoing Native American elders, always "strengthens the state."

"It puts more pressure on the state—which is presided over by the one percent—to step in more and more forcefully, with the middle class saying, 'We care about order. We don't want chaos,' " he said. "That's what happened in Germany. It was a strengthening of the state. This happened in Italy as well. That's what the game plan was for fascists in Norway and Sweden. It didn't work. It didn't work because the left didn't play their game. They didn't allow themselves to be baited into paying attention to them, doing street-fighting.

"Instead, they did what in the civil rights movement we would have called 'they kept their eyes on the prize,' " Lakey said. "They knew the prize was to push away the economic elite, get rid of its dominance, so they can set up a new economic system, which is now called the Nordic model. What they did was: massive strikes, massive boycotts, massive demonstrations. Not only in the urban areas, which is what you expect, but also in the rural areas. During the Depression [in Sweden and Norway], there were lots of farmers who had their farms foreclosed on. Farmers are perennially in debt and had no way of repaying that debt. When the sheriff came, farmers in that county would come to join them and collectively not cooperate—not violently, but very strongly—in such a way that the sheriff couldn't carry out the auction.

"The group I'm involved with [Earth Quaker Action Team] loves to go after corporations," he said. "We went after a bank [PNC], the seventh largest bank in the country, but it was the No. 1 financier of mountaintop removal coal mining in Appalachia. We forced that bank out of the business of financing mountaintop coal mining. Nonviolently. Disrupting. Disrupting. We were in bank branches all over the place. We shut down two shareholder meetings. We led a boycott in which people took out money from that bank and were putting it in their local credit unions. So there's more than one way to go after the one percent.

"These days, a very smart way to do that is to focus on the economic entities that are owned by the one percent, who are basically responsible for the oppression that we experience," he said. "Remember who is actually running things, and we keep our focus on them both politically and economically."

Resistance, he stressed, will come from outside the formal political system. It will not be embraced by the two main political parties or most institutions, which are under corporate control.

"We can make tremendous strides and start building that mass movement," he said, "which in Norway and Sweden was able to push the economic elites away. So that's an indication of the way to build a movement—which is not to take them on the way antifa suggests; instead, [do it] in the way the civil rights movement did. It worked. I was there. The Ku Klux Klan was much stronger than it is now. In the Deep South, the Ku Klux Klan virtually ran the [South]."

Resistance, he said, means movements have to keep "pushing, pushing, pushing. Campaign after campaign after campaign." It must always stay "on the offensive. That's the secret.

"As soon as they lost that sense of going on the offensive, choosing campaign after campaign and winning those campaigns, that was when they lost their momentum," he said of the civil rights movement. "The important thing about what happened in Norway and Sweden was they kept their momentum. The campaigns continued to grow in number and in power until the economic elite was out.

"I was very influenced by Bayard Rustin, who was the chief strategist for Dr. Martin Luther King," he said. "I heard Bayard say over and over and over, 'If we don't get this economic justice thing done, in fifty years we're still going to have rampant racism.' He was right. But Dr. King and the other leaders who understood that were not able to get a sufficient number of people to make it. Now, the '63 march was for jobs and justice. So they were able to do it to some degree. They kept moving in that direction, involving white trade unions in that process. But in the situation of general prosperity, there were many people who were content with our economic system."

The country's economic decline, deindustrialization, austerity, debt peonage, the decay and collapse of social services and infrastructure, and the impoverishment of the working class, Lakey said, have changed the configuration. The working class, in short, can no longer be bought off.

"We're in a very different situation," he said. "We're still in austerity. There's not the degree of [contentment] that there once was. Trump has obviously capitalized on that fact. There's discontent. I think what Dr. King and Bayard and others wanted to happen in the sixties is now realizable.

"The impact of ignoring climate change is going to be more and more disastrous," he added. "We're just through it now with [a devastating hurricane in] Houston. We're going to see more and more money drained off by that [kind of natural disaster]. Again, the one percent won't want to pay their fair share. What that leaves us is a population that is more and more discontented. We see that polarization going on. Polarization always goes along with increased inequality. We can expect more polarization. That's a part of the temptation of antifa: 'I'm more and more upset.'

"When dealing with mountaintop removal coal mining, we went from an organization [Earth Quaker Action Team] that started in a living room to thirteen states," he said. "We were steadfastly nonviolent. And we were targeting something people understood. 'Wow, you're going after the bank that's financing this? I want to join that.' What we were about was making the bank's life so difficult that they would choose instead to get out of the business.

"There's really no need for us to shift our attention from going after the one percent to go after, often, working-class guys on the extreme right," he said. "We [must] look at their real, genuine grievances and address them. How many people on the right are from working-class families who are not being served by our health care system? Many people on the far right are from a demographic that is actually losing life expectancy for the first time in U.S. history. The health care system in the U.S. is a mess. Obamacare is better than previous [health care]. But it's [still] a mess. So what we can do is address the genuine grievances instead of writing people off as if obsession with racism is all that's going on. Fascism grows when the economy declines. So let's address the real thing instead of the symptom."

Nonviolence is not passivity. Wielded astutely, as Lakey said, "it defangs those who want to do us in."

"It's not like the one percent was fond of the civil rights movement," he said. "They had to be dragged kicking and screaming into making concessions. J. Edgar Hoover was even quoted as saying, '[Martin Luther King Jr. is] the most dangerous [Negro] man in America.' "

THE DISCONTENT IN FERGUSON, ATHENS, Cairo, Madrid, and Ayotzinapa is a single discontent. And the emerging revolt, although it will come in many colors, speak many languages, and have different beliefs and values, will be united around a common enemy. Bonds of solidarity and consciousness will unite the wretched of the earth against our global corporate masters.

The leadership for this revolt will not come from institutions of privilege or elite universities, but from the squalid internal colonies that house the poor and usually people of color. The next great revolutionary in America won't look like Thomas Jefferson. He or she will look like the rapper Lupe Fiasco.

The corporate state, no longer concerned with addressing economic and racial inequality, is readying for a confrontation. None of the reforms, increased training, high-powered weaponry, diversity programs, community outreach, SWAT teams, and gimmicks such as body cameras have blunted America's deadly police assault, especially against poor people of color. By the end of 2015, *The Washington Post* counted 995 people shot dead by police.[35] The *Guardian* counted 1,146 people killed.[36] The website Fatal Encounters recorded 1,357 killed.[37] Police are unaccountable, militarized monstrosities that spread fear and terror in poor communities. By comparison, police in England and Wales killed 1,631 people in the twenty-seven years between the start of 1990 and the end of 2016.[38]

Police function as predators in impoverished communities. They indiscriminately seize money, real estate, automobiles, and other assets under forfeiture laws. Traffic, parking, and other fines are often little more than legalized extortion that funds local government and turns jails into debtor prisons.

Millions of young men and women are railroaded into prison, many for nonviolent offenses, without a trial. SWAT teams burst into homes under warrants for nonviolent offenses, sometimes shooting those inside. Trigger-happy police pump multiple rounds into the backs of unarmed men and women and are rarely charged with murder. And basic constitutional rights, including due process for the poor, were effectively abolished decades ago.

Jonathan Simon's *Governing Through Crime* and Michelle Alexander's *The New Jim Crow* argue that what is defined and targeted as criminal activity by the police and the courts is largely determined by racial inequality and class, and most importantly by the potential for targeted groups to cause social and political unrest. Criminal policy, as the sociologist Alex S. Vitale points out in his book *The End of Policing*, "is structured around the use of punishment to manage the 'dangerous classes,' masquerading as a system of justice."[39]

The criminal justice system, at the same time, refuses to hold Wall Street banks, corporations, and oligarchs accountable for crimes that have caused incalculable damage to the global economy, ecosystem, and the lives of tens of millions of Americans. None of the bankers who committed massive acts of fraud that led to the financial collapse in 2008 have gone to prison.[40] Their crimes resulted in widespread unemployment, millions of evictions and foreclosures, homelessness, bankruptcies, and the looting of the U.S. Treasury to bail out these financial speculators at taxpayer expense.

We live in a two-tiered legal system, one where poor people are harassed, arrested, and jailed for absurd infractions, such as selling loose cigarettes—which led to Eric Garner being choked to death by the New York City police in 2014—while crimes of appalling magnitude by the oligarchs and corporations, from oil spills to bank fraud in the hundreds of billions of dollars, which wiped out 40 percent of the world's wealth,[41] are dealt with through tepid administrative controls, symbolic fines, and civil enforcement that give these wealthy perpetrators immunity from criminal prosecution.

The grotesque distortions of the judicial system and aggressive war on the poor by the police will get worse under Trump and Attorney General Jeff Sessions. Already they are rolling back the restrictions President Barack Obama put in place in 2015 for the 1033 Program, allowing the transfer of military-grade weaponry, including grenade launchers, armored personnel carriers, and .50-caliber machine guns, from the federal government to local police forces. Since 1997, the Department of Defense has turned over a staggering $5.1 billion in military hardware to police departments.[42] The Trump administration has also resurrected private prisons in the federal prison system, accelerated the so-called war on drugs, is stacking the courts with right-wing "law and order" judges, and is preaching the divisive politics of punishment and retribution. Many police unions enthusiastically embrace these actions, seeing in them a return to the Wild West mentality that characterized the brutality of police departments in the 1960s and 1970s, when radicals, especially black radicals, were murdered with impunity by law enforcement. The Praetorian Guard of the elites, as in all totalitarian systems, will be beyond the reach of the law. "Our entire criminal justice system has become a gigantic revenge factory," Vitale writes.[43]

The arguments used to justify the expansion of police power, from the racist trope of "superpredators" to the "war on drugs," have no credibility. The abject failure of the war on drugs, along with the vast expansion of the prison system and police powers over the last forty years, has not improved the lives of the poor. The problem is not ultimately in policing techniques and procedures, it is in the increasing reliance on the police as a form of social control. Police sustain a system of corporate capitalism that has turned the working poor into modern-day serfs and abandoned whole segments of society as surplus labor. The government no longer attempts to address racial and economic inequality. Instead, it criminalizes poverty. It turns the poor into another cash crop for the rich. Fyodor Dostoyevsky said that the degree of civilization in a society can be judged by entering its prisons.

"By conceptualizing the problem of policing as one of inadequate training and professionalization, reformers fail to directly address how the very nature of policing and the legal system served to maintain and exacerbate racial inequality," Vitale writes. "By calling for colorblind 'law and order' they strengthen a system that puts people of color at a structural disadvantage. At the root, they fail to appreciate that the basic nature of the police, since its earliest origins, is to be a tool for managing inequality and maintaining the status quo. Police reforms that fail to directly address this reality are doomed to reproduce it. . . . Well-trained police following proper procedures are still going to be arresting people for mostly low-level offenses, and the burden of that will continue to fall primarily on communities of color because *that is how the system is designed to operate*—not because of the biases or misunderstandings of officers."[44]

"We've been waging a war on drugs for forty years by putting people in prison for ever longer sentences," Vitale told me. "Yet drugs are cheaper, easier to get, and at a higher quality than they've ever been. Any high school student in America can get any kind of drugs they want. Yet we persist in this idea that the way to respond to the problem of drugs, and many other social problems, is through arrest, courts, punishments, prisons. This is what Trump is playing to. This idea that the only appropriate role for the state is one of coercion and threats—whether it's in the foreign policy sphere or in the domestic sphere."

Police forces, as Vitale writes in his book, were originally created by the property classes to maintain economic and political dominance and exert control over slaves, the poor, dissidents, and labor unions that challenged the wealthy's hold on power and ability to amass personal fortunes. Yes, they also address crime, but this is not their primary function. The political, cultural, and judicial system in a capitalist state is centered around the protection of property rights. And, as Adam Smith pointed out, when civil government "is instituted for the security of property, [it] is in reality instituted for the defense of the rich against the poor, or of those who have some property against those who have none at all."[45]

Many of America's policing techniques, including widespread surveillance, were pioneered and perfected in American colonies such as the Philippines before being introduced to police departments in the United States. Blacks in the South had to be controlled. Labor unions and radical socialists had to be broken.

"People often point to the London Metropolitan Police, who were formed in the 1820s by Sir Robert Peel," Vitale said when we met. "They are held up as this liberal ideal of a dispassionate, politically neutral police with the support of the citizenry. But this really misreads the history. Peel is sent to manage the British occupation of Ireland. He's confronted with a dilemma. Historically, peasant uprisings, rural outrages were dealt with by either the local militia or the British military. In the wake of the Napoleonic Wars, in the need for soldiers in other parts of the British Empire, he is having more and more difficulty managing these disorders. In addition, when he does call out the militia, they often open fire on the crowd and kill lots of people, creating martyrs and inflaming further unrest. He said, 'I need a force that can manage these outrages without inflaming passions further.' He developed the Peace Preservation Force, which was the first attempt to create a hybrid military-civilian force that can try to win over the population by embedding itself in the local communities, taking on some crime control functions, but its primary purpose was always to manage the occupation. He then exports that model to London as the industrial working classes are flooding the city, dealing with poverty, cycles of boom and bust in the economy, and that becomes their primary mission.

"The creation of the very first state police force in the United States was the Pennsylvania State Police in 1905," Vitale went on. "For the same reasons. It was modeled similarly on U.S. occupation forces in the Philippines. There was a back-and-forth with personnel and ideas. What happened was local police were unable to manage the coal strikes and iron strikes. . . . They needed a force that was more adherent to the interests of capital. . . . Interestingly, for these small-town police forces in a coal mining town there was sometimes sympathy. They wouldn't open fire on the strikers. So, the state police force was created to be the strong arm for the law. Again, the direct connection between colonialism and the domestic management of workers. . . . It's a two-way exchange. As we're developing ideas throughout our own colonial undertakings, bringing those ideas home, and then refining them and shipping them back to our partners around the world who are often despotic regimes with close economic relationships to the United States. There's a very sad history here of the U.S. exporting basically models of policing that morph into death squads and horrible human rights abuses."

The almost exclusive reliance on militarized police to deal with profound inequality and social problems is turning poor neighborhoods in cities such as Chicago into failed states. The "broken windows" policy, adopted by many cities, argues that disorder produces crime. It criminalizes minor infractions, upending decades of research showing that social dislocation leads to crime. It creates an environment where the poor are constantly harassed, fined, and arrested for nonsubstantive activities.

"As poverty deepens and housing prices rise, government support for affordable housing has evaporated, leaving in its wake a combination of homeless shelters and aggressive broken-windows-oriented policing," Vitale writes. "As mental health facilities close, police become the first responders to calls for assistance with mental health crises. As youth are left without adequate schools, jobs, or recreational facilities, they form gangs for mutual protection or participate in the black markets of stolen goods, drugs, and sex to survive and are ruthlessly criminalized."[46]

The corporate state is dismantling the mechanisms that could ameliorate this crisis—affordable housing; well-paying jobs; safe, well-staffed, and well-funded schools and colleges that do not charge tuition; expanded mental health facilities; good public transportation; the rebuilding of the nation's infrastructure; demilitarized police forces; universal, government-funded health care; an end to the predatory loans and practices of big banks; and a campaign to pay reparations to African Americans and end racial segregation.

"We *need* an effective system of crime prevention and control in our communities, but that is not what the current system is," Alexander writes in *The New Jim Crow.* "The system is better designed to create crime, and a perpetual class of people labeled criminal. . . . Saying mass incarceration is an abysmal failure makes sense, though only if one assumes that the criminal justice system is designed to prevent and control crime. But if mass incarceration is understood as a system of social control—specifically, racial control—then the system is a fantastic success."[47]

The indiscriminate murders of young black men and women by police in the United States—a crisis undiminished by the protests of groups such as Black Lives Matter and by the empty rhetoric of black political elites—have given birth to a new young black militant. This militant, rising off the bloody streets of cities such as Baltimore or Ferguson, Missouri, understands that the beast is not simply chronic poverty and the many iterations of racism, but the destructive forces of corporate capitalism. This militant has given up on electoral politics, the courts, and legislative reform, loathes the corporate press, and rejects established black leaders such as Barack Obama, Jesse Jackson, Al Sharpton, and Michael Eric Dyson. This militant believes it is only in the streets and in acts of civil disobedience that change is possible.

T-Dubb-O is a hip-hop artist from St. Louis. He cofounded Hands Up United. The organization was formed in the wake of the murder of Michael Brown on August 9, 2014, in Ferguson. It has built close alliances with radical organizations in Latin America, Europe, and Palestine.

"In my city every day, police is pulling somebody over, harassing

them, extorting them," T-Dubb-O told me. "Because that's what it is—
it's legal extortion. When a government is making 30 to 40 percent of
their yearly budget off of tickets, fines, and imprisonment, it's extortion.
It's the same thing the mob did in the twenties. So we fight. We can't go
back to normal lives. We get followed, harassed, death threats, phones
tapped, social media watched, they hack into our emails, hack into our
social media account, we all got FBI files. They know we here right now.
So I mean it's not a game, but it's either continue to deal with not being
able to just live like a regular person, and dream, and have an opportunity,
or get up and do something about it. And we decided to do something."

"I went to Canfield [Drive, where Brown was killed]," Rika Tyler,
who also founded Hands Up United, told me. "I saw the body. I saw the
blood. I just broke down. And ever since then I've just been out there [as
an activist] every day.

"They left [Brown] in the street for four and a half hours in the
hot sun on concrete, just for display," she said. "That reminded me of a
modern-day lynching. Because you know, they used to lynch slaves and
then have it displayed. And that's basically showing us that this system is
not built for us.

"Just envision a debtor's prison being run by a collusion between
city officials, police, and court judges, who treated our community like
an ATM machine," Tyler said. "Because that's all they did. Ferguson is
in St. Louis County. It's 21,000 people living in 8,100 households. So
it's a small town. Sixty-seven percent of the residents are African American. Twenty-two percent live below poverty level. A total of $2.6 million
[were paid in fines to city officials, the courts, and the police] in 2013.
The Ferguson Municipal Court disposed of 24,532 warrants and 12,018
cases. That's about three warrants per household. One and a half cases
for each household. You don't get $321 in fines and fees and three war-
rants per household from an average crime rate. You get numbers like
this from racist bullshit, arrests from jaywalking, and constant low-level
harassment involving traffic stops, court appearances, high fines, and the
threat of jail for failure to pay. You can get a ticket from walking across
the street, or a ticket from not cutting your grass, and then you're stuck in
this system that they put us in, that is oppressed, and keeps us oppressed.

"I was arrested when I was pregnant, I was thirty-seven weeks and I was arrested in St. Charles County by four white officers," she said. "They took me into custody when I had this big-ass stomach. And I'm like, 'I'm pregnant.' I had a traffic ticket for parking in the wrong meter. And they wrote me a ticket and I never paid it, so they took me. I had a warrant out for my arrest. I sat in jail, pregnant, had my baby a week early because I was stressed out and crying my eyes out in jail."

"No person should have to go through this," T-Dubb-O said, "whether it's in America, Palestine, Mexico, Brazil, Canada. Nobody should have to go through this. You look at a bunch of young people [in Ferguson], their age ranges anywhere from twelve to twenty-eight or twenty-nine, that went against the most powerful military force in this world. That's pretty much what happened. . . . It was tanks on every corner, our phones tapped, they follow us. Every day we was out there we thought we were gonna die. At one point in time they said they were gonna kill us. 'We're not shooting rubber bullets tonight, we're shooting live ammunition.' And these are the things that you don't see on the news. It was just because we was tired of being treated as less than people. Just for opportunity to be able to walk the streets and live and breathe and do what everybody else does.

"In St. Louis, if you've been arrested and you're facing a misdemeanor or felony charges, you're not allowed a Pell Grant to go to college," he said. "So if you can't afford to pay to go to college you're just stuck. If you're on probation and you're trying to get a job—it's a right-to-work state—they have the right to deny you employment because of your past. They don't have to give you an opportunity to work. Where do they leave you, back in the same system that puts you in the same position where you made the first mistake. It's all set up like this."

"I've been tear-gassed six times," Tyler said. "I've been shot at with rubber bullets, live ammo, wooden bullets, bean bag bullets, sound cannons, everything you can think of. I've went up against militarized police, and they did different things like a five-second rule, like I would get arrested if I stood still for longer than five seconds. I would get arrested if I didn't walk longer than five seconds. It was just different things. They don't wear their name badges. . . . Women have been hog-tied, beaten. I got arrested for standing on the sidewalk, just recording them."

T-Dubb-O, after the murder of Brown and the unrest in Ferguson, was invited with other black activists to meet with Obama in the White House. The president, he said, spoke "in clichés" about black-on-black crime, the necessity of staying in school, working hard, and the importance of voting.

"He asked me, 'Did I vote for him,' " he said. "I told him no. I didn't vote for him either time, because I didn't want to vote for him just because he was black. I felt like that would have been shallow on my end. Because he's never honestly spoken and said he was going to do anything for my community or the issues that we face on a daily basis, so why would I vote for somebody like that, whether you white, black, male, female, so on and so forth?

"When you have an eleven-year-old boy whose mother is single, or has a single father who's working two or three jobs just to put food on the table, he has to wake up at 5:30 in the morning, catch public transportation to school," T-Dubb-O said. "Everything around him is damnation. You can't expect an eleven-year-old to have the mental capacity of an adult, to say, 'I'm going to make the mature decisions and not get into trouble.' So I don't care about black-on-black crime. I don't care about the cliché of working hard, 'You can do anything, you can accomplish,' because that's bullshit. And excuse my language, but I can't tell a little boy up the street in my neighborhood, where over a hundred murders happened last year, that he can be an astronaut if he wants to be, because that's not possible.

"I think D.C. is a perfect example of what America is," he said. "You have this big White House representing the government, that was built by slaves, that's beautiful, excellent manicured lawns, and right outside the gate you have fifty homeless people sleeping in a park. Right outside of the gate of the White House. That perfectly describes America.

"The difference between us and those leaders is that we aren't doing it for fame, we aren't doing it for political gain, we aren't doing it for money," he said, speaking of Obama, Sharpton, Jackson, Dyson, and other establishment black leaders. "We're doing it because every day that we've lived we've been denied normal human rights, and we could have lost our life. We don't believe those leaders are properly representing our community. Because they are no longer a part of the community, they don't speak for the community, and honestly, they don't do much for it."

Jackson and Sharpton were heckled by crowds in Ferguson and told to leave, along with crews from CNN. Rika Tyler described CNN and other major news outlets, which often parrot back the official narrative, as "worse than politicians, worse than police."

"So people in Ferguson is basically like, 'Fuck Al Sharpton, and fuck Jesse Jackson, for real,' " Tyler said. "And that's the best way I can put it, for real, because they are co-opted. They had their own movement. Their movement got destroyed. Now they want to come to the new leaders and try to come in our movement and give guidance and stuff, but it's a totally different generation. They marched with suits and ties and sung 'Kumbaya' and stuff. It's people out there that look like him," she said, motioning to T-Dubb-O, "shirtless, tattoos, like Bloods, Crips, whatever, out there just mad, because they was pissed off and they was passionate about it.

"Jesse Jackson came—actually we were in the middle of a prayer for Michael Brown's mother, and we were at the memorial site in Canfield Apartments, where he was killed and laid down in the street for four and a half hours," Tyler said. "Everyone has their heads bowed and [Jackson] comes over and starts shouting 'No justice, no peace' in the middle of a prayer. So instantly the community is pissed the fuck off—like, 'Who the hell is this?' I finally recognized his face. I went over to him, because the guys were ready to fight him. You don't come over here—this mother's grieving, we're all upset—and break up our prayer. And he's all like, 'No justice, no peace!' He has his bullhorn, and his sign and everything, just for a photo op. So I went over and I said to him, 'You probably should leave, because they're really angry and they're gonna get you out of here.' And he was like, 'No justice, no peace!' and he just kept chanting. So I moved out of the way, and the dudes told him, 'Hey bro, if you don't back the fuck up we're gonna make you leave.' And he's like, 'This is what's wrong with us!' and 'Generational divide!' And you know the community wasn't taking it, so he got scared, him and the people he came with, his best-dressed suit on and everything, and everybody [else] was out there shirtless, or tank tops, or just in their normal clothes. And he came out there with a cameraman and everything, like this is just a frenzy or a freaking parade or something to film. So people were pissed off and he instantly left, and he hasn't really been back since."

"Every national organization you can think of is in St. Louis, Mo.," T-Dubb-O said. "We have Urban League. We have the NAACP. We have all these different organizations. But yet for the last two decades we've always had one of the three top murder rates, one of the three highest crime rates. Poverty level is crazy, unemployment, you have all these mission statements on your website saying you do this and you do that, yet those programs aren't available in our city. But you have offices here. You're getting grants. But you're not doing anything. And the community sees that now.

"As far as politics," T-Dubb-O said, "it's going to go either one of two ways. Right now we have a window that's closing pretty fast, to where we can either re-create this system . . . to actually be equal for all people, or they're going to re-create the system to where we'll never be able to punch it in the mouth like we did in Ferguson again.

"We don't know what it's gonna look like, honestly," he said of the coming unrest. "It's been legal to kill a black man in this country. Just since Mike Brown, eleven more people has been killed by police in St. Louis alone, one being a woman who was raped then hung in jail. But none of the other murders got national coverage. It was two standoffs with police yesterday. We know we're dedicated. We're going to continue to fight. It's going to take full-fledged revolution to make a change. The worst of the worst would be civil war. That's just where my mind is.

"I don't see them pulling back," he said of the state and its security forces. "They have no problem killing people. They have no problem shooting gas at babies, pregnant people, old people. They don't have an issue with it. And our politicians are just standing around with their arms folded.

"As long as the powers that be are in control, the oppression isn't going to go anywhere," he said. "It's really going to take people to unite worldwide, not just in America, not just in St. Louis, not just in one particular city or state. It's gonna have to be people identifying their struggles with each other worldwide, internationally, and say enough is enough. That's the only way oppression will ever leave."

PRISON HAS BECOME A RITE of passage for poor people of color. And the conditions in prison are a model for the corporate state.

Prisoners are ideal employees. They do not receive benefits or pensions. They earn under a dollar an hour. Some are forced to work for free. They are not paid overtime. They are forbidden to organize and strike. They must show up on time. They are not paid for sick days or granted vacations. They cannot alter working conditions or complain about safety hazards. If they are disobedient, or attempt to protest their pitiful wages and working conditions, they lose their jobs and are often segregated in isolation cells.

The roughly one million prisoners who work for corporations and government industries in the American prison system are a blueprint for what the corporate state expects us all to become. And corporations have no intention of permitting prison reforms to reduce the size of their bonded workforce. In fact, they are seeking to replicate these conditions throughout the society.

Our prison-industrial complex, which holds 2.3 million prisoners—22 percent of the world's prison population—makes money by keeping prisons full.[48] It demands bodies, regardless of color, gender, or ethnicity. As the system drains the pool of black male bodies, it has begun to incarcerate others. Women—the fastest-growing segment of the prison population—are swelling prisons, as are poor whites, Hispanics, and immigrants.

States, in the name of austerity, have stopped providing prisoners with essential items including shoes, extra blankets, and even toilet paper, while starting to charge them for electricity and room and board. Most prisoners and the families that struggle to support them are chronically short of money. When they go broke—and being broke is a frequent occurrence in prison—prisoners must take out prison loans to pay for medications, legal and medical fees, and basic commissary items such as soap and deodorant. Debt peonage inside prison is as prevalent as it is outside prison.

Prisoners are charged for visits to the infirmary and the dentist.

Prisoners must pay the state for a fifteen-minute deathbed visit to an immediate family member, or for a fifteen-minute visit to a funeral home to view the deceased. New Jersey, like most other states, forces a prisoner to reimburse the system for overtime wages paid to the two guards who accompany him or her to the visit or viewing, plus mileage cost. The charge can be as high as $945.04 in New Jersey. It can take years to pay off a visit with a dying father or mother when you make less than $30 a month.

Fines, often in the thousands of dollars, are assessed against many prisoners when they are sentenced. There are twenty-two fines that can be imposed in New Jersey, including the Violent Crime Compensation Assessment (VCCA), the Law Enforcement Officers Training & Equipment Fund (LEOT), and Extradition Costs (EXTRA). The state takes a percentage each month out of a prisoner's wages to pay for penalties. It can take decades to pay fines. Some 10 million Americans owe $50 billion in fees and fines because of their arrest or imprisonment, according to a 2015 report by the Brennan Center.

If a prisoner who is fined $10,000 at sentencing relies solely on a prison salary, he or she will owe about $4,000 after making monthly payments for twenty-five years. Prisoners often leave prison in debt to the state. And if they cannot continue to make regular payments—difficult because of high unemployment among ex-felons—they are sent back to prison. High recidivism is part of the design.

Most of the prison functions once handled by governments have become privatized. Corporations run prison commissaries and, since the prisoners have nowhere else to shop, often jack up prices by as much as 100 percent. Corporations have taken over the phone systems and grossly overcharge prisoners and their families. They demand exorbitant fees for money transfers from families to prisoners. And corporations, with workshops inside prisons, pay little more than a dollar a day to prison laborers. Food and merchandise vendors, construction companies, laundry services, uniform companies, prison equipment vendors, cafeteria services, manufacturers of pepper spray, body armor, and the array of medieval-looking instruments used for the physical control of prisoners, and a host of other contractors feed like jackals off prisons. Prisons, in America, are big business.

Slavery is legal in prisons under the Thirteenth Amendment of the U.S. Constitution, which reads: "Neither slavery nor involuntary servitude, except as punishment for crime whereof the party shall have been duly convicted, shall exist within the United States."[49] Prisoners are not covered under the Fair Labor Standards Act requiring workers to be paid the minimum wage. The highest hourly wage in prison rarely exceeds $2 and most prisoners earn less than a dollar an hour. In Alabama, Arkansas, Florida, Georgia, and Texas most prisoners are not paid for their work. Once you enter prison you become, in essence, a slave of the state.

Corporate investors, who have poured billions into the business of mass incarceration, expect long-term returns. And they will get them. It is their lobbyists who write the draconian laws that demand absurdly long sentences, deny paroles, determine immigrant detention laws, and impose minimum-sentence and Three-Strikes laws, which mandate life sentences after three felony convictions.

Corrections Corporation of America (CCA), the largest owner of for-profit prisons and immigration detention facilities in the country, earned $1.7 billion in revenues and collected $300 million in profits in 2013.[50] CCA holds an average of 81,384 inmates in its facilities on any one day.[51] Aramark Holdings Corp., a Philadelphia-based company that contracts through Aramark Correctional Services, provides food for six hundred correctional institutions across the United States.[52] Goldman Sachs and other investors acquired it in 2007 for $8.3 billion.[53] The three top for-profit prison corporations spent an estimated $45 million over a recent ten-year period for lobbying to keep the prison business flush.[54] The resource center In the Public Interest documented in its report "Criminal: How Lockup Quotas and 'Low-Crime Taxes' Guarantee Profits for Private Prison Corporations" that private prison companies often sign state contracts that guarantee prison occupancy rates of 90 percent.[55] If states fail to meet the quota they have to pay the corporations for the empty beds.

CCA in 2011 gave $710,300 in political contributions to candidates for federal or state office, political parties, and so-called 527 groups (PACs and super PACs), the American Civil Liberties Union reported.[56] The corporation also spent $1.07 million lobbying federal officials plus undisclosed sums to lobby state officials.[57] The GEO Group, one of the nation's largest for-profit prison management companies, donated $250,000 to Donald Trump in 2017.[58]

The United States, from 1970 to 2005, increased its prison population by about 700 percent, the ACLU reported.[59] Private prisons account for nearly all newly built prisons.[60] And nearly half of all immigrants detained by the federal government are shipped to for-profit prisons, according to Detention Watch Network.[61]

But corporate profit is not limited to building and administering prisons. Corporations rely on prison labor. Federal prisoners, who are among the highest paid in the U.S. prison system, making as much as $1.25 an hour, produce the military's helmets, uniforms, pants, shirts, ammunition belts, ID tags, and tents. Prisoners work, often through subcontractors, for major corporations such as Chevron, Bank of America, IBM, Motorola, Microsoft, McDonald's—which makes its uniforms in prison—AT&T, Starbucks, which manufactures holiday products, Nintendo, Victoria's Secret, JC Penney, Sears, Walmart, Kmart, Eddie Bauer, Wendy's, Procter & Gamble, Johnson & Johnson, Fruit of the Loom, Caterpillar, Sara Lee, Quaker Oats, Mary Kay, Microsoft, Texas Instruments, Dell, Honeywell, Hewlett-Packard, Nortel, Nordstrom's, Revlon, Macy's, Pierre Cardin, and Target. Prisoners in some states run dairy farms. They staff call centers, take hotel reservations, or work in slaughterhouses. They carry out public services such as collecting highway trash in states such as Ohio.

A Louisiana sheriff in October 2017 held a press conference to denounce a prisoner release program because it cost his department free labor. He lamented the prison will lose "some good [prisoners] that we use every day to wash cars, to change oil in the cars, to cook in the kitchen."[62] At the same time, it was revealed that up to 40 percent[63] of the firefighters battling the catastrophic forest fires sweeping across California in the fall of 2017 were prisoners earning $2 an hour.[64]

"Correctional industries" are run by Departments of Corrections to produce goods and provide services used by state employees. Former New Jersey governor Chris Christie, like many state employees, had his office furniture refurbished by prisoners in East Jersey State Prison. Products produced in correctional industries are sold to government departments and nonprofit organizations.

States, with shrinking budgets, share in the corporate exploitation. They get kickbacks of as much as 40 percent from corporations that prey on prisoners. This kickback money is often supposed to go into "inmate welfare funds," but prisoners say they rarely see any purchases made by the funds to improve life inside prison. The wages paid to prisoners for labor inside prisons have remained stagnant, and in real terms have declined over the past three decades. In New Jersey a prisoner made $1.20 for eight hours of work—yes, $1.20 for eight hours of work—in 1980 and today makes $1.30 for a day's labor. Prisoners earn, on average, $28 a month. Those incarcerated in for-profit prisons earn as little as 17 cents an hour.

However, items for sale in prison commissaries have risen in price over the past two decades by as much as 100 percent. Scrip, rather than money, was once paid to coal miners, and it could be used only at the company store. Prisoners live in a similar environment. And new rules in some prisons, including those in New Jersey, prohibit families from sending packages to prisoners, forcing prisoners to rely exclusively on prison vendors. This is as much a psychological blow as a material one—it leaves families feeling powerless to help loved ones trapped in the system.

A bar of Dove soap in 1996 cost New Jersey prisoners 97 cents. Today it costs $1.95, an increase of 101 percent. A tube of Crest toothpaste cost $2.35 in 1996 and today costs $3.49, an increase of 48 percent. AA batteries have risen by 184 percent, and a stick of deodorant has risen by 95 percent. The only two items I found that remained the same in price from 1996 were Frosted Flakes cereal and Cup O'Noodles, but these items in prisons have been switched from brand names to generic products. The white Reebok shoes that most prisoners wear, which last about six months, cost about $45 a pair. Those who cannot afford the Reebok brand must buy, for $20, substandard shoes with cardboard soles that shred easily. Keefe Supply Co., which runs commissaries for an estimated half a million prisoners in states including Florida and Maryland, is notorious for price gouging. It sells a single No. 10 white envelope for 15 cents—$15 per 100 envelopes. The typical retail cost outside prison for a box of 100 envelopes is $7. The company marks up a 3-ounce packet of noodle soup, one of the most popular commissary items, to 45 cents from 26 cents. There is a 10 percent charge imposed by New Jersey on every commissary purchase, including postage stamps.

Global Tel Link, a private phone company, jacks up phone rates in New Jersey to 15 cents a minute, although some states, such as New York, have relieved the economic load on families by reducing the charge to 4 cents a minute. The Federal Communications Commission determined that a fair rate for a fifteen-minute interstate call by a prisoner is $0.21 for debit and $0.25 for collect.[65] But a federal court ruled in June 2017 that the Federal Communications Commission did not have the authority to cap prison phone rates.[66] The high phone rates imposed on prisoners, who do not have a choice of carriers and must call either collect or by using debit accounts that hold prepaid deposits made by them or their families, are especially damaging to the two million children with a parent behind bars.

Monopolistic telephone contracts give kickbacks to the state amounting, on average, to 42 percent of gross revenues from prisoner phone calls, according to *Prison Legal News*.[67] The companies with exclusive prison phone contracts not only charge higher phone rates but add to the phone charges the cost of the kickbacks, called "commissions" by state agencies.[68] The phone market in state prison systems generates an estimated $362 million annually in gross revenues for the states, and costs prisoners' families, who put money into phone accounts, some $143 million a year.[69]

When strong family ties are retained, there are lower rates of recidivism and fewer parole violations. But that is not what the corporate architects of the prison system want. High recidivism, now at over 60 percent, keeps the cages full.[70] This is one reason, I suspect, that prisons make family visitations humiliating and difficult. It is not uncommon for the prisoners I teach in the New Jersey prison system to tell their families—especially those that include small children traumatized by the security screening, long waits, body searches, clanging metal doors, and gruff orders from the guards—not to visit. Prisoners with life sentences frequently urge loved ones to sever all ties and consider them as dead.

The rise of what Marie Gottschalk, the author of *Caught: The Prison State and the Lockdown of American Politics*, calls "the carceral state" is ominous.[71] It will not be reformed through elections or by appealing to political elites or the courts. Prisons are prototypes for the future, an example of the disempowerment and exploitation corporations seek to inflict on all workers.

Melvin Ray, James Pleasant, and Robert Earl Council led work stoppages in Alabama prisons in January 2014 as part of the Free Alabama Movement. After the uprising they were all placed in indefinite solitary confinement. Authorities were unnerved by the organized protests that engulfed three prisons in the state, as well as by videos and pictures of abusive conditions smuggled out by the movement.

The prison strike leaders are denied televisions and reading material in solitary confinement. They spend at least three days a week, sometimes longer, without leaving their tiny cells. They eat their meals sitting on steel toilets. They are allowed to shower once every two days, although temperatures routinely rise above 90 degrees in the summer.

The men are symbols of a growing resistance movement inside American prisons. The prisoners' work stoppages and refusal to cooperate with authorities in Alabama are modeled on actions that shook the Georgia prison system in December 2010. The strike leaders argue work stoppages are the only mechanism left to prisoners across America. By refusing to work—a tactic that forces prison authorities to hire compensated labor or to induce the prisoners to return to their jobs by paying a fair wage—the slavery that defines the prison system will be broken. Prisoners are organizing work stoppages in Arizona, California, Florida, Illinois, Ohio, Pennsylvania, Mississippi, Texas, Virginia, and Washington.

"WE HAVE TO SHUT DOWN the prisons," Council, known as Kinetik, one of the founders of the Free Alabama Movement, told me by phone from the Holman Correctional Facility in Escambia County, Alabama. He has been in prison for twenty-one years, serving a sentence of life without parole. "We will not work for free anymore. All the work in prisons, from cleaning to cutting grass to working in the kitchen, is done by inmate labor. [Almost no prisoner] in Alabama is paid. Without us the prisons, which are slave empires, cannot function. . . . The state gets from us millions of dollars in free labor and then imposes fees and fines.

You have brothers that work in kitchens twelve to fifteen hours a day and have done this for years and have never been paid."

"We do not believe in the political process," said Ray, who spoke from the St. Clair Correctional Facility in Springville, Alabama. He is also serving life without parole. "We are not looking to politicians to submit reform bills. We aren't giving more money to lawyers. We don't believe in the courts. We will rely only on protests inside and outside of prisons and on targeting the corporations that exploit prison labor and finance the school-to-prison pipeline. We have focused our first boycott on McDonald's. McDonald's uses prisoners to process beef for patties and package bread, milk, [and] chicken products. We have called for a national Stop Campaign against McDonald's. We have identified this corporation to expose all the others. There are too many corporations exploiting prison labor to try and take them all on at once.

"We are not going to call for protests outside of statehouses," Ray went on. "Legislators are owned by corporations. To go up there with the achy breaky heart is not going to do any good. These politicians are in it for the money. If you are fighting mass incarceration, the people who are incarcerated are not in the statehouse. They are not in the parks. They are in the prisons. If you are going to fight for the people in prison, join them at the prison. The kryptonite to fight the prison system, which is a $500 billion enterprise, is the work strike. And we need people to come to the prisons to let guys on the inside know they have outside support to shut the prison down. Once we take our labor back, prisons will again become places for correction and rehabilitation rather than centers of corporate profit."

The three prisoners said that until the prison-industrial complex was dismantled, there would be no prison reform. They said books such as Stokely Carmichael's *Ready for Revolution* and Alexander's *The New Jim Crow*, along with the failure of prison reform movements, convinced them that the only hope was to organize campaigns of noncooperation.

"The politicians are the ones who orchestrated this system," Ray said. "They are either directly involved as businessmen—many are already millionaires or billionaires, or they are controlled by millionaires and billionaires. We are not blindsided by titles. We are looking at what is going on behind the scenes. We see a coordinated effort by the Koch brothers, ALEC [American Legislative Exchange Council], and political action committees that see in prisons a business opportunity. Their goal is to increase earnings. And once you look at it like this, it does not matter if we have a black or white president. That is why the policies have not changed. The laws, such as mandatory minimum [sentences], were put in place by big business so they would have access to cheap labor. The antiterrorism laws were enacted to close the doors on access to justice so people would be in prison longer. Big business writes the laws and legislation."

In Alabama prisons, as in nearly all such state facilities across the United States, prisoners do nearly every job, including cooking, cleaning, maintenance, laundry, and staffing the prison barbershop. In the St. Clair prison there is also a chemical plant, a furniture company, and a repair shop for state vehicles. Other Alabama prisons run printing companies and recycling plants, stamp license plates, make metal bed frames, operate sand pits, and tend fish farms. Only a few hundred of Alabama's 26,200 prisoners—the system is designed to hold only 13,130 people—are paid to work—they get 17 to 71 cents an hour. The rest are slaves.

The men bemoaned a lack of recreational and educational programs and basic hygiene supplies, the poor ventilation that sends temperatures in the cells and dormitories to over 100 degrees, crumbling infrastructure, cockroach and rat infestations, and corrupt prison guards who routinely beat prisoners and sell contraband, including drugs and cell phones. An estimated 80 percent of prisoners entering the Alabama prison system are functionally illiterate.[72]

"The worst thing is the water," said Pleasant, a St. Clair prisoner who has served thirteen years of a forty-three-year sentence. "It is contaminated. It causes kidney, renal failure and cancer. The food causes stomach diseases. We have had three to four outbreaks of food poisoning in the last four months.

"Sleeping on a concrete slab is not going to teach you how to read or write," Pleasant said. "Sleeping on a concrete slab will not solve mental health issues. But the system does not change. It does what it is designed to do. It makes sure people are driven back into the system to work without pay."

"For years we were called niggers to indicate we had no value or worth and that anything could be done to us," Ray said. "Then the word 'nigger' became politically incorrect. So they began calling us criminals. When you say a person is a criminal it means that what happens to them does not matter. It means he or she is a nigger. It means they deserve what they get."

Prisons, the men said, have increasingly placed larger and larger financial burdens on families.

"If you don't get money from your family, your poverty blocks you out from buying items at the commissary or making phone calls," Council said. "You can't communicate with your family. If you don't have someone to send you money, you can't even buy stamps to write home. They [authorities] are supposed to give us two free stamps a week, but I have never seen them do it in my sixteen years of incarceration. We pay a $4 medical copay if we make a sick call. Every additional medication we receive is $4. If you have a cold and you get something for sinuses, pain meds, and something for congestion, that becomes a $16 visit. And if you get $20 from a family member, the state will take $16 off the top to pay for the [medical] visit. You end up with $4 to spend at a jacked-up canteen. There are a lot of brothers walking around in debt."

"It takes brutality and force to make a person work for free and live in the type of conditions we live in and not do anything about it," Ray said. "The only way they made slavery work was to use force. It is no different in the slave empire of prisons. They use brutality to hold it together. And this brutality will not go away until the system goes away."

"They stood me up against the wall [with my hands cuffed behind me]," Pleasant said. "There were about ten officers. They started swinging, punching, and hitting me with sticks. They knocked my legs out from under me. My face hit the floor. They stomped on my face. They sent me to the infirmary to hide what they did, for thirty days. When I looked in the mirror I could not recognize my facial features. This was the fourth time I was beaten like this."

I asked the three men, speaking to me on a conference call on their illegal cell phones, what prison conditions said about America. They all laughed.

"It says America is what it has always been—America!" said Ray. "It says if you are poor and black you will be exploited, brutalized, and murdered. It says most of American society, especially white society, is indifferent. It says nothing has really changed for us since slavery."

SIDDIQUE HASAN, HIS LEGS SHACKLED to a chair, sat in the fourth-floor visiting room of the Ohio State Penitentiary, a supermax prison in Youngstown. The room, surrounded by thick glass windows, had a guard booth in the center and food vending machines flanking a microwave on one wall. There was a line of small booths, entered through a door behind Hasan, where families, including children, were talking to prisoners through plexiglass partitions.

Hasan, five feet ten inches tall, fifty-two years old, bearded with wire-rim glasses, had a white kufi on his head. He wore a short-sleeve shirt over a long-sleeve shirt, light blue prison pants, and white Nikes. His 209-pound frame was taut and compact, the result of his exercise regime. He has been on death row since he was convicted for his actions in leading, along with four others, the April 1993 uprising at the Southern Ohio Correctional Facility at Lucasville. They are known as the Lucasville Five.

The uprising saw prisoners take control of the prison for eleven days to protest numerous grievances, including deaths that occurred allegedly from beatings by guards. It was one of the longest prison uprisings in U.S. history. By the time it was over, nine prisoners, many suspected of being informants or "snitches," had been killed along with a prison guard.

Hasan, born Carlos Sanders, has been in juvenile detention facilities or prison since he was an adolescent. His early life was unstable and marked by extreme poverty. His mother had her first child at twelve and her fourth and final child at nineteen. His father, who was physically abusive to Hasan's mother, abandoned the family when Hasan was five. The children and their mother survived on her meager pay from cooking and cleaning jobs. Hasan, the third of the four children, lived briefly in foster homes. He never went beyond fifth grade. He ran the streets with his older brother and engaged in petty crime. Since his first incarceration, in his early teens in Georgia—where he was nicknamed Savannah Slim or Savannah Red, and where he worked with other convicts on Georgia prison highway details—until today, he has spent only seventeen months outside prison walls. He always rebelled. He masterminded a mass escape from a juvenile detention facility when he was fifteen years old and, a year later, a mass escape from a county jail. In 2013 he took part in a hunger strike with other death row prisoners that saw prison authorities agree to expand the range of items at the prison commissary, permit physical contact in visits with relatives, allow prisoners to use computers to do legal research, increase the length of phone conversations, and increase recreation time.

"I am a human being," Hasan said. "I don't like being locked up, deprived of my rights, told when to go to bed, when to eat, when to shower. These things hurt a person physically, emotionally, and psychologically."

Before he converted to Islam in 1981, he said, he was "a materialist freak and a monster that sold drugs and protected people for payment in prison." He organized prison gambling rings and extortion rackets. He oversaw a small army of enforcers.

"I would have thirty pairs of shoes, thirty bottles of lotion, thirty bottles of shampoo, thirty bottles of baby oil, and two hundred bars of soap in my cell," he said. "But once I came into Islam and put into practice the knowledge I acquired, I changed."

He is one of the leaders of the effort to organize a nationwide work stoppage in prisons. His demands include raising the roughly $1 a day that prisoners now receive for eight hours of labor to the legal minimum wage. He calls for boycotts of overpriced commissaries. He said prisoners should purchase only the bare necessities, such as soap and toothpaste, and forgo the "zoozoos and wamwams," prison slang for junk food. He also places no hope in the courts and the legislatures. Prisoners, like the rest of the country, will have to start carrying out acts of mass civil disobedience for any justice, he said—that is the only mechanism left.

"Prison authorities never give you anything without a fight," he said, clutching white prayer beads. "Those prisoners who can should refuse to go to work to demand the minimum wage, although the first thing the prison will do is try and break it up by transferring the leaders to another prison or remove them from the general population. But if any protest is done right, with unity, they may not lock anyone down. Let the prison authorities know in advance what will be done. Let them know the demands. Don't surprise them. Give them an opportunity to resolve it, say sixty days. If you catch them by surprise all you will get is a lockdown. If you put them on notice they can't say they didn't know it was coming.

"The beauty of a work stoppage is that the prison administrators have to bring in compensated labor," he said. "This is what happened in the Georgia prison system in 2010 when the prisoners held a work stoppage for six days. It cost the state a lot of money. The prisoners got a lot of concessions. The issue of state pay cannot be solved expeditiously. That takes time. It is best to have other demands and other tactics. We can [first] lower commissary prices and the price of phone calls through boycotts."

Those who rebel, he said, must make a careful study of how power works. They must create a disciplined and hierarchical organization. They must ensure that leaders are incorruptible. They must remain nonviolent. They must prevent personal, racial, or religious animosities, including bigotry toward homosexuals and hatred of informants, or "snitches," from dividing them. Divisions among the oppressed, Hasan said, are gifts to the oppressor.

Successful revolt, he said, requires transparency, including informing the authorities in advance of a protest and articulating demands. Prisoners who mobilize an entire prison cannot hope to keep anything secret given the swarms of informants, just as protesters outside prison cannot hope to keep many secrets from the security surveillance organs of the state. There must be a clear set of achievable demands and an active support network outside the prison willing to mobilize on behalf of the rebels and publicize its struggles and demands.

Finally, he said, any revolt requires a willingness on the part of the rebel leaders to sacrifice themselves. For Hasan, this last element is made possible by his Muslim faith.

Hasan, who had been only months away from being released at the time of the uprising, lived in the Lucasville prison honor wing, reserved for prisoners with good disciplinary records. He worked as an imam among the prison population. During the uprising he repeatedly minimized or prevented violence. He is credited with saving several lives, a fact that came up in his trial. The state, as always, was far more concerned with removing from the general prison population a charismatic and incorruptible prison leader, regardless of what he or she did.

Prisoners in sworn affidavits after the uprising told of Ohio State Highway Patrol officers moving through the institution's population and offering deals for reduced sentences to those who would name and testify against revolt leaders. One of those who testified against the leaders of the uprising, Anthony Lavelle, the head of the Black Gangster Disciples inside the Lucasville facility, is widely believed to have carried out the murder of the prison guard, Robert Vallandingham. For that killing, Hasan was sentenced to death with George Skatzes, Namir Abdul Mateen, and Jason Robb. Keith LaMar was sentenced to death on a charge of having led a group that killed fellow prisoners during the uprising. Despite intense pressure by the state and promises to spare them from the death penalty, the five men refused to incriminate each other. That the five are mixed racially—Skatzes and Robb at the time were members of the Aryan Brotherhood and had to reject white solidarity to stand with the black defendants—was remarkable.

"They rose above their status as prisoners, and became, for a few days in April 1993, what rebels in Attica had demanded a generation before them: men," Mumia Abu Jamal wrote in the foreword to *Lucasville: The Untold Story of a Prison Uprising*, by Staughton Lynd, "As such, they did not betray each other, they did not dishonor each other, they reached beyond their prison 'tribes' to reach the commonality."[73]

It was the Muslims, the most disciplined and politically conscious segment of the prison population, who organized the Lucasville revolt. And the uprising was, from its inception, designed to be nonviolent. Guards would be seized, as had happened five years earlier in the prison during a protest. They would be held until prisoners were permitted to speak to the press. Once the press reported the prisoners' grievances, and once the state agreed to address the abuses, the guards would be released.

"We were dealing with a warden, Arthur Tate Jr., who was very hardline," Hasan said. "The convicts called him King Arthur. We wanted to bring enough pressure on the system to take it out of his hands and get his superiors in Columbus at the ODRC [Ohio Department of Rehabilitation and Correction] to respond. The goal was always to resolve this amicably."

No one in Lucasville, Hasan said, wanted to replicate the bloodbath that took place in New York State in September 1971 during the four-day uprising at the Attica prison, in which over forty-three people were killed, including ten correctional officers and civilian employees, along with thirty-three prisoners who died at the hands of state police officers who stormed the institution.[74] But uprisings, as Hasan swiftly found out, are very difficult to control.

The catalyst for the revolt was a decision by the prison administration to test the prisoners for tuberculosis by injecting them with a substance the Muslims believed contained alcohol, which is forbidden to followers of Islam. Hasan and other Muslim leaders asked the prison authorities to do the testing by X-ray or sputum sample. The prison refused. Hasan said the testing, especially because it was scheduled during Ramadan, was "the final straw."

"Muslims were fasting," he said. "They couldn't take a shot."

Conditions in the prison were already barbaric. There was severe overcrowding. White and black prisoners often physically clashed, sometimes within a single cell. Medical facilities were inadequate. Families that attempted to visit prisoners were harassed and insulted by the guards. Commissary items were overpriced. Phone calls were limited to one five-minute conversation a year, usually at Christmas. Guards routinely beat prisoners, at times fatally. A group of prisoners known as the "Lucasville 14" had earlier attempted to renounce their U.S. citizenship. Three of them, to illustrate their seriousness, cut off fingers and mailed them to the United Nations and the U.S. Department of Justice. Prisoners had also attempted to organize a branch of the Industrial Workers of the World to demand that prison laborers receive the national minimum wage. Every attempt to organize or resist was met with harsher conditions.

"There were several incidents where a prisoner did something like masturbate in front of a female guard, spit on a guard, or become verbally and physically abusive," Hasan said. "In situations like these the guards are supposed to file a conduct report. But instead the guards took the liberty of physical abuse, and in some cases this was fatal. They would take a prisoner to isolation or administrative segregation, go into the cell, close the door, and jump the prisoner while he was handcuffed and shackled."

In the 1993 revolt, the Muslims seized a dozen guards at the end of the recreation period around 3:00 p.m. Prisoners, freed from their cells and prison control, grabbed baseball bats and fire extinguishers. They attacked the guards. Some prisoners wanted to murder the "snitches" and the "fags," which Hasan blocked, telling them "that would mean killing half the prison population." Prisoners began to barricade hallways with ice machines and locker boxes. They used forty-five-pound weight bars and pickaxes to smash windows and doors to capture guards sheltering in a secure area known as a "safewell."

"Me and some of the other Muslims had congregated in the barbershop," he said. "A brother told us they were killing snitches in [Block] L6. We went down to L6 and saw bodies on top of bodies. Not all were dead. Some were gagging for air, some survived.

"It was mass chaos," he said. "People were beating the guards and beating convicts. It was pandemonium. Blood was in the hallway. It was like a massacre. Blood does not have a nice smell. I remembered snapping at the Muslims and telling them to secure these guys."

Hasan moved the captured guards to the shower stalls. He stationed Muslims outside to protect them. Those who committed rape during the initial stages of the uprising were also put in locked cells.

He placed vulnerable prisoners, including the informants, in cells for their safety. The Muslims had drawn up an organizational plan before the uprising, with groups assigned to security, legal matters, food distribution, and education. They struggled to impose order.

I asked him how he felt when he saw the bodies and the bloodbath, something he had hoped to avoid.

"I didn't feel anything, maybe because I have a different perception about death than other people," he said. "Stabbin'. Killin'. Hangin'. This was not [an intended] part of the uprising. Things got out of hand. You had a lot of prisoners with a lot of grudges, animosities, and hatred in their hearts for prisoners and nonprisoners. These people had snitched on them or abused them. People settled old scores with other prisoners and with guards. That's what happened. That's what went wrong."

Hasan said one black prisoner, Bruce Harris, raped a white prisoner. Other white prisoners, when they heard of the rape, wanted to kill Harris. Hasan intervened.

It was agreed that a prisoner from each of the three main prison factions—the Aryan Brotherhood, the Muslims, and the Black Gangster Disciples—would punish Harris. They took Harris to the corridor and beat him for three minutes. Then they took him to the gym and beat him again for three minutes. After that, they locked him in a cell.

"Bruce was nervous that they were going to kill him and he started tearing up the cell," Hasan said. "He tore the porcelain toilet off the wall and smashed it to pieces, disturbing the Muslims, who were praying. I went to Bruce. I asked him to stop. I assured Bruce that he was not going to die. I told him I would escort him out to the prison authorities when the time came to end the riot. He promised to stop making a ruckus."

Harris, however, was killed later by fellow prisoners. The state attempted to charge Hasan with the murder, but during the trial a video was produced showing Hasan in negotiations with prison authorities at the time of Harris's killing.

"When there is disorder and no law, people have the tendency to do evil things," Hasan said.

"What is the cause of any uprising?" he asked. "Simply put, it's man's injustice to man. We could not expect freedom, but we could expect freedom from oppression, tyranny, persecution, and gross miscarriages of justice that go on in institutional life. Prisons are here to stay. Be realistic. It's about the money, the control, and the power. But if you take over a prison you can confront the evil and the corruption, you can make some changes."

The captured guards, the power dynamic now reversed, began calling Hasan Mr. Sanders, his legal name.

"The guards were all saying they were sorry, they were just doing their jobs," he said.

The white prisoners, many of them members of the Aryan Brotherhood, gathered nervously in the gym in the first hours of the revolt. They feared that the blacks would turn on them. All of the alleged snitches killed in the first few hours were white. A few blacks believed to be snitches were beaten but survived. Hasan called the Muslims to prayer in the gym. He demanded that the non-Muslim prisoners be quiet and respectful during prayer. When it was over he announced that any other religious group that wanted to worship would be given the same respect shown to the Muslims. That promise of respect broke down racial animosities. It made an alliance between whites and blacks possible. Prisoners began to paint slogans such as "Convict Race," "Convict Unity," and "White and Black Together" on the walls.

"I did what I did with the choices that were available," Hasan said. "I had to do something. I am a revolutionary. To be a revolutionary is to be an agent of change, which is impossible if one doesn't know what needs to be changed. For there to be a revolution there must be revolutionary consciousness. A prison-wide hunger strike, a prison-wide work stoppage, would have been more effective. But then it would not have been about the Muslims. You would have had to take it to the whole convict body."

On death row, all who rebel against empire are comrades.

"People, Muslim and non-Muslim, admire ISIS [Islamic State]," he said. "They are happy to see ISIS stand up against the U.S. government and Israel. A lot of us may not agree with all their tactics, but we know what it is like to be pushed to the edge. We also know that al Qaeda carried out the attacks of 9/11 against the symbols of American power, the Pentagon, and the financial institutions. If they only wanted to kill Americans they could have flown the planes into a stadium with eighty thousand or ninety thousand people during a pro football game. Prisoners, because they are oppressed, like seeing anyone stand up to the big bad wolf."

After the Lucasville uprising was settled, the state promised not to carry out reprisals against the leaders—a promise it broke once it regained control.

What can one make of a state that places a person such as Hasan on death row when it knows he never committed murder? Did the state cut a plea deal with the actual killer of the corrections officer so it could execute Hasan? The message sent by the state is clear: It does not fear criminals. It fears rebels.

Hasan, who is fighting his own death sentence in the courts, has seen several men taken to the death chamber. Two of those executed—Abdul-Hakim Zakiy and Abdullah Sharif Kaazim Mahdi—were close friends. The last conversations before execution haunt him.

"Brother Mahdi didn't get a lot of visits in prison," he said. "He would not participate in the final process. He didn't want a last meal. He spent the day fasting and reading the Koran. He asked for a little olive oil and some Islamic dates. I told him he would be dearly missed. I told him I knew he had a strong faith. I told him I knew he believed in Allah. I told him to accept that all life is transitory. I told him to hope that Allah would accept his worship, the sincerity of his belief and grant him paradise. I told him I loved him. I felt helpless.

"He did not want his family to get his body," he went on. "He wanted his body washed and buried according to Islam. He wanted to rest in the prison burial plot with the other Muslim prisoners. It is hard to see someone you love and admire go through that. I believe I will see him in the next life. I can't imagine going through that without my faith."

THE AMERICAN EMPIRE IS COMING to an end. The nation has lost the power and respect needed to induce allies in Europe, Latin America, Asia, and Africa to do its bidding. Add the mounting destruction caused by climate change and you have a recipe for an emerging dystopia. Overseeing this descent at the highest levels of the federal and state governments is a motley collection of imbeciles, con artists, thieves, opportunists, and warmongering generals. And to be clear, I include Democrats.

The empire will limp along, steadily losing influence until the dollar is dropped as the world's reserve currency, plunging the United States into a crippling depression and instantly forcing a massive contraction of its military machine.

Short of a sudden and widespread popular revolt, the death spiral appears unstoppable, meaning the United States as we know it will no longer exist within a decade or, at most, two. The global vacuum we leave behind will be filled by China, already establishing itself as an economic and military juggernaut, or perhaps there will be a multipolar world carved up among Russia, China, India, Brazil, Turkey, South Africa, and a few other states. Or maybe the void will be filled, as the historian Alfred W. McCoy writes in his book *In the Shadows of the American Century: The Rise and Decline of US Global Power* by "a coalition of transnational corporations, multilateral military forces like NATO, and an international financial leadership self-selected at Davos and Bilderberg" that will "forge a supranational nexus to supersede any nation or empire." [75]

Under every measurement, from financial growth and infrastructure investment to advanced technology, including supercomputers, space weaponry, and cyber warfare, we are being rapidly overtaken by the Chinese. "In April 2015 the U.S. Department of Agriculture suggested that the American economy would grow by nearly 50 percent over the next 15 years, while China's would triple and come close to surpassing America's in 2030," McCoy noted. [76] China became the world's second largest economy in 2010, the same year it became the world's leading manufacturing nation, pushing aside a United States that had dominated the world's manufacturing for a century. [77] The Department of Defense issued a sober report titled, "At Our Own Peril: DoD Risk Assessment in a Post-Primary World." It found that the U.S. military "no longer enjoys an unassailable position versus state competitors," and "it no longer can . . . automatically generate consistent and sustained local military superiority at range." [78] McCoy predicts the collapse will come by 2030. [79]

Empires in decay, blinded by their hubris and unable to accept their diminishing power, refuse to confront hard and unpleasant facts. They replace diplomacy, multilateralism, and politics with unilateral threats and the blunt instrument of war.

This inability to face reality saw the United States make the greatest strategic blunder in its history—the invasion of Afghanistan and Iraq. The architects of the war in the George W. Bush White House, and the array of useful idiots in the press and academia who were cheerleaders for it, knew very little about the countries being invaded, were stunningly naive about the effects of industrial warfare, and were blindsided by the ferocious blowback. They stated, and probably believed, that Saddam Hussein had weapons of mass destruction, although they had no valid evidence to support this claim. They insisted that democracy would be implanted in Baghdad and spread across the Middle East. They assured the public that U.S. troops would be greeted as liberators by grateful Iraqis and Afghans. They promised that oil revenues would cover the cost of reconstruction. They insisted that the bold and quick military strike—"Shock and Awe"—would restore American hegemony in the region and dominance in the world. It did the opposite. As Zbigniew Brzezinski, President Jimmy Carter's national security advisor, noted, this "unilateral war of choice against Iraq precipitated a widespread delegitimation of U.S. foreign policy." [80]

Historians of empire call these military fiascos, a feature of all late empires, "micro-militarism." [81] The Athenians engaged in micro-militarism in 413 BC during the Peloponnesian War when they invaded Sicily, suffering the loss of two hundred ships and thousands of soldiers, and triggering revolts throughout the empire. [82] Britain did so in 1956 when it attacked Egypt in a dispute over the nationalization of the Suez Canal and then quickly had to withdraw in humiliation, empowering a string of Arab nationalist leaders such as Egypt's Gamal Abdel Nasser, and dooming British rule over the nation's few remaining colonies. [83] Neither of these empires recovered.

"While rising empires are often judicious, even rational in their application of armed force for conquest and control of overseas dominions, fading empires are inclined to ill-considered displays of power, dreaming of bold military masterstrokes that would somehow recoup lost prestige and power," McCoy writes. "Often irrational even from an imperial point of view, these micro-military operations can yield hemorrhaging expenditures or humiliating defeats that only accelerate the process already under way." [84]

Empires need more than force to dominate other nations. They need a mystique. This mystique—a mask for imperial plunder, repression, and exploitation—seduces some native elites, who become willing to do the bidding of the imperial power or at least remain passive. And it provides a patina of civility, even nobility, to justify to those at home the costs in blood and money needed to maintain empire. The parliamentary system of government that Britain replicated in appearance in the colonies, and the introduction of British sports such as polo, cricket, and horse racing, along with elaborately uniformed viceroys and the pageantry of royalty, were buttressed by what the colonialists said was the invincibility of their navy and army. England was able to hold its empire together from 1815 to 1914 before being forced into a steady retreat.[85]

America's high-blown rhetoric about democracy, liberty, and equality, along with basketball, baseball, and Hollywood, as well as our own deification of the military, entranced and cowed much of the globe in the wake of World War II. Behind the scenes, of course, the CIA used its dirty tricks to orchestrate coups, fix elections, and carry out assassinations, black propaganda campaigns, bribery, blackmail, intimidation, and torture. But none of this works anymore.

The loss of the mystique is crippling. It makes it hard to find pliant surrogates to administer the empire, as we have seen in Iraq and Afghanistan. The photographs of physical abuse and sexual humiliation imposed on Arab prisoners at Iraq's Abu Ghraib prison inflamed the Muslim world. They fed al Qaeda and later Islamic State with new recruits. The assassination of Osama bin Laden and a host of other jihadist leaders, including the U.S. citizen Anwar al-Awlaki, openly mocked the rule of law. The hundreds of thousands of dead, the millions of refugees fleeing our debacles in the Middle East, and the near-constant threat from militarized aerial drones, have exposed us as state terrorists. We have repeated in the Middle East the widespread atrocities, indiscriminate violence, lies, and blundering miscalculations that led to our defeat in Vietnam.

The brutality abroad is matched by a growing brutality at home. The disillusionment and anger that led to Trump's election—a reaction to the corporate coup d'état and the poverty afflicting at least half of the country—have discredited American democracy.

"The demise of the United States as the preeminent global power could come far more quickly than anyone imagines," McCoy writes.

Despite the aura of omnipotence empires often project, most are surprisingly fragile, lacking the inherent strength of even a modest nation-state. Indeed, a glance at their history should remind us that the greatest of them are susceptible to collapse from diverse causes, with fiscal pressures usually a prime factor. For the better part of two centuries, the security and prosperity of the homeland has been the main objective for most stable states, making foreign or imperial adventures an expendable option, usually allocated no more than 5 percent of the domestic budget. Without the financing that arises almost organically inside a sovereign nation, empires are famously predatory in their relentless hunt for plunder or profit—witness the Atlantic slave trade, Belgium's rubber lust in the Congo, British India's opium commerce, the Third Reich's rape of Europe, or the Soviet exploitation of Eastern Europe.[86]

When revenues shrink or collapse, McCoy points out, "empires become brittle."[87]

"So delicate is their ecology of power that, when things start to go truly wrong, empires regularly unravel with unholy speed: just a year for Portugal, two years for the Soviet Union, eight years for France, eleven years for the Ottomans, seventeen for Great Britain, and, in all likelihood, just twenty-seven years for the United States, counting from the crucial year 2003 [when the U.S. invaded Iraq]," he writes.[88]

Many of the estimated sixty-nine empires[89] that have existed throughout history lacked competent leadership in their decline. They ceded power to monstrosities such as the Roman emperors Caligula and Nero or imbecile narcissists like Trump.

"For the majority of Americans, the 2020s will likely be remembered as a demoralizing decade of rising prices, stagnant wages, and fading international competitiveness," McCoy writes.[90] The loss of the dollar as the global reserve currency will see the U.S. unable to pay for its huge deficits by selling Treasury bonds, which will be drastically devalued at that point. There will be a massive rise in the cost of imports. Unemployment will explode. Domestic clashes over what McCoy calls "insubstantial issues"[91] will fuel a dangerous hypernationalism that could morph into an American fascism.

The array of instruments created for global dominance—wholesale surveillance, the evisceration of civil liberties, sophisticated torture techniques, militarized police, the massive prison system, the thousands of militarized drones and satellites—will become ubiquitous in the homeland.

As the German socialist Karl Liebknecht wrote during the First World War: "The main enemy is at home." [92]

The elites use war, as they always have, as a safety valve for class conflict. War, as W. E. B. Du Bois said, creates an artificial community of interest between the oligarchs and the poor, diverting the poor from their natural interests and obscuring the class struggle. The redirecting of national frustrations and emotions into an epic struggle of good and evil against a common enemy, the cant of patriotism, the racism that is part of all nationalist ideologies that sustain war, the false bonding that comes with comradeship, seduces those on the margins of society. They feel in wartime they belong. They feel they have a place. They are offered the chance to be heroes. And off they march like sheep to the slaughter. By the time they find out, it is too late.

"Modern totalitarianism can integrate the masses so completely into the political structure, through terror and propaganda, that they become the architects of their own enslavement," wrote the social critic Dwight Macdonald. "This does not make slavery less likely, but on the contrary more—a paradox there is no space to unravel here. Bureaucratic collectivism, not capitalism, is the most dangerous future enemy of socialism." [93]

War allows the state to accrue to itself power and resources that in peacetime a citizenry would never permit. And that is why the war state, like the one we live in, must keep us afraid. Constant surveillance, a loss of civil liberties, and police control are essential for our safety.

It was the militarists and the capitalists that at the end of World War II conspired to roll back the gains made by working women and men under the New Deal. They used the rhetoric of the Cold War to cement into place an economy geared toward total war, even in peacetime. This permitted the arms industry to continue making weapons, with guaranteed profits from the state, and permitted the generals to continue presiding over a massive military.

The manufacturing of weapons systems and the waging of war are the chief activities of the state today. They are no longer one among other means of advancing the national interest but have become the sole national interest. These corporatists and militarists bankrolled and promoted movements in the twentieth century that spoke of the "politics of productivism," eschewed the language of class conflict and talked only about economic growth and a partnership with the capitalist class. The NAACP, for example, was formed to lure African Americans away from the Communist Party, the only radical organization in the early twentieth century that did not discriminate. The AFL-CIO was later fed CIA money to help crush and supplant radical unions abroad and at home. The AFL-CIO, like the NAACP, is today a victim of its own corruption and bureaucratic senility. Its bloated leadership pulls down huge salaries as its dwindling rank and file is stripped of benefits and protections. The capitalists no longer need what they once called "responsible" unionism—which meant pliable unionism. And once the capitalists and the militarists killed off the radical movements and unions, they finished off the dupes who had helped them do it. Surplus labor, desperate for work and too frightened to challenge the bosses, is the bulwark of corporate capitalism.

Fear is the only language the power elite understands. This is a dark fact of human nature. It is why Richard Nixon was our last liberal president. Nixon was not a liberal personally. He was devoid of empathy and lacked a conscience. But he was frightened of movements. You do not make your enemy afraid by selling out. You make your enemy afraid by refusing to submit, by fighting for your vision, and by organizing. It is not our job to take power. It is our job to build movements to keep power in check. Without these movements nothing is possible.

"You get freedom by letting your enemy know that you'll do anything to get your freedom; then you'll get it," Malcolm X said.

When you get that kind of attitude, they'll label you as a "crazy Negro," or they'll call you a "crazy nigger"—they don't say Negro. Or they'll call you an extremist or a subversive, or seditious, or a red, or a radical. But when you stay radical long enough, and get enough people to be like you, you'll get your freedom. . . . So don't you run around here trying to make friends with somebody who's depriving you of your rights. They're not your friends, no, they're your enemies. Treat them like that and fight them, and you'll get your freedom; and after you get your freedom, your enemy will respect you. And I say that with no hate. I don't have hate in me. I have no hate at all. I don't have any hate. I've got some sense. I'm not going to let anybody who hates me tell me to love him.[94]

The New Deal, as Franklin Delano Roosevelt said, saved capitalism. It was put in place because socialists were a strong and serious threat. The oligarchs understood that with the breakdown of capitalism—something I expect we will again witness in our lifetimes—there was a possibility of a socialist revolution. They did not want to lose their wealth and power. Roosevelt, writing to a friend in 1930, said there was "no question in my mind that it is time for the country to become fairly radical for at least one generation. History shows that where this occurs occasionally, nations are saved from revolution."[95]

In other words, Roosevelt went to his fellow oligarchs and said, "Hand over some of your money or you will lose all your money in a revolution." And they complied. That is how the government created fifteen million jobs, Social Security, unemployment benefits, and public works projects. The capitalists did not do this because the suffering of the masses moved them to pity. They did this because they were scared.

We must stop looking for salvation from strong leaders. Strong people, as the civil rights leader Ella Baker said, do not need strong leaders. Politicians, even good politicians, play the game of compromise and are seduced by the privileges of power.

Revolutions, Rosa Luxemburg argued, were as much the product of mass struggle as its instigator. A revolution was a "living" entity. "It was formed not from above," but from the "consciousness of the masses." And this consciousness took years to build. A revolutionary had to respond to the unpredictable moods and sentiments that define any revolt, to the unanticipated responses of a population in revolt. Luxemburg denounced terror as a revolutionary tool. She detested the domination of revolutionary elites such as the Bolshevik Party's vanguard. She warned that revolutionary movements that were not democratic swiftly became despotic. She also understood the peculiar dynamics of revolution.

"It is extremely difficult for any directing organ of the proletarian movement to foresee and calculate which occasions and factors can lead to explosions and which cannot," she wrote. "Those who were rigidly tied to an ideology or those who believed they could shape events through force, were crippled by a rigid, mechanical, bureaucratic conception." [96]

Vladimir Lenin, to achieve power during the 1917 revolution, was forced to follow her advice, abandoning many of his most doctrinaire ideas to respond to the life force of Russian Revolution itself. "Lenin," the civil rights leader Robert Looker wrote, "was a Luxemburgist in spite of himself." [97]

A population rises up against a decayed system not because of revolutionary consciousness, but because, as Luxemburg pointed out, it has no other choice. It is the obtuseness of the old regime, not the work of revolutionaries, that triggers revolt. Revolt is usually lit by some small, even banal, injustice that snaps the lethargy of the public. No one can predict such events or where they will go. And, as Luxemburg pointed out, all revolutions are in some sense failures, events that begin, rather than culminate, a process of social transformation.

"There was no predetermined plan, no organized action, because the appeals of the parties could scarcely keep pace with the spontaneous rising of the masses," she wrote of the 1905 uprising in Russia. "The leaders had scarcely time to formulate the watchwords of the on-rushing crowd." [98]

"Revolutions," she wrote, "cannot be made at command. Nor is this at all the task of the party. Our duty is only at all times to speak out plainly without fear or trembling; that is, to hold clearly before the masses their tasks in the given historical moment, and to proclaim the political program of action and the slogans which result from the situation. The concern with whether and when the revolutionary mass movement takes up with them must be left confidently to history itself. Even though socialism may at first appear as a voice crying in the wilderness, it yet provides for itself a moral and political position the fruits of which it later, when the hour of historical fulfillment strikes, garners with compound interest."[99]

As a reporter I covered uprisings and revolutions, including the insurgencies in Central America in the 1980s, the two Palestinian uprisings, the revolutions in 1989 in East Germany, Czechoslovakia, and Romania, and the street demonstrations that brought down Slobodan Milosevic in Serbia. Luxemburg's understanding of the autonomous nature of revolt is correct. A central committee, like Lenin's Bolsheviks, because it is ruthless, secretive, highly disciplined, and willing to use violence and terror, is capable of carrying out a counterrevolution to crush the democratic aspirations of a population—which is what happened in 1917 in Russia. But these organizations are not the primary engine of revolution. The messiness of democracy, with all its paralysis, diffusion of power, and reverses, keeps revolution alive and vibrant. It protects the population from the abuse of centralized power.

"Without general elections, without unrestricted freedom of the press and of assembly, without the free struggle of opinion, life in every public institution dies down and becomes a mere semblance of itself in which bureaucracy remains as the only active element," Luxemburg wrote.[100]

As a socialist I am not concerned with what is expedient or what is popular. I am concerned with what is right and just. I am concerned with holding fast to the core ideals of socialism, if for no other reason than keeping this option alive for future generations. And these ideals are the only ones that will make possible a better world. "To succeed would be the Greatest Transformation of all time," writes the Boston College sociologist Charles Derber. "To fail will ultimately guarantee the end of the human experiment."[101]

The lies of the corporate state are transparent. This has thrown us into what Antonio Gramsci called an interregnum—a time when the reigning ideology has lost efficacy but has yet to be replaced by a new one. "The crisis consists," Gramsci wrote, "precisely in the fact that the old is dying and the new cannot be born, [and] in this interregnum a great variety of morbid symptoms appear." [102] Hence political mutations such as Donald Trump, or in Gramsci's time, Benito Mussolini.

Gramsci warned that the ruling elites will continually mutate ideas, laws, institutions, language, and systems of control, as African Americans have experienced under white supremacy, to maintain the status quo. This requires the constant vigilance of the critical, revolutionary theorist. There will be a never-ending battle of ideas, those spun out by the elites to justify their privilege and power and the radical theorists who will expose the ideas as tools of repression and hold up an alternative.

We cannot pick and choose whom among the oppressed it is convenient to support. We must stand with all the oppressed or none of the oppressed. This is a global fight for life against corporate tyranny. We will win only when we see the struggle of working people in Greece, Spain, and Egypt as our own struggle. This will mean a huge reordering of our world, one that turns away from the primacy of profit to full employment and unionized workplaces, inexpensive and modernized mass transit, especially in impoverished communities, universal single-payer health care and a banning of for-profit health care corporations. The minimum wage must be at least $15 an hour and a weekly income of $500 provided to the unemployed, the disabled, stay-at-home parents, the elderly, and those unable to work. Anti-union laws, like the Taft-Hartley Act, and trade agreements such as NAFTA, will be abolished. All Americans will be granted a pension in old age. A parent will receive two years of paid maternity leave, as well as shorter work weeks with no loss in pay and benefits. The Patriot Act and Section 1021 of the National Defense Authorization Act, which permits the military to be used to crush domestic unrest, as well as government spying on citizens, will end. Mass incarceration will be dismantled. Global warming will become a national and global emergency. We will divert our energy and resources to saving the planet through public investment in renewable energy and end our reliance on fossil fuels. Public utilities, including the railroads, energy companies, the arms industry, and banks, will be nationalized. Government funding for the arts, education, and public broadcasting will create places where creativity, self-expression, and voices of dissent can be heard and seen. We will terminate our nuclear weapons programs and build a nuclear-free world. We will demilitarize our police, meaning that police will no longer carry weapons when they patrol our streets but instead, as in Great Britain, rely on specialized armed units that have to be authorized case by case to use lethal force. There will be training and rehabilitation programs for the poor and those in our prisons, along with the abolition of the death penalty. We will grant full citizenship to undocumented workers. There will be a moratorium on foreclosures and bank repossessions. Education will be free from day care to university. All student debt will be forgiven. Mental health care, especially for those now caged in our prisons, will be available. Our empire will be dismantled. Our soldiers and marines will come home.

The weak and the vulnerable, especially children, will no longer be sacrificed on the altars of profit and the needs of empire. The measure of a successful society will not be the GDP or the highs of the stock market but human rights. Children will never go to bed hungry. They will live in safety and security, be nurtured and educated, and grow up to fulfill their potential.

The forces arrayed against us are frightening. The struggle will be difficult. But we will never succeed if we attempt to accommodate the current structures of power. Corporate capitalism cannot be reformed. Our strength lies in our steadfastness and our integrity. It lies in our ability to hold fast to our ideals, as well as our willingness to sacrifice for those ideals. We must refuse to cooperate.

Resistance entails suffering. It requires self-sacrifice. It accepts that we may be destroyed. It is not rational. It is not about the pursuit of happiness. It is about the pursuit of freedom. Resistance accepts that even if we fail, there is an inner freedom that comes with defiance, and perhaps this is the only freedom and true happiness we will ever know. To resist evil is the highest achievement of human life. It is the supreme act of love. It is to carry the cross, as the theologian James Cone reminds us, and to be acutely aware that what we are carrying is also what we will die upon.

Most of those who resist—Sitting Bull, Harriet Tubman, Emma Goldman, Elizabeth Cady Stanton, Malcolm X, and Martin Luther King Jr.—are defeated, at least in the cold calculation of the powerful. The final, and perhaps most important quality of resistance, as Cone writes in *The Cross and the Lynching Tree*, is that it "inverts the world's value system."[103] Hope rises up out of defeat. Those who resist stand, regardless of the cost, with the crucified. This is their magnificence and their power.

The seductive inducements to conformity—money, celebrity, prizes, grants, book contracts, hefty lecture fees, important academic and political positions, and a public platform—are scorned by those who resist. The rebel does not define success the way the elites define success. Those who resist refuse to kneel before the idols of mass culture and the power elites. They are not trying to get rich. They do not want to be part of the inner circle of the powerful. They accept that when you stand with the oppressed you are treated like the oppressed. The inversion of the world's value system makes freedom possible. Those who resist are free not because they have attained many things or high positions, but because they have so few needs. They sever the shackles used to keep most people enslaved. And this is why the elites fear them. The elites can crush them physically, but they cannot buy them off.

The power elites attempt to discredit those who resist. They force them to struggle to make an income. They push them to the margins of society. They write them out of the official narrative. They deny them the symbols of status. They use the compliant liberal class to paint them as unreasonable and utopian. "What is possible would never have been achieved if, in this world, people had not repeatedly reached for the impossible," the sociologist Max Weber wrote.[104]

The visionaries and utopian reformers such as the abolitionists and socialists brought about real social change, not the "practical" politicians. The abolitionists destroyed what the historian Eric Foner calls "the conspiracy of silence by which political parties, churches and other institutions sought to exclude slavery from public debate."[105]

"For much of the 1850s and the first two years of the civil war, Lincoln—widely considered the model of a pragmatic politician—advocated a plan to end slavery that involved gradual emancipation, monetary compensation for slave owners, and setting up colonies of freed blacks outside the United States. The harebrained scheme had no possibility of enactment," Foner writes. "It was the abolitionists, still viewed by some historians as irresponsible fanatics, who put forward the program—an immediate and uncompensated end to slavery, with black people becoming U.S. citizens—that came to pass (with Lincoln's eventual help, of course)."[106]

The political squabbles that dominate public discourse almost never question the sanctity of private property, individualism, capitalism or imperialism. They hold as sacrosanct American "virtues." They insist that Americans are a "good" people steadily overcoming any prejudices and injustices that may have occurred in the past. The debates between the Democrats and the Whigs, or today's Republicans and Democrats, are rooted in the same allegiance to the dominant structures of power, myth of American exceptionalism, and white supremacy.

"It's all a family quarrel without any genuine disagreements," Foner told me.

Those who challenge these structures, who reach for the impossible, who dare to speak the truth, have been, throughout American history, dismissed as "fanatics." But as Foner pointed out, it is often the "fanatics" who make history.

Resistance is not, fundamentally, political. It is cultural and spiritual. It is about finding meaning and expression in the transcendent and the incongruities of life. Music, poetry, theater, and art sustain resistance by giving expression to the nobility of rebellion against the overwhelming forces, what the ancient Greeks called *fortuna*, which can never ultimately be overcome. Art celebrates the freedom and dignity of those who defy malignant evil. Victory is not inevitable, or at least not victory as defined by the powerful. Yet in every act of rebellion we are free. It was the raw honesty of the blues, spirituals, and work chants that made it possible for African-Americans to endure.

Power is a poison. It does not matter who wields it. The rebel, for this reason, is an eternal heretic. He or she will never fit into any system. The rebel stands with the powerless. There will always be powerless people. There will always be injustice. The rebel will always be an outsider.

Resistance requires eternal vigilance. The moment the powerful are no longer frightened, the moment the glare of the people is diverted and movements let down their guard, the moment the ruling elites are able to use propaganda and censorship to hide their aims, the gains made by resisters roll backward. We have been steadily stripped of everything that organized working men and women—who rose up in defiance and were purged, demonized and killed by the capitalist elites—achieved with the New Deal. The victories of African-Americans, who paid with their bodies and blood in making possible the Great Society and ending legal segregation, also have been reversed.

The corporate state makes no pretense of addressing social inequality or white supremacy. It practices only the politics of vengeance. It uses coercion, fear, violence, police terror and mass incarceration as forms of social control while it cannibalizes the nation and the globe for profits. Our cells of resistance have to be rebuilt from scratch.

The corporate state, however, is in trouble. It has no credibility. All the promises of the "free market," globalization and trickle-down economics have been exposed as a lie, an empty ideology used to satiate greed. The elites have no counterargument to their anti-capitalist and anti-imperialist critics. The attempt to blame the electoral insurgencies in the United States' two ruling political parties on Russian interference, rather than massive social inequality—the worst in the industrialized world—is a desperate ploy. The courtiers in the corporate press are working feverishly, day and night, to distract us from reality. The moment the elites are forced to acknowledge social inequality as the root of our discontent is the moment they are forced to acknowledge their role in orchestrating this inequality.

The U.S. government, subservient to corporate power, has become a burlesque. The last vestiges of the rule of law are evaporating. The kleptocrats openly pillage and loot. Programs instituted to protect the common good—public education, welfare, and environmental regulations—are being dismantled. The bloated military, sucking the marrow out of the nation, is unassailable. Poverty is a nightmare for half the population. Poor people of color are gunned down with impunity in the streets. Our prison system, the world's largest, is filled with the destitute. There is no shortage of artists, intellectuals, and writers, from Martin Buber and George Orwell to James Baldwin, who warned us that this dystopian era was fast approaching. But in our Disneyfied world of intoxicating and endless images, cult of the self and willful illiteracy, we did not listen. We will pay for our negligence.

Søren Kierkegaard argued that it was the separation of intellect from emotion, from empathy, that doomed Western civilization. The "soul" has no role in a technocratic society. The communal has been shattered. The concept of the common good has been obliterated. Greed is celebrated. The individual is a god. The celluloid image is reality. The artistic and intellectual forces that make transcendence and the communal possible are belittled or ignored. The basest lusts are celebrated as forms of identity and self-expression. Progress is defined exclusively by technological and material advancement. All that is human is obliterated. This creates a collective despair and anxiety that is fed by glitter, noise, and false promises of consumer-culture idols. The despair grows ever-worse, but we never acknowledge our existential dread. As Kierkegaard understood, "the specific character of despair is precisely this: it is unaware of being despair."[107]

Those who resist are relentlessly self-critical. They ask the hard questions that mass culture, which promises an unachievable eternal youth, fame and financial success, deflects us from asking. What does it mean to be born? What does it mean to live? What does it mean to die? How do we live a life of meaning? What is justice? What is truth? What is beauty? What does our past say about our present? How do we defy radical evil?

We are in the grip of what Kierkegaard called "sickness unto death"— the numbing of the soul by despair that leads to moral and physical debasement. Those who are ruled by rational abstractions and an aloof intellectualism, Kierkegaard argued, are as depraved as those who succumb to hedonism, cravings for power, violence, and predatory sexuality. We achieve salvation when we accept the impediments of the body and the soul, the limitations of being human, yet despite these limitations seek to do good. This burning honesty, which means we always exist on the cusp of despair, leaves us, in Kierkegaard's words, in "fear and trembling."[108] We struggle not to be brutes while acknowledging we can never be angels. We must act and then ask for forgiveness. We must be able to see our own face in the face of the oppressor.

The theologian Paul Tillich did not use the word "sin" to mean an act of immorality. He, like Kierkegaard, defined sin as estrangement. For Tillich, it was our deepest existential dilemma. Sin was our separation from the forces that give us ultimate meaning and purpose in life. This separation fosters the alienation, anxiety, meaninglessness, and despair that are preyed upon by mass culture. As long as we fold inward and embrace a hyper-individualism that is defined by selfishness and narcissism, we will never overcome this estrangement. We will be separated from ourselves, from others and from the sacred.

Resistance is not only about battling the forces of darkness. It is about becoming a complete human being. It is about overcoming estrangement. It is about our neighbor. It is about honoring the sacred. It is about dignity. It is about sacrifice. It is about courage. It is about freedom. It is about the capacity to love. Resistance must become our vocation.

ACKNOWLEDGMENTS

Eunice once again oversaw every draft of this book. She spent many hours editing, revising, and critiquing it. She is my most important critic and editor, improving not only the flow and language of the text but the ideas and organization. I would be helpless without her. I was also assisted during the last six months of the writing of the book by the skilled journalist and researcher Amelia Pang. She not only edited, fact-checked, did footnoting and research, and typed out dozens of hours of transcripts, but carried out reporting with me when we wrote the chapter on the alt-right and antifa and the chapter on gambling. She taped and transcribed the interviews she carried out in Rockford, Illinois, while I was reporting four hours away in Anderson, Indiana. She also covered the events at Charlottesville and interviewed the Proud Boys in Maryland.

There is material in the book that made up some of the columns I wrote for the online magazine *Truthdig*, along with *The Walrus* magazine. My weekly *Truthdig* columns are edited by Thomas Caswell. Tom, who worked for many years at the *Los Angeles Times*, is one of the most gifted editors I have ever worked with. He not only ensures accuracy and fluidity, but makes sure that each column strikes the right tone. Bob Bender at Simon & Schuster edited each chapter as they were completed, offering invaluable ideas and suggestions. He then sat down with the final manuscript and provided the guidance and advice to shape it into its final form. I benefited immensely from his skill and work. I would like to thank Philip R. Metcalf, Johanna Li, and Fred Chase at Simon & Schuster, who carried out the meticulous fact-checking and copyediting. I would also like to thank Naila Kauser, who took on the very unpleasant task of typing up the many hours of tape collected for the sadism chapter, including the sadistic porn scenes quoted in the book. My son Thomas and Naila provided invaluable help editing the final manuscript.

The book could not have been written without the generous support of the NoVo Foundation, which provided a grant to *Truthdig* to fund my weekly columns, as well as the Wallace Change Makers Fund, which made it possible to hire Amelia and cover the expenses of much of my travel around the country.

I have spent nearly a decade writing a weekly column for *Truthdig*. The editor of the site, Robert Scheer, is one of the finest reporters and columnists in the country. His integrity and courage are what all of us hope to achieve. The publisher, Zuade Kaufmann, has arguably built one of the most important sites on the Internet, one that is fearless in taking on the powerful and entrenched interests, including the Israel lobby and the Democratic Party establishment. I am fortunate to write for her and Bob. I would like to thank Dwayne Booth, aka Mr. Fish, who usually illustrates my columns. Dwayne is the finest political cartoonist in the country. He has paid for his courage and integrity. I rely heavily on my friendships with Ralph Nader, who has fought the abuses of corporate power longer and with more integrity than anyone else in the country; Cornel West, and James Cone, two of our most important intellectuals, who keep alive the Black Prophetic tradition, our most important intellectual tradition; and the cartoonist Joe Sacco, who has produced graphic novels of stunning power and brilliance that transform reporting into art and lift up the voices of the oppressed. Several people in this book opened wounds that will never heal to tell their stories of loss and tragedy. Christine Pagano had the guts to speak openly about her long nightmare as an addict and prostituted woman. She now works in a rehab facility helping recovering addicts, is engaged to her boyfriend, and has given birth to a gorgeous little girl. Boris Rorer, a friend, fellow lover of books, and activist, and Sue and Bob Miller, along with their daughters, Megan and Camarie, allowed me into their homes to speak of their irrevocable loss of Shannon Miller. This was very hard for them. I owe them a tremendous debt. Kevin Zeese, Dr. Margaret Flowers, Steve Kinzer, Narda Zacchino, Kasia Anderson, Eric Ortiz, Donald Kaufman, Ben Norton, Max Blumenthal, Bonnie Kerness, Ojore Lutalo, Ann and Walter Pincus, Jennifer and Peter Buffett, Marty Brest, Roy Singham, Jodie Evans, Randall Wallace, Richard Wolff, June Ballinger, Michael Goldstein, Tom Artin, the Rev. Michael Granzen, the Rev. Karen Hernandez, the Rev. Mel White, Joe and Heidi Hough; the courageous feminists Lee Lakeman and Alice Lee; Sheik Hamza Yusuf, one of the country's most important religious scholars; my former Shakespeare professor, Margaret Maurer, the intrepid attorneys Bruce Afran and Carl Mayer; Ajamu Baraka, Kshama Sawant; Katie Fisher, the highly talented producer of my show *On Contact*; Anya Parampil, Priya Reddy, John Richard, Dr. Jill Stein, Emily Allen-Hornblower, Don Roden, Jean Ross, Chris Agans, Anthony Arnove, Margaret Atkins, Irene Brown; Sam Hynes, my neighbor and fellow author; Sonali Kolhatkar, Francine Prose, Russell Banks, Celia Chazelle, Toby Sanders; Boris Franklin, my former student, friend, and weightlifting partner (which is humbling given that he benches 415 pounds), and fellow author of the play *Caged*, which he and other students wrote about mass incarceration; Ron Pierce, another former student and friend who is now finishing his degree at Rutgers; Walter Fortson, Larry Hamm, Peter Hershberg, Derrick Jensen, Henry Klapper, Lola Mozes, Abby Martin, Gary Francione, Jeff Wise, and John Ralston Saul are all friends and colleagues. Dorothea von Molke and Cliff Simms, who run one of the finest bookstores in the country and donated more than 700 books to the prison library in New Jersey for my students, are vital to my work as a writer and a teacher. I would like to especially thank the students in my college classes at East Jersey State Prison and the Edna Mahan Correctional Facility for Women. Our classes, which in the spring of 2017 included Princeton University undergraduates who traveled to the women's prison for an accredited course, are the highlight of my week.

Lisa Bankoff, my agent, has handled all of my books. I have long relied on her skill, patience, and expertise. I would also like to thank Kristine Dahl at ICM Partners for her help in preparing the manuscript and promoting the book.

Eunice; my four children Thomas, Noëlle, Konrad, and Marina; and our adopted greyhounds Marlow and Row are the fulcrum of my life. I hope I have not asked Konrad and Marina, exuberant and playful children, to be quiet too often because I was writing. They bring joy, awe, beauty, and unrivaled happiness into our lives. In a bleak age they hold up hope and remind me why we must resist. We are responsible for the world they inherit.

NOTES

Epigraphs

1. Hannah Arendt, ed., *Walter Benjamin Illuminations: Essays and Reflections* (New York: Schocken Books, 1968), 37–38.
2. Dietrich Bonhoeffer, *Ethics* (Minneapolis: Fortress Press, 2015), 65.

Chapter 1 – DECAY

1. Plato, *The Republic* (London: Oxford University Press, 1972), 546a.
2. Jim Lockwood, "Scranton City Council accepts $555K gaming grant for Scranton Lace redevelopment," *The Times Tribune*, October 26, 2012, http://thetimes-tribune.com/news/scranton-city-council-accepts-555k -gaming-grant-for-scranton-lace-redevelopment-1.1394220.
3. Elizabeth Flock, "In 'Scranton Lace,' nostalgia for a time and place that no longer exist," *PBS*, May 15, 2017, http://www.pbs.org/newshour/poetry/ scranton-lace-nostalgia-time-place-no-longer-exist/.
4. Ibid.
5. Borys Krawczeniuk, "Clinton visits Scranton for fundraiser; visited father's grave earlier," *The Times Tribune*, July 30, 2015, http://thetimes -tribune.com/news/clinton-visits-scranton-for-fundraiser-visited-father-s -grave-earlier-1.1919601.
6. "The sadness of Scranton," *The Economist*, July 21, 2012, http://www .economist.com/node/21559382.

7. Jeff Brady, "Scranton's Public Workers Now Paid Minimum Wage," *NPR*, July 7, 2012, http://www.npr.org/2012/07/07/156416876/scrantons-public-workers-pay-cut-to-minimum-wage.

8. "The sadness of Scranton," *The Economist*, July 21, 2012, http://www.economist.com/node/21559382.

9. Josh Mrozinski and Borys Krawczeniuk, "Doherty's 2012 Scranton budget raises real estate taxes 29 percent, lays off 29 firefighters," *The Times-Tribune*, November 16, 2011, http://thetimes-tribune.com/doherty-s-2012-scranton-budget-raises-real-estate-taxes-29-percent-lays-off-29-firefighters-1.1232738.

10. Jeff Brady, "Scranton's Public Workers Now Paid Minimum Wage."

11. Jim Lockwood, "Scranton eyes its seven largest nonprofits for contributions," *The Times-Tribune*, August 2, 2012, http://thetimes-tribune.com/news/scranton-eyes-its-seven-largest-nonprofits-for-contributions-1.1353318.

12. Jim Lockwood, "As University of Scranton expands, so does tension," *The Times-Tribune,* December 1, 2013, http://thetimes-tribune.com/news/as-university-of-scranton-expands-so-does-tension-1.1590681.

13. Ibid.

14. Stacy Lange, "Scranton School District under State's 'Financial Watch,' " *WNEP*, June 23, 2017, http://wnep.com/2017/06/23/scranton-school-district-under-states-financial-watch/.

15. Jim Lockwood, "North Pocono municipalities hear battle cry against Scranton's commuter tax," *The Citizens' Voice*, September 20, 2012, http://citizensvoice.com/news/north-pocono-municipalities-hear-battle-cry-against-scranton-s-commuter-tax-1.1376215.

16. "Scranton, Pennsylvania Income and Salaries," Sperling's Best Places, http://www.bestplaces.net/economy/city/pennsylvania/scranton.

17. "Department of Defense (DoD) Releases Fiscal Year 2017 President's Budget Proposal," U.S. Department of Defense, https://www.defense.gov/News/News-Releases/News-Release-View/Article/652687/department-of-defense-dod-releases-fiscal-year-2017-presidents-budget-proposal/.

18. William Hartung, "A Guide to Trump's $1 Trillion Defense Bill," *The Nation*, July 25, 2017, https://www.thenation.com/article/a-guide-to-trumps-1-trillion-defense-bill/.

19. "Scranton (City of) PA," Moody's Investors Service, https://www.moodys.com/credit-ratings/Scranton-City-of-PA-credit-rating-600030181.

20. Andrew Ross Sorkin and Mary William Walsh, "A.I.G. Reports Loss of $617. Billion as U.S. Gives More Aid," *The New York Times*, March 2, 2009. http://www.nytimes.com/2009/03/03/business/03aig.html.

21. Hilary Russ, "Scranton, Pennsylvania to sell sewer utility for $195 million," *Reuters*, March 29, 2016, http://www.reuters.com/article/us-pennsylvania-scranton-pa-amer-water-idUSKCN0WV2BI.

22. Ibid.

23. Jim Lockwood, "Scranton Sewer Authority approves sale of system to water company," *The Times-Tribune*, March 29, 2016, http://thetimes-tribune.com/news/scranton-sewer-authority-approves-sale-of-system-to-water-company-1.2024344.

24. Jim Lockwood, "Attorney fees in sewer sale top $3.1 million," *The Times-Tribune*, February 16, 2017, http://thetimes-tribune.com/news/attorney-fees-in-sewer-sale-top-3-1-million-1.2155594.

25. Hilary Russ, "Scranton, Pennsylvania to sell sewer utility for $195 million," *Reuters*, March 29, 2016, http://www.reuters.com/article/us-pennsylvania-scranton-pa-amer-water-idUSKCN0WV2BI.

26. Ibid.

27. "The National Development Council and Scranton Finalize $32M Parking System Transaction," The National Development Council, https://ndconline.org/2016/09/12/the-national-development-council-and-scranton-finalize-32m-parking-system-transaction/.

28. Jim Lockwood, "Scranton to get $28 million from lease of parking garages to nonprofit," *The Times-Tribune*, June 16, 2016, http://thetimes-tribune.com/news/scranton-to-get-28-million-from-lease-of-parking-garages-to-nonprofit-1.2055690.

29. Karl Marx, *Capital* (New York: Vintage Books, 1977), 14.

30. Karl Marx, *The German Ideology* (New York: International Publishers, 1970), 64.

31. Ibid.

32. Stuart Hall, Charles Critcher, and Tony Jefferson, Policing the Crisis: Mugging, the State and Law and Order (New York: Palgrave Macmillan, 2013), 20.

33. Meghnad Desai, *Marx's Revenge: The Resurgence of Capitalism and the Death of Statist Socialism* (New York: Verso, 2004), 10.

34. Karl Marx, *A Contribution to the Critique of Political Economy*, translated from the Second German Edition by N. I. Stone, (Chicago: Charles H. Kerr & Company, 1911), 12–13.

35. Jake Bernstein, "The Paradise Papers Hacking and the Consequences of Privacy," *New York Times*, November 7, 2017, https://www.nytimes.com/2017/11/07/opinion/paradise-papers-hacking-privacy.html.

36. Karl Marx and Friedrich Engels, *Manifesto of the Communist Party* (Chicago: Charles H. Kerr & Company, 1906), 17.

37. The Editorial Board, "Banks as Felons, or Criminality Lite," *New York Times*, May 22, 2015, https://www.nytimes.com/2015/05/23/opinion/banks-as-felons-or-criminality-lite.html.

38. "Projected Costs of U.S. Nuclear Forces, 2015 to 2024," Congressional Budget Office, https://www.cbo.gov/sites/default/files/114th-congress-2015-2016/reports/49870-nuclearforces.pdf.

39. "New Class Of Ballistic Missile Submarines Reaches Milestone," The Office of Military Affairs, http://www.ct.gov/oma/cwp/view.asp?a=3422&q=589070.

40. Thomas Hedges, "The Pentagon has never been audited," *The Guardian*, March 20, 2017, https://www.theguardian.com/commentisfree/2017/mar/20/pentagon-never-audited-astonishing-military-spending.

41. Robert O'Harrow Jr., "The outsourcing of U.S. intelligence raises risks among the benefits," *Washington Post*, June 9, 2013, https://www.washingtonpost.com/world/national-security/the-outsourcing-of-us-intelligence-raises-risks-among-the-benefits/2013/06/09/eba2d314-d14c-11e2-9f1a-1a7cdee20287_story.html?utm_term=.923b38ddd517.

42. Neil Irwin, "Seven facts about Booz Allen Hamilton," *Washington Post*, June 10, 2013, https://www.washingtonpost.com/news/wonk/wp/2013/06/10/seven-facts-about-booz-allen-hamilton/?utm_term=.958958c6986c.

43. "How Large Are Global Energy Subsidies?" International Monetary Fund, http://www.imf.org/external/pubs/ft/wp/2015/wp15105.pdf.

44. Ibid.

45. The Editors, "Why Should Taxpayers Give Big Banks $83 Billion a Year?" *Bloomberg News*, February 20, 2013, https://www.bloomberg.com/view/articles/2013-02-20/why-should-taxpayers-give-big-banks-83-billion-a-year-.

46. "The Damaging Rise in Federal Spending and Debt Statement of Chris Edwards, Director of Tax Policy Studies, Cato Institute, before the Joint Economic Committee September 20, 2011," United States Congress Joint Economic Committee, https://www.jec.senate.gov/public/_cache/files/5c2ebe54-218c-4946-b012-7b62cd1d3f19/jec-testimony—9.202.011—statement-of-chris-edwards-director-of-tax-policy-studies-cato-institute.pdf.

47. Drew DeSilver, "For most workers, real wages have barely budged for decades," *Pew Research Center*, http://www.pewresearch.org/fact tank/2014/10/09/for-most-workers-real-wages-have-barely-budged-for-decades/.

48. Drew Harwell, "Workers endured long hours, low pay at Chinese factory

used by Ivanka Trump's clothing-maker," *Washington Post*, April 25, 2017, https://www.washingtonpost.com/business/economy/workers-endured -long-hours-low-pay-at-chinese-factory-used-by-ivanka-trumps-clothing -maker/2017/04/25/b6fe6608-2924-11e7-b605-33413c691853_story .html?utm_term=.45d2d9c6c60b.

49. Ashley Westerman, "4 Years After Rana Plaza Tragedy, What's Changed For Bangladeshi Garment Workers?" *NPR*, April 30, 2017, https://www.npr .org/sections/parallels/2017/04/30/525858799/4-years-after-rana-plaza -tragedy-whats-changed-for-bangladeshi-garment-workers.

50. Karl Marx, *Capital: A Critique of Political Economy, Volume 3* (New York: Vintage Books, 1981), 525.

51. Andrew P. Wilper, Steffie Woolhandler, David U. Himmelstein et al. (2009). Health Insurance and Mortality in US Adults. *American Journal of Public Health*, 99(12): 2289–2295. Doi: 102.105/AJPH.20081.57685.

52. Philip Rucker and Robert Costa, "Bannon vows a daily fight for 'decon- struction of the administrative state,' " *Washington Post*, February 23, 2017, https://www.washingtonpost.com/politics/top-wh-strategist-vows-a -daily-fight-for-deconstruction-of-the-administrative-state/2017/02/23 /03f6b8da-f9ea-11e6-bf01-d47f8cf9b643_story.html?utm_term= .01faf6ef1114.

53. William S. Burroughs, *Naked Lunch: The Restored Text* (New York: Grove Press, 1959), 46.

54. Ibid.

55. A. J. Katz, "Fox News and MSNBC in Top 5 Most-Watched Cable Nets," *Adweek*, March 21, 2017, http://www.adweek.com/tvnewser/cable-net work-ranker-week-of-march-13/324331.

56. Paul Farhi, "One billion dollars profit? Yes, the campaign has been a gusher for CNN," *Washington Post*, October 27, 2016, https://www .washingtonpost.com/lifestyle/style/one-billion-dollars-profit-yes-the -campaign-has-been-a-gusher-for-cnn/2016/10/27/1fc879e6-9c6f-11e6 -9980-50913d68eacb_story.html?utm_term=.ea69c5e0d529.

57. Michael Barthel, "Despite subscription surges for largest U.S. newspapers, circulation and revenue fall for industry overall," *Pew Research Center*, June 1, 2017, http://www.pewresearch.org/fact-tank/2017/06/01/circula tion-and-revenue-fall-for-newspaper-industry/.

58. Laurel Wamsley, "Big Newspapers Are Booming: 'Washington Post' to Add 60 Newsroom Jobs," *NPR*, December 27, 2016, http://www.npr.org /sections/thetwo-way/2016/12/27/507140760/big-newspapers-are -booming-washington-post-to-add-sixty-newsroom-jobs.

59. Jeffrey A. Trachtenberg, "The New Yorker Tests Readers' Willingness to Pay Up," *Wall Street Journal*, April 4, 2016, https://www.wsj.com/articles/the -new-yorker-tests-readers-willingness-to-pay-up-1459767600.

60. Ken Doctor, "Trump Bump Grows Into Subscription Surge—and Not Just for the New York Times," *The Street*, March 3, 2017, https://www.thes treet.com/story/14024114/1/trump-bump-grows-into-subscription-surge .html.

61. Kim LaCapria, "Kellyanne Conway Explains Microwave Oven Surveillance Remarks," *Snopes*, March 13, 2017, http://www.snopes.com/2017/03/13/ kellyanne-conway-microwave-spying/.

62. Alastair Jamieson, "Betsy DeVos Cites Grizzly Bears During Guns-in-Schools Debate," *NBC*, January 18, 2017, https://www.nbcnews.com/news /us-news/betsy-devos-schools-might-need-guns-due-potential-grizzlies -n708261.

63. Matt Taibbi, *Insane Clown President: Dispatches from the 2016 Circus* (New York: Spiegel & Grau, 2017), 154.

64. Jeffrey Frank, "The Gong Show, With Donald Trump," *New Yorker*, March 28, 2017, https://www.newyorker.com/news/daily-comment/the-gong -show-with-donald-trump.

65. Gabriel García Márquez, *The Autumn of the Patriarch* (New York: Penguin Books, 1975), 163.

66. "Presidential Address: Clinton Urges Passage Of Free-Trade Pact," CQ Alma-nac, https://library.cqpress.com/cqalmanac/document.php?id=cqal93-844 -25162-1104274.

67. Hannah Arendt, *The Origins of Totalitarianism* (New York: Harcourt, 1976), xxxiv.

68. Mark Murray, "Trump and his family could save more than $1 billion under House tax bill," *NBC*, November 16, 2017, https://www.nbcnews .com/politics/first-read/trump-his-family-could-save-more-1-billion-un der-house-n821491.

69. Paul Krugman, "Republicans' Tax Lies Show the Rot Spreads Wide and Runs Deep," *New York Times*, November 30, 2017, https://www.nytimes .com/2017/11/30/opinion/republican-tax-lies-fed.html.

70. "The Latest: Natural resources chairman lauds Trump decision," *ABC*, December 4, 2017, http://abcnews.go.com/amp/Politics/wireStory/latest -trump-defends-scaling-back-utah-monuments-51562064.

71. Dino Grandoni, "The Energy 202: Legal battle over national monuments is just beginning," *Washington Post*, December 6, 2017, https://www.wash ingtonpost.com/news/powerpost/paloma/the-energy-202/2017/12/06/

the-energy-202-legal-battle-over-national-monuments-is-just-begin ning/5a27242530fb0469e883fa3d/?utm_term=.b45f9155b180.

72. Chris Enloe, "FCC chairman Ajit Pai drops truth bomb on Jimmy Kimmel after 'hysteria' over net neutrality repeal," *The Blaze*, December 16, 2017, http://www.theblaze.com/news/2017/12/16/fcc-chairman-ajit-pai-drops truth-bomb-on-jimmy-kimmel-after-hysteria-over-net-neutrality-repeal.

73. Ledyard King, " 'Transgender,' 'fetus,' 'science-based' reportedly on CDC list of banned words," *USA Today*, December 16, 2017, https://www.usato day.com/story/news/politics/2017/12/16/transgender-fetus-science-based -cdc-list-banned-words-per-report/957996001/.

74. Joost A. M. Meerloo, *The Rape of the Mind: The Psychology of Thought Control, Menticide, and Brainwashing* (New York: Martino Fine Books, 2015), 80-81.

75. Voltaire, *Miracles and Idolatry* (London: Penguin UK, 2005), 42.

76. Horace B. Davis, ed., *The National Question: Selected Writings by Rosa Luxemburg* (New York: Monthly Review Press, 1976), 294.

77. David Forgacs, ed., *The Gramsci Reader Selected Writings1916–1935* (New York: New York University Press, 2000), 38.

78. Joseph A. Buttigierg, *Antonio Gramsci Prison Notebooks,* vol. 2 (New York: Columbia University Press, 2010), 45.

79. Antonio Gramsci, *The Gramsci Reader Selected Writings* 1916–5, 312.

80. Antonio A. Santucci, ed., *Antonio Gramsci* (New York: Monthly Review Press, 2010), 63.

81. Samuel P. Huntington, Michel J. Crozier and Joji Watanuki, "The Crisis of Democracy," Trilateral Commission, http://trilateral.org/download/doc/ crisis_of_democracy.pdf.

82. Bill Blum, "The Right-Wing Legacy of Justice Lewis Powell, and What It Means for the Supreme Court Today," *Truthdig*, https://www.truthdig .com/articles/the-right-wing-legacy-of-justice-lewis-powell-and-what-it -means-for-the-supreme-court-today/.

83. Emily Willingham, "Why Did Mylan Hike EpiPen Prices 400%? Because They Could," *Forbes*, August 21, 2016, https://www.forbes.com/sites/ emilywillingham/2016/08/21/why-did-mylan-hike-epipen-prices-400-be cause-they-could/#3abe17d6280c.

84. Irving Howe, "Faulkner: End of a Road," *New Republic*, December 7, 1959, https://newrepublic.com/article/92609/faulkner-end-road.

85. Lewis Carroll, *Lewis Carroll: The Complete Illustrated Works* (New York: Gramercy Books, 1982), 6–7.

86. John Gray, *Heresies: Against Progress And Other Illusions* (London: Granta Publications, 2004), 106–107.

87. Jeff Goodell, *The Water Will Come: Rising Seas, Sinking Cities, and the Remaking of the Civilized World* (New York: Little, Brown and Company, 2017), 195.

88. "The US Military on the Front Lines of Rising Seas," Union of Concerned Scientists, http://www.ucsusa.org/sites/default/files/attach/2016/07/front-lines-of-rising-seas-key-executive-summary.pdf.

89. James Howard Kunstler, *The Long Emergency: Surviving the End of Oil, Climate Change, and Other Converging Catastrophes of the Twenty-First Century* (New York: Grove Press, 2006), 1.

90. Goodell, *The Water Will Come,* 149.

91. "An Abrupt Climate Change Scenario and Its Implications for US National Security," Greenpeace International, http://www.greenpeace.org/international/Global/international/planet-2/report/2006/3/an-abrupt-climate-change-scena.pdf.

92. Goodell, *The Water Will Come,* 208.

93. "The Age of Consequences: The Foreign Policy and National Security Implications of Global Climate Change," Center for a New American Security, https://www.scribd.com/document/9854638/The-Age-of-Consequences-The-Foreign-Policy-and-National-Security-Implications-of-Global-Climate-Change.

94. Hannah Arendt, *The Origins of Totalitarianism* (New York: Harcourt, 1976), 426.

95. "Fact Sheet: Extraordinary Rendition," American Civil Liberties Union, https://www.aclu.org/other/fact-sheet-extraordinary-rendition.

96. Spencer Ackerman, "US cited controversial law in decision to kill American citizen by drone," *The Guardian,* June 23, 2014, https://www.theguardian.com/world/2014/jun/23/us-justification-drone-killing-american-citizen-awlaki.

97. See "Room Information," Scranton Cultural Center, http://www.scrantonculturalcenter.org/index.php/weddingsevents/room-matrix/.

98. Josh Mrozinski, "Scranton's population decline bottoming out; growth led by minority population," *The Times-Tribune,* March 13, 2011, http://the-times-tribune.com/scranton-s-population-decline-bottoming-out-growth-led-by-minority-population-1.1118232.

99. See "Scranton city, Pennsylvania," United States Census Bureau, https://www.census.gov/quickfacts/fact/table/scrantoncitypennsylvania/PST045216.

100. See "Scranton Iron Furnaces," Pennsylvania Anthracite Heritage Museum, http://www.anthracitemuseum.org/explore/iron-furnaces/.

101. Nella Van Dyke and Holly J. McCammon, *Strategic Alliances: Coalition Building and Social Movements Vol. 34* (Minneapolis: University of Minnesota Press, 2010), 32.

102. Ibid.

103. Brian Greenberg et al., *Social History of the United States* (Santa Barbara, CA: ABC-CLIO, 2008), 94.

104. Ibid.

105. Ibid.

106. William T. Moye, "The end of the 12-hour day in the steel industry," http://digitalcollections.library.cmu.edu/awweb/awarchive?type=file&item=430142.

107. Albert J. Churella, *The Pennsylvania Railroad, Volume 1: Building an Empire, 1846–1917* (Philadelphia: University of Pennsylvania Press, 2012), 658.

108. Quoctrung Bui, "50 Years Of Shrinking Union Membership, In One Map," *NPR*, February 23, 2015, http://www.npr.org/sections/money/2015/02/23/385843576/50-years-of-shrinking-union-membership-in-one-map.

109. Jason Miller, *That Championship Season* (New York: Atheneum, 1972), 21–22.

110. Ibid., 114–116.

111. Daniel J. Boorstein, *The Image: A Guide to Pseudo-Events in America* (New York: Atheneum, 1961), 37.

112. Ibid., 240.

113. See "Local Area Unemployment Statistics June 2017," Pennsylvania Center For Workforce Information & Analysis, http://www.workstats.dli.pa.gov/Documents/County%20Profiles/Lackawanna%20County.pdf.

114. C.D.C. Reeve, *Plato: The Republic*, translated by G.M.A. Grube, (Indianapolis: Hackett Publishing Company, Inc., 1992), 2.

115. C.D.C. Reeve, *The Republic*, 7.521.

116. Ibid., 7.520.

117. See "Number of Municipal Governments & Population Distribution," National League of Cities, http://www.nlc.org/number-of-municipal-governments-population-distribution.

118. Detlev Clemens and Brendan M. Purcell, *The Collected Works of Eric Voegelin: Volume 31: Hitler and the Germans* (Columbia: University of Missouri Press), 15.

119. Ibid., 89.

120. Ibid.

121. Ibid.

122. Ibid., 99.

123. Terry Gross, "Megyn Kelly on Trump and the Media: 'We're In A Dangerous Phase Right Now,'" *NPR*, December 7, 2016, http://www.npr.org/templates/transcript/transcript.php?storyId=504622630.

124. Walter Benjamin, *Illuminations* (New York: Schocken Books, 1968), 257–258.

125. Émile Durkheim, *On Suicide* (New York: Penguin Classics, 2006).

126. Katherine Stewart, "Eighty-One Percent of White Evangelicals Voted for Donald Trump. Why?" *The Nation*, November 17, 2016, https://www.thenation.com/article/eighty-one-percent-of-white-evangelicals-voted-for-donald-trump-why/.

127. "Annotated: Trump's Executive Order On Religious Liberty," *NPR*, May 4, 2017, http://www.npr.org/2017/05/04/526840823/annotated-trumps-executive-order-on-religious-liberty.

128. See "DONATIONS," EX Ministries, http://www.exministries.com/donations/.

129. Peter Applebome, "Bakker Is Convicted on All Counts; First Felon Among TV Evangelists," *New York Times,* October 6, 1989, http://www.nytimes.com/1989/10/06/us/bakker-is-convicted-on-all-counts-first-felon-among-tv-evangelists.html?mcubz=3.

130. Julie Johnson, "Jessica Hahn: Shifting Views of a Sudden Celebrity," *New York Times,* October 21, 1987, http://www.nytimes.com/1987/10/21/nyregion/jessica-hahn-shifting-views-of-a-sudden-celebrity.html?page-wanted=all&mcubz=3.

131. See "The Jim Bakker Show's Store," https://store.jimbakkershow.com/.

132. Ed Mazza, "Jim Bakker: Making Fun of Trump Is the 'Spirit of the Antichrist,' " *Huffington Post,* May 15, 2017, http://www.huffingtonpost.com/entry/jim-bakker-antichrist_us_59195cfbe4b0031e737ebff7.

133. Akbar Shahid Ahmed, "Trump Copied Another Family's Coat Of Arms," *Huffington Post,* May 29, 2017, http://www.huffingtonpost.com/entry/trump-mar-a-lago-crest-a-scam-new-york-times-finds_us_592c6f40e4b053f2d2ad7e75.

134. William Lobdell, "Pastor's Empire Built on Acts of Faith, and Cash," *Los Angeles Times*, September 23, 2004, http://www.latimes.com/local/california/la-na-paul-crouch-story-20160531-snap-htmlstory.html.

135. Ibid.

136. Ibid.

137. Ibid.

138. Chris Hedges, *American Fascists: The Christian Right and the War on America* (New York: Free Press, 2006), 170.

139. Ibid., 172–173.

140. Ibid., 12–13, 14–15, 136.

141. Gill Troy, "She Was the Steve Bannon of the Great Depression," *Daily Beast*, February 4, 2017, http://www.thedailybeast.com/she-was-the-steve-bannon-of-the-great-depression.

142. "In U.S., 42% Believe Creationist View of Human Origins," Gallup Polls, http://www.gallup.com/poll/170822/believe-creationist-view-human-origins.aspx.

143. Brian Vines, "The evangelical vote: will 94 million Americans sit out this year's election?" *The Guardian,* June 21, 2016, https://www.theguardian.com/us-news/2016/jun/21/evangelical-vote-us-elections.

144. Simone Weil, *Gravity and Grace* (London: Routledge & Kegan Paul, 1952), 71.

145. See "2018 Budget Blueprint," https://www.whitehouse.gov/sites/whitehouse.gov/files/omb/budget/fy2018/2018_blueprint.pdf.

146. James Strachey, ed., *Civilization and Its Discontents* (New York: W. W. Norton & Company, 1961).

147. Ibid., 81.

148. Ernst Jünger, *Storm of Steel,* translated by Michael Hofmann (London: Penguin Classics, 2004).

149. Quoted in Raoul Peck, "I Am Not Your Negro."

150. James Baldwin, *The Fire Next Time* (New York: The Dial Press, 1963), 115–116.

151. James Baldwin, *I Am Not Your Negro: A Companion Edition to the Documentary Film Directed by Raoul Peck* (New York: Vintage International, 2017), 56–58.

152. James Baldwin, *The Price of the Ticket: Collected Nonfiction, 1948–1985* (New York: St. Martin's Press, 1985), 478.

153. Quoted in Raoul Peck, "I Am Not Your Negro."

154. James Baldwin, *The Devil Finds Work* (New York: Vintage Books, 2011), 75.

155. Ibid., 11.

156. Ibid.

157. Ibid.

158. Ibid., 16–17.

159. Quoted in Raoul Peck, "I Am Not Your Negro."

160. Ibid.

Chapter 2 – HEROIN

1. David Foster Wallace, *Infinite Jest* (New York: Back Bay Books, 1996), 347.
2. Ailsa Chang, "Crime-Ridden Camden To Dump City Police Force," *NPR*, December 6, 2012, http://www.npr.org/2012/12/06/166658788/crime-ridden-camden-to-dump-city-police-force.
3. Josh Katz, "Drug Deaths in America Are Rising Faster Than Ever," *New York Times*, June 5, 2017, https://www.nytimes.com/interactive/2017/06/05/upshot/opioid-epidemic-drug-overdose-deaths-are-rising-faster-than-ever.html.
4. Ibid.
5. "America's Pain Points," Express Scripts, December 9, 2014, http://lab.express-scripts.com/lab/insights/drug-safety-and-abuse/americas-pin-points.
6. Dina Gusovsky, "Americans Consume Vast Majority of the World's Opioids," *CNBC*, April 27, 2016, http://www.cnbc.com/2016/04/27/americans-consume-almost-all-of-the-global-opioid-supply.html.
7. Sam Quinones, *Dreamland: The True Tale of America's Opiate Epidemic* (New York: Bloomsbury Press, 2015), 190.
8. Dina Gusovsky, "Americans Consume Vast Majority of the World's Opioids."
9. John Tozzi, "More Pot, Less Cocaine: Sizing Up America's Illicit Drug Market," *Bloomberg BusinessWeek*, March 10, 2014, https://www.bloomberg.com/news/articles/2014-03-10/more-pot-less-cocaine-sizing-up-americas-illicit-drug-market.
10. Molly Triffin, "Hospitalizations Among Teens for Opioid Poisonings Increase, Study Shows," *Teen Vogue*, Feb 13, 2017, www.teenvogue.com/story/teens-opioid-poisonings-painkillers-hospitalizations-teen-story.
11. Sam Quinones, *Dreamland: The True Tale of America's Opiate Epidemic*, 135.
12. Harriet Ryan, Lisa Girion And Scott Glover, " 'You Want a Description of Hell?' OxyContin's 12-Hour Problem," *Los Angeles Times*, May 5, 2016, www.latimes.com/projects/oxycontin-part1/.
13. Barry Meier, *"In Guilty Plea, OxyContin Maker to Pay $600 Million,"* *New York Times*, May 10, 2007, http://www.nytimes.com/2007/05/10/business/11drug-web.html.
14. *OxyContin Goes Global — "We're Only Just Getting Started," Los Angeles Times* (Dec. 18, 2016) (online at: www.latimes.com/projects/la-me-oxycontin-part3/).
15. Online at: http://katherineclark.house.gov/_cache/files/a577bd3c-29ec-4bb9-bdba-1ca71c784113/mundipharma-letter-signatures.pdf.
16. Sam Quinones, *Dreamland: The True Tale of America's Opiate Epidemic*, 39.
17. Delray Beach was once an acclaimed sanctuary for young recovering heroin

addicts. Then the sober home owners realized it would be more profitable if addicts relapsed in their care. Ever since the Affordable Care Act began permitting parents to keep their children on their health insurance policy until age 26, which includes some coverage for drug relapses, many treatment centers and sober houses have gotten involved in insurance fraud. It has become common practice for sober house supervisors to bring in heroin because drug treatment centers use the insurance money to pay sober house owners illegal bonuses for referring outpatients to their centers for therapy. Sober houses—which do not require certification in Florida—receive thousands of dollars a month for each recovering addict they house. Paramedics sometimes treat the same person several times on the same day. They often rescue several people in a sober house who shared a laced batch. Palm Beach County dealt with 5,000 overdoses in 2016. Most of the victims were white, under the age of 26, and from out of state. Florida has a billion-dollar drug treatment industry with minimal oversight. Thousands of substance abusers pour in from the Northeast and Midwest to get help each year. Source: Alvarez, Lizette. "Haven for Recovering Addicts Now Profits From Their Relapses," *The New York Times*. June 20, 2017. Accessed July 4, 2017, https://www.nytimes.com/2017/06/20/us/delray-beach-addiction.html.

18. Richard Branson, "War on drugs a trillion-dollar failure," *CNN*, December 7, 2012, http://www.cnn.com/2012/12/06/opinion/branson-end-war-on-drugs/index.html.

19. "The Annual Cost of The War on Drugs," Elevations Health, https://elevationshealth.com/annual-cost-war-on-drugs/.

20. Marc Lewis, "Why are so many people dying from opiate overdoses? It's our broken society," *The Guardian*, July 10, 2017, https://www.theguardian.com/commentisfree/2017/jul/10/people-dying-opiate-overdoses-society-drugs.

21. Ibid.

22. Nicholas Kristof, "How to Win a War on Drugs: Portugal treats addiction as a disease, not a crime," *New York Times*, September 22, 2017, https://www.nytimes.com/2017/09/22/opinion/sunday/portugal-drug-decriminalization.html?mtrref=www.google.com&assetType=opinion.

23. Ibid.

24. Ibid.

Chapter 3 – WORK

1. Émile Durkheim, *On Suicide* (New York: Penguin Classics, 2006), 230.

2. Lindsey Holden, "Sock monkeys and miniature cars relics of Rockford's

manufacturing past," *Rockford Register Star*, March 17, 2016, http://
www.rrstar.com/special/20160317/sock-monkeys-and-miniature-cars
-relics-of-rockfords-manufacturing-past.

3. Conor Dougherty, "Welcome to Rockford, Ill, the Underwater Mortgage
Capital of America," *Wall Street Journal*, September 8, 2013, https://www.wsj
.com/articles/welcome-to-rockford-ill-the-underwater-mortgage-capital
-of-america-1378506072.

4. Data obtained from Winnebago County Coroner's Office.

5. "U.S.A. SUICIDE: 2015 OFFICIAL FINAL DATA," American Association
of Suicidology, http://www.suicidology.org/Portals/14/docs/Resources/
FactSheets/2015/2015datapgsv1.pdf?ver=2017-01-02-220151-870.

6. Mary Emily O'Hara, "It's Not Just Chris Cornell: Suicide Rates Highest
Among Middle-Aged Men," *NBC News*, May 20, 2017, http://www.nbcnews
.com/news/us-news/it-s-not-just-chris-cornell-suicide-rates-highest
-among-n762221.

7. Ibid.

8. "Suicide: 2016 Facts and Figures," The American Foundation for Suicide
Prevention, http://afsp.org/wp-content/uploads/2016/06/2016-National
-Facts-Figures.pdf.

9. Anne Case and Angus Deaton, "Mortality and Morbidity in the 21st Century," *Brookings Papers on Economic Activity*, Spring 2017, https://www
.brookings.edu/wp-content/uploads/2017/08/casetextsp17bpea.pdf.

10. Ibid.

11. Émile Durkheim, *On Suicide*, 226.

12. Cheryl Corley, "Skeletons Of The Auto Industry Linger Across U.S.,"
NPR, July 15, 2009, http://www.npr.org/templates/story/story.php?sto
ryId=106655302.

13. Jeremy W. Peters and Micheline Maynard, "Company Town Relies on G.M.
Long After Plants Have Closed," *The New York Times*, Feb. 20, 2006, http://
www.nytimes.com/2006/02/20/business/company-town-relies-on-gm
-long-after-plants-have-closed.html?mcubz=3.

14. Ibid.

15. Ken de la Bastide, "Madison County, Anderson continue to lose population," *The Herald Bulletin*, Jun 22, 2016, http://www.heraldbulletin.com/
news/local_news/madison-county-anderson-continue-to-lose-population/
article_362969d8-38d9-11e6-a221-4791405b4db5.html.

16. *LABOREM EXERCENS*, The Holy See, http://w2.vatican.va/content/
john-paul-ii/en/encyclicals/documents/hf_jp-ii_enc_14091981_laborem
-exercens.html.

17. Ibid.
18. Jeffrey St. Clair, *Grand Theft Pentagon: Tales of Corruption and Profiteering in the War on Terror* (Monroe: Common Courage Press, 2005), 171.
19. Ibid.
20. Sidney Fine, *Sit-down: The General Motors strike of 1936–1937* (Ann Arbor: University of Michigan Press, 1969), 317.
21. Ibid., 61.
22. Ibid.
23. Ibid., 156.
24. "1936 Sit-down strike begins in Flint," This Day in History, http://www.history.com/this-day-in-history/sit-down-strike-begins-in-flint.
25. Sidney Fine, *Sit-down: The General Motors strike of 1936–1937*, 1.
26. Ibid.
27. Ibid., 4.
28. Ibid., 266.
27. "1936 Sit-down strike begins in Flint," This Day in History, http://www.history.com/this-day-in-history/sit-down-strike-begins-in-flint.
28. Sidney Fine, *Sit-down: The General Motors strike of 1936–1937*, 309.
29. Ibid.
30. Ibid.
31. Ibid.
32. Ibid.
33. "The 1936–37 Flint, Michigan Sit-Down Strike," *BBC*, January 28, 2002, http://www.bbc.co.uk/dna/place-london/A672310.
34. Ibid.
35. Ibid.
36. Ibid.
37. Ibid.
38. Steven Greenhouse, "In Indiana, Clues to Future of Wisconsin Labor," *New York Times*, February 26, 2011, http://www.nytimes.com/2011/02/27/business/27collective-bargain.html?mcubz=3.
39. Ibid.
40. Kylee Wierks and Matt Adams, "Donald Trump rails against Carrier during rally at Indiana State Fairgrounds," *Fox News*, April 20, 2016, http://fox59.com/2016/04/20/live-updates-donald-trump-rally-in-indianapolis.
41. Ronald Radosh, ed., *Debs* (Englewood Cliffs, NJ: Prentice-Hall, 1971), 1.
42. Barbara W. Tuchman, *The Proud Tower: A Portrait of the World Before the War, 1890–914* (New York: Random House, 2014), 471.
43. Ibid.

44. Ibid.
45. Ibid., 472.
46. Ibid.
47. Ibid.
48. Eugene Victor Debs, *Debs: His Life, Writings and Speeches* (Chicago: Press of John F. Higgins, 1908), 84.
49. Ibid., 30.
50. Nick Salvatore, *Eugene V. Debs: Citizen and Socialist* (Chicago: University of Illinois Press, 1984), 148.
51. Ibid.
52. Ibid., 151.
53. Ibid., 311.
54. Ibid.
55. Ibid., 165.
56. Ibid., 155.
57. Ibid.
58. Ibid.
59. Ibid., 345.
60. J. Robert Constantine, ed., *Gentle Rebel: Letters of Eugene V. Debs* (Champaign: University of Illinois Press, 1995), xxx–xxi.
61. Ibid., xxix.
62. Ibid.
63. Ibid.
64. Ibid., xxx.
65. Nick Salvatore, *Eugene V. Debs: Citizen and Socialist*, 264.
66. Howard Zinn and Anthony Arnove, *Voices of a People's History of the United States* (New York: Seven Stories Press), 291.
67. Constantine, ed., *Gentle Rebel*, xxviii.
68. Ibid., xxxii.
69. Nick Salvatore, *Eugene V. Debs: Citizen and Socialist*, 161.
70. Constantine, ed., *Gentle Rebel*, xxxiii–xxxiv.
71. "The Sedition Act of 1918 From The United States Statutes at Large, V. 40. (April 1917–arch 1919)," PBS, http://www.pbs.org/wnet/supremecourt/capitalism/sources_document1.html.
72. Ibid.
73. Nick Salvatore, *Eugene V. Debs: Citizen and Socialist*, 295.
74. Eugene V. Debs, *Debs*, 82–4.
75. Constantine, ed., *Gentle Rebel*, 200.

76. Bernard J. Brommel, *Eugene V. Debs: Spokesman For Labor And Socialism* (Chicago: Charles H Kerr, 1978), 190–191.

77. Victor Hugo, translated by Norman Denny, *Les Misérables* (New York: Penguin Classics, 1976), 1,230.

Chapter 4 – SADISM

1. Wilhelm Reich, *The Mass Psychology of Fascism* (New York: Farrar, Straus and Giroux,1980), xv.

2. "San Francisco's Ten Year Plan to End Chronic Homelessness: Anniversary Report Covering 2004 to 2014," San Francisco Human Services Agency City and County of San Francisco, http://sfmayor.org/sites/default/files/FileCenter/Documents/404-Ten%20Year%20Plan%20Anniversary%20Report%20-%20Final%20Draft.pdf.

3. Jesse McKinley, "A Neighbor Moves in With Ropes and Shackles, and Some Are Not So Pleased," *New York Times,* February 12, 2007, http://www.nytimes.com/2007/02/12/us/12armory.html.

4. Jack Leibman, San Francisco Armory in the Mission, San Francisco City Guides, http://www.sfcityguides.org/public_guidelines.html?article=506&submitted=TRUE&srch_text=&submitted2=&topic=.

5. Sam Levin, " 'End of an era': porn actors lament the loss of legendary San Francisco Armory," *The Guardian,* January 25, 2017, https://www.theguardian.com/culture/2017/jan/25/porn-bdsm-kink-armory-closing-san-francisco.

6. Gail Dines, *Pornland: How Porn Has Hijacked Our Sexuality* (Boston: Beacon Press, 2011), 47.

7. Ibid.

8. Rebecca Solnit, *Men Explain Things to Me* (Chicago: Haymarket Books, 2014), 19.

9. Ibid., 23.

10. Rachel Moran, *Paid For* (New York: W.W. Norton & Company, 2013), 100.

11. Aimee Allison and David Solnit, *Army of None: Strategies to Counter Military Recruitment, End War and Build a Better World* (New York: Seven Stories Press, 2007), 3–7.

12. Rachel Moran, *Paid For,* 175.

13. Ibid., 122.

14. Ibid., 52.

15. Molly Freedenberg, "Kink Dreams," *San Francisco Bay Guardian,* September 24, 2008, http://48hills.org/sfbgarchive/2008/09/23/kink-dreams/.

16. Nicholas Iovino, "Porn Factory Must Defend Itself Against HIV Claims," *Courthouse News*, December 18, 2017, https://www.courthousenews.com/porn-factory-must-defend-itself-against-hiv-claims/.

17. Edward W. Said, *Orientalism* (New York: Vintage Books, 1979), 3.

18. "Canada 2014 Human Rights Report," U.S. Department of State, https://www.state.gov/documents/organization/236884.pdf.

19. Seo-Young Cho, Axel Dreher, and Eric Neumayer (2012). Does Legalized Prostitution Increase Human Trafficking? *World Development*, 41 (1), 2013, pp. 67–82. https://papers.ssrn.com/sol3/papers.cfm?abstract_id=1986065.

20. "ILO says forced labour generates annual profits of US$ 150 billion," International Labour Organization, http://www.ilo.org/global/about-the-ilo/newsroom/news/WCMS_243201/lang—en/index.htm.

21. Ibid.

22. Michael Shively, Kristina Kliorys, Kristin Wheeler, Dana Hunt, "A National Overview of Prostitution and Sex Trafficking Demand Reduction Efforts, Final Report," The National Institute of Justice, https://www.ncjrs.gov/pdffiles1/nij/grants/238796.pdf.

23. John J. Potterat, Devon D. Brewer, Stuart Brody. (2004). Mortality in a Long-term Open Cohort of Prostitute Women. *American Journal of Epidemiology,* 159 (8): 778–785. DOI: https://doi.org/101.093/aje/kwh110.

24. "How profitable is the exploitation of people? Sadly, extraordinarily so," International Labour Organization, http://www.ilo.org/newyork/voices-at-work/WCMS_244965/lang—en/index.htm.

Chapter 5 – HATE

1. Hannah Arendt, *The Origins of Totalitarianism* (New York, Harcourt, Inc., 1976), 474.

2. Albert Camus, *The Plague*, translated from the French by Stuart Gilbert (New York: Vintage Books, 1991), 308.

3. German Lopez, "The trial of Dylann Roof for the Charleston church shooting, explained," *Vox*, January 10, 2017, https://www.vox.com/identities/2016/12/7/13868662/dylann-roof-trial-verdict-charleston-church-shooting.

4. Rachel Kaadzi Ghansah, "A Most American Terrorist: The Making of Dylann Roof," *GQ*, August 21, 2017, https://www.gq.com/story/dylann-roof-making-of-an-american-terrorist.

5. Ibid.

6. "Last Rhodesian Manifesto," Document Cloud, https://www.document-cloud.org/documents/2108059-lastrhodesian-manifesto.html.

7. Frances Robles, "Dylann Roof Photos and a Manifesto Are Posted on Website," *New York Times,* June 20, 2015, https://www.nytimes.com/2015/06/21/us/dylann-storm-roof-photos-website-charleston-church-shooting.html.

8. Rachel Kaadzi Ghansah, "*A Most American Terrorist: The Making of Dylann Roof.*"

9. "Last Rhodesian Manifesto," Document Cloud, https://www.document cloud.org/documents/2108059-lastrhodesian-manifesto.html.

10. James West, "Decoding the Scene From Dylann Roof's 'Favorite Film,'" *Mother Jones,* June 21, 2015, http://www.motherjones.com/politics/2015/06/dylann-roof-favorite-film-scene-himizu/.

11. "Last Rhodesian Manifesto," Document Cloud, https://www.document cloud.org/documents/2108059-lastrhodesian-manifesto.html.

12. Rachel Kaadzi Ghansah, "*A Most American Terrorist: The Making of Dylann Roof.*"

13. Ibid.

14. Ibid.

15. Felicia Lee, "Bench of Memory at Slavery's Gateway," *New York Times,* July 28, 2008, http://www.nytimes.com/2008/07/28/arts/design/28benc.html.

16. "Contents of Cell Search 8-3-15," United States Courts, http://www.us courts.gov/courts/scd/cases/2-15-472/exhibits/GX500.pdf.

17. Ibid.

18. Kristine Phillips, "Dylann Roof loses bid to fire Jewish, Indian lawyers — his 'political and biological enemies,'" *Washington Post,* September 19, 2017, https://www.washingtonpost.com/news/post-nation/wp/2017/09/19/dylann-roof-wants-to-fire-jewish-and-indian-lawyers-his-political-and-biological-enemies/?utm_term=.2910aa3f679c.

19. Ibid.

20. Rachel Kaadzi Ghansah, "*A Most American Terrorist: The Making of Dylann Roof.*"

21. Ibid.

22. Ibid.

23. "Contents of Cell Search 8-3-15," United States Courts, http://www.uscourts.gov/courts/scd/cases/2-15-472/exhibits/GX500.pdf.

24. "Hate Crime Analysis & Forecast," Center for the Study of Hate and Extremism, https://csbs.csusb.edu/sites/csusb_csbs/files/Final%20Hate%20Crime%2017%20Status%20Report%20pdf.pdf.

25. Jesse Singal, "Undercover With the Alt-Right," *New York Times*, September 19, 2017, https://www.nytimes.com/2017/09/19/opinion/alt-right-white-supremacy-undercover.html.

26. "Contents of Cell Search 8-3-15," United States Courts, http://www.uscourts.gov/courts/scd/cases/2-15-472/exhibits/GX500.pdf.

27. See "Deposit village, New York," United States Census Bureau, https://factfinder.census.gov/faces/nav/jsf/pages/community_facts.xhtml?src=bkmk.

28. Laila Kearney, "A tranquil Muslim hamlet in the Catskills—until the attack plot," *Reuters*, June 1, 2015, https://www.reuters.com/article/us-usa-islamberg-insight/a-tranquil-muslim-hamlet-in-the-catskills-until-the-attack-plot-idUSKBN0OH1D920150601.

29. Ibid.

30. Ibid.

31. Ibid.

32. Ibid.

33. "US Islamist group arming up in anticipation of Trump, report claims," *Fox News*, November 29, 2016, http://www.foxnews.com/us/2016/11/29/us-islamist-group-arming-up-in-anticipation-trump-report-claims.html.

34. Peter Finn, "Khalid Sheik Mohammed killed U.S. journalist Daniel Pearl, report finds," *Washington Post*, January 20, 2011, http://www.washingtonpost.com/wp-dyn/content/article/2011/01/20/AR2011012000057.html.

35. "Guerilla training of women at Islamberg, Hancock, N.Y., headquarters of Muslims of the Americas," Clarion Project, https://www.youtube.com/watch?v=bxoykqCSruY.

36. "America's First Islamic Government," Christian Action Network, https://can-test.squarespace.com/blog/2013/12/13/2nd-placeholder-postadmin christianactionorg.

37. Ibid.

38. Tim Ghianni, "Tennessee man sentenced over plot to attack Muslim community," *Reuters*, June 15, 2017, https://www.reuters.com/article/us-tennessee-muslim-crime/tennessee-man-sentenced-over-plot-to-attack-muslim-community-idUSKBN1962R7.

39. Ibid.

40. Ryan Mauro and Martin Mawyer, "Exclusive: Jihadi Cult Associate Arrested in NY With Firearms Stockpile," *Clarion Project*, July 2, 2017, https://clarionproject.org/exclusive-jihadi-cult-associate-arrested-ny-firearms-stockpile/.

41. "New Alt-Right 'Fight Club' Ready for Street Violence," Southern Poverty Law Center, https://www.splcenter.org/hatewatch/2017/04/25/new-alt right-fight-club-ready-street-violence.

42. PawL BaZiLe, "Proud Boys visiting Islamic training ground in NY this Saturday," *Proud Boy Magazine*, July 2017, http://officialproudboys.com/col umns/proud-boys-visiting-islamic-training-ground-in-ny-this-saturday/.

43. Adam Gabbatt, "Five anti-Muslim protesters and 400 peace supporters meet at New York rally," *The Guardian*, May 16, 2016, https://www .theguardian.com/us-news/2016/may/16/anti-muslim-protest-bikers -new-york-islamberg-peace-rally.

44. Evan Osnos, "Doomsday Prep for the Super-Rich," *New Yorker,* January 30, 2017, https://www.newyorker.com/magazine/2017/01/30/doomsday -prep-for-the-super-rich.

45. Pankaj Mishra, *Age of Anger: A History of the Present* (New York: Farrar, Straus and Giroux, 2017), 274.

46. Ibid., 8.

47. Ibid., 28.

48. Ibid., 27.

49. Ibid., 123.

50. Hannah Arendt, *Men in Dark Times* (New York: Harcourt, Brace & Company, 1970), 83.

51. Pankaj Mishra, *Age of Anger: A History of The Present,* 77.

52. Gal Tziperman Lotan, Paul Brinkmann and Rene Stutzman, "Witness: Omar Mateen had been at Orlando gay nightclub many times," *Orlando Sentinel,* June 13, 2016, http://www.orlandosentinel.com/news/pulse -orlando-nightclub-shooting/os-orlando-nightclub-omar-mateen-profile -20160613-story.html.

53. Pankaj Mishra, *Age of Anger: A History of the Present,* 77.

54. Robin Wright, "Abu Muhammad al-Adnani, the Voice of ISIS, Is Dead," *New Yorker,* August 30, 2016, http://www.newyorker.com/news/news desk/abu-muhammad-al-adnani-the-voice-of-isis-is-dead.

55. Pankaj Mishra, *Age of Anger: A History of the Present,* 230.

56. Ibid.

57. Ibid., 77.

58. Ibid., 135.

59. Ibid., 275–276.

60. Ibid., 288.

61. Ibid., 125.

62. Ibid., 81.

63. Chris Kyle, *American Sniper: The Autobiography of the Most Lethal Sniper in U.S. Military History* (New York: HarperCollins, 2013), 4.

64. Ibid.

65. Ibid., 220.

66. Ibid., 6.

67. Ibid., 86.

68. Ibid.

69. Ibid.

70. Ibid., 231.

71. Ibid., 219.

72. Ibid., 199.

73. Ibid., 53–54.

74. Ibid., 86.

75. Manny Fernandez and Kathryn Jones, " 'American Sniper' Jury Finds Chris Kyle's Killer Guilty of Murder," *New York Times,* February 24, 2015, https://www.nytimes.com/2015/02/25/us/american-sniper-trial-jury -finds-ex-marine-guilty-of-murder.html.

76. Ibid.

77. Pankaj Mishra, *Age of Anger: A History of the Present,* 280.

78. Ibid.

79. Ibid., 271.

80. Ibid.

81. Ibid., 295.

82. Oriana Fallaci, "The Rage and the Pride," *Corriere della Sera,* September 29, 2001 http://users.ecs.soton.ac.uk/harnad/Temp/oriana.html.

83. Diana Johnstone, "Antifa in Theory and Practice," *Counterpunch*, October 9, 2017, https://www.counterpunch.org/2017/10/09/antifa-in-theory-and -in-practice/.

84. Ibid.

85. Quoted in Paul Mattick, *Anti-Bolshevik Communism* (Pontypool, UK: Merlin Press, 1978), 21.

86. Richard J. Evans, *The Coming of the Third Reich* (New York: Penguin, 2003), 268–269.

87. Ibid.

88. Ibid., 269–70.

89. Jan Valtin, *Out of the Night: The Memoir of Richard Julius Herman Krebs Alias Jan Valtin* (Oakland, CA: AK Press, 2004), 216.

90. Richard J. Evans, *The Coming of the Third Reich,* 270.

91. Ibid., 272.

92. Theodore Roszak, *The Making of a Counter Culture* (New York: Anchor Books,1969), 40.

93. Joseph Goldstein, "*Inspector Who Pepper-Sprayed Protesters Is Ordered to Appear Before Panel,*" New York Times, November 27, 2013, http://www.nytimes.com/2013/11/28/nyregion/inspector-who-pepper-sprayed-protesters-is-ordered-to-appear-before-panel.html.

94. Ibid.

95. Libby Nelson, "Why we voted for Donald Trump": David Duke explains the white supremacist Charlottesville protests," *Vox,* https://www.vox.com/2017/8/12/16138358/charlottesville-protests-david-duke-kkk.

96. "I Was Beaten By White Supremacists," Go Fund Me, https://www.gofundme.com/i-was-beaten-by-white-supremacists.

97. Ibid.

98. "New Castle town, Virginia," United States Census Bureau, https://factfinder.census.gov/faces/nav/jsf/pages/community_facts.xhtml?src=bkmk.

99. Luke Barnes, "Proud Boys founder disavows violence at Charlottesville but one of its members organized the event," *Think Progress*, August 24, 2017, https://thinkprogress.org/proud-boys-founder-tries-and-fails-to-distance-itself-from-charlottesville-6862fb8b3ae9/.

100. See the Redneck Revolt website, https://www.redneckrevolt.org/.

101. Joanna Walters, "Militia leaders who descended on Charlottesville condemn 'rightwing lunatics,'" *The Guardian*, August 14, 2017, https://www.theguardian.com/us-news/2017/aug/15/charlottesville-militia-free-speech-violence.

102. Ibid.

103. Ibid.

104. National Council, "The Three Percenters Official Statement Regarding the Violent Protests in Charlottesville," *The Three Percenters*, August 12, 2017, http://www.thethreepercenters.org/single-post/2017/08/12/The-Three-Percenters-Official-Statement-Regarding-the-Violent-Protests-in-Charlottesville.

105. Sigmund Freud, *Civilization and Its Discontents*, translated by Joan Riviere (New York: Dover Publications, 1994), 42.

106. Christopher Lasch, *The Culture of Narcissism: American Life in an Age of Diminishing Expectations* (New York: W. W. Norton & Company, 1979), 15.

107. Sophia Burns, "Catharsis Is Counter-Revolutionary," Gods & Radicals,

August 2017, https://godsandradicals.org/2017/08/09/catharsis-is-count er-revolutionary/.

108. Aviva Chomsky, "How (Not) to Challenge Racist Violence," *Common Dreams*, August 21, 2017, https://www.commondreams.org/views/2017/08/21/how-not-challenge-racist-violence.

109. Jana Winter, "FBI and DHS Warned of Growing Threat From White Supremacists Months Ago," *Foreign Policy*, August 14, 2017, http://foreignpolicy.com/2017/08/14/fbi-and-dhs-warned-of-growing-threat-from-white-supremacists-months-ago/.

110. *Ten Ways to Fight Hate: A Community Response Guide*, *Southern Poverty Law Center*, https://www.splcenter.org/20170814/ten-ways-fight-hate-community-response-guide.

111. Ibid.

112. Benjamin Oreskes and Paige St. John, "After 'antifa' violence, Berkeley debates whether Milo Yiannopoulos and other conservatives are welcome," *Los Angeles Times*, August 30, 2017, http://www.latimes.com/local/lanow/la-me-berkeley-far-left-protests-milo-20170830-story.html.

113. Frances Robles, "As White Nationalist in Charlottesville Fired, Police 'Never Moved,'" *New York Times*, August 25, 2017, https://www.nytimes.com/2017/08/25/us/charlottesville-protest-police.html.

114. Jazmine Ulloa, John Myers, Emily Alpert Reyes, and Victoria Kim, "7 stabbed at neo-Nazi event outside Capitol in Sacramento," *Los Angeles Times*, June 26, 2016, http://www.latimes.com/local/lanow/la-me-neo-nazi-stabbed-20160626-snap-htmlstory.html.

115. Joseph Serna, "Neo-Nazis didn't start the violence at state Capitol, police say," *Los Angeles Times*, June 27, 2016, http://www.latimes.com/local/lanow/la-me-ln-neo-nazi-event-stabbings-capitol-20160627-snap-story.html.

116. Natasha Lennard, "Neo-Nazi Richard Spencer Got Punched—You Can Thank the Black Bloc," *The Nation*, January 22, 2017, https://www.thenation.com/article/if-you-appreciated-seeing-neo-nazi-richard-spencer-get-punched-thank-the-black-bloc/.

117. Ibid.

118. Walter Benjamin, *The Work of Art in the Age of Its Technological Reproducibility, and Other Writings on Media* (Cambridge: Belknap Press, 2008), 42.

Chapter 6 – GAMBLING

1. Quoted in Brad Thomas, *The Trump Factor: Unlocking the Secrets Behind the Trump Empire* (New York: Post Hill Press, 2016), 112.

2. Mark Berman, "Atlantic City's casino revenue was cut in half in less than a decade," *Washington Post*, January 14, 2015, https://www.washingtonpost.com/news/post-nation/wp/2015/01/14/atlantic-citys-casino-revenue-was-cut-in-half-in-less-than-a-decade/?utm_term=.74af58649c78.

3. Ibid.

4. Ed Davis, Tim Murphy and Geoff Freeman, "The federal sports betting ban has failed: Let's legalize and regulate it," *The Hill*, June 12, 2017, http://thehill.com/blogs/congress-blog/politics/337367-the-federal-sports-betting-ban-has-failed-lets-legalize-and.

5. Ellen Mutari and Deborah M. Figart, *Just One More Hand: Life in the Casino Economy* (New York: Rowman & Littlefield, 2015), 3–4

6. "2017 AGA Survey of the Casino Industry," American Gaming Association, https://www.americangaming.org/sites/default/files/research_files/2017%20State%20of%20the%20States.pdf.

7. "2013 AGA Survey of Casino Entertainment," American Gaming Association, https://www.americangaming.org/sites/default/files/research_files/aga_sos2013_rev042014.pdf.

8. John Rosengren, "How Casinos Enable Gambling Addicts," *The Atlantic*, December 2016, https://www.theatlantic.com/magazine/archive/2016/12/losing-it-all/505814/.

9. Ibid.

10. "2013 AGA Survey of Casino Entertainment," American Gaming Association, https://www.americangaming.org/sites/default/files/research_files/aga_sos2013_rev042014.pdf.

11. Ibid.

12. Lorenzo Ferrigno, Brian Vitagliano, and Amanda Wills, "The Atlantic City summer that nearly ruined Donald Trump," *CNN*, July 7, 2016, http://www.cnn.com/2016/07/06/politics/donald-trump-atlantic-city-taj-mahal/index.html.

13. Paul Goldberger, "It's 'Themed,' It's Kitschy, It's Trump's Taj," *New York Times*, April 6, 1990, http://www.nytimes.com/1990/04/06/nyregion/it-s-themed-it-s-kitschy-it-s-trump-s-taj.html.

14. John Rosengren, "How Casinos Enable Gambling Addicts."

15. "Gambling and Suicide," National Council on Problem Gambling, http://www.ccpg.org/problem-gambling/more/gambling-and-suicide/.

16. Jon Nordheimer, "In Atlantic City, Suspicion Is a Way of Life; Casino Agents Keep an Eye on Things . . . and People, and Machines," *New York Times*, March 22, 1994, http://www.nytimes.com/1994/03/22/nyregion/atlantic-city-suspicion-way-life-casino-agents-keep-eye-things-people-ma chines.html?pagewanted=all.

17. Natasha Dow Schüll, *Addiction by Design: Machine Gambling in Las Vegas* (Princeton, NJ: Princeton University Press, 2012),164.

18. Ibid., 154.

19. Lisa Fletcher, Jen Wlach, Sarah Netter, Monica Escobedo, "Biggest Loser? Gambler Dropped $127M in a Year," *ABC*, December 8, 2009, http://abcnews.go.com/GMA/gambler-dropped-127-million-vegas-blames-casi no-losses/story?id=9272730.

20. Natasha Dow Schüll, *Addiction by Design*, 147.

21. Ibid.

22. Brian Pempus, "Americans Lost $1169.B Gambling In 2016: Report," *Card Player*, February 14, 2017, https://www.cardplayer.com/poker -news/21342-americans-lost-116-9b-gambling-in-2016-report.

23. "2017 AGA Survey of the Casino Industry," *American Gaming Association*, https://www.americangaming.org/sites/default/files/research_ files/2017%20State%20of%20the%20States.pdf.

24. Adam Silver, "Legalize and Regulate Sports Betting," *The New York Times*, November 13, 2014, https://www.nytimes.com/2014/11/14/opinion/nba-commissioner-adam-silver-legalize-sports-betting.html.

25. Lucy Dadayan, "State Revenues from Gambling," *The Blinken Report*, April 2016, http://www.rockinst.org/pdf/government_finance/2016-04 -12-Blinken_Report_Three.pdf.

26. Derek Thompson, "Lotteries: America's $70 Billion Shame," *The Atlantic*, May 11, 2015, https://www.theatlantic.com/business/archive/2015/05/lotteries-americas-70-billion-shame/392870/.

27. Natasha Dow Schüll, *Addiction by Design,* 104.

28. Ibid., 5.

29. Roger Caillois, *Man, Play, and Games* (Champaign: University of Illinois Press, 1958), ix.

30. Natasha Dow Schüll, *Addiction by Design*, 18.

31. Quoted in Rick Green, "Gamblers Fight Back to Even the Score," *Hartford Courant*, May 10, 2004, http://articles.courant.com/2004-05-10/news/0405100328_1_video-poker-electronic-slot-machines-gambling -industry.

32. Natasha Dow Schüll has heard Howard Shaffer, A Harvard scientist who

studies addictions, and others use the "crack cocaine" metaphor when speaking of gambling machines (Bulkeley 1992; Simurda 1994; Dyer 2001).

33. Natasha Dow Schüll, *Addiction by Design,* 19.

34. Ibid., 116.

35. Andrew Thompson, "Engineers of Addiction, Slot Machines Perfected Addictive Gaming. Now, Tech Wants Their Tricks," *The Verge,* May 6, 2015, https://www.theverge.com/2015/5/6/8544303/casino-slot-machine-gambling-addiction-psychology-mobile-games.

36. Bryant Simon, *Boardwalk of Dreams: Atlantic City and the Fate of Urban America* (New York: Oxford University Press, 2004), 194.

37. Bill Moyers, "Big Gamble in Atlantic City," *CBS News Special Report,* July 28, 1986, Heston Room, The Atlantic City Free Public Library.

38. David Cay Johnston, *The Making of Donald Trump* (Brooklyn, NY: Melville House, 2016), 60.

39. Ibid., 64.

40. Hal Rothman and Mike Davis, *The Grit Beneath the Glitter: Tales from the Real Las Vegas* (Berkeley: University of California Press, 2002), 5.

41. Bryant Simon, *Boardwalk of Dreams,* 205.

42. Bill Kent, "ATLANTIC CITY; To the Lighthouse," *New York Times,* November 16, 1997, http://www.nytimes.com/1997/11/16/nyregion/atlantic-city-to-the-lighthouse.html.

43. Bryant Simon, *Boardwalk of Dreams,* 205.

44. Russ Buettner and Charles V. Bagli, "How Donald Trump Bankrupted His Atlantic City Casinos, but Still Earned Millions," *New York Times,* June 11, 2016, https://www.nytimes.com/2016/06/12/nyregion/donald-trump-atlantic-city.html.

45. Ibid.

46. Robert O'Harrow Jr., "Trump's bad bet: How too much debt drove his biggest casino aground," *Washington Post,* January 18, 2016, https://www.washingtonpost.com/investigations/trumps-bad-bet-how-too-much-debt-drove-his-biggest-casino-aground/2016/01/18/f67cedc2-9ac8-11e5-8917-653b65c809eb_story.html?utm_term=.7a2ee17125ba.

47. Russ Buettner and Charles V. Bagli, "How Donald Trump Bankrupted His Atlantic City Casinos, but Still Earned Millions."

48. Ibid.

49. Michelle Celarier, "Why Carl Icahn Is The Donald Trump of Finance," *Fortune Magazine,* March 14, 2016, http://fortune.com/2016/03/14/carl-icahn-donald-trump/.

50. Ibid.

51. Ibid.

52. Ibid.

53. Ibid.

54. Tanya Agrawal, "Another Atlantic City casino company files for bankruptcy," *Reuters,* September 9, 2014, http://www.reuters.com/article/us-trump-bankruptcy-casinos-idUSKBN0H413E20140909.

55. Noah Shachtman, "Trump Taj Mahal Slashed Security. Then the Murders Started," *Daily Beast,* June 2, 2016, http://www.thedailybeast.com/trump-taj-mahal-slashed-security-then-the-murders-started.

56. Ibid.

57. Ibid.

58. Ibid.

59. Ellen Mutari and Deborah M. Figart, *Just One More Hand: Life in the Casino Economy,* 98.

60. "Trump Entertainment files for bankruptcy; Taj Mahal could close in November," *NJ.com,* September 09, 2014, http://www.nj.com/business/index.ssf/2014/09/trump_entertainment_files_for_bankruptcy_taj_mahal_could_close_in_november.html.

61. Patrick McGeehan, "Uncertainty for Workers Losing Jobs at Atlantic City Casinos," *New York Times,* August 25, 2014, https://www.nytimes.com/2014/08/26/nyregion/uncertainty-for-workers-losing-jobs-at-atlantic-city-casinos.html.

62. Wayne Parry, "Icahn rejects union bid to keep Trump Taj Mahal casino open," *Associated Press,* August 29, 2016, https://apnews.com/36d5370b83fe4d2da8562b9fde6f964a/union-makes-proposal-icahn-it-says-will-save-taj.

63. David Cay Johnston, *The Making of Donald Trump,* x.

64. Ibid., 86.

65. Ibid., 87.

66. Ibid., 87–88.

67. Ibid., 89.

68. Ibid., 90.

69. Ibid., 93.

70. Ibid.

71. "This complaint, however, of the scarcity of money, is not always confined to improvident spendthrifts. It is sometimes general through a whole mercantile town, and the country in its neighborhood. Overtrading is the common cause of it . . . When the profits of trade happen to be greater than

ordinary, overtrading becomes a general error both among great and small dealers . . . They buy upon credit . . . an unusual quantity of goods . . . They run about everywhere to borrow money . . . and they have nothing at hand with which they can either purchase money or give solid security for borrowing . . . the difficulty which such people find in borrowing, and which their creditors find in getting payment . . . a particular merchant, with abundance of goods in his warehouse, may sometimes be ruined by not being able to sell them in time," Adam Smith, *The Wealth of Nations, Part Two* (New York: P.F. Collier & Son, 1902), 135–137.

72. Neil Postman, *Amusing Ourselves to Death: Public Discourse in the Age of Show Business* (New York: Penguin Books, 1985),155–156.

Chapter 7 – FREEDOM

1. George Eliot, *Middlemarch* (New York: The Modern Library, 1992), 799.
2. Willard Gaylin, *In the Service of Their Country: War Resisters in Prison* (New York: Viking Press, 1970), 330.
3. Rob Kall, "Chomsky Talks about Psychopaths and Sociopaths," *Op Ed News*, February 15, 2014, www.opednews.com/articles/Chomsky-Talks -about-Psych-by-Rob-Kall-Corporations_Health-Mental-Sociopath-Nar cissim_Narcissism_Psychopath-140215-378.html.
4. Walker Percy, *Love In the Ruins* (New York: Farrar, Straus and Giroux, 1971), 107.
5. Reinhold Niebuhr, *Beyond Tragedy: Essays on the Christian Interpretation of History* (New York: C. Scribner's Sons, 1937), 41.
6. Ibid., 83.
7. Ibid., 14.
8. Ibid., 6.
9. Ibid., 16.
10. Ibid., 221.
11. Ibid., 132.
12. Ibid., 136.
13. Ibid., 186.
14. Ibid., 18.
15. Ibid.
16. Ibid., 15.
17. Ibid., 17.
18. Ibid., 107.
19. Ibid., 19.

20. Ibid., 12.

21. Ibid., 233.

22. Walker Percy, *Love In the Ruins*, 56–57.

23. Saul Alinsky paraphrasing British Prime Minister Lord Palmerston in David Brown, *Palmerston and the Politics of Foreign Policy, 1846–1855* (Manchester: Manchester University Press, 2002), 82–83.

24. Michael Gecan, "Back of the Yards: Lessons from a Community Organizer on Building Political Power," *Boston Review,* January 4, 2017, http://bostonreview.net/politics/michael-gecan-back-yards.

25. William Yardley, "The $3.7-billion pipeline that became a rallying cry for tribes across America," *Los Angeles Times*, September 13, 2016, http://www.latimes.com/nation/la-na-sej-dakota-access-pipeline-20160912-snap-story.html.

26. Serena Marshall, Evan Simon, and Morgan Winsor, "Trump Moves to Advance Keystone XL, Dakota Access Pipelines," *ABC News*, January 24, 2017, http://abcnews.go.com/Politics/trump-advances-keystone-xl-dakota-access-pipelines/story?id=45008003.

27. Julia Carrie Wong, "Police remove last Standing Rock protesters in military-style takeover," *The Guardian*, February 23, 2017, https://www.theguardian.com/us-news/2017/feb/23/dakota-access-pipeline-camp-cleared-standing-rock.

28. Blake Nicholson, "Tribal head who led Dakota Access pipeline fight voted out," *Associated Press*, September 28, 2017, https://www.apnews.com/8c6c1a5bb28e48beab1bac4c1b2bfc60/Tribal-head-who-led-Dakota-Access-pipeline-fight-voted-out.

29. Gregor Aisch and K. K. Rebecca Lai, "The Conflicts Along 1,172 Miles of the Dakota Access Pipeline," *New York Times*, March 20, 2017, https://www.nytimes.com/interactive/2016/11/23/us/dakota-access-pipeline-protest-map.html.

30. Ibid.

31. Mark Trahant, "Blood and Land: The Story of Native America by JCH King – review," *The Guardian*, December 15, 2016, https://www.theguardian.com/books/2016/dec/15/blood-and-land-the-story-of-native-america-jch-king-review.

32. Ibid.

33. Charlie Northcott, "Standing Rock: What next for protests?" *BBC News*, December 5, 2016, http://www.bbc.com/news/world-us-canada-38214636.

34. Catherine Thorbecke, "141 Arrested at Dakota Access Pipeline Protest as Police Move In," *ABC News,* October 28, 2016, http://abcnews

.go.com/US/tensions-mount-protesters-police-controversial-pipeline/sto
ry?id=43078902.

35. "995 people shot dead by police in 2015," *Washington Post,* https://www
.washingtonpost.com/graphics/national/police-shootings/.

36. "The Counted People killed by police in the US," *The Guardian,* https://
www.theguardian.com/us-news/ng-interactive/2015/jun/01/the-count
ed-police-killings-us-database/

37. Daniel Bier, "How Many Americans Do the Cops Kill Each Year?" *Newsweek,* July 16, 2016, http://www.newsweek.com/how-many-americans-do
-cops-kill-each-year-480712.

38. "Deaths in Police Custody," INQUEST, http://inquest.gn.apc.org/statis
tics/deaths-in-police-custody.

49. Alex S. Vitale, *The End of Policing* (New York: Verso, 2017), 52.

40. William D. Cohan, "How Wall Street's Bankers Stayed Out of Jail," *The
Atlantic,* September 2015, https://www.theatlantic.com/magazine/ar
chive/2015/09/how-wall-streets-bankers-stayed-out-of-jail/399368/.

41. NPR Staff, "In Book's Trial Of U.S. Justice System, Wealth Gap Is Exhibit
A," *NPR,* April 6, 2014, http://www.npr.org/2014/04/06/297857886/in
-books-trial-of-u-s-justice-system-wealth-gap-is-exhibit-a.

42. David Nakamura and Niraj Chokshi, "Obama orders review of military
equipment supplied to police," *Washington Post,* August 23, 2014, https://
www.washingtonpost.com/politics/obama-orders-review-of-military
-equipment-supplied-to-police/2014/08/23/6316b8aa-2b03-11e4-8593
-da634b334390_story.html?utm_term=.453e6d9165fc.

43. Alex S. Vitale, *The End of Policing,* 28.

44. Ibid., 14–15.

45. Adam Smith, *An Inquiry Into the Nature and Causes of the Wealth of Nations*
(Chicago: University of Chicago Press, 1977), 299.

46. Alex S. Vitale, *The End of Policing,* 53.

47. Michelle Alexander, *The New Jim Crow* (New York: The New Press, 2012),
224–225.

48. Michelle Ye Hee Lee, "Does the United States really have 5 percent of the
world's population and one quarter of the world's prisoners?" *Washington
Post,* April 30, 2015, https://www.washingtonpost.com/news/fact-checker/
wp/2015/04/30/does-the-united-states-really-have-five-percent-of
-worlds-population-and-one-quarter-of-the-worlds-prisoners/?utm_ter
m=.2715e6056446.

49. "The Thirteenth Amendment," https://constitutioncenter.org/interac
tive-constitution/amendments/amendment-xiii.

50. Valerie Strauss, "Update: Columbia University divesting from private prison companies. Why other schools should too," *Washington Post*, September 13, 2015, https://www.washingtonpost.com/news/answer-sheet/wp/2015/07/15/columbia-university-divesting-from-private-prison-companies-why-other-schools-should-too/?utm_term=.157a9d486e2d.

51. "CCA Announces 2012 Third Quarter Financial Results and Provides Update on Potential REIT Conversion," Corrections Corporations of America and Subsidiaries website, http://ir.correctionscorp.com/phoenix.zhtml?c=117983&p=irol-newsArticle&ID=1755801.

52. Al Lewis, "How insiders will feast on Aramark's third IPO," *Market Watch*, September 11, 2013, https://www.marketwatch.com/story/third-time-may-not-be-the-charm-for-aramark-ipo-2013-09-11.

53. "Aramark Completes Merger News Release," U.S. Securities and Exchange Commission website, January 26, 2007, https://www.sec.gov/Archives/edgar/data/1144528/000119312507014322/dex99a10.htm.

54. Sadhbh Walshe, "How lawmakers and lobbyists keep a lock on the private prison business," *The Guardian*, September 27, 2012, https://www.theguardian.com/commentisfree/2012/sep/27/lawmakers-lobbyists-keep-lock-private-prison-business.

55. "Criminal: How Lockup Quotas and 'Low-Crime Taxes' Guarantee Profits for Private Prison Corporations," In the Public Interest, https://www.inthepublicinterest.org/criminal-how-lockup-quotas-and-low-crime-taxes-guarantee-profits-for-private-prison-corporations/.

56. Carl Takei, "Happy Birthday to the Corrections Corporation of America? Thirty Years of Banking on Bondage Leaves Little to Celebrate," *ACLU*, January 29, 2013, https://www.aclu.org/blog/mass-incarceration/happy-birthday-corrections-corporation-america-thirty-years-banking-bondage.

57. Ibid.

58. Fredreka Schouten, "Private prisons back Trump and could see big payoffs with new policies," *USA Today*, February 23, 2017, https://www.usatoday.com/story/news/politics/2017/02/23/private-prisons-back-trump-and-could-see-big-payoffs-new-policies/98300394/.

59. Carl Takei, "Anonymous Exposes U.S.'s Biggest Private Prison Company as a Bad Financial Investment."

60. "Private Prisons in the United States," The Sentencing Project, August 28, 2017, https://www.sentencingproject.org/publications/private-prisons-united-states/.

61. "The Influence of the Private Prison Industry in the Immigration Detention

Business," Detention Watch Network, http://www.detentionwatchnet work.org/pressroom/reports/2011/private-prisons.

62. Sebastian Murdock and Hayley Miller, "Louisiana Sheriff Wants 'Good' Prisoners to Stay Jailed for Their Free Labor," *Huffington Post*, October 12, 2017, https://www.huffingtonpost.com/entry/louisiana-sheriff-steve -prator-prisoners_us_59dfa0bee4b0fdad73b2cded.

63. Celina Fang, "The California Inmates Fighting The Wine Country Wildfires," *The Marshall Project*, October 23, 2017, https://www .themarshallproject.org/2017/10/23/the-california-inmates-fight ing-the-wine-country-wildfires.

64. Matt Wotus and Monte Plott, California inmates help battle raging wildfires, *CNN*, October 18, 2017, http://www.cnn.com/2017/10/13/us/cali fornia-fires-inmate-firefighters/index.html.

65. "Inmate Telephone Service," Federal Communications Commission, https://www.fcc.gov/consumers/guides/inmate-telephone-service.

66. Cecilia Kang, "Court Strikes Obama-Era Rule Capping Cost of Phone Calls from Prison," *New York Times*, June 13, 2017, https://www.nytimes .com/2017/06/13/technology/fcc-prison-phone-calls-regulations.html.

67. John Dannenberg, "Nationwide PLN Survey Examines Prison Phone Contracts, Kickbacks," *Prison Legal News*, April 15, 2011, https://www .prisonlegalnews.org/news/2011/apr/15/nationwide-pln-survey-exam ines-prison-phone-contracts-kickbacks/.

68. Ibid.

69. Ibid.

70. "Recidivism," Office of Justice Programs, https://www.nij.gov/topics /corrections/recidivism/Pages/welcome.aspx.

71. Marie Gottschalk, *Caught: The Prison State and the Lockdown of American Politics* (Princeton, NJ: Princeton University Press, 2015), 20.

72. Melvin Ray, "Free Alabama Movement," http://www.freealabamamove ment.com/FREE%20ALABAMA%20MOVEMENT.pdf.

73. Staughton Lynd, *Lucasville: The Untold Story of a Prison Uprising* (Oakland, CA: PM Press, 2011),12.

74. Mark Oppenheimer, " 'Blood in the Water,' a Gripping Account of the Attica Prison Uprising," *New York Times*, August 18, 2016, https://www .nytimes.com/2016/08/19/books/blood-in-the-water-a-gripping-account -of-the-attica-prison-uprising.html.

75. Alfred McCoy, *In the Shadows of the American Century: The Rise and Decline of US Global Power* (Chicago: Haymarket Books, 2017), 234.

76. Ibid., 235–236.

77. Ibid., 235.

78. "At Our Own Peril: DoD Risk Assessment in a Post-Primacy World," Strategic Studies Institute, https://ssi.armywarcollege.edu/pdffiles/PUB1358.pdf.

79. Alfred McCoy, *In the Shadows of the American Century*, 230.

80. Zbigniew Brzezinski, *Strategic Vision: America and the Crisis of Global Power* (New York: Basic Books, 2012), 44–45.

81. Alfred McCoy, *In the Shadows of the American Century*, 241.

82. Ibid.

83. Ibid.

84. Ibid.

85. Arthur Donald Innes, *A History of England and the British Empire. VOL. IV: 1802–1914* (Charleston, SC: Nabu Press, 2010), 55.

86. Alfred McCoy, *In the Shadows of the American Century*, 227.

87. Ibid.

88. Ibid., 227–228.

89. Niall Ferguson, *Colossus: The Rise and Fall of the American Empire* (New York: Penguin Books, 2004), 14.

90. Alfred McCoy, *In the Shadows of the American Century*, 239.

91. Ibid., 240.

92. Karl Liebknecht, *Ausgewählte Reden und Aufsätze (Selected Speeches and Essays)* (Berlin: Dietz Verlag,1952), 296–301.

93. Dwight Macdonald, *The Root is Man: Two Essays in Politics* (New York: Cunningham Press, 1953), 30.

94. George Breitman, ed., *Malcolm X Speaks: Selected Speeches and Statements* (New York: Grove Press, 1965), 145.

95. Elliott Roosevelt, ed., *F.D.R., His Personal Letters 1928–1945* (New York: Kraus Reprint Company, 1970), 118.

96. Peter Hudis and Kevin B. Anderson, ed., *The Rosa Luxemburg Reader* (New York: Monthly Review Press, 2004), 198.

97. Robert Looker, ed., *Rosa Luxemburg: Selected Political Writings* (London: Jonathan Cape, 1972), 45.

98. Peter Hudis and Kevin B. Anderson, ed., *The Rosa Luxemburg Reader*, 180.

99. Quoted in Paul Mattick, *Anti-Bolshevik Communism* (Pontypool, UK: Merlin Press, 1978), 143–44.

100. Paul Frölich, *ed., Rosa Luxemburg*, translated by Johanna Hoornweg (Chicago: Haymarket Books, 2010), 249.

101. Charles Derber, *Welcome to the Revolution: Universalizing Resistance for Social Justice and Democracy in Perilous Times* (New York: Routledge, 2017), 289.

102. Joseph A. Buttigieg, ed., *Antonio Gramsci Prison Notebooks, vol. 2* (New York: Columbia University Press, 1996), 32–33.

103. James H. Cone, *The Cross and the Lynching Tree* (New York: Orbis Books, 2011), 2.

104. Sam Whimster, ed., *The Essential Weber: A Reader* (New York: Routledge, 2004), 269.

105. Eric Foner, *Battles for Freedom: The Use and Abuse of American History* (New York: The Nation Company, 2017), 201.

106. Ibid., 206.

107. Søren Kierkegaard, *The Sickness Unto Death* (New York: Start Publishing LLC, 2012), 19.

108. Ibid., 143.

BIBLIOGRAPHY

Alexander, Michelle. *The New Jim Crow.* New York: The New Press, 2012.

Allison, Aimee, and David Solnit. *Army of None: Strategies to Counter Military Recruitment, End War and Build a Better World.* New York: Seven Stories Press, 2007.

Arendt, Hannah. *Men in Dark Times.* New York: Harcourt, Brace & Company, 1970.

———. *The Origins of Totalitarianism.* New York: Harcourt, 1976.

Baldwin, James. *The Devil Finds Work.* New York: Vintage Books, 2011.

———. *The Fire Next Time.* New York: The Dial Press, 1963.

——— *I Am Not Your Negro: A Companion Edition to the Documentary Film Directed by Raoul Peck.* New York: Vintage International, 2017.

———. *Notes of a Native Son.* Boston: Beacon Press, 1955.

———. *The Price of the Ticket: Collected Nonfiction, 1948–985.* New York: St. Martin's Press, 1985.

Becker, Ernest. *The Denial of Death.* New York: Free Press, 1973.

Benjamin, Walter. *Illuminations.* New York: Schocken Books, 1968.

———. *The Work of Art in the Age of Its Technological Reproducibility, and Other Writings on Media.* Cambridge, MA: Belknap Press, 2008.

Boorstin, Daniel J. *The Image: A Guide to Pseudo-Events in America*, New York: Vintage Books, 1987.

Bonhoeffer, Dietrich. *Ethics.* Minneapolis: Fortress Press, 2015.

Bray, Mark. *Antifa: The Anti-Fascist Handbook.* New York: Melville House, 2017.

Breitman, George, ed. *Malcolm X Speaks: Selected Speeches and Statements.* New York: Grove Press, 1965.

Brommel, Bernard J, ed. *Eugene V. Debs: Spokesman for Labor And Socialism*. Chicago: Charles H Kerr, 1978.

Brzezinski, Zbigniew. *Strategic Vision: America and the Crisis of Global Power*. New York: Basic Books, 2012.

Burroughs, William S. *Naked Lunch: The Restored Text*. New York: Grove Press, 1959.

Butler, Paul. *Chokehold: Policing Black Men*. New York: The New Press, 2017.

Buttigieg, Joseph A, ed. *Antonio Gramsci Prison Notebooks, Volume 2*. New York: Columbia University Press, 1996.

Caillois, Roger. *Man, Play, and Games*. Champaign: University of Illinois Press, 1958.

Camus, Albert. *The Plague*. Translated by Stuart Gilbert. New York: Vintage, 1991.

Carmichael, Stokely. *Ready for Revolution*. New York: Scribner, 2005.

Carroll, Lews. *The Complete Illustrated Works*. New York: Gramercy Books, 1982.

Churella, Albert J. *The Pennsylvania Railroad, Volume 1: Building an Empire, 1846–1917*. Philadelphia: University of Pennsylvania Press, 2012.

Cohn, Norman. *The Pursuit of the Millennium: Revolutionary Messianism in Medieval and Reformation Europe and Its Bearing on Modern Totalitarian Movements*. New York: Harper & Row, 1961.

Cone, James H. *The Cross and the Lynching Tree*. New York: Orbis Books, 2011.

Constantine, J. Robert, ed. *Gentle Rebel: Letters of Eugene V. Debs*. Champaign: University of Illinois Press, 1995.

Davis, Horace B, ed. *The National Question: Selected Writings by Rosa Luxemburg*. New York: Monthly Review Press, 1976.

Debs, Eugene V. *His Life, Writings and Speeches*. Chicago: Press of John F. Higgins, 1908.

Derber, Charles. *Welcome to the Revolution: Universalizing Resistance for Social Justice and Democracy in Perilous Times*. New York: Routledge, 2017.

Desai, Meghnad. *Marx's Revenge: The Resurgence of Capitalism and the Death of Statist Socialism*. New York: Verso, 2004.

Detlev Clemens and Brendan M. Purcell, eds. *The Collected Works of Eric Voegelin: Volume 31: Hitler and the Germans*. Columbia: University of Missouri Press, 1999.

Dilling, Elizabeth. *The Red Network: A "Who's Who" and Handbook of Radicalism for Patriots*. CreateSpace Independent Publishing Platform, 2010.

Dines, Gail. *Pornland: How Porn Has Hijacked Our Sexuality*. Boston: Beacon Press, 2011.

Dombrink, John, and William Norman Thompson. *The Last Resort: Success and Failure in Campaigns for Casinos*. Reno: University of Nevada Press, 1990.

Durkheim, Émile. *The Division of Labour in Society.* New York: Free Press, 1984.

———. *On Suicide.* New York: Penguin Classics, 2006.

Dyke, Nella Van, and Holly J. McCammon. *Strategic Alliances: Coalition Building and Social Movements Vol. 34.* Minneapolis: University of Minnesota Press, 2010.

Eliot, George. *Middlemarch.* New York: The Modern Library, 1992.

Evans, Richard J. *The Coming of the Third Reich.* New York: Penguin, 2003.

Foner, Eric. *Battles for Freedom: The Use and Abuse of American History.* New York: The Nation Company, 2017.

Ferguson, Niall. *Colossus: The Rise and Fall of the American Empire.* New York: Penguin Books, 2004.

Fine, Sidney. *Sit-down: The General Motors strike of 1936–1937.* Ann Arbor: University of Michigan Press, 1969.

Forgacs, David. *Antonio Gramsci The Gramsci Reader Selected Writings 1916–1935.* New York: New York University Press, 2000.

Forman, James. *Locking Up Our Own: Crime and Punishment in Black America.* New York: Farrar, Straus and Giroux, 2017.

Freud, Sigmund. *Beyond the Pleasure Principle.* New York: W. W. Norton & Company, 1990.

Freud, Sigmund. *Civilization and Its Discontents.* Translated by James Strachey. New York: W. W. Norton & Company, 1961.

Frölich, Paul, ed. *Rosa Luxemburg.* Translated by Johanna Hoornweg. Chicago: Haymarket Books, 2010.

Gaylin, Willard. *In the Service of Their Country: War Resisters in Prison.* New York: Viking Press, 1970.

Gecan, Michael. *Going Public: An Organizer's Guide to Citizen Action.* New York: Anchor, 2004.

Goodell, Jeff. *The Water Will Come: Rising Seas, Sinking Cities and the Remaking of the Civilized World.* New York: Little, Brown and Company, 2017.

Gottschalk, Marie. *Caught: The Prison State and the Lockdown of American Politics.* Princeton, NJ: Princeton University Press, 2015.

Gramsci, Antonio. *Selections from the Prison Notebooks of Antonio Gramsci.* London: Lawrence & Wishart, 1971.

Gray, John. *Heresies: Against Progress And Other Illusions.* London: Granta UK Publications, 2004.

Greenberg, Brian, Gordon Reavley, Richard Greenwald, Linda S. Watts, Alice George, Scott Beekman, Cecelia Bucki, Mark Ciabattari, John Charles Stoner, Troy D. Paino, Laurie Mercier, Peter C. Holloran, Andrew Hunt, and Nancy Cohen. *Social History of the United States.* Santa Barbara, CA: ABC-CLIO, 2008.

Hall, Stuart, Charles Critcher and Tony Jefferson. *Policing the Crisis: Mugging, the State and Law and Order.* New York: Palgrave Macmillan, 2013.

Hedges, Chris. *American Fascists: The Christian Right and the War on America.* New York: Free Press, 2006.

Hobbes, Thomas. *The Elements of Law, Natural and Politic: Part I, Human Nature, Part II, De Corpore Politico; With Three Lives.* New York: Oxford University Press, 1999.

Hoyt, Edwin Palmer. *The Palmer Raids, 1919–1920: An Attempt to Suppress Dissent.* New York: Seabury Press, 1969.

Hudis, Peter and Kevin B. Anderson, eds. *The Rosa Luxemburg Reader.* New York: The Monthly Review Press, 2004.

Hugo, Victor. *Les Misérables.* Translated by Norman Denny. New York: Penguin, 1976.

Innes, Arthur Donald. *A History of England and the British Empire. Volume 4: 1802–1914.* Charleston, SC: Nabu Press, 2010.

Jensen, Derrick. *The Culture of Make Believe.* Hartford, VT: Chelsea Green Publishing, 2004.

Johnston, David Cay. *The Making of Donald Trump.* Brooklyn, NY: Melville House, 2016.

Jünger, Ernst. *Storm of Steel.* Translated by Michael Hofmann. London: Penguin Classics, 2004.

Kierkegaard, Søren. *Sickness Unto Death.* New York: Start Publishing LLC, 2012.

Kyle, Chris. *American Sniper: The Autobiography of the Most Lethal Sniper in U.S. Military History.* New York: William Morrow, 2012.

Lakey, George and Martin Oppenheimer. *A Manual for Direct Action: Strategy and Tactics for Civil Rights and All Other Nonviolent Protest Movements.* Chicago: Quadrangle Books, 1965.

Lasch, Christopher. *The Culture of Narcissism: American Life in an Age of Diminishing Expectations.* New York: W. W. Norton & Company, 1979.

Lesieur, Henry. *The Chase.* Rochester, VT: Schenkman Books Inc., 1984.

Liebknecht, Karl. *Ausgewählte Reden und Aufsätze.* Berlin: Dietz Verlag, 1952.

Lifton, Robert Jay. *The Broken Connection: On Death and the Continuity of Life.* Arlington, VA: American Psychiatric Publishing, 1996.

Lifton, Robert Jay. *Death in Life: Survivors of Hiroshima.* Chapel Hill: University of North Carolina Press, 1991.

Lifton, Robert Jay, and Richard A. Falk. *Indefensible Weapons: The Political and Psychological Case Against Nuclearism.* New York: Basic Books, 1982.

Looker, Robert, ed. *Rosa Luxemburg: Selected Political Writings.* London: Jonathan Cape, 1972.

Lynd, Staughton. *Lucasville: The Untold Story of a Prison Uprising*. Oakland, CA: PM Press, 2011.

Macdonald, Dwight. *The Root Is Man: Two Essays in Politics*. Cunningham Press, 1953.

Mattick, Paul. *Anti-Bolshevik Communism*. Pontypool, UK: Merlin Press, 1978.

Márquez, Gabriel García. *The Autumn of the Patriarch*. Penguin Books, 1975.

Marx, Karl. *A Contribution to the Critique of Political Economy*. Translated from the Second German Edition by N. I. Stone. Chicago: Charles H. Kerr & Company, 1911.

Marx, Karl. *Capital: A Critique of Political Economy, Volume 3*. Translated by David Fernbach. New York: Vintage Books, 1981.

Marx, Karl. *Capital*. Translated by Ben Fowkes. New York: Vintage Books, 1977.

Marx, Karl. *The German Ideology*. Edited by C. J. Arthur. New York: International Publishers, 1970.

Marx, Karl, and Friedrich Engel. *Manifesto of the Communist Party*. Chicago: Charles H. Kerr & Company, 1906.

Mattick, Paul. *Anti-Bolshevik Communism*. Pontypool, UK: Merlin Press, 1978.

McCoy, Alfred W. *In the Shadows of the American Century: The Rise and Decline of US Global Power*. Chicago: Haymarket Books, 2017.

Meerloo, Joost A. M. *The Rape of the Mind: The Psychology of Thought Control, Menticide, and Brainwashing*. New York: Martino Fine Books, 2015.

Miller, Jason. *That Championship Season*. New York: Atheneum, 1972.

Mishra, Pankaj. *Age of Anger: A History of The Present*. New York: Farrar, Straus and Giroux, 2017.

Moran, Rachel. *Paid For*. New York: W. W. Norton & Company, 2013.

Morris, Brian. *Religion and Anthropology: A Critical Introduction*. Cambridge, UK: Cambridge University Press, 2006.

Mutari, Ellen, and Deborah M. Figart. *Just One More Hand: Life in the Casino Economy*. New York: Rowman & Littlefield, 2015.

Niebuhr, Reinhold. *Beyond Tragedy: Essays on the Christian Interpretation of History*. New York: C. Scribner's Sons, 1937.

Niebuhr, Reinhold. *The Structure of Nations and Empires*. New York: Scribner, 1959.

Parker, Carleton Hubbell. *The Casual Laborer: And Other Essays*. New York: Harcourt, Brace and Howe, 1920.

Pascal, Blaise. *Pascal's Pensées*. New York: E. P. Dutton & Co., 1958.

Percy, Walker. *Love In the Ruins*. Farrar, Straus and Giroux: New York, 1971.

Plato. *The Republic*. London: Oxford University Press, 1972.

———. *The Republic*. Translated by G.M.A. Grube, revised by C.D.C. Reeve. Indianapolis: Hackett Publishing Company, Inc., 1992.

Postman, Neil. *Amusing Ourselves to Death: Public Discourse in the Age of Show Business.* New York: Penguin Books, 1985.

Quinones, Sam. *Dreamland: The True Tale of America's Opiate Epidemic.* New York: Bloomsbury Press, 2015.

Radosh, Ronald, ed. *Debs.* Englewood Cliffs, NJ: Prentice-Hall, 1971.

Rauschenbusch, Walter. *A Theology for the Social Gospel.* New York: The Macmillan Company, 1917.

Reich, Wilhelm. *The Mass Psychology of Fascism.* New York: Farrar, Straus and Giroux, 1980.

Rondinone, Troy. *The Great Industrial War: Framing Class Conflict in the Media, 1865–1950.* New Brunswick: Rutgers University Press, 1973.

Roosevelt, Elliot, ed. (assisted by Joseph P. Lash), *F.D.R. His Personal Letters, 1928–1945.* New York: Duell, Sloan and Pearce, 1950.

Roszak, Theodore. *The Making of a Counter Culture.* New York: Anchor Books, 1969.

Rothman, Hal, and Mike Davis. *The Grit Beneath the Glitter: Tales from the Real Las Vegas.* Berkeley: University of California Press, 2002.

Said, Edward W. *Orientalism.* New York: Vintage Books, 1979.

Salvatore, Nick. *Eugene V. Debs: Citizen and Socialist.* Chicago: University of Illinois Press, 1984.

Santucci, Antonio A., ed. *Antonio Gramsci.* New York: Monthly Review Press, 2010.

Schmidt, Regin. *Red Scare: FBI and the Origins of Anticommunism in the United States, 1919–1943.* Copenhagen: Museum Tusculanum Press, 2000.

Schorske, Carl. *Fin-de-Siècle Vienna: Politics and Culture.* New York: Alfred A. Knopf, 1980.

Schumpeter, Joseph. *Capitalism, Socialism, and Democracy.* Crows Nest, Australia: Allen & Unwin, 1976.

Schüll, Natasha Dow. *Addiction by Design: Machine Gambling in Las Vegas.* Princeton, NJ: Princeton University Press, 2012.

Shaw, George Bernard. *Pygmalion and Major Barbara.* New York: Random House, 2008.

Simon, Bryant. *Boardwalk of Dreams: Atlantic City and the Fate of Urban America.* New York: Oxford University Press, 2006.

Simon, Jonathan. *Governing Through Crime: How the War on Crime Transformed American Democracy and Created a Culture of Fear.* Oxford, UK: Oxford University Press, 2009.

Smith, Adam. *An Inquiry Into the Nature and Causes of the Wealth of Nations.* Chicago: University of Chicago Press, 1977.

Smith, Adam. *The Wealth of Nations, Part Two.* New York: P.F. Collier & Son, 1902.

Solnit, Rebecca. *Men Explain Things to Me.* Chicago: Haymarket Books, 2014.

St. Clair, Jeffrey. *Grand Theft Pentagon: Tales of Corruption and Profiteering in the War on Terror.* Monroe: Common Courage Press, 2005.

Stewart, H. F., ed. *Pascal's Apology for Religion: Extracted from the Pensées.* Cambridge, UK: Cambridge University Press, 1942.

Taibbi, Matt. *Insane Clown President: Dispatches from the 2016 Circus.* New York: Spiegel & Grau, 2017.

Tainter, Joseph. *The Collapse of Complex Societies.* Cambridge: Cambridge University Press, 1990.

Theweleit, Klaus. *Male Fantasies, Vol. 2: Male Bodies—Psychoanalyzing the White Terror.* Minneapolis: University Of Minnesota Press, 1989.

Thomas, Brad. *The Trump Factor: Unlocking the Secrets Behind the Trump Empire.* New York: Post Hill Press, 2016.

Tuchman, Barbara W. *The Proud Tower: A Portrait of the World Before the War, 1890–1914.* New York: Random House, 2014.

Valtin, Jan. *Out of the Night: The Memoir of Richard Julius Herman Krebs Alias Jan Valtin.* Oakland, CA: AK Press, 2004.

Van Dyke, Nella, and Holly J. McCammon. *Strategic Alliances: Coalition Building and Social Movements Vol. 34.* Minneapolis: University of Minnesota Press, 2010.

Vitale, Alex S. *The End of Policing.* New York: Verso, 2017.

Voltaire. *Miracles and Idolatry.* London: Penguin UK, 2005.

Wallace, David Foster. *Infinite Jest.* New York: Back Bay Books, 1996.

Weil, Simone. *Gravity and Grace.* London: Routledge & Kegan Paul, 1952.

Whimster, Sam, ed. *The Essential Weber: A Reader.* New York: Routledge, 2004.

Wolin, Sheldon S. *Democracy Incorporated: Managed Democracy and the Specter of Inverted Totalitarianism.* Princeton, NJ: Princeton University Press, 2008.

Wolin, Sheldon S. *Politics and Vision: Continuity and Innovation in Western Political Thought.* Princeton, NJ: Princeton University Press, 2004.

Wright, Ronald. *A Short History of Progress.* New York: Carroll & Graf, 2005.

Zinn, Howard. *A People's History of the United States.* New York: Harper Perennial Modern Classics, 2015.

Zinn, Howard, and Anthony Arnove. *Voices of a People's History of the United States.* New York: Seven Stories Press, 2009.

INDEX

Also by Pulitzer Prize–winning journalist and bestselling author

Chris Hedges

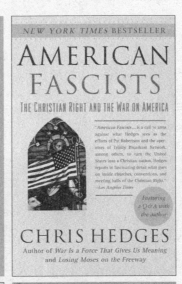

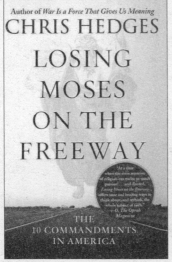

Pick up or download
your copies today!